Xiaxia Xue has written an important and challenging book on intertextuality in Romans 9–11. She does not define intertextuality as do most of her colleagues in New Testament studies, by simply equating it with how the Old Testament is used in the New, but instead she fully embraces both the dialogical nature of intertexts and the role that a robust theory of linguistics can play in engaging such interactive voices. However, this is not intertextuality practiced for its own sake. Xiaxia brings her theory to bear on interpreting Paul's deep concern for how God, Israel and the Gentiles are presented in Romans 9–11. I warmly recommend this book as providing a major step forward both in method and in understanding how Paul creates his argument in this important part of his letter to the Romans. This is a book to be read and contemplated.

Stanley E. Porter
President, Dean and Professor of New Testament,
Roy A. Hope Chair in Christian Worldview,
McMaster Divinity College, Canada

Paul's Viewpoint on God, Israel, and the Gentiles in Romans 9–11

An Intertextual Thematic Analysis

Xiaxia E. Xue

MONOGRAPHS

© 2015 by Xiaxia E. Xue

Published 2015 by Langham Monographs
an imprint of Langham Creative Projects

Langham Partnership
PO Box 296, Carlisle, Cumbria CA3 9WZ, UK
www.langham.org

ISBNs:
978-1-78368-047-4 Print
978-1-78368-048-1 Mobi
978-1-78368-049-8 ePub
978-1-78368-050-4 PDF

Xiaxia E. Xue has asserted her right under the Copyright, Designs and Patents Act, 1988 to be identified as the Author of this work.

All rights reserved. No part of this publication may be reproduced, stored in a retrieval system or transmitted, in any form or by any means, electronic, mechanical, photocopying, recording or otherwise, without the prior written permission of the publisher or the Copyright Licensing Agency.

Unless otherwise stated, Scripture quotations are from the New Revised Standard Version Bible, copyright © 1989 National Council of the Churches of Christ in the United States of America. Used by permission. All rights reserved.

British Library Cataloguing in Publication Data

Xue, Xiaxia, author.
  Paul's viewpoint on God, Israel, and the Gentiles in Romans
9-11 : an intertextual thematic analysis.
  1. Bible. Romans, IX-XI--Hermeneutics. 2. Bible. Romans,
IX-XI--Language, style. 3. Paul, the Apostle, Saint--
Teachings. 4. Gentiles in the New Testament. 5. Jews in the
New Testament. 6. Israel (Christian theology)
  I. Title
  227.1'066-dc23

ISBN-13: 9781783680474

Cover & Book Design: projectluz.com

Langham Partnership actively supports theological dialogue and a scholar's right to publish but does not necessarily endorse the views and opinions set forth, and works referenced within this publication or guarantee its technical and grammatical correctness. Langham Partnership does not accept any responsibility or liability to persons or property as a consequence of the reading, use or interpretation of its published content.

Contents

Abstract ix

Abbreviations xi

Chapter One 1
Introduction
    1.1 Situating Romans 3
        1.1.1 Paul's Own Situation 3
        1.1.2 The Situation of the Christians in Rome 5
    1.2 A Survey of the Literature of Romans 9–11 6
        1.2.1 Survey of General Studies of Romans 9–11 7
            1.2.1.1 Theological-exegesis Approach 8
            1.2.1.2 Literary Approach 10
        1.2.2 Intertextual Research on Romans 9–11 12
            1.2.2.1 Focus on Motifs 12
            1.2.2.2 Focus on Paul's Role in his Understanding of Scripture 13
    1.3 The Objective of this Study and its Thesis 20
    1.4 Value of this Research 23
    1.5 Outline of the Present Study 23

Chapter Two 25
Research Methodology: An Intertextual Thematic Analysis
    2.1 Introduction 25
    2.2 Lemke's Concept of Intertextuality 26
        2.2.1 Introduction 26
        2.2.2 Lemke's Concept of Thematic Formations 30
            2.2.2.1 The Definition 30
            2.2.2.2 Its Constructions 31
        2.2.3 Lemke's Concept of Intertextual Thematic Formation 32
            2.2.3.1 The Definition 32
            2.2.3.2 Relations of Intertextual Thematic Formations 33
            2.2.3.3 Heteroglossic Voices and Projection Clauses 36
        2.2.4 Thematic Organization 38
        2.2.5 Multiple Voices and Intertexts 39
    2.3 Evaluation of Lemke's Intertextual Thematic Model 40
    2.4 An Adaptation of Lemke's Intertextual Thematic Analysis to our Analytical Procedure 42

  2.4.1 An Adaptation of Lemke's Intertextual Thematic Analysis 42
  2.4.2 Analytical Procedure..43
 2.5 Conclusion 45

Chapter Three 47
 An Intertextual Thematic Analysis of Romans 9:1–29:
 The Nature of God and Who are God's People
 3.1 Introduction 47
 3.2 Romans 9:1–5 48
  3.2.1 Presentational Meaning 48
  3.2.2 Scriptural Voices..58
  3.2.3 Thematic-organizational Meaning 61
  3.2.4 Multiple Voices: Viewpoints of Paul's Jewish
   Contemporaries on Intercession for Israel 62
 3.3 Romans 9:6–13 67
  3.3.1 Presentational Meaning: God's Promise and Who are
   God's People..67
  3.3.2 Scriptural Voices..74
  3.3.3 Thematic-organizational Meaning 77
  3.3.4 Multiple Voices: Viewpoints of Paul's Jewish
   Contemporaries on God's Word and Human's Doing...............78
 3.4 Romans 9:14–29 83
  3.4.1 Presentational Meaning: God's Authority, God's Mercy
   and God's People 83
  3.4.2 Scriptural Voices..95
  3.4.3 Thematic-organizational Meaning 102
  3.4.4 Multiple Voices: Paul's Jewish Contemporaries'
   Viewpoints on God's Nature and God's People 103
 3.5 Conclusion 109

Chapter Four.. 113
 Paul's Critique of Israel:
 An Intertextual Thematic Analysis of Romans 9:30–10:21
 4.1 Introduction 113
 4.2 Romans 9:30–10:4 116
  4.2.1 Presentational Meaning: Israel's Failure to Attain
   Righteousness 116
  4.2.2 Scriptural Voices..124
  4.2.3 Thematic-organizational Meaning 127
  4.2.4 Multiple Voices: Paul's Jewish Contemporaries
   Viewpoints on Law, Righteousness, and Faith...................129

    4.3 Romans 10:5–13 133
        4.3.1 Presentational Meaning 134
        4.3.2 Scriptural Voices...143
        4.3.3 Thematic-organizational Meaning 150
        4.3.4 Multiple Voices: Paul's Jewish Contemporaries'
            Viewpoints on the Scope of Salvation 151
        4.3.5 Conclusion..157
    4.4 Romans 10:14–21 158
        4.4.1 Presentational Meaning 158
        4.4.2 Scriptural Voices...165
        4.4.3 Thematic-organizational Meaning 173
        4.4.4 Multiple Voices: Paul's Jewish Contemporaries'
            Viewpoints Concerning Israel's Sin in Relation to the Gentiles 174
        4.4.5 Conclusion..178
    4.5 Conclusion 179

Chapter Five.. 181
Paul's Warning to the Gentiles and the Salvation of All God's People:
An Intertextual Analysis of Romans 11
    5.1 Introduction 181
    5.2 Romans 11:1–10 182
        5.2.1 Presentational Meaning: The Remnant of Israel................182
        5.2.2 Scriptural Voices...192
        5.2.3 Thematic-organizational Meaning 200
        5.2.4 Multiple Voices: Paul's Jewish Contemporaries'
            Viewpoints on God's Faithfulness and Israel's Sinfulness..........200
    5.3 Romans 11:11–32 204
        5.3.1 Presentational Meaning 204
        5.3.2 Scriptural Voices...223
        5.3.3 Thematic-organizational Meaning 225
        5.3.4 Multiple Voices: Paul's Jewish Contemporaries' Viewpoints
            on the Role of the Gentiles in the Salvation of Israel................226
    5.4 Conclusion 231
    5.5 Additional Note: Verses 33–36 233

Chapter Six 237
Conclusion

Appendix 1... 241

Appendix 2... 249
    Chart for Romans 9:1–5

Appendix 3 253
    Charts for Romans 9:6–13

Appendix 4 255
    Charts for Romans 9:14–29

Appendix 5 263
    Charts for Romans 9:30–10:4

Appendix 6 265
    Charts for Romans 10:4–13

Appendix 7 269
    Baruch Text

Appendix 8 273
    Charts for Romans 10:14–21

Appendix 9 277
    Charts for Romans 11:1–10

Appendix 10 281
    Charts for Romans 11:11–32

Appendix Endnotes 288

Bibliography 289

Abstract

Romans 9–11 has been investigated through varied methods during the past two decades. One of the most prominent approaches is an intertextual reading of Romans 9–11. However, most discussions of intertextual studies do not adequately treat the discourse in Romans 9–11 by closely investigating Paul's discourse patterns and that of his Jewish contemporaries regarding God, Israel, and the Gentiles due to lack of an appropriate intertextual methodological control. Therefore, this study adapts Lemke's linguistic intertextual thematic theory as a methodological control to analyze Paul's intertextual discourse patterns in Romans 9–11. Paul's unique way of using Scripture as one part of his discourse pattern will be investigated as well. Through the intertextual thematic study of Paul's discourse in Romans 9–11, we demonstrate the divergence of Paul's viewpoints on some typical Jewish issues, which suggests that the discontinuities between Paul and his Jewish contemporaries are obvious and – sometimes – radical.

We conclude the findings of our investigation of Romans 9–11 as follows: First, we have adjusted Lemke's intertextual thematic analysis, as an indispensable tool, to analyze Paul's viewpoints of the relationships of God, Israel and the Gentiles in Romans 9–11 within the backdrop of Second Temple Literature. Second, Paul re-contextualizes the Jewish discourse patterns regarding the topics of intercession, Israel, God's promise, God's people, righteousness and law. It can be seen that Paul's discourse patterns share some continuity with his Jewish contemporaries, but the core of his value regarding how to include the Gentiles as God's people stands in a discontinuous relationship with contemporary Judaism(s). Third, this study has demonstrated that although Paul uses Jewish styles of scriptural hermeneutics, and though his discourse patterns resemble some Jewish literature in important aspects, Paul's viewpoint on the relationship of God, Israel and the Gentiles in Romans 9–11 is dissociated from his Jewish contemporaries in key ways. In other words, the core value of early Christian discourse has been embedded in Romans 9–11. Paul's viewpoint on the relationship of God, Israel and the Gentiles takes a divergent stance away from his Jewish contemporaries since Gentile inclusion is rooted in the gospel of Christ. Finally, Romans 9–11 not only provides Paul's self-presentation as a Mosaic prophet figure, but also its overall discourse patterns appears as a prophetic discourse: In each section (Rom 9:1–29; 9:30–10:21; 11:1–36) Paul designates his identity or his concerns of Israel (Rom 9:1–3, 10:1; 11:1–2) before he enters into the argumentation, which demonstrates the relation between Paul's self-understanding and his message in these three chapters; also, the overall discourse pattern in Romans 9–11 resembles a prophetic discourse pattern, which expresses the idea that Paul's self-understanding as a prophetic figure serves to confirm that his word comes from divine authority.

Abbreviations

AB	The Anchor Bible
ABC	Ariel's Bible Commentary
ADP	Advances in discourse processes
AJEC	Ancient Judaism and Early Christianity
AOTC	Apollos Old Testament Commentary
AUMSR	Andrews University Monographs: Studies in Religion
BCOTWP	Baker Commentary on the Old Testament Wisdom and Psalms
BHHB	Baylor Handbook on the Hebrew Bible
Bib	*Biblica*
BibInt	*Biblical Interpretation*
BDF	Blass, F., A. Debrunner, and R. W. Funk. *A Greek Grammar of the New Testament and Other Early Christian Literature.* Chicago, 1961.
BDAG	Danker, Frederick W., Walter Bauer, William Arndt, and F. Gingrich. *A Greek-English Lexicon of the New Testament and Other Early Christian Literature.* 3rd ed. Chicago: University of Chicago Press, 2000
BLG	Biblical Languages: Greek Series
BO	Berit Olam
BZNWK	Beihefte zur Zeitschrift für die neutestamentliche Wissenschaft und die Kunde der älteren Kirche
CBCA	The Cambridge Bible Commentary on the Apocrypha
CBQ	*Catholic Biblical Quarterly*
ConBNT	Coniectanea biblica: New Testament Series
CSCD	Cambridge Studies in Christian Doctrine
CSCO	Corpus scriptorum christianorum orientalium

CTJ	*Calvin Theological Journal*
CurBS	*Currents in Research: Biblical Studies*
CPLE	Critical perspectives on literacy and education
DSBOT	Daily Study Bible – Old Testament
ECC	Eerdmans Critical Commentary
FOTL	Forms of the Old Testament Literature
FRLANT	Forschungen zur Religion und Literatur des Alten und Neuen Testaments
Hermeneia	Hermeneia-A critical and historical commentary on the Bible
JSNT	*Journal for the Study of the New Testament*
JSNTSup	Journal for the Study of the New Testament: Supplement Series
JBL	*Journal of Biblical Literature*
JSP	*Journal for the Study of the Pseudepigrapha*
JSOT	*Journal for the Study of the Old Testament*
ICC	International Critical Commentary
Int	*Interpretation*
IBC	Interpretation: A Bible Commentary for Teaching and Preaching
LBC	Linguistic biblical studies
LNTS	Library of New Testament Studies
MAJT	*Mid-America Journal of Theology*
MNTC	The Moffatt New Testament Commentary
NAC	New American Commentary
NCBC	New Century Bible Commentary
NCamBC	New Cambridge Bible Commentary
NCI	The New Critical Idiom
NIBCOT	New International Biblical Commentary on the Old Testament
NICOT	New International Commentary on the Old Testament
NTS	*New Testament Studies*
OB	Oxford Bible
OBC	Oxford Bible Commentary
OL	Open Linguistics

OTL	Old Testament Library
OTP	The Old Testament Pseudepigrapha
PBTM	Paternoster Biblical and Theological Monographs
PCC	Paul in Critical Contexts
PAC	Philo of Alexandria Commentary
PSB	Princeton Seminary Bulletin
Readings	Readings: A New Biblical Commentary
RevExp	*Review & Expositor*
RQ	*Restoration Quarterly*
SBG	Studies in Biblical Greek
SBL	Society of Biblical Literature
SBLDS	Society of Biblical Literature Dissertation Series
SI	*Semiotic Inquiry*
SHBC	Smyth & Helwys Bible commentary
SJT	*Scottish Journal of Theology*
SNT	Supplements to Novum Testamentum
SNTSMS	Society for New Testament Studies Monograph Series
SJSJ	Supplements to the Journal for the Study of Judaism
SRB	Studies in Rewritten Bible
SP	Sacra Pagina
THL	Theory and History of Literature
TMSJ	*The Master's Seminary Journal*
T&TCLBS	T & T Clark Library of Biblical Studies
WBC	Word Biblical Commentary
WBT	Word Biblical Themes
WestBC	Westminster Bible companion
WTJ	*Westminster Theological Journal*
WUNT	Wissenschaftliche Untersuchungen zum Neuen Testament
UBS	United Bible Societies
USFISFCJ	University of South Florida international studies in formative Christianity and Judaism
ZECNT	Zondervan Exegetical Commentary on the New Testament

CHAPTER ONE

Introduction

In recent decades, the study of Romans 9–11 has become a very heated topic, for more and more scholars have realized the significance of Romans 9–11 in the overall scheme of Paul's thought. One of the reasons for valuing these three chapters arises from the recognition of the significance of Jewish literature in understanding Paul's letters, particularly since Sanders' *Paul and Palestinian Judaism: A Comparison of Patterns of Religion* (1977). It can be seen that, among all of Paul's letters, Romans 9–11 is the most pronounced in incorporating Scripture. An understanding of this fact is important for studying Paul and his viewpoint on the relationship of God, Israel, and the Gentiles through his discourse patterns and his use of these Jewish Scriptures.[1] Therefore, a great deal of intertextual study on Romans 9–11 has been attempted.

Some studies focus on the relationship of Jewish Scriptures with their New Testament use, considering their interconnectedness with tradition-historical methods, while employing the term "intertextuality."[2] However, this diachronic method has been fiercely challenged by those scholars who insist on the post-structuralist roots of intertextuality.[3] In the

---

1. Note that, according to Paul's own usage of Scripture(s), this study will use "Jewish Scriptures," "Scriptures of Israel," or "Scripture(s)" to refer to "Old Testament," except when it is inside a quotation.
2. Biblical scholars have used many terms to describe the connection with previous texts and host texts, and intertextuality is among one of them. See Mark Boda, "Quotation and Allusion," in *Dictionary of Biblical Criticism and Interpretation*, ed. Stanley E. Porter, (London: Routledge, 2007), 296.
3. The term "Intertextuality" is coined by Kristeva, who views intertexts as transpositions, from one sign system to another. As she indicates, "it may be borrowed from different signifying materials: the transposition from a carnival scene to the written text, for

post-structuralist view of intertextuality, "Intertextuality is an 'anonymous' and 'impersonal' process of blending, clashing, and intersecting. Texts 'blend and clash,' not people." [4] Therefore, from the perspective of post-structuralism, intertextuality should not be seen as "a linear adaptation of another text but as a complex of relationships."[5] Under influence of this post-structuralist concept of "intertextuality," some biblical scholars have been able to identify certain literary connections between biblical texts, but most biblical studies of intertextuality mix literary theory with historical concerns. One of these representatives is Hays' *Echoes of Scriptures*, whose study has exerted a lot of influence on subsequent intertextual study.[6] However, Hays' intertextual methodology is much more a literary concept than an interpretive tool.[7] Therefore, this study will develop a

---

instance. In this connection we examined the formation of a specific signifying system – the novel – as the result of a redistribution of several different sign systems: carnival, courtly poetry, scholastic discourse. The term intertextuality denotes this transposition of one (or several) sign system(s) into another." See Julia Kristeva, *Revolution in Poetic Language*, translated by Margaret Walker, (New York: Columbia University Press, 1984), 59–60.

4. Susan Friedman, "Weavings: Intertextuality and the (Re)Birth of the Author," in *Influence and Intertextuality in Literary History*, ed. Jay Clayton and Eric Rothstein, (Madison: University of Wisconsin Press, 1991), 149; and George Aichele, "Canon as Intertext: Restraint or Liberation?" in *Reading the Bible Intertextually*, ed. Richard B. Hays, Stefan Alkier and Leroy Andrew Huizenga, (Waco: Baylor University Press, 2009), 142.

5. Ellen Van Wolde, "Trendy Intertextuality?" in *Intertextuality in Biblical Writings: Essays in Honour of Bas Van Ierse*, ed. Sipke Draisma, (Kampen: Kok, 1989) 47.

6. For instance, Christopher A. Beetham, *Echoes of Scripture in the Letter of Paul to the Colossians*, BibInt 96, (Leiden: Brill, 2008); J. Ross Wagner, *Heralds of the Good News: Isaiah and Paul "in Concert" in the Letter to the Romans*, NovTSup 101, (Leiden: Brill, 2002); Brian J. Abasciano, *Paul's Use of the Old Testament in Romans 9:1–9: An Intertextual and Theological Exegesis*. LNTS 301, (New York: T&T Clark, 2005); Brian J. Abasciano, *Paul's Use of the Old Testament in Romans 9:10–18: An Intertextual and Theological Exegesis*, LNTS 317, (New York: T & T Clark, 2011); Guy Prentiss Waters, *The End of Deuteronomy in the Epistles of Paul*, WUNT 221, (Tübingen: Mohr Siebeck, 2006); Frank Thielman, "Unexpected Mercy: Echoes of a Biblical Motif in Romans 9–11," *SJT* 47 (1994), 169–181.

7. In the survey section, we will indicate more of our critique of Hays' intertextual methodology. For other scholars' comments on Hays' approach, see Evans and Sanders, *Paul and the Scriptures of Israel*, ed. Craig A. Evans and James A. Sanders, (Sheffield: JSOT Press, 1993), 79–96. For critiques of Hays' seven criteria, see Stanley Porter, "The Use of the Old Testament in the New Testament: A Brief Comment on Method and Terminology," in *Early Christian Interpretation of the Scriptures of Israel*, ed. Craig A. Evans and James A. Sanders, (Sheffield: Sheffield Academic, 1997), 82–88. Other profound critiques can be found in Christopher Stanley, "Paul's Use of Scripture: Why the Audience

new perspective on Paul's use of intertexts in Romans 9–11 by employing Lemke's intertextual thematic analysis as a methodological control.[8]

In the following section, we will first situate Paul's letter to the Romans by investigating both Paul's own situation and the situation in the churches of Rome. A survey of recent research on Romans 9–11 will follow. Next, after observing the weaknesses in the recent intertextual studies on Romans 9–11, the objective of this study and our thesis will be provided. In the last two sections, the value and the outline of this study will be offered.

1.1 Situating Romans

1.1.1 Paul's Own Situation

Paul writes his letters first of all from the perspective of who he is, from his worldview regarding the issues that concern him, along with his awareness of the situation of the intended audience. Therefore, Paul's role, position, and identity are significant for understanding his writings. Paul is both a Jew (Rom 9:3) and apostle to the Gentiles (11:13). These two dimensions of his identity are clearly expressed in his letter to the Romans, particularly in Romans 9–11 and 14–15. From this perspective, it is not surprising that Paul labors to deal with the relationship of God, Israel, and the Gentiles in Romans 9–11.

Paul's own situation in writing Romans can be detected in the letter. He describes his situation and future plans at the beginning and the end of Romans (1:8–15; 15:14–33). Paul intends to visit Rome, but has been prevented from doing so (1:8–15). After many years of longing to visit the Christians at Rome, he finally will be able to do so (15:14 –33), because

---

Matters," in *As It Is Written: Studying Paul's Use of Scripture*, ed. Stanley E. Porter and Christopher D. Stanley, (Atlanta: SBL, 2008), 127–136.

8. Lemke's theory of intertextuality is influenced by Hallidayan Systemic Functional Linguistics (henceforth SFL) and postmodern critical theory. For details about this methodology, see chapter two. Hallidayan Systemic Functional Linguistics refers to the way of viewing language as a social semiotic system that was developed by Michael Halliday. For further discussions of SFL, see M. A. K. Halliday and Christian M. I. M. Matthiessen, *An Introduction to Functional Grammar*, 3rd ed. (London: Arnold, 2004), 19–31.

he has fulfilled his goal of preaching the gospel "from Jerusalem . . . as far around as Illyricum" (15:19). He thus plans to stay in Rome for a little while on his way to Spain.[9] However, at the present time, he has to bring the collection from the Christians of Macedonia and Achaia to the poor members in the church of Jerusalem (15:25–26). It is this collection, which came from the Gentile Christians to the Jewish Christians of Jerusalem, that Paul has written about at length; this suggests the significance of the unity of the Gentile Christians and the Jewish Christians. Particularly, Paul describes the contribution of the Gentile Christians as the Gentiles' debt to the Jewish Christians (15:27). Later, he even fears that the Jewish Christians in Jerusalem may not accept the collection (15:32b). These remarks may indicate the tense relationship between the Gentile and the Jewish Christians, which is also the situation in the Roman churches.[10]

Paul not only demonstrates the tension between the Gentile and the Jewish Christians, he also indicates his personal conflict with the non-believing Jews in his request for prayer to the Christians in Rome (15:30–33). Starting with an urgent request that they join in with prayers for him (παρακαλῶ δὲ ὑμᾶς [, ἀδελφοί,] . . . συναγωνίσασθαί μοι ἐν ταῖς προσευχαῖς ὑπὲρ ἐμοῦ πρὸς τὸν θεόν),[11] Paul mentions two immediate requests for prayer shared between himself and the Roman churches. The first is about delivery from the danger of the unbelieving Jews in Judea: ἵνα ῥυσθῶ ἀπὸ τῶν ἀπειθούντων ἐν τῇ Ἰουδαίᾳ (Rom 15:31a).[12] The second relates to the hope that the Jewish Christians in Jerusalem would accept him and his collection. In other words, when Paul wrote the letter to Romans, his relationship with his kinsmen was highly tense.[13] This explains Paul's heartfelt

---

9. Paul intends to present himself to the Christians in Rome for their support in his traveling to Spain.

10. Cf. Thomas H. Tobin, *Paul's Rhetoric in Its Contexts: The Argument of Romans*, (Peabody, MA: Hendrickson, 2004), 52–53.

11. Italics mine. This is to emphasize the urgent request.

12. The participle ἀπειθούντων refers to the unbelieving Jews. See Robert Jewett, *Romans: A Commentary*, Hermeneia, (Minneapolis: Fortress, 2007), 935; Douglas J. Moo, *The Epistle to the Romans*, NICOT, (Grand Rapids: Eerdmans, 1996), 910. Also, cf. Acts 21:27–36 (Paul needs to be protected from the Jews' desire to kill him).

13. Some scholars indicate that Paul accepted Gentiles through a law-free gospel, which may have challenged the distinctive Jewish way of life. In other words, Paul's controversies

concern for the salvation of his kinsmen in Romans 9–11, together with his critique of their unbelief (9:1–5 and10:1; 9:30–10:21).

1.1.2 The Situation of the Christians in Rome

It is generally accepted that Paul wrote his letter to the Romans between AD 55 and 59 (most likely around AD 56 or 57).[14] The composition of the Roman churches most likely consisted of both Gentiles and Jewish Christians.[15] After the Claudian edict of AD 49, the Jews were expelled from Rome. On the death of Claudius at AD 54, the next emperor, Nero, allowed the Jews to return to Rome. When the Jewish Christians arrived back in the churches of Rome, the Gentiles were dominant. This occasioned the friction between the Jewish Christians, who still observe the Jewish lifestyle, and the Gentile Christians, who lived a "liberated" life from the viewpoint of the Jews.[16] Therefore, the unity of the Roman churches in overcoming their growing divergence and conflict becomes the object of Paul's concern in the letter.[17]

In sum, the situation of Paul and the Roman churches demonstrates that the relationship between the Jews and the Gentiles is in high tension. This situation presses Paul to articulate his viewpoint on the relationship

---

with the Jews were due to the law-free gospel. See William S. Campbell, *Paul and the Creation of Christian Identity*, LNTS 322, (New York: T & T Clark, 2008), 6.

14. Tobin, *Paul's Rhetoric*, 70; Lee Martin McDonald and Stanley E Porter, *Early Christianity and Its Sacred Literature*, (Peabody: Hendrickson, 2000), 451.

15. Cf. McDonald and Porter, *Early Christianity and Its Sacred Literature*, 451–455. There are other opinions. For instance, some scholars argue that the Christians in the Roman church were predominantly Jewish or Jewish shaped. Bell contends that "the dominant Christianity at Rome had been shaped by the Jerusalem Christianity associated with James and Peter, and hence was a Christianity appreciative of Judaism and loyal to its customs." A Petrine party, who opposed Paul, may have existed in Rome. Therefore, Paul answers the accusations of this party. See Richard H. Bell, *Provoked to Jealousy: The Origin and Purpose of the Jealousy Motif in Romans 9–11*, WUNT 63, (Tübingen: Mohr Siebeck, 1994), 74. For a critique of this type of position, see McDonald and Porter, *Early Christianity and Its Sacred Literature*, 453. Recently, there are some scholars arguing that the Christians in the Roman church were essentially Gentile. See Andrew A. Das, *Solving the Romans Debate*, (Minneapolis: Fortress Press, 2007), 53–114.

16. Cf. Gordon Zerbe, "Jews and Gentiles as People of the Covenant: The Background and Message of Romans 11," *Direction* 12 (1983), 21.

17. The issue regarding the purpose of Romans is very controversial. The different viewpoints can be seen in Karl P Donfried's edited book, *The Romans Debate*, (Grand Rapids: Baker Academic, 1991).

between God, Israel, and the Gentiles so as to reduce tensions and improve the relations of the two people groups (the Jews and the Gentiles).

1.2 A Survey of the Literature of Romans 9–11

Romans 9–11 has been seen as an excursus or addendum to chapters 1–8.[18] This view was proposed because scholars assumed that the topic of chapters 1–8 was justification by faith: Jesus Christ inaugurated a new age to save all through faith. Chapters 9–11 seem to depart from this trajectory. However, most recent commentators reject this view, seeing them as the climax of Paul's argument, or even of the book as a whole.[19] We believe that these three chapters play a significant role in understanding the whole book in full depth. As Cranfield has rightly commented, "A closer study reveals the fact that there are very many features of chapters 1 to 8 which are not understood in full depth until they are seen in the light of chapters 9–11. . . . These chapters may be seen to be an integral part of the working out of the theme of the epistle."[20]

In the past two decades, much research has been done, from different perspectives, on Romans 9–11. There exist at least two approaches in studying Romans 9–11. The first focuses on the host text, namely, Paul's own argumentation and his theology indicated in Romans 9–11. Within

---

18. C. H. Dodd treats it as an appendix, "It has been suggested that the three chapters were originally a separate treatise which Paul had by him, and which he used for his present purpose." C. H. Dodd, *The Epistle of Paul to the Romans*, MNTC, (London: Hodder & Stoughton, 1932), 148; see also Andrew H. Wakefield, "Romans 9–11: The Sovereignty of God and the Status of Israel," RevExp 100 (2003): 66; James D. G. Dunn, *Romans 9–16*, WBC 38, (Dallas: Word Books, 1988), 519.

19. Hays indicates that they are not some excursus or appendix peripheral to the letter's theme, but are the heart of the matter (Richard B. Hays, *Echoes of Scripture in the Letters of Paul*, [New Haven: Yale University Press, 1989] 63). For Wright, "Romans 9–11 functions as the climax of the theological argument" (N. T. Wright, *The Climax of the Covenant: Christ and the Law in Pauline Theology*, [Minneapolis: Fortress Press, 1992], 234). O'Neill, Stendahl, etc., regard Romans 9–11 as the climax of Romans (Shiu-Lun Shum, *Paul's Use of Isaiah in Romans: A Comparative Study of Paul's Letter to the Romans and the Sibylline and Qumran Sectarian Texts*. WUNT 156, [Tübingen: Mohr Siebeck, 2002], 203; see also Wakefield, "Romans 9–11, 65.

20. C. E. B. Cranfield,. *A Critical and Exegetical Commentary on the Epistle to the Romans*, ICC 31A, (Edinburgh: T. & T. Clark, 1979), 445.

this trend, some scholars approach the text from theological motifs; others are interested in Paul's rhetorical or his structural argumentation. The second approach focuses on intertextual research, in that related scriptural contexts and the Second Temple literature are brought in to interpret Paul's discourse in Romans 9–11. In the following subsection, we will give a selective survey of the general studies on Romans 9–11 first, and in the next subsection, the focus will shift to the current intertextual research on these three chapters.

1.2.1 Survey of General Studies of Romans 9–11

Some scholars tend to engage with the host text itself. They do not seriously deal with previous scriptural texts, let alone the related Second Temple literature. For them, the main lines of Paul's thought in these three chapters can be sketched without reference to the Scriptures of Israel he cites.[21] Although some current researchers have given their attention to the scriptural background, the governing rule for their analysis relies on the host texts. In the following, we will do a brief survey of this camp, and then subsequently turn to the intertextual study of Romans 9–11. There are at least two approaches to focusing on the host texts.[22]

---

21. Sanday and Headlam think the Scriptures are of little significance in Paul's argumentation, as they have stated: "The Apostle does not intend to base any argument on the quotation from the O.T., but only selects the language as being familiar, suitable, and proverbial, in order to express what he wishes to say." See W. Sanday and Arthur C. Headlam, *A Critical and Exegetical Commentary on the Epistle to the Romans*, ICC 32, (New York: C. Scribner's Sons, 1923), 289.

22. There is another approach that will not be listed here: a reader-response reading of Romans 9–11 conducted by Lodge. According to my knowledge, there is no other reading with this approach, so I will not consider it as significant. However, we will give a brief summary and comments on the book here: Lodge attempts to give an account of the sequential, chronological impact of the reading experience as a report of the reading process. He deliberately refrains from presenting his conclusion or "thesis" as such about the "meaning" or "point" of Romans 9–11until well into the account of his reading of Romans 11. He contends that conclusions and reports of the "point" of a text are often reductionistic. For Lodge, ambiguity, not resolution, is the point of reading. The ambiguity is not to be resolved but experienced as a strategy of indirection (see John G. Lodge, *Romans 9–11: A Reader-Response Analysis*, USFISFCJ, [Atlanta: Scholars, 1996], xv). This postmodern reader-response reading relies heavily on readers' personal experience and their ability to interweave the text with their understanding, which is too subjective, in my opinion.

1.2.1.1 Theological-exegesis Approach

Paul raises a number of controversial theological issues in Romans 9–11 that are important for ancient and modern readers, for instance, election, the righteousness of God, the salvation of Israel, and the role of the law in salvation. Therefore, there are quite a number of articles and monographs focusing on the theological topics of Romans 9–11.

Piper's monograph, *The Justification of God: An Exegetical and Theological Study of Romans 9:1–23* (1983), is an attempt to argue for Paul's understanding of the righteousness of God in Romans 9:1–23 as "his [God's] unswerving commitment to preserve the honor of his name and display his glory."[23] As a matter of fact, Piper is aware of the scriptural co-texts.[24] He devotes two chapters to them: chapter 4, "Exodus 33:19 in its Old Testament Context" and chapter 6, "The Righteousness of God in the Old Testament," and also some other small sections. However, his treatment of the scriptural texts is governed by his theological question of God's righteousness, which prevents him from dealing with the scriptural texts in their own right. Moreover, he has not explored the exegetical traditions available to Paul outside the Scripture.[25]

---

23. John Piper, *The Justification of God: An Exegetical and Theological Study of Romans 9:1–23* (Grand Rapids: Baker Pulbishing, 1983), 203. Piper tries to grasp what Paul means by the righteousness of God in Romans 9, and also attempts to answer the subordinate question of election and predestination: "Does election in Romans 9:1–23 concern nations or individuals? And does it concern historical roles or eternal destinies?" See Piper, *Justification of God*, 1. Regarding the motif of the righteousness of God, see C. Müller, *Gottes Gerechtigkeit und Gottes Volk: Eine Untersuchung zu Römer 9–11*, Göttingen: Vandenhoeck & Ruprecht, 1964, which focuses on God's righteousness. Actually, Müller has compared Paul's expressions with the Scripture as well as rabbinical and apocalyptic literature, but this comparison is governed by his theological concern about the motif of God's righteousness.

24. Note that I use scriptural co-text instead of scriptural context. In this study, we will use "co-text" to refer to the literary context of the Scriptures. For us, "context" refers to situational context of social events that the texts refer to or about the author's writing context. The use of the term "co-text" was developed by Halliday, whose systematic functional grammar of language will be adapted into part of our methodological system. According to Halliday, the extra-linguistic environment relevant to the total text is considered as "context"; the linguistic environment, "the language accompanying the linguistic unit under focus", is viewed as "co-text". See M. A. K. Halliday and Ruqaiya Hasan, *Language, Context, and Text: Aspects of Language in a Social-Semiotic Perspective*, 2nd ed. Language Education, (Oxford: Oxford University, 1989), 75–76.

25. Cf. Abasciano, "Paul's Use of the Old Testament in Romans 9:1–9," 122. For the sake of the style and requirements of the publishing company, Abasciano revised and cut

Quite a number of articles argue that Romans 9–11 concerns the salvation of Israel. We will briefly speak of a few as representative. Hofius, in his article "All Israel Will be Saved" (1990), examines Paul's theology of the salvation of Israel in Romans 9–11, barely even consulting Israel's scriptural texts, let alone other Jewish literature. He tends to consider that "all Israel" (in the diachronic sense) will encounter the *Kyrios* at the parousia and thus believe in Jesus Christ.[26] Also concerned about the theological theme "salvation," Spencer, in his current article "Metaphor, Mystery, and the Salvation of Israel in Romans 9–11" (2006), develops the metaphors of the foot race and the olive tree to explain Paul's hope of the salvation of "all Israel," and to affirm God's faithfulness to save all of God's people: Jew (first) and Gentile (also).[27] A related article by Wakefield, "Romans 9–11: The Sovereignty of God and the Status of Israel" (2003), sketches out the stages of Paul's argument in Romans 9–11,[28] and concludes, as others have done previously, "God will accomplish his plan of salvation, even in spite of – indeed, by means of – human disobedience and rebellion."[29] Wakefield's concern with these three chapters is about its theological arguments without considering scriptural context issues. In other words, most of the works focusing on the theological motifs of Romans 9–11 neglect the role that the Scriptures play in Paul's discourse, since the focus of those works is motivated by their theological interest in Romans 9–11.

---

down some parts of his dissertation. However, there are some significant references in his dissertation that I find useful. This is why I sometimes refer to his thesis, and do not limit myself to the published book.

26. Otfried Hofius, "'All Israel Will Be Saved': Divine Salvation and Israel's Deliverance in Romans 9–11," *PSB* 11 (1990), 37.

27. F. Scott Spencer, "Metaphor, Mystery and the Salvation of Israel in Romans 9–11: Paul's Appeal to Humility and Doxology." *RE* 103 (2006)" 113–138.

28. He divides Romans 9–11 into six sections in terms of their theological topics: the introduction (9:1–6a); the logic and history of election (9:6b–13); the sovereignty of God (9:14–29); Jewish misunderstanding and/or rejection (9:30–10:21); the possibility of restoration (11:1–24); and salvation through jealousy and rebellion (11:11–36). He provides the four key issues in Romans 9–11: predestination versus free will, theodicy, the role of the law in salvation, and Paul's use of Scripture. See Wakefield, "Romans 9–11," 68–78.

29. Wakefield, "Romans 9–11," 78.

1.2.1.2 Literary Approach

The use of literary analysis is an important development in Pauline studies. Several works have been produced which deal with the literary issue of argumentative structure in Romans 9–11. In the following, we will select a few of them as representative.

Kim's dissertation,[30] *God, Israel, and the Gentiles: Rhetoric and Situation in Romans 9–11* (2000), is a study that aims to examine the way Paul presents his argumentation in Romans 9–11 in the context of Graeco-Roman rhetorical conventions.[31] Kim employs rhetorical criticism[32] to demonstrate that "Paul is indeed consistent and that he follows through on his thesis clearly and methodically,"[33] a conclusion that is already widely accepted by most scholars. In addition, this is a study of Romans 9–11, but the investigation of the actual text of these three chapters is slim (only 27 pages). It is no surprise that Kim's work does not deal sufficiently with the Scripture, let alone the Jewish extra-biblical literature.

Another book on these chapters, *Called from the Jews and from the Gentiles* (2009), is a revised version of Gadenz's doctoral dissertation supervised by Jean-Noël Aletti at the Pontifical Gregorian University. It employs rhetorical analysis to examine Paul's ecclesiology in Romans 9–11. Although Gadenz's reading is guided by a rhetorical analysis of the sections' argumentation (*dispositio, elocutio* and *inventio*), he is attentive to the scriptural references that form its interpretive background.[34] However, Gadenz's treatment of the Scriptures is governed by his concern with

---

30. The dissertation was completed at Union Theological Seminary.
31. Johann D. Kim, *God, Israel, and the Gentiles: Rhetoric and Situation in Romans 9–11* (Atlanta: SBL, 2000), 1. As he states, "Our understanding of Romans 9–11 can only be advanced if we pay more attention to Paul's argumentative structure from the perspective of his sophisticated use of Greco-Roman rhetorical theories." See also Kim, *God, Israel, and the Gentiles*, 8.
32. Kim's rhetorical criticism can be summarized as follows: (1) determination of the *rhetorical unit*; (2) determination of the *rhetorical situation*; (3) determination of the *rhetorical problem*; (4) determination of the *arrangement of material*: the subdivisions of material (*exordium, narration, proposition, probation, refutation, peroration*, etc.); (5) determination of *invention* and *style*; (6) evaluation of *rhetorical effectiveness*. See Kim, *God, Israel, and the Gentiles*, 11–13. Italics original.
33. Ibid., 143.
34. Pablo T. Gadenz, *Called from the Jews and from the Gentiles: Pauline Ecclesiology in Romans 9–11*, WUNT 267 (Tübingen: Mohr Siebeck, 2009), 7.

Pauline ecclesiology in Romans 9–11,[35] which explains why his dealing with the Scriptures is uneven.

One year later, Belli's book, *Argumentation and Use of Scripture in Romans 9–11*, was published. Through ancient rhetoric, Belli identifies the nature of the discourse as invention, disposition and elocution, conclusions similar to Gadenz's. Moreover, he establishes the distinctive type of argument, called "scriptural argumentation." Belli attempts to prove that the Scriptures are decisive for Paul's argument in Romans 9–11.[36] However, Belli is not really interested in how the scriptural traditions affect Paul's argumentation, since Belli treats the scriptural co-texts only briefly.

In sum, there stands a trend in researching Romans 9–11 that focuses on the host texts themselves. Some of the recent research work may have an awareness of the scriptural co-texts, but the discussion of these is governed by theological or literary-structural concerns; that is, the scriptural texts are not really treated in their own right. Also, these works concerning Paul's host text in Romans 9–11 restrict their interpretation to the stance of Christian communities, an approach that fails to provide any understanding of how Paul's view of God, Israel, and the Gentiles is positioned within the first-century Jewish world.

Nevertheless, the weakness of this trend of study has been overcome to some extent by some current biblical scholars who realize the value and significance of placing Paul's text within its intertextual background. In the following, intertextual research on Romans 9–11 will be examined.

---

35. In the view of Gadenz, the scriptural references "are at the service of Paul's argumentation as part of his rhetorical strategy." Also, the Scriptures basically function as proofs for Paul's arguments. Gadenz, *Called from the Jews and from the Gentiles*, 40, 321–22.

36. Filippo Belli, *Argumentation and Use of Scripture in Romans 9–11*, Anbib 183, (Rome: Gregorian & Biblical Press, 2010), 409–410. Belli points out the distinguished way that Paul uses Scriptures in the course of his argumentation: "the Scriptures at times sustain the arguments; other times they prepare them; still other times, however, they remain in the background of the treatment." He then concludes, "It is the argumentation that determines the use of the Scriptures and not vice-versa." Moreover, Belli proposes that, "The point of departure of the discourse . . . is not the Scriptures but Christian experience, the gospel that he [Paul] wishes to communicate."

1.2.2 Intertextual Research on Romans 9–11

1.2.2.1 Focus on Motifs

Munck identified scriptural themes throughout Romans in his book *Christ & Israel: An Interpretation of Romans 9–11* (original German in 1956, English translation in 1967).[37] Munck is aware of Paul's situation when he was writing Romans. That is, Paul, as a Jewish apostle to the Gentiles, has to face the tension between Israel's unbelief and the Gentiles' acceptance of the gospel.[38] He offers the schema of salvation of the Jews and the Gentiles: no-yes-yes.[39] The Jews' no to the gospel leads to the yes to the salvation to the Gentiles, which in turn brings in salvation for the Jews because of their jealousy.[40] Munck's exegesis of Romans 9–11 gives attention to the scriptural texts, although his interpretation of the Scriptures seems governed by his theological schemata. Note that Munck is aware of Paul's role as a prophetic apostle, as he states that Paul sees himself as a prophet, like Elijah, who "confronts a majority of the people, alone and in danger of death."[41]

Bell engaged in research on Romans 9–11,[42] focusing on the motif of jealousy. He argued in his book *Provoked to Jealousy* that Paul borrowed the jealousy motif from Deuteronomy 32, the "Song of Moses." He

---

37. See Johannes Munck, *Christ & Israel: An Interpretation of Romans 9–11*, (Philadelphia: Fortress, 1967), 3.
38. Ibid., 8.
39. Murray Baker's article "Paul and the Salvation of Israel: Paul's Ministry, the Motif of Jealousy, and Israel's Yes." *CBQ* 67 (2005) 469–484, argues against the schema of no-yes-(jealousy)-yes, saying that "no direct line can be drawn that will intersect all three points [Paul's ministry, the motif of jealousy, and the salvation of Israel]" Baker contends that "jealousy is the mark of hardening," which "has no connection with Israel's salvation." See Baker, "Paul and the Salvation of Israel," 484. Cf. Mary Ann Getty, "Paul and the Salvation of Israel: A Perspective on Romans 9–11." *CBQ* 50 (1988) 456–469.
40. Krister Stendahl in the forward of the book rightly summarizes Munck's understanding of Paul on the issue of the salvation of Jews and Gentiles: "Paul's special revelation, the mystery and the gospel which he had received, was a reversal of the expected timetable as to the salvation of Jews and Gentiles: rather than letting the Yes of the Jews – which was not forthcoming at the time – lead to the Yes of the Gentiles, Paul announced that the very No of the Jews was God's strange way of bringing salvation to the Gentiles right then. And this in turn would, in God's own time, lead to the Yes of the Jews." Munck, *Christ & Israel*, xiii.
41. Ibid., 13.
42. Bell, *Provoked to Jealousy*.

investigated the "Song of Moses" in the light of its Jewish use (The *Song* in the OT, the Dead Sea Scrolls, the books of *Maccabees*, Philo, and Josephus, etc.) and its Christian use, in order to indicate the influence of the *Song* on Paul's understanding of salvation history. The aim of Bell's study is to investigate the jealousy motif in the argument of Romans 9–11, which limits his analysis to this very motif. Also, he relies too much on the role of the "Song" in Paul's understanding of the salvation-historical scheme.

1.2.2.2 Focus on Paul's Role[43] in his Understanding of Scripture

The publication of Hays' book *Echoes of Scripture in the Letters of Paul* (1989) has had a significant impact on subsequent research on Paul's use of Scripture.[44] He stresses Paul's role as a reader or interpreter of Scripture,[45] and sees Paul's reading of Scripture as a hermeneutical model for our Christian hermeneutics of Scripture.[46] Among all the Pauline letters, Hays spends most space on Romans, particularly on Romans 9–11 (ch. 2 and some passages on Romans throughout the book). Hays' intertextual echo reading of Romans 9–11 is articulated poetically and is well designed to bring in larger scriptural co-texts. However, his way of locating intertextual meaning remains confusing. That is, Hays mixes his intertextual reading of Paul and Paul's own intertextual discourse – in his terms, it is "intertextual fusion"[47] – as he attempts to hold together all the five different approaches

---

43. It is considered to be scriptural interpreter or/and apostle to the Gentiles.

44. Quite a number of works have been written since Hays' book was published that either offer critique, explicit use, or modifications of his approach. Cf. Kenneth D. Litwak, "Echoes of Scripture? A Critical Survey of Recent Works on Paul's Use of the Old Testament," *CurBS* 6 (1998), 264–275. Beetham, *Echoes of Scripture*; Wagner, *Heralds of the Good News*; Abasciano, *Paul's Use of the Old Testament in Romans 9:1–9* and *Paul's Use of the Old Testament in Romans 9:10–18*. For the critiques, see Porter, "Use of the Old Testament," 79–96; Stanley, "Paul's Use of Scripture," 127–136.

45. Hays says, "My investigation is . . . animated by the question, How did Paul interpret Israel's Scriptures?" He further states the task of his book "is to retrace some of Paul's readings, seeking to grasp their novelty and to follow the intricate hermeneutical paths along which he led his readers." See Hays, *Echoes of Scripture in the Letters of Paul*, x, 5.

46. Ibid., 178–192.

47. Ibid., 28.

to locate meaning.[48] It is difficult to make this fusion methodology work, therefore Hays seems to intend to depend on his own reading, as well as giving attention to historical exegesis.[49] Note that although his seven criteria,[50] which are meant to determine intertextual echoes in the texts, have been widely discussed and more or less adopted by scholars in speaking of Paul's use of Scripture, they function more like concepts in understanding intertextual echoes than a methodological measure for the intertextuality of texts; this means that the seven criteria cannot work as a methodological control to measure intertextual interconnectedness. In addition, Hays does not distinguish quotations from echoes. He seems to examine all the scriptural texts (including quotation texts) as echoes or allusions.[51]

Influenced by Hays, Wagner argues in his book *Heralds of the Good News: Isaiah and Paul "in Concert" in the Letter to the Romans* (2002) that Isaiah and Paul are in symphonic harmony as they each address a resistant and contrary people.[52] He pays attention to the Scriptures' own texts and their co-texts, and compares Paul's wording of Scripture with the various

---

48. Here are the five options: (1) The hermeneutic event occurs in Paul's mind; (2) the hermeneutical event occurs in the original readers of the letter; (3) the intertextual fusion occurs in the text itself; (4) the hermeneutical event occurs in current reader's act of reading; (5) the hermeneutical event occurs in a community of interpretation. See Hays, *Echoes of Scripture in the Letters of Paul*, 26–27.

49. Ibid., 27–28.

50. Ibid., 29–32. Here are the seven criteria: availability, volume, recurrence, thematic coherence, historical plausibility, history of interpretation, and satisfaction.

51. As we have mentioned above, a critique of Hays also can be found in Porter's article and some other articles. See Porter, "Use of the Old Testament," 79–96. See also Stanley, "Paul's Use of Scripture," 127–136.

52. In the same year, another book on Paul and Isaiah by Shiu-Lun Shum was published, entitled *Paul's Use of Isaiah in Romans*. In contrast to Wagner, Shum seems to go back to the traditional source-influence approach to doing intertextuality, although he mentions Hays' theory of intertextual echo in his methodology. In the book, he detects and examines the influence of the Isaianic tradition upon three sets of materials (by the Sibyls, the Qumran sectarians, and Paul). Shum spends 172 pages on non-Roman literature and less than 100 pages on Paul's use of Isaiah in Romans, although the book is titled as *Paul's Use of Isaiah in Romans*. Moreover, he spends a great deal of time on the Isaianic tradition in the Jewish literature, but he does not explain how Jewish literature's usage of Isaianic tradition would influence his interpretation of Paul's use of Isaiah in Romans. The relations of the two parts are loose. Finally, his conclusion drawn from his analysis is too general to be new. He concludes that "despite some dissimilarities shown in the way they utilized and handled the Isaianic material, Paul, the Qumran sectarians and the Sibyls basically shared the same interpretive traditions and techniques. However, Paul set himself apart from the sectarians and the Sibyls in messianic belief, which in turn affected

readings in the manuscript tradition of the LXX and MT. In particular, he closely examines some passages of the manuscripts of the LXX, 1 QIsa^a, Targum, and Peshitta in relation "to Paul's reading of Isaiah in its wider cultural and historical context."[53] Wagner provides a closer examination of the Isaianic texts than Hays' general discussion of the larger scriptural co-text. Moreover, Wagner shows awareness of the need to set Paul's reading of Scripture in its wider cultural context, but he does not bring in Paul's Jewish contemporaries' reading of Scripture, except sporadically in his discussion of the related exegetical activity for some passage in Second Temple literature.[54] In sum, Wagner has depicted a consonant picture of Paul and Isaiah: that Paul's mission to the Gentiles leads to the redemption of Israel and that this story of Israel's final deliverance can be heard in Isaiah. Note that before Wagner's *Heralds of the Good News*, Chilton, in his article "Romans 9–11 as Scriptural Interpretation and Dialogue with Judaism" (1988), had already argued for the harmony of the two tracks – Paul's own discourse and the Hebrew Scripture.[55]

In current study of Paul's use of the Scriptures, a growing number of scholars locate Paul's letters within the Second Temple Period with its religious texts and beliefs. In other words, the literature of Second Temple Judaism has been employed in important ways in the study of Paul's letters. Aageson's Oxford dissertation, "Paul's Use of Scripture" (1984),[56] represents an important work on Paul's use of Scripture in Romans 9–11. He

---

greatly his understanding of the Isaianic prophecies." See Shum, *Paul's Use of Isaiah in Romans*, 268.

53. Wagner, *Heralds of the Good News*, 17–18.

54. Ibid., 17.

55. He says that, "We may set out mentally, as it were side by side, two analyzes of Romans 9–11. Followed along one track, the chapters instance protreptic discourse. . . . He [Paul] wishes to convince them that God's inclusion of believing Gentiles with Jews who accept Jesus as Christ represents a fulfillment of the promise to Israel. Followed along the second track, the same chapters represent a carefully orchestrated argument from all the main sections of the Hebrew canon, cited in translation. . . . It is obvious that the two tracks of analysis are complementary, and neither alone would adequately account for the chapters as a whole. But it is equally obvious that the chapters are crafted as a whole." See Bruce D. Chilton, "Romans 9–11 as Scriptural Interpretation and Dialogue with Judaism," *ExAud* 4 (1988): 30–31.

56. The full name of the dissertation, which was completed at Oxford University, is: "Paul's Use of Scripture: A Comparative Study of Biblical Interpretation in Early Palestinian Judaism and the New Testament with Special Reference to Romans 9–11."

not only argues that the interpretive methods that Paul applies to Scripture can be found in the early Jewish sources, but also that "Paul's method of scriptural interpretation and argumentation is fundamental to the theological development of the discussion in Romans 9–11."[57] First, Aageson compares the early Jewish use of Scripture to Paul's and asserts that Paul's interpretive methods of Scripture are not different from that of his Jewish contemporaries. This assertion is far too general and broad to be helpful.[58] This dissertation came before Hays' *Echoes of Scripture*; and the dissertation indicates that the larger scriptural context may not be important for Paul.[59] Moreover, Aageson's exegesis of the texts of Romans 9–11 is very brief. For instance, less than one page serves to treat the whole section of Romans 9:1–5. In addition, the discussion of the last chapter of the dissertation, which covers Paul's use of Scripture in comparison with the pertinent Jewish sources, is governed by some sporadic themes – such as "not all those descended from Israel are really Israel," "the 'potter' and his 'clay,'" "a 'remnant,'" and "Christ and the commandment of God" – rather than a literary-systematic comparison of Paul's discourse in Romans 9–11 and the pertinent Second Temple Jewish literature.[60] Although Aageson

---

57. James W. Aageson, "Paul's Use of Scripture: A Comparative Study of Biblical Interpretation in Early Palestinian Judaism and the New Testament with Special Reference to Romans 9–11," unpublished D Phil thesis, University of Oxford, 1983, 2. Note that Aageson shares some awareness of the relation between Paul's writing and Paul's role. He says, "Paul writes as one of God's 'elect'. His heart has not been hardened; he has not been given a spirit of stupor. Concerning the righteousness of God he has 'knowledge'; he does not attempt to establish his own righteousness." See Aageson, "Paul's Use of Scripture," 242. However, Aageson's view of Paul's role sounds like a plain counterpart to his opponents, which are described in Romans 9–10.

58. Hays' comment on Pauline Exegesis as Midrash would also fit here, "The claim is true but trivial. . . . All readings of Scripture by Jews and Christians always and everywhere are instances of midrash." See Hays, *Echoes of Scripture in the Letters of Paul*, 10–11. Regarding a midrashic reading of Romans 9–11, see William R. Stegner's article "Romans 9:6–29 – A Midrash," *JSNT* 22 (1984): 37–52. The purpose of the article "is to show that Romans 9: 6–29 is a midrash both because of its midrashic form and because of its content." He establishes a formal definition of midrash, and shows that the passage is similar to rabbinic midrashim in both form and content. See Stegner, "Romans 9:6–29," 38–45.

59. Contrary to Hays' theory of Paul's use of Scripture, Aageson states, "Among the explicit quotations . . . we discover that there appears to be little or no direct evidence that the larger scriptural contexts were thematically important for Paul." See Aageson, "Paul's Use of Scripture," 111.

60. Ibid., 244–276.

is aware of the need to compare Paul's use of Scripture with the Second Temple literature, he lacks the methodological control to do the comparison, which results in his study being less integrated.

Sharing similar interests with Aageson, Johnson also investigates Romans 9–11 in relation to Jewish literature.[61] In the work, she seeks to answer questions about the nature of Paul's relationship to Jewish apocalyptic thought and how it is "that tradition from two so different kinds of literature – apocalyptic and wisdom – can co-exist in the same text."[62] Johnson also argues, in regard to the function of apocalyptic and wisdom traditions in Romans 9–11, that Paul's confluence of the two traditions maintains "a balanced tension between God's impartial treatment of all and God's faithfulness to Israel."[63] However, Johnson's three criteria vocabulary, ideas or themes,[64] and forms[65] for testing a passage involving the wisdom tradition are too broad to specify the genre of a text. It is surprising that when she enters into exegesis of Romans 9–11 in order to establish the sapiential characteristics, the three criteria are not applied in her analysis; instead, she simply lays out two passages, Romans 10:6–8 and 11:33–36, which other scholars have considered to be sapiential texts.

If the analysis in both Aageson's dissertation and Johnson's work on Romans 9–11 remains too general and all inclusive to demonstrate the specific relationships of Pauline texts and the Jewish literature, then Abasciano's work stands at the other pole. Abasciano's exegesis is too detailed to see the whole picture of Romans 9–11, although he may be aware of this

---

61. In 1989, E. Elizabeth Johnson's dissertation (completed at Princeton Theological Seminary) on Romans 9–11 was turned into a book, *The Function of Apocalyptic and Wisdom Tradition in Romans 9–11,* (Atlanta: Scholars, 1989).

62. Ibid., 206.

63. Ibid., 175, 208.

64. Those themes are concerning "correct human social behavior and relationships, the order of the social and natural worlds, questions of theodicy and the purpose of human life, and the divine origin of Wisdom and its essentially revelatory nature." See Johnson, *Function of Apocalyptic*, 65.

65. According to Johnson, the typical forms of wisdom literature are: "proverbs, riddles, fables and allegories, hymns and prayers, disputations and dialogues, autobiographical narratives and confessions, lists, and didactic poetry and narratives" (Johnson, *Function of Apocalyptic*, 66). This list is too broad to decide whether a passage is a wisdom literature or not.

limitation.⁶⁶ He considers Paul to be a serious interpreter of Scripture, so he enters into a detailed analysis of the relevant Old Testament texts and the related Jewish exegetical traditions. For instance, he uses 26 pages (pp. 46–72) to depict the larger context of Exodus 32:32 (Exod 32–34) and 15 pages (pp. 74–89) to explain the interpretive traditions surrounding Exodus 32:32.⁶⁷ Therefore, it is not a surprise that he has had to write three books to analyze Paul's use of the Old Testament in Romans 9 (Rom 9:1–9 [2005]; Romans 9:10–18 [2011]; and Romans 9:19–33 [2015]).⁶⁸ Even so, the analysis of the co-text of Romans 9:3 is shorter than it deserves. For instance, Abasciano uses less than 3 pages (pp. 90–93) to analyze Romans 9:1–2, which suggests that his analysis depends heavily on the larger scriptural co-text, neglecting the significant role of Paul's own discourse within it.

In addition, there are some current scholars who value Paul's self-awareness of his role in the use of Scripture. In his monograph (published in 1997), *Paul as Apostle to the Gentiles*, Chae argues that "Paul's self-awareness of being apostle to the *Gentiles* functions as the controlling factor for the shape of his argument."⁶⁹ Chae structures the content of Romans 1–11 according to his understanding of the subject matter of Paul's argument in Romans, that is, the equality of Jew and Gentile.⁷⁰ He also claims to "adopt Paul's use of the OT as a crucial interpretative key for his argument

---

66. He sets aside a chapter to introduce Romans 9–11. However, his whole analysis is drowning in detail.

67. I do not see how these interpretive traditions contribute to our understanding of Paul's use of Scripture.

68. It is rather arbitrary to divide Romans 9:1–18 as vv. 1–9 and vv. 10–18, since Abasciano acknowledges that the logical structure of Romans 9 is as follows: vv. 1–5, vv. 6–13, vv. 14–18, vv. 19–29, vv. 30–33. See Abasciano, *Paul's Use of the Old Testament in Romans 9:1–9*, 37–38.

69. Daniel Jong-Sang Chae, *Paul as Apostle to the Gentiles: His Apostolic Self-Awareness and Its Influence on the Soteriological Argument in Romans*, PBTM, (Carlisle: Paternoster, 1997), 2. Italics original.

70. In this sense, he divides Romans 9–11 into the following parts: Romans springs from Paul's apostolic self-awareness (1:1–15); the equal inclusion of Gentiles in God's salvation (1:16–17); the equality of Jew and Gentile in sinfulness (1:18–3:20); the equality of Jew and Gentile in justification (3:21–4:25); the equality of Jew and Gentile in the new status (5:1–8:39); the equality of Jew and Gentile in the plan of God (9:1–11:36). See Chae, *Paul as Apostle to the Gentiles*, 38–301.

in the letter [to the Romans]."[71] Given Chae's focus, the most important characteristic of Paul's use of Scripture in Romans 9–11 is that "he chooses some of the most severely critical passages in the OT" to apply to Jews, and "he applies to *Gentiles* some of the passages most affirmative of Israel."[72] A German scholar, Wilk, also gives attention to Paul's self-understanding of his role as an apostle to the Gentiles. He investigates Paul's use of Isaiah in the seven undisputed Pauline letters "with regard to his self-understanding as an apostle and his proclamation of the gospel."[73]

Paul's role as an apostle to the Gentiles represents a common consensus among biblical scholars; however, when speaking of Paul's self-understanding of his role represented in Romans 9–11, it is too general to say that Paul identifies himself as the Gentiles' apostle. How should we explain his serious concern about his kinsmen if Paul understands himself just as an apostle for Gentiles? Therefore, Paul's self-awareness of his role can be specified as expressed in Romans 9–11. Evans' article on the relation of Paul and the prophets with special reference to Romans 9–11, with its implication that Paul's role as a prophet is related to the discourse in these chapters, has not been given enough attention.[74] Evans' analysis is based on two elements: the relationship between apostle and prophet (prophetic call, visions, manner of speaking of himself and his ministry, apostolic obligation, and comparison with Elijah), and the hermeneutics of prophetic criticism. He views Paul's employment of the hermeneutics of prophetic criticism in his use of Scripture in Romans 9–11 as a way to attest to "an important aspect of the apostle's understanding of his apostleship. . . . Paul's calling placed him in the tradition of the prophets."[75] However, there

---

71. Ibid., 13.
72. Ibid., 218.
73. Florian Wilk, *Die Bedeutung des Jesajabuches für Paulus*, FRLANT 179, (Göttingen: Vandenhoeck & Ruprecht, 1998), 1. He states, "Angesichts dieser Zusammenhänge besteht die Intention der vorliegenden Studie darin, den Einfluß des Jesajabuches auf die Ausformung des paulinischen Selbstverständnisses und der ihm anvertrauten Verkündigung Jesu Christi unter den Heiden zu bestimmen."
74. See C. A. Evans, "Paul and the Prophets: Prophetic Criticism in the Epistle to the Romans," in *Romans and the People of God: Essays in Honor of Gordon D. Fee on the Occasion of His 65th Birthday*, ed. Sven Soderlund, Gordon D. Fee and N. T. Wright, (Grand Rapids: Eerdmans, 1999),115–128.
75. Ibid., 128.

has not been much research done on the relationship of Paul's discourse in Romans 9–11 and his self-understanding as a prophet,[76] even though there are some studies on Paul's role as a prophet in his other letters, such as Aernie's *Is Paul Also among the Prophets?* and Sandnes' *Paul – One of the Prophets?* However, neither of these two books deals with Romans 9–11, let alone Paul's discourse patterns and his use of Scriptures in comparison with early Jewish literature.

In conclusion, in their approach to intertextual research, some scholars use motifs to discuss the interaction of the host and precursor texts, others see Paul as the scriptural interpreter, and still others view Paul as the apostle to the Gentiles, a role which influences Paul's use of Scripture. Moreover, some other Pauline researchers realize the significance of other Jewish literature in understanding Paul's reading of Scripture. Therefore, more and more scholars are focusing on the comparative study of Paul's, as well as his Jewish contemporaries', use of Scripture. Unfortunately, some of these comparative studies are very broad in scope, while others are too detailed. This is because most of these comparative studies do not utilize an appropriate methodological measure to do the analysis.

1.3 The Objective of this Study and its Thesis

So far, we have demonstrated that previous studies of Romans 9–11 have attempted to deal with the theological arguments of Paul, analyze Paul's rhetorical argumentation, and use intertextual approaches on Paul's use of Scriptures with varying degrees of success. Among these studies, there are some scholars who are aware of the relationship between Paul's self-understanding and his writings. Among scholars who use intertextual approaches, there is a growing awareness of the larger co-text of Scripture,

---

76. Munck, in his book *Christ and Israel*, has some occasional descriptions of Paul as a prophet. Also, Hall's dissertation (Winfield Scott Hall, "Paul as a Christian Prophet in His Interpretation of the Old Testament in Romans 9–11." Unpublished PhD Dissertation. Lutheran School of Theology at Chicago, 1982) deals with Paul as a Christian prophet, whose interpretation of the Old Testament is by means of charismatic exegesis. However, his viewpoint on prophetic discourse is too restrictive to confine Paul's interpretation to charismatic exegesis.

with some scholars setting Paul's use of Scripture against the background of the literature of Second Temple Judaism. However, no one up to now has employed an appropriate intertextual methodological control which is based on an intertextual principle of meaning making in analyzing Paul's discourse.[77] In other words, intertextual reading does not just happen when Paul uses Scripture; the whole discourse of Romans 9–11 must be examined within an intertextual thematic system.[78] In order to understand Paul's viewpoint better, we have to place his discourse within the context of his social communities, which include the communities of the Second Temple period, particularly those of Paul's period.

Therefore, most discussions do not adequately treat the discourse in Romans 9–11 by closely investigating Paul's discourse patterns and his Jewish contemporaries' discourses regarding God, Israel, and the Gentiles due to lack of an appropriate intertexutal methodological control. Our attempt will show how an intertextual thematic methodology can be beneficial for a proper understanding of Paul's viewpoint on the relationship of God, Israel, and the Gentiles in Romans 9–11.

This study will focus on Paul's discourse patterns regarding the relationships of God, Israel, and the Gentiles in Romans 9–11 by means of intertextual thematic analysis. Paul's unique way of using Scripture as one part of his discourse pattern will be investigated as well. We will argue that, although Paul uses a Jewish style of interpretation of Scripture, and though his discourse patterns resemble some of those in Jewish literature to a certain degree, Paul's viewpoint on the relationship of God, Israel, and the Gentiles in Romans 9–11 is in key ways dissociated from, and in fact even opposes, that of his Jewish contemporaries. In other words, although the new and creative nuances of Paul's viewpoint on God, Israel, and the Gentiles in Romans 9–11 are held in traditional wine bottles, this fact does

---

77. As Lemke has pointed out, "All meaning is intertextual. No text is complete or autonomous in itself; it needs to be read, and it is read, in relation to other texts" (See J. L. Lemke, *Textual Politics: Discourse and Social Dynamics*, CPLE, [London: Taylor & Francis, 1995], 41). However, it has not been developed as a methodological term since Kristeva, when it was more a theoretical term. See Timothy K. Beal, "Ideology and Intertextuality: Surplus of Meaning and Controlling the Means of Production," in *Reading between Texts*, ed. Danna Nolan Fewell, (Louisville: Westminster John Knox, 1992), 27.
78. We will explain in detail in the next chapter about "intertextual thematic systems."

not diminish the divergence of his own stance being away from that of his Jewish contemporaries. This conclusion is contrary to many current studies, which claim that the conflict between Paul (along with his communities) and the Jews is still an inner-Jewish polemic.[79] Some scholars portray Paul's viewpoint as one of many available Jewish traditions, and argue that the early Christian community functioned merely as one of the sects of Judaism. However, through an intertextual study of Paul's discourse in Romans 9–11, we will demonstrate the divergence of Paul's viewpoints on some typical Jewish issues, which suggests that the discontinuities between Paul and his Jewish contemporaries are obvious, and sometimes radical.

This investigation indicates that the core values of Pauline Christian communities have been embedded in Paul's discourse in Romans, and differ from contemporary Jewish beliefs at their core. In addition, the overall discourse pattern in Romans 9–11 resembles a prophetic discourse pattern, which indicates that Paul's self-understanding as a prophetic figure serves to confirm that his word comes from God,[80] the divine authority.[81] In sum, through the detailed intertextual analysis of Paul's discourse patterns with those of the Jewish tradition and Paul's Jewish contemporaries, we will

---

79. Regarding the inner-Jewish polemic, see James D. G. Dunn, *The Partings of the Ways: Between Christianity and Judaism and Their Significance for the Character of Christianity*, 2nd ed. (London: SCM, 2006); and Terence L. Donaldson, *Jews and Anti-Judaism in the New Testament: Decision Points and Divergent Interpretations* (Waco: Baylor University Press, 2010).

80. The concept of Paul as an apostle is not different from the Old Testament conception of a prophet. They are both, in essence, sent by God and speaking for God. The term "prophet" expresses the meaning of "being sent by God as a messenger . . . The verb 'send' (shalah) appears at the heart of God's commissioning of Moses, Isaiah, Jeremiah, and Ezekiel. In the New Testament 'apostle' means 'one who is sent' (ἀπόστολος is etymologically related to the verbal root ἀποστέλλω) and so the New incorporates within its depiction of those who foundationally speak for God in Christ the conceptuality of the Old" (R. W. L. Moberly, *Prophecy and Discernment*, CSCD, [Cambridge: Cambridge University Press, 2006] 4). According to Sawyer, "Prophets are first and foremost 'proclaimers'" (John F. A. Sawyer, *Prophecy and the Biblical Prophets*, rev. ed. OB, [Oxford: Oxford University Press, 1993], 1). Sawyer points out that "'prophecy' means both prediction (foretelling) and proclamation (forthtelling), so that 'prophets' include not only people with supernatural powers . . . but preachers like St Francis of Assisi, John Wesley, Martin Luther King and other 'proclaimers' as well".

81. The three main authorial self-references (9:3; 10:1; 11:1–2) attest to Paul's consciousness of being in the tradition of Israel's prophets. This prophetic role would legitimate Paul's right to proclaim that God's people are not only from the Jews but also from the Gentiles on the basis of the gospel of Jesus Christ.

demonstrate that Paul's viewpoint on the relationship of God, Israel, and the Gentiles shares both continuity and discontinuity with that of contemporary Judaism(s).

1.4 Value of this Research

This study is hopefully of interest for the following four reasons. First, the study is useful for highlighting the value of intertextual thematic analysis as an indispensable tool for understanding Paul's viewpoints against the backdrop of Jewish contemporary literature. Second, it offers a deeper understanding of Paul's discourse patterns and how the patterns ally with or oppose his Jewish contemporaries' discourses. Third, it generates better understanding of Paul's use of Scripture in Romans 9–11. Finally, the study provides a new insight into the overall discourse patterns in Romans 9–11, which appears to be prophetic discourse.

1.5 Outline of the Present Study

This study is divided into six chapters, along with an introduction and a conclusion. This introduction provides the situation of Paul's letter to the Romans, including Paul's own situation and the situation of the Roman churches. Also, this introductory chapter gives a selective survey of important previous studies of Romans 9–11 and presents the objectives and the thesis of this study, including the value and the plan of the study, which serve as an overall view of the whole project. Then, in chapter 2, we demonstrate our methodology, adapting Lemke's intertextual thematic analysis so it can be better applied in Romans 9–11. Chapters 3 to 5 offer an intertextual thematic analysis of Romans 9–11, arranged according to the discourse structure that enjoys consensus among scholars: 9:1–29; 9:30–10:21; and 11:1–32 (36). A summary of the findings in each chapter will be presented at the end of each chapter. The final chapter concludes with a synthesis of all the findings of our intertextual thematic analysis of Romans 9–11. It will demonstrate the nature of the (dis)association of

Paul's viewpoints on the relationship of God, Israel, and the Gentiles from that of his Jewish contemporaries.

CHAPTER TWO

Research Methodology: An Intertextual Thematic Analysis

2.1 Introduction

Much research has been done on Romans 9–11. However, what remains lacking is an appropriate intertextual methodological control in order to identify the thematic patterns of Paul's argumentations in Romans 9–11 and to compare these patterns with the argumentation of Paul's Jewish contemporaries in regard to the relationship of God, Israel, and the Gentiles. This study will employ Lemke's intertextual thematic formation theory to approach Romans 9–11.[1] In the following, Lemke's theory of intertextuality will first be introduced, including the general idea of intertextuality, thematic formations, intertextual thematic formations, and heteroglossic voices. Next, our evaluation of Lemke's intertextual thematic model will be provided including its strengths and weakness as well as its usefulness and limitations for the study of Romans 9–11. Finally, an adaptation of Lemke's model and our full analytical procedure will be outlined in order to offer a complete picture for the process of analysis in this study.

---

1. Note that the word "thematic" here is not identitcal with the meaning of Halliday's Theme-Rheme. It refers to a topic which occurs from text to text. See Lemke, "Intertextuality and Text Semantics," in *Discourse in Society Systemic Functional Perspectives*, ed. Peter Howard Fries, Michael Gregory and M. A. K. Halliday, (Norwood: Ablex, 1995), 91.

2.2 Lemke's Concept of Intertextuality

2.2.1 Introduction

Lemke's concept of intertextuality is different from the traditional view of a linear adaption of one text in another and the post-structuralist concept of intertextuality. Lemke's theory of general intertextuality is a way of meaning making in communities, which enhances the register theory of analysis for text meaning.

Many biblical scholars employ the term "intertextuality" to describe the relationship created when an Old Testament text is used in a New Testament text.[2] Traditionally, when speaking of biblical intertextual relationships, the focus is upon the wording found within the texts. The treatment of textual adaptation involves the analysis of phenomena such as verbatim copying, near-verbatim copying, explicit or near-explicit reference, paraphrase, or allusion in the host text in relation to previous texts.[3] Lemke, however, considers intertextual relations differently. As he has stated, two texts that "share only one or a few key words is not enough,

---

2. Biblical scholars have used many terms to describe the connection between previous texts and later texts, and intertextuality is one of them (see Boda, "Quotation and Allusion," 296). For instance, Hays, *Echoes of Scripture in the Letters of Paul* (1989); Steve Moyise, ed., *The Old Testament in the Book of Revelation*. JSNTSup 115. (Sheffield: Sheffield Academic, 1995); Rikki Watts, *Isaiah's New Exodus and Mark* (Tübingen: Mohr Siebeck, 1997); G. K. Beale, *John's Use of the Old Testament in Revelation*, JSNTSup 166, (Sheffield: Sheffield Academic, 1998); David W. Pao, *Acts and the Isaianic New Exodus*. WUNT 130 (Tübingen: Mohr Siebeck, 2000); Gary T. Manning, *Echoes of a Prophet: The Use of Ezekiel in the Gospel of John and in Literature of the Second Temple Period*. JSNTSup 270 (London: T & T Clark International, 2004); Francis Watson, *Paul and the Hermeneutics of Faith* (Edinburgh: T & T Clark, 2004); Litwak, *Echoes of Scripture in Luke-Acts: Telling the History of God's People Intertextually* (2005); Beetham, *Echoes of Scripture in the Letter of Paul to the Colossians* (2008); Steve Moyise, *Paul and Scripture* (Grand Rapids: Baker Academic, 2010). It is worth noting that the use of the term is not restricted to New Testament studies; and it is beginning to emerge in Old Testament studies as well. According to Hatina, "Historically oriented Old Testament scholars generally use the term in much the same way as their New Testament counterparts, namely as a designation for the appropriation of prior texts by later texts." See Thomas R. Hatina, "Intertextuality and Historical Criticism in New Testament Studies : Is There a Relationship?" *BibInt* 7 (1999): 1, n. 2.

3. See Thomas L. Brodie, Dennis Ronald MacDonald, and Stanley E. Porter, "Conclusion: Problems of Method," in *The Intertextuality of the Epistles: Explorations of Theory and Practice*, ed. Brodie, MacDonald and Porter, 284–296, (Sheffield: Sheffield Phoenix, 2006), 288–290.

and may be quite irrelevant if those words are being used with different thematic meanings in the different texts."[4] In addition, he points out that "the texts may not share words, but use thematically equivalent synonyms or even figurative expressions. It is semantic patterns that the texts must share."[5]

The traditional diachronic approach to intertextuality has been challenged by those scholars who insist on the post-structuralist roots of intertextuality. From this perspective, intertextuality should not be seen as "a linear adaptation of another text but as a complex of relationships."[6] This understanding of "intertextuality" derives from a particular view of text.[7] That is, a text is never wholly one's own, for it is always already permeated with traces of other texts or other discourses.[8] However, since this view of intertextuality does not provide a way to analyze the complex of relations within texts, post-structural intertextuality is much more a literary concept than an interpretive tool. Lemke views texts as "arenas where we may hear the conflicts being fought out, or being contained."[9] He develops a way of doing intertextual relations so as to locate text semantics, which is viewed "differently from different social positions within the community."[10]

---

4. Lemke, "Intertextuality and Text Semantics," 91.
5. Ibid.
6. Wolde, "Trendy Intertextuality?," 47.
7. Here is the view of the text in post-structural literary circles: According to Bakhtin, "any text is an intertext; other texts are present in it, at varying levels. . . . Any text is a new tissue of past citations, bits of codes, formulae, rhythmic models, fragments of social languages, etc. passed into the text and redistributed within it, for there is always language before and around the text" (Roland Barthes, "Theory of the Text," in *Untying the Text: A Post-Structuralist Reader*, ed. Robert Young, [London: Routledge & Kegan Paul, 1981], 39).
8. Graham Allen, *Intertextuality*, NCI, (New York: Routledge, 2000), 28–30: Bakhtin identified the dialogic, heteroglossic quality of language so as to argue against "any unitary, authoritarian, and hierarchical conception of society, art, and life." Under this vision of human society and communication, Kristeva was able to coin the term "intertextuality" as part of her account of Bakhtin's work.
9. J. L. Lemke, "Discourses in Conflict: Heteroglossia and Text Semantics," in *Systemic Functional Approaches to Discourse: Selected Papers from the 12th International Systemic Workshop*, ed. James D. Benson and William S. Greaves (Norwood: Ablex 1988), 39. He states, "Every text combines ITFs whose thematic and actional intertextual ties enmesh it in the social heteroglossia of the community."
10. Ibid., 33.

Lemke's way of doing intertextual analysis is more executable than that of post-structural literary critics.

As a social semiotician, Lemke places intertextuality on the level of a system of social meaning-making practices that are characteristic of the community.[11] This is not just situational context, since he indicates that intertextual relations transcend the context of situation and depend on the context of culture.[12] This is a significant contribution to the relationship between text and context. For Lemke, a complete account of textual meaning does not only depend on the grammatical and situational context, but also on the context of culture.[13] In other words, Lemke sees the particular role of intertextuality as bridging "the use of lexicogrammatical resources in a text and the use of discourse patterns in a culture."[14] Moreover, Lemke views the theory of intertextuality as compensating for register theory.[15] That is, the system of intertextual relations can enhance for register theory in capturing socially dynamic points of view. As he indicates, the notion of register "does not capture many of the socially most important kinds of relationship among the texts made in a community."[16] So Lemke's theory of intertextuality aims to capture the socially dynamic voices represented in the systems of intertextual relations of texts by using the resources of systemic-functional grammar. In Lemke's words, "It [intertextual thematic

---

11. Lemke, "Intertextuality and Text Semantics," 85.

12. Ibid., 86.

13. Ibid., 85. Lemke's description of the culture of a community is: "[It] is as a complex system of relations among social practices, the socially meaningful 'doings' in the community" (Lemke, "Intertextuality and Text Semantics," 86).

14. Ibid., 86. Later, Lemke explains the discourse pattern in detail: "In addition to the lexico-grammar of a community's language, we need to know its recurrent forms of argument, rhetorical patterns, and ways of doing things, its recognizable activity types as well as the meaning potentials of its actional semiotic systems." See Lemke, "Intertextuality and Text Semantics," 86.

15. According to Halliday, "a register is a functional variety of language – the patterns of instantiation of the overall system associated with a given type of context." (See Halliday, *An Introduction to Functional Grammar*, 27). In another place, he further defines it as "a configuration of meanings that are typically associated with a particular situational configuration of field, mode, and tenor." See Halliday, *Language, Context, and Text*, 38–39.

16. J. L. Lemke, "Ideology, Intertextuality, and the Notion of Register," in *Systemic Perspectives on Discourses*, ed. J. D. Benson and W.S. Greaves (Norwood: Ablex, 1985), 280.

formation] recognized the role of grammar and textual cohesion, but it was far more 'local,' more register-specific."[17]

Lemke's intertextuality is concerned with text semantics (text meaning).[18] As he states, "the theory of intertextuality has profound implications for text semantics, providing an alternative model for text meaning from that of lexicogrammatical semantics."[19] If Halliday's register theory aims for use meaning (in Lemke's terms),[20] corresponding to the contextualized meaning made with the words of a text, then Lemke's theory of intertextuality aims for thematic meaning, "corresponding to the meaning the word realizes in a recurrent discourse pattern that is familiar in many texts and which forms the basis of cothematic intertextual relations."[21] Therefore, the study of intertextuality focuses on "the recurrent discourse and activity patterns of the community and how they are constituted by, instanced in, and interconnected or disjoined through particular texts."[22] When intertextuality is applied to a biblical text, for example, in order to understand the meaning of "Israel who pursued the righteousness of law did not succeed in fulfilling the law" (Rom 9:31), we not only need to analyze the lexicogrammar of the text, but we also need to know the recurrent pattern of argument used by Paul and his communities to speak of the relations of Israel, righteousness, and the law, and how this discourse pattern is interconnected with, or disjoined from, the way in which Paul's fellow Jews speak of them in each of their own communities. This would enable a construction of intertextual relations among these particular texts in order to locate Paul's viewpoint within the diverse textual data.

---

17. J. L. Lemke, "Intertextuality and the Project of Text Linguistics," *TEXT* 20 (2000):223.

18. Text semantics, for Lemke, is complementary to lexicogrammatical semantics, which is "both a textual and an intertextual semantics" (Lemke, "Intertextuality and Text Semantics," 90–91). "It [text semantics] is a model of semantics in which larger discourse wholes contextualize the meanings of grammatical structures (e.g. clause-like units) and words." See Lemke, "Intertextuality and Text Semantics," 90.

19. Ibid., 87–88.

20. Note that Halliday uses the term "functional meaning."

21. Lemke, "Intertextuality and Text Semantics," 89.

22. Ibid., 86.

2.2.2 Lemke's Concept of Thematic Formations

Before we start to discuss Lemke's concept of "intertextual thematic formations" (ITFs), which plays a key role in Lemke's analysis of intertextual relations, it is very significant to make note of his definition of a *thematic formation* and its constructions. Only after this an understanding of ITF can be developed.

2.2.2.1 The Definition

Lemke's descriptions of thematic formations are spread throughout his articles on intertextuality, and his voice best captures their meanings. In one place, he explains it as follows: "Patterns of semantic relations among the same or closely related words and phrases are regularly repeated over and over again in many texts in a given community. These patterns are called thematic formations."[23] In another place, Lemke artfully describes it as follows: "A thematic formation can be represented in general as a web-like diagram with **thematic items** at the nodes and **thematic relations** connecting the nodes."[24] It should be noted that Lemke acknowledges an interchangeability between thematic items and thematic formations. As he expressly states, "In some cases . . . a small thematic formation may itself be treated as a thematic item in a larger formation."[25] Thematic formations are units of meaning; Lemke indicates, "They [thematic formations] are . . . elements of the system of grammatical resources which we use to construct meanings."[26]

---

23. Ibid., 165. This definition has been simplified as follows: "a recurrent pattern of semantic relations used in talking about a specific topic from text to text." Lemke, "Intertextuality and Text Semantics," 91.
24. See Lemke, "Intertextuality and Text Semantics," 92, emphasis original. Regarding a thematic item, it "glosses the repeated semantic features of the lexical items in the texts that realized a particular Process or Participant role in clause, group, or phrase structure (e.g., Actors, Goals, Classifiers, Mental Processes, Ranges, etc.)"; regarding thematic relation, it "states the lexicogrammatical semantic relation between two thematic items (e.g., Process-to-Range, Classifier-to-Thing, Carrier-to-Attribute, hypernym-to-hyponym, etc.)" See Lemke, "Intertextuality and Text Semantics," 92.
25. Ibid., 92.
26. Lemke, *Textual Politics*, 42.

2.2.2.2 *Its Constructions*

There is now one important question to be raised: how do we construct thematic formations? According to Lemke, thematic formations are built up by using multivariate structural relations, a multidimensional network consisting of essentially non-linear thematic relations.[27] For instance, if I see "deliver" and "gospel" in the same clause, then my encounter with other texts leads me to expect "Jesus Christ" nearby. If I do see them, the semantic relationships among them will be realized by such expressions as "deliver the gospel of Jesus Christ." Moreover, there can be included a few more other terms, e.g. sin, forgiveness, reconciliation. The whole typical pattern is an instance of a thematic formation, which can be called [gospel of Jesus Christ]. Lemke has provided the following example to explain the construction of a thematic formation: "If . . . we come across the lexical item 'electron,' and also 'atom,' 'orbital,' and valence,' then we can construct semantic relations among these items, according to a pattern we have encountered in many other texts."[28] These items can be recognized from the formation [Electron Configurations] for the discourse of chemistry.

Another possible way to build up a thematic formation is based on covariate ties. Covariate relations build connectivity between segments of texts or actions based on the fact that the segments are part of a system of meaning relations which indicates a specific relation among them.[29] For instance, if two segments of a text A and B (which may be words, clauses, stretches of text, etc.) are "both members of the same class (i.e. share a type feature z) then there is a z-relation between A and B, and between them and any other member of the z-class."[30] Here is one example: "This disease is a physical condition caused by biological factors." The nominal groups – the disease, the physical condition, and biological factors – share a covariate

---

27. According to Lemke, "The thematic relation states the lexicogrammatical semantic relation between two thematic items (e.g. Process-to-Range, Classifier-to-Thing, Carrier-to-Attribute, hypernym-to-hyponym, etc.). See Lemke, "Intertextuality and Text Semantics," 92–93; cf. Lemke, "Thematic Analysis: Systems, Structures, and Strategies," *SI* 3 (1983):162.
28. Lemke, "Text Structure and Text Semantics," in *Pragmatics, Discourse and Text*, ed. Erich H. Steiner (London: Pinter, 1988), 165.
29. Lemke, "Ideology, Intertextuality, and the Notion of Register," 287–288.
30. Ibid., 288.

tie; that is, they can belong to a recognizable sort of discourse, called [Biomedical]. In this way, covariate ties can help illumine constructions of thematic formations. Moreover, the covariate relations can be more complex: member A and B may not belong to the same class, but to contrasting classes (e.g. human, animal). Third, in Lemke's words, "A and B may have a covariate tie by virtue of belonging to a common thematic system."[31] For instance, book and author can have a covariate relation through the same thematic system, but their specific relations are not of a class-and-member or whole-and-part kind of relation.[32]

Besides multivariate and covariate ties, clausal and clause complexing relations are also important in establishing thematic formations. Examples of relations of clause complexes that Lemke provides are "Exemplification, Replacement ('not this, but that'), and Cause-Consequence."[33] I will use Halliday's description of the patterns of clause complexes, a more systematic description of clause complex relationships, in the appendixes to the analysis chapters.[34] A more detailed explanation of these relations will be provided in appendix 1, in which we provide Halliday's three main conjunctive relations and their subtype-relations with examples of Greek clauses from the New Testament.

2.2.3 Lemke's Concept of Intertextual Thematic Formation

2.2.3.1 *The Definition*
Now let us describe what is meant by an *intertexutal thematic formation* (ITF). According to Lemke, "It [an ITF] abstracts from a set of thematically related texts their common semantic patterns insofar as these mattered to *a particular community* for a particular set of social purposes."[35] In other words, ITFs are these co-thematic texts that build similar semantic relations

---

31. Ibid.
32. Ibid.
33. Lemke, "Intertextuality and Text Semantics," 95.
34. See the appendices 2, 3, 4, 5, 6, 8, 9, 10 in this dissertation, which analyze Romans 9–11.
35. Lemke, "Intertextuality and the Project of Text Linguistics," 223; italics mine.

from equivalent/same thematic objects.[36] For instance, if a discourse states the pro-life arguments against abortion, then all texts or discourses which share this view or provide supportive evidences against abortion become potentially relevant to making sense of this discourse.[37] Those texts or discourses would belong to the same ITFs. If other texts contain arguments for a positive view of abortion, then they would belong to different ITFs. It is worth noting that ITFs carry distinct social viewpoints in the form of beliefs and values to which the text responds in regard to their correctness and propriety.[38] In addition, it is worth mentioning the distinction between a text-specific thematic formation (TTF) and an intertextual thematic formation. The former is specific to a text, the latter is shared with some set of other texts.[39]

2.2.3.2 Relations of Intertextual Thematic Formations

The relationships among ITFs can be divided into three types: co-actional relations, linking texts that belong to parts of the same larger social activity;[40] co-thematic relations, joining texts that speak of the same things in the same manner;[41] and heteroglossic relations, which are the relations between the discourse and activity patterns of people occupying different positions within a social structure (economic roles, gender roles, age roles, etc.).[42] Among all these types of intertextual connections, the heteroglossic relations are the most important for Lemke in his intertextual analysis.

There are two main kinds of heteroglossic relations: Opposition and Alliance. In Opposition, the texts posit a common discursive object shared between two ITFs with the same topic, but construct opposite

---

36. See Lemke, "Discourses in Conflict," 30–31.
37. Cf. Lemke, "Discourses in Conflict," 34.
38. Ibid., 31.
39. Lemke, "Thematic Analysis," 160.
40. Lemke, "Discourses in Conflict," 30. See also Lemke, "Intertextuality and Text Semantics," 87: There are two cases for co-actional intertextuality: they belong to different functionally related parts of the same social activity (e.g. indictment and verdict in a trial); and they can be taken to be texts of different instances of the same social action (e.g., two instructions to the jury). The relation of co-thematic intertextuality: they construct at least in part the same pattern of semantic relations among their themes.
41. Lemke, "Discourses in Conflict," 30.
42. Lemke, "Intertextuality and Text Semantics," 87.

value-orientations, posing them as being in conflict (incompatible, contradictory, or mutually inconsistent);[43] in Alliance, the two ITFs share similar value-orientations toward their respective themes.[44] There are three subtypes of Alliance: (1) Complementarity, "where the intertextual thematic formations are construed as talking about 'different aspects of the same thing'"; (2) Affiliation of the ITFs, "within which there are subtypes depending on whether the affiliated ITFs are used as if one included the other, as if one is merely semantically linked as an extension of the other, or as if there were an indirect relation enabling the same portion of a text to mean polysemically through both ITFs at once"; and (3) "a distinct dialectical relation of ITFs, involving mutually metadiscursive relations."[45] In another place, Lemke has explained this more specifically: "Such a [Dialectical] relationship involves making each formation explicitly metadiscursive to the other; i.e. each formation is set up as accounting for, as providing the framework within which to compare or relate, alternative versions of the other."[46] In brief, the defining feature of Alliance relations is as follows for all three subtypes: there exists a shared value direction toward formations that are related; they offer support in a way that is mutual, consistent, and compatible.[47]

In addition to these two intertextual relations, a relation of Alignment establishes a definite correspondence between parts of ITFs. If Alliance and Opposition are the heteroglossic relations among whole formations, then Alignment deals with the relations that are constructed between parts of formations. Lemke defines it as "the establishment of a correspondence between particular items and relations in two formations."[48] There are two forms of Alignment relations: one is the "establishment of a Contrast relation in which a semantic difference (*not* a value opposition) functions to create

---

43. Ibid., 99; Lemke, "Discourses in Conflict," 48.
44. Lemke, "Discourses in Conflict," 48.
45. Ibid.
46. Lemke, "Intertextuality and Text Semantics," 100. Lemke has given an example to refer to the *dialectical* relationship, that is, the discourse of the [Interaction System] and that of the [Meaning System] of a community.
47. Ibid., 99.
48. Ibid., 100.

a pair (or set) of inconsistent or contrasted corresponding alternatives."⁴⁹ For instance, a key sentence of two formations of righteousness is presented in Romans 9:30–31: ἔθνη τὰ μὴ διώκοντα δικαιοσύνην κατέλαβεν δικαιοσύνην, δικαιοσύνην δὲ τὴν ἐκ πίστεως, Ἰσραὴλ δὲ διώκων νόμον δικαιοσύνης εἰς νόμον οὐκ ἔφθασεν (The Gentiles who did not pursue righteousness have attained it, that is, righteousness through faith; but Israel who pursued the righteousness which is based on law did not get it). The thematic formation of [Gentiles Attained Righteousness] is different in the semantic sense from that of [Israel Did Not Get Righteousness],⁵⁰ but they establish a pair of contrasted corresponding formations of [Righteousness] and share the transitivity pattern of Actor-Process-Goal (material: action). The second subtype of Alignment is Homology: between the parts of formations, their elements that correspond to one another possess the equivalent or similar meanings.⁵¹ For example, in εἰ δὲ ἡ ἀπαρχὴ ἁγία, καὶ τὸ φύραμα· καὶ εἰ ἡ ῥίζα ἁγία, καὶ οἱ κλάδοι (Rom 11:16), the formation of [Dough-Whole lump] is taken to have closely similar meaning of that of [Root-Branches]. In conclusion, the above are the basic terminologies employed to describe the intertextual relations among ITFs.

In sum, among the three main intertextual relations, co-actional, co-thematic and heteroglossic, Lemke has addressed heteroglossic relations in detail. There are two kinds of heteroglossic relations, Opposition and Alliance. The latter can be further described in three subtypes, Complementarity, Affiliation and Dialectical. Regarding the relations between parts of two ITFs, a relation of Alignment has been employed, which is categorized into two subtypes by Lemke, Contrast and Homology. It is worthy of mention that Lemke does not provide exhaustive details of linguistic features or resources to construct all these relations, but he has briefly spoken of them.⁵²

---

49. Ibid.
50. Note that we use [] to denote a thematic formation or ITF.
51. Lemke, "Discourses in Conflict," 48; Lemke, "Intertextuality and Text Semantics," 101.
52. Lemke, "Discourses in Conflict," 48–49.

2.2.3.3 Heteroglossic Voices and Projection Clauses

The previous discussions have demonstrated that heteroglossic relations are essential for intertextual thematic analysis. Besides the two main relations (Opposition and Alliance) for the analysis of the relationships of ITFs, it is necessary to explore *heteroglossia* further.

Bakhtin defines *heteroglossia* as "the diversity of social languages, socially defined discourse types in a community."[53] Lemke attempts to further develop the concept so as to build up the systematic relations of the different social discourses in a community.[54] This heteroglossic analysis helps to detect the different voices embedded in a text, the voices of different classes, genders, philosophical and religious views, political opinions, and so on.[55] It is important to listen to Lemke's own words on this topic: "It [heteroglossic analysis] foregrounds the mechanisms of semantic neogenesis whereby new thematic formations, new ways of speaking, and new discursive objects are produced."[56]

Therefore, each discourse tradition in a community has its own customs regarding which texts are most relevant to the interpretation of any one text.[57] Although Lemke has noticed the phenomenon of discourse within discourse – for instance, scriptural discourse in Paul's discourse – he does not deal with this field in his writings. Regarding Paul's discourse about Scriptures, Paul's community[58] has its own pattern of reading Scriptures and determining which texts are most relevant to which. This system of intertextuality in turn embodies Paul's community's beliefs and evaluative attitudes.[59] Although Hays' intertextual echo is not accurate in textual analysis, his following description of the two voices expresses that he

---

53. Lemke, *Textual Politics*, 38.
54. He states, "In a more fully developed social theory of the role of language and discourse in society, however, we need to understand these different discourse voices are not simply different; they are also systematically related to one another, and related in ways that depend on the wider social relations between the subcommunities that use them." See Lemke, *Textual Politics*, 38.
55. Lemke, "Discourses in Conflict," 30.
56. Ibid., 31.
57. Lemke, *Textual Politics*, 41.
58. Those share similar viewpoints of scriptural discourses with Paul.
59. Cf. Lemke, *Textual Politics*, 45.

has an awareness of the differentiation between Paul's voice and the voice of Scripture.

> Paul's allusive manner of using Scripture leaves enough silence for the voice of Scripture to answer back. Rather than filling the intertextual space with explanations, Paul encourages the reader to listen to more of Scripture's message than he himself voices. The word that Scripture speaks where Paul falls silent is a word that still has the power to contend against him.[60]

In this sense, there are heteroglossic voices in Paul's discourse of which the scriptural voice is one. In order to discern Paul's viewpoint toward the scriptural voice, the co-texts of the Scriptures shall not only be examined in their own right, but also Paul's use of projecting clauses or introductory formulae shall be addressed.

Since Lemke does not provide an analysis for projection clauses,[61] we will consider Halliday's proposal of types of projection as well as Thibault's development of Halliday's proposal of projection in order to identify the relations between the projecting and projected contexts. Halliday provides four types of projection clauses and Thibault gives six. In the following, only three types that are highly related to Paul's projecting formulas will be examined. The first type is the paratactic direct quotation, for instance, "David says, 'Let their table become a snare and a trap, a stumbling block and a retribution for them . . .'" (Rom 11:9). The paratactic relations between the projecting and projected contexts entail a clear separation between the two contexts in which one viewpoint is insulated from the other.[62] In this case, it can be seen that the speaker, Paul, keeps a distance by means of direct quotation from what the sayer, David, has said in his context. Paul

---

60. Hays, *Echoes of Scripture in the Letters of Paul*, 177.
61. Lemke has an article close to this field, Lemke, "Resources for Attitudinal Meaning: Evaluative Orientation in Text Semantics," *Functions of Language* 5 (1998):33–56, but this is not really what we want to do here.
62. According to Thilault, for paratactic relations "there is strong insulation in the projected clause between the Speaker and the Sayer, namely, the one who is quoted" (Paul J. Thibault, *Social Semiotics as Praxis: Text, Social Meaning Making, and Nabokov's Ada* [Minneapolis: University of Minnesota Press, 1991], 101).

may or may not identify his stance with David; his stance is dependent on the surrounding co-texts in which Paul places the sayer's discourse.

The second type represents indirect report. The hypotactic relation between the projecting and projected contexts makes the boundaries between two contexts indistinct.[63] "The hypotactic subordination of the projected clause to the projecting clause tends . . . to weaken the insulation between the two. The effect is to increase the identification of the Speaker with the Sayer."[64] It seems that the second type does not have any corresponding cases in Romans 9–11. However, there is one type of projecting formula, "it is written," which has been called the standard formula, and is similar to the indirect report in regard to the relation of projecting and projected contexts. The boundary between two contexts is weakened in the standard formula. At least, the projected utterance would be viewed as definitive and permanently valid.[65]

The third type is a non-projecting projection (there is no verbal or mental process that projects the projected text). For instance, "He has mercy on whomever he wills, and he hardens whomever he wills" (Rom 9:18). There is no projecting introductory formula, no sayer doing the projecting, but it is a projection (the Saying is probably from Exod 4:21). In this case, the insulation disappears, and the speaker and the sayer are identified.[66] In other words, what Moses said in Exodus is completely dissolved into Paul's voice, the speaker in his current situation.

2.2.4 Thematic Organization

Now let us turn to an integrated way of seeing thematic organization. There are several significant elements of a text that we shall examine in order to have a complete picture of the overall text thematic structure (i.e.

---

63. Thibault, *Social Semiotics as Praxis*, 101.
64. Ibid.
65. Watson also makes a good observation, "If attribution to a specific author highlights the text's individuality and distinctiveness, anonymous citation [the standard formula] emphasizes its representative character." Also, he states, "The standard formula presents a citation as a completed utterance that is definitive and permanently valid." See Watson, *Paul and the Hermeneutics of Faith*, 45.
66. Thibault, *Social Semiotics as Praxis*, 102.

overall thematic organization, carrier formation, thematic prosodies, and thematic interactions).

According to Lemke, the thematic organization of a text is seen in the complete pattern of the interconnecting thematic formations across it.[67] That is, the thematic organization can be seen as waves rippling through the text.[68] Among these thematic waves, there is a carrier wave of the whole text, with other formations connected to it, syntagmatically and intertextually, sharing linkages of mediation.[69] In other words, the carrier wave is "a nexus in thematic organization," which is "a place in the text where a local maximum of thematic relations or whole formations are discursively or metadiscursively connected."[70]

In contrast to multivariate structure, the covariate structure is essentially a synonym for a prosodic pattern.[71] The thematic prosodies "are like 'chains' or 'strands' appearing and reappearing, or rising and falling in prominence, through a text in a non-connected fashion."[72] Regarding thematic interactions, Lemke's system of heteroglossic relations (Opposition, Alliance, and their subtypes) are actually about thematic interactions, which may be usefully applied here.

2.2.5 Multiple Voices and Intertexts

Most texts are embedded with different voices, therefore even if a text seems to speak in a purely single voice, it "speaks and is heard in a community of many voices and its meanings are made in relation to them."[73] In order to understand better Paul's voice in Romans 9–11, it is necessary to place his discourse in the cultural context of his time. Lemke provides an appropriate insight on bringing in other texts:

---

67. Lemke, "Intertextuality and Text Semantics," 101.
68. Ibid., 107.
69. Ibid., 101.
70. Ibid., 103.
71. J. L. Lemke, "Interpersonal Meaning in Discourse: Value Orientations," in *Advances in Systemic Linguistics: Recent Theory and Practice*, ed. Martin Davies and Louise Ravelli (London: Pinter, 1992), 93.
72. Ibid.
73. Lemke, "Discourses in Conflict," 30.

> Every text requires that we bring to it a knowledge of other texts (its intertexts) to create or interpret it, and members of different social groups will in general bring different intertexts to bear, will speak with different discourse voices and listen with different discourse dispositions.[74]

Therefore, this study will bring in other examples of Second Temple Period Jewish literature in order to do a comparative study with Paul's discourse patterns in each section of Romans 9–11. In this way, Paul's unique voice and his discourse patterns regarding the relationship of God, Israel, and the Gentiles can be better demonstrated.

2.3 Evaluation of Lemke's Intertextual Thematic Model

It is significant and productive to analyze the letter to the Romans with the Intertextual Thematic Model, since Paul lived in a pluralistic and complex world, replete with different communities with conflicting viewpoints. As a Jew of the first century, Paul lived during an age dominated by Greek culture and Roman power.[75] Paul's world is constituted by multiple worlds and thus different overlapping cultures.[76] Recent research has presented arguments for reading Romans against the background of Roman political rhetoric in a broad sense, while at the same time, other studies of Paul have recognized that Paul's words and message belong to Jewish culture to an

---

74. Lemke, *Textual Politics*, 38.
75. Neil Elliott, *The Arrogance of Nations: Reading Romans in the Shadow of Empire* (Minneapolis: Fortress, 2008), x.
76. Wright has described the world of Paul in terms of its multiple overlapping and competing narratives: "The story of God and Israel from the Jewish side; the pagan stories about their gods and the world, and the implicit narratives around which individual pagans constructed their identities, from the Greco-Roman sides; and particularly the great narratives of empire, both the large-scale ones we find in Virgil and Livy and elsewhere and the smaller, implicit ones of local culture. Likewise, this world could be described in terms of its symbols: within Judaism, Temple, Torah, Land and family identity; within paganism, the multiple symbols of nation, kingship, religion, and culture; in Rome in particular, the symbols which spoke of the single great world empire." See N. T. Wright, *Paul: In Fresh Perspective* (Minneapolis: Fortress Press, 2005), 6–9.

even greater extent.[77] Moreover, Paul himself has experienced transformation from one community to another, from a committed observant Jewish group to a group within the Jesus Movement. In the first century, the followers of Jesus were composed of several sub-groups, for example, the Matthean community, the Johannine community, the Jerusalem church, and what may be called the Pauline churches. How Paul spoke and wrote the letters to the first-century churches should indicate his identity or his viewpoints toward different cultures, religions, and groups.[78] Therefore, Lemke's intertextual thematic analysis is sound and holds promise for handling Paul's views on the relationship of God, Israel, and the Gentiles by comparing him to his Jewish compatriots in his Hellenized world.

The intertextual thematic model is helpful in many ways. First, it provides methodological control for the analysis and interpretation of intertextual relations within biblical texts. Second, it establishes criteria for such comparative studies. Third, it is useful in locating Paul's viewpoints on important topics related to Judaism, which, in turn, will help in controversial discussions regarding Paul's relationship with Judaism.

However, Lemke's intertextual thematic analysis is not without limitations. First, his theory is developing, which means that sometimes his terminology and analysis are not adequately consistent. In his early article, "Thematic Analysis," ITFs were called intertextual thematic systems (ITSs), and text-specific thematic formations (TTFs) were labeled as a text thematic system (TTS).[79] In addition, he uses the example of homosexuality at least four times in his analysis in different articles, but he uses different

---

77. Ekkehard W. Stegemann, "Coexistence and Transformation: Reading the Polictics of Identity in Romans in an Imperial Context," in *Reading Paul in Context: Explorations in Identity Formation: Essays in Honour of William S. Campbell*, ed. Kathy Ehrensperger and J. Brian Tucker (London: T & T Clark International, 2010), 5–6.

78. According to Lemke, "Distinct social groups (classes, genders, religious sects, etc.) often speak distinct discourses which they take, metadiscursively, to be allied with or opposed to the discourses of other groups. Social identity, the relations among social positions and roles, and social alliances and conflicts are maintained and in part constituted by the relations construed between usual ways of speaking about various subjects." See Lemke, "Intertextuality and Text Semantics," 97.

79. Lemke, "Thematic Analysis," 160–161.

terminology to analyze the same phenomenon, which is confusing.[80] This dissertation, however, will employ his later, more developed theory, which is consistent in terminology, in the adaptation of Lemke's core concept of intertextual thematic analysis as applied to Romans 9–11.

Second, although his analysis of intertextual meaning in each case is convincing, his methodological model lacks an analysis for projection clauses, which are significant in Paul's use of the Scriptures. Therefore, it has been necessary to integrate part of Halliday's proposal for projection types and Thilbault's categorization of six types of projection clauses for analysis of the projecting formulas in this study. Doing so enables the heteroglossic voices to sound forth, and the way that Paul deals with those different voices can be detected through his method of formulating the projection in the introductory formulas.

Finally, the obvious language difference makes it challenging to apply Lemke's intertextual thematic model to the study of Pauline texts. Writing constructions may be quite different in New Testament Greek than in English. However, the essential ideas about the functions of language are similar in both. In addition, a well-defined procedure will be given to incorporate Lemke's intertextual theories.

2.4 An Adaptation of Lemke's Intertextual Thematic Analysis to our Analytical Procedure

2.4.1 An Adaptation of Lemke's Intertextual Thematic Analysis

From the previous discussion of the construction of thematic formations, it can be seen that the establishment of formations is mostly concerned with the ideational (presentational) meaning in terms of Halliday's three metafunctions of language.[81] Lemke has indicated that the specific meaning in

---

80. Lemke, "Semantic and Social Values," *Word* 40 (1989):41–45; Lemke, "Discourses in Conflict," 33–49; Lemke, "Intertextuality and Text Semantics," 99–100; Lemke, *Textual Politics*, 38–46.

81. According to Lemke, "Halliday's ideational (or experiential) resources, deal mainly with specifying what kind of process or relationship we are talking about (material

a text depends on the pattern of presentational meanings. He aptly says, "I take these thematic patterns, appropriately modified or subclassified where necessary to take into account the dependence of presentational meaning on the orientational stance of the discourse, as the irreducible units of text meaning."[82] Therefore, in his analysis of the relationships of thematic formations, he focuses on the transitivity features, clause-complexing relationships, and cohesive ties, etc. It seems that Lemke does not stress the role of organizational meaning (textual meaning), for he admits that such dimensions of meaning-creation "are least considered."[83] It is true that for intertextual thematic analysis the overall organizational meaning is not very significant; however, the thematic-organizational meaning of a text remains important from many perspectives, particularly in providing text-specific thematic formations that demonstrate the specific text semantics of a text. Although Lemke is aware of text thematic organization, we still need to develop a model for analysis of thematic organizations that is workable for Greek argumentative text.

2.4.2 Analytical Procedure

The intertextual thematic meaning between two texts cannot be deduced solely on the basis of what is said in the texts; nevertheless, it must be done with reference to what is said in the texts.[84] Therefore, two interdependent uses of language should be examined: (1) the discourse's construction of "the way the world is" (its presentational meaning), and (2) the discourse's construction of the heteroglossic relations between it and other possible discourses.[85]

---

action, sensory perception, identity, location, etc.), what the participants in the process or relationships are (agents, beneficiaries, targets, sensors, phenomena, locations, etc.), and various relevant circumstances (time, place, manner, etc.)." See Lemke, *Textual Politics*, 33. Note that Lemke re-names Halliday's three meta-functions of language (ideational, interpersonal, textual) as presentational, orientational, and organizational. See Lemke, *Textual Politics*, 34.

82. Lemke, *Textual Politics*, 35.
83. Ibid.
84. Ibid., 33.
85. Ibid.

The procedure for the analysis of Romans 9–11 will cover the above two aspects. Four steps will be utilized in approaching the texts. The first step will focus on presentational meaning. Presentational meaning concerns the construction of how things are in the natural and social worlds, and is similar to Halliday's ideational or experiential meaning. It establishes the topics and the themes of the discourses, which can be realized by discursive explicit description as "participants, processes, relations, and circumstances standing in particular semantic relations to one another across meaningful stretches of text, and from text to texts."[86] In this part, Halliday's analysis of experiential systems will be considered,[87] especially the process type and the participant structures. Moreover, the clausal, clause-complexing, and thematic relations will be examined in order to establish the text-specific thematic formations of the discourse.

The second step deals with scriptural voices. First the scriptural texts employed by the host text will be examined in their own co-texts; and then Paul's viewpoints toward these scriptural texts will be demonstrated.

The third step serves to analyze the thematic-organizational meaning.[88] The purpose for investigation of the thematic-organizational meaning is to understand the complex relations within text-specific thematic formations. We will investigate Paul's dominant discourse formations (presented in the texts), or the carrier thematic formation. Moreover, the intertextual relations of Alliance, Opposition, Alignment, etc., will be represented in order to demonstrate the viewpoints embedded in the text and to form the framework of intertextual relations for Paul's Jewish contemporaries' voices in the subsequent section, in which the various thematic views of the world and the views of other communities and their discourses will be represented.

The fourth step focuses on the multiple voices beyond the text. We will take a synoptic reading of the literature of Paul's Jewish contemporaries so as to represent their viewpoints/voices on the topics that Paul has presented

---

86. Ibid., 34.
87. Halliday and Hasan, *Language, Context, and Text* 32.
88. Note that "thematic-organizational meaning" is different from Halliday's textual-structural meaning. The former is more concerned with the thematic relations that are constructed in the text.

in Romans 9–11. Finally, in each section, there will be a summary to conclude the main findings or the key issues that have been discussed.

2.5 Conclusion

In the above, we first introduced Lemke's concept of intertextuality, which is not restricted to the traditional view of a linear adaptation of one text in another. His intertextual theory enhances register theory in text analysis, since intertextual theory is very helpful in capturing the heteroglossic voices embedded in the text. In this part, Lemke's concepts of thematic formation, intertextual thematic formations, and heteroglossic voices and projection clauses will be discussed. We have strengthened Lemke's analysis in heteroglossic voices by employing an appropriate way to deal with the projection clauses. Second, we provide our evaluation of Lemke's intertextual thematic model, demonstrating its strengths and weakness. Finally, our adaptation of Lemke's model and full analysis procedure has been offered. Note that the thematic-organizational meaning will be provided after the presentational meaning. This will strengthen Lemke's intertextual thematic theory and make it a suitable analytical tool for the analysis of a biblical text. In short, the integrated intertextual thematic analysis will better equip the reader to understand Paul's text in Romans 9–11.

CHAPTER THREE

An Intertextual Thematic Analysis of Romans 9:1–29: The Nature of God and Who are God's People

3.1 Introduction

During the development of early Christianity in the first half of the first century, disciples of Jesus proclaimed Jesus as the future returning Messiah and proclaimed the renewed relationships among God, Israel, and the Gentiles. This message alone would astonish most contemporary Jews, but, to make it more complicated, Paul declared a law-free gospel to the Gentiles. Paul, as one of the apostles, lived in the first-century Jewish and Hellenistic world, replete with different faith communities with conflicting viewpoints.[1] In this new age, Paul faced many challenges. How could he deliver the message of the gospel and justify his law-free Gentile mission? Such a proclamation would be hard for Jews to accept, including some law abiding Jewish Christians. Helping him in this regard is Paul's understanding of himself as a prophet, which is expressed through the manner in which he speaks about himself and through the discourse patterns of speeches he presents to his audience.

Romans 9 will be divided into three sections: verses 1–5, verses 6–13 and verses 14–29. The procedure for each section is as follows. First, the presentational meaning will be demonstrated through the analysis of the

---

1. Elliott, *The Arrogance of Nations*, x.

relationships among the clauses or clause complexes of each section.² Second, the scriptural voice, including the Scriptures' own co-texts and Paul's usage of them, will be considered. Third, the thematic-organizational meaning will be examined in order to view the inner discourse patterns that Paul establishes. Fourth, through a comparative reading with some related literature of the Second Temple Period, the multiple voices on the topics that Paul has presented in Romans 9:1–29 will be discussed.

3.2 Romans 9:1–5

3.2.1 Presentational Meaning

The presentational meaning (the ideational meaning in SFL terms) refers to what is "going on" in the text with respect to what is going on outside of the text.³ The grammar of clauses that are used to express the presentational meaning is primarily realized by means of processes, participants in a process, and circumstances associated with a process.⁴ According to chart 2 of appendix 2, the participants can be classified into three types: implied participant reference (the morphological features of person and number with a finite verb form), reduced participant reference (the use of a pronoun or other referring expression to point to a participant), and grammaticalized participant reference (a full, substantive reference to a participant). Paul, as the speaker, "I," appears as the implied participant reference in all three main primary clauses, which suggests that Paul is a leading participant. Moreover, the pronoun ἐγώ (the reduced participant reference) appears explicitly six times in verses 1–3. Consequently, it is evident that Paul is the leading participant reference.⁵ The term "Christ," with whom Paul's identity has formed a bond (grammaticalized participant reference), is found in

---

2. See my analysis charts in appendices 2, 3, and 4.
3. Cf. Jeffrey T. Reed, *A Discourse Analysis of Philippians: Method and Rhetoric in the Debate over Literary Integrity*. JSNTSup 136 (Sheffield: Sheffield Academic, 1997), 331.
4. Ibid.
5. The use of person and number does not change until v. 6, which gives a clue that vv. 1–5 is a section.

the adjunct of two primary clauses (vv. 1 and 3), and in the subject slot of a relative clause in verse 5.

Romans 9:1–5 consists of three primary clauses (vv. 1, 3; c1A, c2A, c3A)[6] in which the semantic domains of three main finite verbs are close to each other, all belonging to verbal clauses (λέγω, ψεύδομαι, and ηὐχόμην).[7] Also, all three finite verbs in the three primary clauses use imperfective aspect (the first two present tense, and imperfect tense in v. 3), indicating that this is a marked section for the author, for he emphasizes the process with an ongoing status.[8] The second primary clause paratactically elaborates the first one. In other words, the first two primary clauses express the same meaning in a positive and a negative way respectively (ἀλήθειαν λέγω, οὐ ψεύδομαι), to stress Paul's speech in the following projected clauses. That is, the combination of the verbal clauses of ἀλήθειαν λέγω (speak the truth) and οὐ ψεύδομαι (not lie) orients us to the emphatic, marked, and solemn statement that Paul is going to make, the projection of his locution in verse 2.[9] The participle clause c2B, συμμαρτυρούσης μοι τῆς συνειδήσεώς μου ἐν πνεύματι ἁγίῳ (v. 1), again emphasizes the solemn statement in the subsequent ὅτι clause in verse 2 (c2Ca, c2Cb). The prepositional phrase ἐν Χριστῷ grammatically is a spherical use, "according to which it is said that one is in the sphere of Christ's control."[10] In other words, the spherical

---

6. See chart 1 of appendix 2.
7. According to Halliday, there are six process types of verbal groups: material, mental, relational (the three principal types); and three other subsidiary process types: behavioral (at the boundary between material and mental), verbal (at the boundary between mental and relational), and existential (at the boundary between relational and material). See Halliday and Matthiessen, *An Introduction to Functional Grammar*, 179–263.
8. According to Porter, each choice of verb tense reflects an attempt by the speaker to grammaticalize his conception of the process. See Stanley E. Porter, *Verbal Aspect in the Greek of the New Testament: With Reference to Tense and Mood*. SBG 1 (New York: P. Lang, 1989), 86. Porter' definition of verbal aspect is: "Greek verbal aspect is a synthetic semantic category (realized in the forms of verbs) used of meaningful oppositions in a network of tense systems to grammaticalize the author's reasoned subjective choice of conception of a process." Porter, *Verbal Aspect*, 88. In contrast to the imperfective aspects, perfective verbs occur most frequently to provide the background information within expositional passages.
9. Cf. Dunn, *Romans 9–16*, 522, Cranfield, *Romans*, 452. It is worth noting that the combination of these two verbal clauses appears in 1 Tim 2:7, in which it is emphasized that Paul was appointed as a teacher, preacher, and apostle to the Gentiles.
10. Stanley Porter, *Idioms of the Greek New Testament* (Sheffield: Sheffield Academic, 1994), 159.

sense makes it appear very likely that the speaker belongs to a particular community in union with Christ.[11] The prepositional phrase ἐν πνεύματι ἁγίῳ has similar function to that of ἐν Χριστῷ. The spherical use indicates that that which will be confirmed is located within the sphere of control or domain of the Holy Spirit.[12] The combinational use of Christ and Holy Spirit is very common in early Christian literature,[13] which confirms that Paul's solemn statement is from the stance of early Christian communities. Therefore, Paul's discourse stands within a Christian position.

The projected clause ὅτι in verse 2 immediately begins to orient the reader to the thematic content to which the speaker repeatedly points. The semantic chains of sorrow, anxiety, and psychological faculties in this projected clause can be recognized in Jewish and apocalyptic literature, which belong to a recognizable sort of discourse. For instance, Isa 35:10; 51:11; Jer 4:19; 14:17; *T. Jud.* 23:1; *4 Ezra* 8:16; 10:24, 39; *2 Apoc. Bar.* 10:5; 35:1–4; 81:1–4; Par. Jer. 4:10; 6:17, etc.[14] Let us call this sort of discourse formation [Lament over Israel].[15] In this first thematic formation, the doubling of λύπη and ὀδύνη intensifies the strong emotive force

---

11. Porter has provided a good example for this spherical sense of the clause: ἤμην . . . ἀγνοούμενος τῷ προσώπῳ ταῖς ἐκκλησίαις τῆς Ἰουδαίας ταῖς ἐν Χριστῷ (Gal 1:22: I was . . . unknown by face to the churches in Christ of Judea). See Porter, *Idioms of the Greek New Testament*, 159. Contra Dunn, *Romans 9–16*, 523.

12. Porter, *Idioms of the Greek New Testament*, 157.

13. E.g. Matt 1:18; Luke 2:26; Act 2: 38; Rom 1:4; 8:2, 9–11; 9:1; 15:16, 19, 30; 1 Cor 6:11; 2 Cor 3:3; 13:13; Gal 3:14; 6:18; Eph 1:17, 19, 27; 2:1; 3:3; 4:23; Col 2:5; 1 Thess 5:23; Phlm 1:25; Heb 9:14; 1 Pet 1:2, 11; 3:18; 4:14; 1 John 4:2; 5:6.

14. Cf. Dunn, *Romans 9–16*, 524.

15. The thematic formation [Lament over Israel] is not uncommon in Jewish and apocalyptic literature. The sayer of the speech is often a prophet. For instance, the prophet Jeremiah offers a Lament over Jerusalem in Jer 4:19–21. The semantic chains of sorrow, pain, and psychological faculties in Jer 4:19 LXX have a similar discourse pattern as here: "My anguish, my anguish! I am pained at my very heart; my heart is beating wildly; and I cannot keep silent . . . (τὴν κοιλίαν μου τὴν κοιλίαν μου ἀλγῶ καὶ τὰ αἰσθητήρια τῆς καρδίας μου μαιμάσσει ἡ ψυχή μου σπαράσσεται ἡ καρδία μου οὐ σιωπήσομαι . . .)." In Jeremiah, the prophet suffered from pain over the destruction of Jerusalem. The prophet's expression of anguish may be because of the unbelief of God's people, Israel. Craigie and Kelley comment, this confessional unit is related to "a portion of an oracle (v. 22) in which God laments the stupidity of his chosen people." The oracular verse provides in part the basis of the prophet's expression of anguish. Thus, we can infer that Paul may identify himself with a certain type of prophet in his lament over Israel in Rom 9:1–2. See Peter C. Craigie, Page H. Kelley and Joel F. Drinkard, *Jeremiah 1–25* (Dallas: Word Books, 1991), 79–80.

of Paul's statement;[16] and the term ἀδιάλειπτος (constantly, unceasingly) increases the emotional intensity.[17] Regarding modal systems of [Lament over Israel], all the verbal moods are Indicative, which, according to Porter, "is used for assertive or declarative statements."[18] Note that the assertions or the declarations are not about the reality but "grammaticalize simply the 'will' of the speaker."[19] Therefore, Paul's assertion of his worry about Israel states his subjective attitude toward Israel, which has been explicitly stated in the following clauses.

With the escalating progress of the expressions of Paul's concern for his kinsmen, the third primary clause arrives at an apex. First, the γὰρ in c3A (v. 3) hints that Paul is going to confirm his concern for Israel with even more specific description.[20] Also, prominent expressions are outstanding in verse 3: besides the grammatical subject (first person singular) implied within the verb ηὐχόμην, Paul mentions himself again with the intensive and personal nominative pronouns αὐτὸς ἐγὼ; the imperfect tense form (ηὐχόμην) departs from the first two present tense forms in the primary clauses; the use of middle voice "expresses more direct participation, specific involvement" by Paul;[21] and the structure of verse 3 – a main verb (ηὐχόμην) goes with an infinitive phrase (ἀνάθεμα εἶναι) – departs from others in this section. In other words, it is the focal point of verse 3 (ηὐχόμην γὰρ ἀνάθεμα εἶναι αὐτὸς ἐγὼ . . .) which presents the formation that somebody, for the sake of those for whom he has great concern, is willing to be excluded from someone or some community important to her/himself. Through the use of the semantic chains of kinship, e.g. my brothers, my kinsmen, according to flesh (by race), it is evident that participants in this section do not only include the speaker, but also some social group or community, that is, Paul's kinsmen, ethnic Israel.

---

16. Dunn, *Romans 9–16*, 523.
17. Ibid. 524.
18. Porter, *Verbal Aspect*, 166.
19. Ibid.
20. See BDAG, "γὰρ": 1d, "the General is confirmed by the specific."
21. Porter, *Idioms of the Greek New Testament*, 67; Stanley E. Porter, Jeffrey T. Reed, and Matthew Brook O'Donnell, *Fundamentals of New Testament Greek*. Grand Rapids: Eerdmans, 2010, 40.

This sort of discourse formation can be established as a thematic formation of a martyr-like sacrifice, which is not uncommon in Jewish literature, for instance, the stories of the Maccabean martyrs, "whose deaths were sometimes thought to have atoning value for the nation of Israel as a whole."[22] Another example is Moses' prayer in Exodus 32:30–32. He prayed that God would forgive the sin of Israel and asked that his own name be excluded if God chose not to forgive.[23] Here Paul probably evokes Moses' intercession for Israel, identifying himself with Israel: "Moses asks Yahweh to forgive Israel or to erase his own name from the book Yahweh has written."[24] Thus, this type of self-sacrifice formation can be labeled as [Martyr-like Intercession for Israel]. It should be noted that there are some nuances in Paul's view of Israel's sin and his martyr-like intercession for Israel. For Paul, to be cursed is to be cut away from the Messiah, Jesus Christ in the ITF [Martyr-like Intercession for Israel: Paul]. However, for Moses, or the Jewish tradition, to be blotted out of the book meant to be separated from YHWH's blessing or from relationship with YHWH.[25] Moreover, in the time of Moses, Israel's sin was to worship YHWH in her own way, with the golden calf, but in Paul, the Israelites sinned because they refused Jesus as their Messiah. Interestingly, Paul aligns these actions as the same sin, with which most of his Jewish contemporaries would not agree. Apparently, Paul attempts to marry this Jewish tradition with the viewpoint of the early Christian community. The one common link between Israel's sin with the golden calf and her later sin of unbelief is that both sins focus on their own way of worshipping God.

The thematic formation [Martyr-like Intercession for Israel] in this cotext of Romans 9:1–5 declares Paul's willingness to sacrifice himself for his Jewish contemporaries; it strengthens a greater identification of Paul with

---

22. Moo, *The Epistle to the Romans*, 558.
23. Dunn, *Romans 9–16*, 558–559.
24. John I. Durham, *Exodus* (Waco: Word Books, 1987), 432. Exodus 32 focuses on YHWH's and Moses' responses to Israel's sin of worship of the golden calf, that is, Israel asks for a new point of focus for their worship of Yahweh: "The calf represented Yahweh on *their* terms. Yahweh had made clear repeatedly that he would be received and worshiped only on *his* terms." See Durham, *Exodus*, 422.
25. Durham, *Exodus*, 433–435; Douglas K. Stuart, *Exodus* (Nashville: Broadman & Holman, 2006), 683–689.

the Jewish people.²⁶ We demonstrated earlier that Paul's solemn statement is from a Christian position (in Christ and in Spirit); now Paul explicitly confirms his caring for his kinsmen, ethnic Israel. So far, Paul's concern for his Jewish people is based on his identity in Christ.

The last two verses (vv. 4–5) are used to describe τῶν ἀδελφῶν μου τῶν συγγενῶν μου in verse 3. The linguistic features of the enumeration of Israel's blessings are shown in verses 4–5: the sequence of the embedded clauses ὧν . . . ὧν . . . καὶ ἐξ ὧν . . . (cc3Da-c; vv. 4–5) modifies the plural noun Ἰσραηλῖται (c3C, v. 4), which is identical in reference to the nominal phrase τῶν ἀδελφῶν μου τῶν συγγενῶν μου (Paul's kinsmen according to the flesh, c3B, v. 3). The following eight predicate nominatives indicate God's blessing to Israel, the special gifts the Israelites owned: ἡ υἱοθεσία καὶ ἡ δόξα καὶ αἱ διαθῆκαι καὶ ἡ νομοθεσία καὶ ἡ λατρεία καὶ αἱ ἐπαγγελίαι . . . οἱ πατέρες . . . ὁ Χριστός.²⁷

With a series of relative clauses to modify τῶν ἀδελφῶν μου, a semantic chain of elements of Israelite's heritage is enumerated in verses 4–5: the adoption, the glory, the covenants, the law, the worship, the promises, the patriarchs, and the Christ.²⁸ We will call it ITF [Heritage of Israel]. In this ITF, there are three occurrences of the relative pronoun ὧν to demonstrate the heritage of the Israelites: "The first ὧν embraces the six items listed in verse 4; the second refers to οἱ πατέρες; and the last, which is written ἐξ ὧν, indicates that the Messiah came from Israel."²⁹ The first six items can be classified into three pairs by their feminine noun endings:³⁰

---

26. Abasciano, *Paul's Use of the Old Testament in Romans 9:1–9*, 100.
27. Regarding textual variation of αἱ διαθῆκαι, the singular noun ἡ διαθήκη has good manuscript evidence, like P⁴⁶ B D F G b, etc. According to Metzger, the singular form of covenant refers to "God's covenant with Moses, made at Mount Sinai." The plural form refers to "the covenants made with Israel's ancestors: Abraham (Gen 15:18; 17:2, 7, 9), Isaac (Gen 26:3–5; Exod 2:24), the three patriarchs (Exod 6:4–5; Lev 26:42), Moses (Exod 24:7–8), and David (2 Sam 23:5)." See Roger L. Omanson, *A Textual Guide to the Greek New Testament* (Stuttgart: Deutsche Bibelgesellschaft, 2006), 307–308; also Joseph A. Fitzmyer, *Romans: A New Translation with Introduction and Commentary* (New York: Doubleday, 1993), 546.
28. Cf. Herman C. Waetjen, *The Letter to the Romans: Salvation as Justice and the Deconstruction of Law* (Sheffield: Sheffield Phoenix, 2011), 230.
29. Thomas R. Schreiner, *Romans*. BECNT. (Grand Rapids: Baker, 1998), 483.
30. Cf. Dunn, *Romans 9–16*, 522; Schreiner, *Romans*, 483–485. According to Dunn, the key words like "adoption," "glory," and "promise" are important in the preceding

υἱοθεσία (sonship)	νομοθεσία (the giving of the law)
δόξα (glory)	λατρεία (worship)
διαθῆκαι (covenants)	ἐπαγγελίαι (promises)

Both **sonship** and **the giving of the law** can refer back to the Exodus events when Israel was redeemed as God's son (cf. Exod 4:22), for in Judaism there existed a close relationship between the law and Israel's sonship.[31] However, instead of υἱοθεσία, it is the term υἱός that has been utilized in Exodus 4:22.[32] Note that the term υἱοθεσία is nowhere used in the LXX nor other ancient Jewish literature; Paul has an explicitly Christian use of this term (cf. 8:15, 23; Gal 4:5; Eph 1:5).[33] Paul's use of this term υἱοθεσία here as one aspect of Israel's heritage must be expressing that the way for Israel to be God's children is no different from the way of the Christians to be God's children. The second pair (δόξα and λατρεία) suggests that the glory of God is manifested in his people's worship of him.[34] "The glory" as part of the heritage refers to God's presence with the people of Israel (cf. Exod 33:16, 18),[35] and "the worship" in view is particularly the temple cult.[36] The two lexical items of the last pair, διαθῆκαι and ἐπαγγελίαι, can mutually interpret one another: the covenants are those promises contained in them and the promises are the covenant promises.[37] Covenant in most discussions means the salvific relationship established between God and his

---

argument: adoption (8:15, 23; 9:4), glory (5:2; 8:18, 21), promise (4:13–14, 16, 20). See James D. G. Dunn, "Did Paul Have a Covenant Theology? Reflections on Romans 9. 4 and 11.27," in *The Concept of the Covenant in the Second Temple Period*, ed. Stanley E. Porter and Jacqueline C. R. De Roo (Leiden: Brill, 2003), 302.

31. Schreiner, *Romans*, 483.

32. See also Isa 1:2; Jer 31:9, which identify Israel as God's firstborn son.

33. Jewett, *Romans*, 562; Moo, *The Epistle to the Romans*, 562. Scholars consider Paul's usage of this term as surprising or puzzling. However, this is not the case.

34. As Schreiner points out, "Israel has been blessed with the glorious presence of God and access to him through the cult." Schreiner, *Romans*, 484.

35. In Exod 33:16, Moses points out that YHWH's presence made Israel distinct from every other people on earth; and in the following verse 18, Moses asked for God's glory, which was his plea for YHWH's presence. Cf. Durham, *Exodus*, 455.

36. Moo, *The Epistle to the Romans*, 564; Dunn, *Romans 9–16*, 527.

37. Schreiner, *Romans*, 484–485.

people.³⁸ As Porter has rightly observed, because they belong to the same semantic domains in the Louw-Nida lexicon, ἐπαγγελ- words are closely related to that of covenant.³⁹ The covenants here most probably refer to the covenants with Abraham (Gen 15, 17), with Moses at Mount Sinai (Exod 19:5–6) and in the plains of Moab (Deut 29–31), since all these passages are referred to again within Romans 9–11. The promises may focus on the promises given to Abraham, Isaac, and Jacob/Israel,⁴⁰ for they have been discussed by Paul in Romans 9:6–13.

The second ὧν references οἱ πατέρες most likely referring to the patriarchs (cf. Rom 11:28),⁴¹ who are those to whom God gave promises (cf. Rom 9:6–13). The promises to Abraham, Isaac, and Israel, are mentioned by Moses in Exodus 32:13 to appeal to God to forgive Israel's sin with the golden calf. Therefore, the patriarchs are one part of the valuable heritage inherited by Israel. The last inheritance mentioned here is distinct from the others, since it has its own clause and is introduced by ἐξ ὧν instead of ὧν, suggesting that "rather than 'belonging' to the Israelites, the Messiah 'is from' them."⁴² We should note that the structure of the clause complex (καὶ ἐξ ὧν ὁ Χριστὸς τὸ κατὰ σάρκα) ὁ ὢν ἐπὶ πάντων θεὸς εὐλογητὸς εἰς τοὺς αἰῶνας, ἀμήν has been disputed among scholars.⁴³ Two main opin-

---

38. Stanley E. Porter, "The Concept of Covenant in Paul," in *The Concept of the Covenant in the Second Temple Period*, ed. Stanley E. Porter and Jacqueline C. R. De Roo (Leiden: Brill, 2003), 275.

39. Ibid., 281–283. Also, it is worth noting what the plural usage of 'covenants' here refers to. Do they refer to the sequence of covenants mentioned in the Scriptures (with Abraham [Gen 15, 17], with Israel at Mount Sinai [Exod 19:5–6], in the plains of Moab [Deut 29–31], with David [2 Sam 23:5; Jer 33:21] and so on)? Or do they refer to the two covenants, old and new? Dunn prefers the latter option. See Dunn, "Covenant Theology," 302.

40. Cf. Moo, *The Epistle to the Romans*, 564.

41. Cranfield, *Romans*, 464; Moo, *The Epistle to the Romans*, 564.

42. Cf. Moo, *The Epistle to the Romans*, 565.

43. As Moo has rightly observed, there are two main possibilities for putting a comma in the clause complex; one is after σάρκα and the alternative is after Χριστὸς. Here we prefer the former option, on which our following discussion is based. See Moo, *The Epistle to the Romans*, 566–568; For a more detailed discussion, see Murray J. Harris, *Jesus as God: The New Testament Use of Theos in Reference to Jesus* (Grand Rapids: Baker, 1992), 143–172; George Carraway, *Christ Is God over All: Romans 9:5 in the Context of Romans 9–11*. LNTS 489. (London: T & T Clark, 2013), 21–57.

ions have been presented:[44] the first is to view the article ὁ as a relative pronoun, which refers to the antecedent Χριστὸς and governs until θεὸς. Then it can be read as "who (referring to Christ) is God over all, be blessed forever! Amen." In this sense, "God" is taken as a designation of Christ.[45] An alternative reading is also to view the article ὁ as a relative pronoun, but to punctuate a full stop after πάντων.[46] It reads as, "who (referring to Christ) is over all. May God be blessed forever! Amen." By doing this, we would have an independent doxology to God in the co-text, which is rare in Paul's writings.[47] Therefore, Paul is probably pointing out the particular meaning "Messiah as God" from his stance within a Christian community, while he still considers this particular meaning of Messiah as aligning with the current Jewish thought.[48] In a word, Paul lists the Jewish advantage and regards "Christ as God" as one of the privileges, which is not common among his Jewish contemporaries.

Therefore, Paul's voice in Romans 9:1–5 labors to ally with the prophet, Moses, and the Israelites and their heritage, which includes the legislation of the law at Mount Sinai. Does this illustrate that his stance is on the side

---

44. Dunn, *Romans 9–16*, 528–529.

45. That Paul may call Jesus "God" was accepted by most of the church fathers and a number of scholars. See Moo, *The Epistle to the Romans*, 566–568. Cf. Dunn, *Romans 9–16*, 528–529. For the newest discussion about "Christ is God over all," see Carraway, *Christ Is God* (2013).

46. The phrase ὁ ὢν is very possible to be construed as relative in v. 5b. See Harris, *Jesus as God*, 157–159.

47. Moo, *The Epistle to the Romans*, 567. There are two types of doxologies in the New Testament: a volitive or exclamatory doxology; and a descriptive or declarative doxology. See Harris, *Jesus as God*, 145–146.

48. Charlesworth has an excellent explanation for the issue of the relationships of Messianology with Christology in early Judaism and Christianity. See James H. Charlesworth, "From Messianology to Christology: Problems and Prospects," In *The Messiah: Developments in Earliest Judaism and Christianity*, ed. James H. Charlesworth (Minneapolis: Fortress, 1992), 3–35. This is a heated topic in considering the Messiah in early Judaism and Christianity. For example, Stanley Porter, ed., *The Messiah in the Old and New Testaments* (Grand Rapids: Eerdmans, 2007); Magnus Zetterholm, *The Messiah: In Early Judaism and Christianity* (Minneapolis: Fortress, 2007); Jacob Neusner, Wiliam S. Green, and Ernest Frerichs, eds., *Judaisms and Their Messiahs: At the Turn of the Christian Era* (Cambridge: Cambridge University Press, 1987); William Horbury, *Jewish Messianism* Horbury, William. *Jewish Messianism and the Cult of Christ* (London: SCM, 1998); Dan Cohn-Sherbok, *The Jewish Messiah* (Edinburgh: T&T Clark, 1997); Richard Bauckham, *Jesus and the God of Israel: God Crucified and Other Studies on the New Testament's Christology of Divine Identity*, (Grand Rapids: Eerdmans, 2008).

of, and shares the same ideological values with, contemporary Jewish communities? Yes and no. Then whose voice and what community does the speaker represent? It is worth noting that all three ITFs include the participant "Christ."[49] In [Lament over Israel], the speaker's statement/speech is ἐν Χριστῷ, who has the authority/power to guarantee the truth of the statement the speaker makes. In [Martyr-like Intercession for Israel], in view of Paul's stance, εἶναι . . . ἀπὸ τοῦ Χριστοῦ is a great curse, like Moses' name being blotted out of the book of life (Exod 32:30–32). In other words, to be in Christ or away from Christ is a matter of life and death, and is the basis of all other identities. This text-specific thematic formation [Heritage of Israel] enumerates "Christ who is God over all" as part of Israel's rich heritage. Some of the Jewish apocalyptic literature of early Judaism may refer to the origin of the Messiah from King David, but rarely connect the Messiah(s) to Jesus, as Paul and his community did.[50] Thus far, it is evident that Paul's stance is from within a Christian community. At the same time, Paul labors to align with his Jewish kinsmen through his heartfelt concern for them, his willingness to offer a Martyr-like sacrifice, and his acknowledgement of their rich heritage. In other words, Paul considers himself as a member of his kinsmen's circle, as one who shares in Israel's heritage, but he identifies himself with a Christian community first.

To summarize, the main presentational meaning of this discourse consists of Paul's strong concern for the Israelites (his kinship group): the Israelites' separation from Christ creates great sorrow for Paul, who is willing to pay any price in order to bring his kinsfolk to Christ. Paul speaks as one of the prophets of Israel: Moses, who lamented over Israel's sinful or fallen state.[51] His concern over the spiritual state of Israel has escalated,

---

49. For Paul, this "Christ" refers to Jesus.
50. For the four early Jewish documents in the Pseudepigrapha that contain the term "Messiah," see, *Psalms of Solomon*, the *Parables of Enoch*, *4 Ezra*, and *2 Baruch*, which date from 50 BC to AD 100. See the discussions in James Charlesworth's edited book, *The Messiah: Developments in Earliest Judaism and Christianity* (Minneapolis: Fortress, 1992) and Porter (ed.), *The Messiah in the Old and New Testaments* (2007).
51. Cf. Moo, *The Epistle to the Romans*, 557. See Jer 4:19; 14:17; Dan 9:3; and also 2 *Apoc. Bar.* 14:8–9; 35:3; *T. Jud.* 23:1; *4 Ezra* 8:16; 10:24, 39; *Par. Jer.* 4:10; 6:17. Note that Johnson has shown that many of the themes and motifs of Rom 9–11 are reminiscent of Jewish apocalyptic (Johnson, *Function of Apocalyptic*, 124–131). See Moo, *The Epistle to the Romans*, 557, n. 11.

which is manifested in [Martyr-like Intercession for Israel]. Paul embraces Israel by being willing to take the place of those who are under the curse of God. It is worth noticing that Paul associates curse with separation from Christ. In this section, Paul does not only express love for his kinsmen and God's blessing to Israel, but also presents himself particularly as a Mosaic figure for Israel (v. 3). Therefore, Paul specifically sees Moses as his own model. The nuanced difference from Mosaic expression, however, lies in three significant items of the early Christian discourse pattern: the Spirit, Christ (x2), and God. Finally, Paul acknowledges the privileges of the Israelites, and includes Jesus Christ as one part of their great heritage. This last privilege (Christ being from them) must be Paul or his community's new contribution for [Heritage of Israel], since it cannot be found in the Jewish literature as one of their privileges.

3.2.2 Scriptural Voices

We have mentioned that Paul's intercession for his Jewish contemporaries shares some similarities with Moses' intercession for the ancient Israelites at Mount Sinai when Israel sinned with the golden calf (Exod 32:30–32). In the following, we will examine Exodus 32:30–32 in its own co-text, and then Paul's voice's use of Moses' intercession will be analyzed.

Exodus 32–34 is considered a whole unit in its final narrative form,[52] which is a large co-text for Exodus 32:30–32. However, its more immediate co-text is Exodus 32,[53] which is called the golden calf episode and which has been interpreted and retold in early Judaism literature (e.g. Philo, Josephus, Pseudo-Philo).[54] It is this immediate co-text that we will focus on to explore its discourse pattern:

(1) Israel's sin of the construction of the golden calf (32:1–6);

(2) YHWH threatens destruction and Moses intercedes (vv. 7–14);

---

52. See Thomas B. Dozeman, *Commentary on Exodus* (Grand Rapids: Eerdmans, 2009), 697; Abasciano, *Paul's Use of the Old Testament in Romans 9:1–9*, 46–47.
53. The composition of Exod 32 has undergone supplementation and revision. It has been determined that the original story of the golden calf consists of 32:1–6 ("the construction of the golden calf"), 15–21 ("its destruction by Moses"), and 35 ("plague"), see Dozeman, *Exodus*, 696–98. However, it is the final compositional form that we will explore.
54. Pekka Lindqvist, *Sin at Sinai: Early Judaism Encounters Exodus 32* (Winona Lake: Eisenbrauns, 2008), 117–155.

(3) Moses brings punishments on Israel (vv. 15–29);[55]
(4) Moses' intercession to atone for Israel (vv. 30–35).[56]

This text concerning Israel's sin, God's judgment, and restoration is captured in Deuteronomy 32 and Isaiah 65 as well, which seems to be part of the discourse progression of Romans 9–11.[57] For now we will focus on Moses' intercession in atoning for Israel in regard to Paul's intercession in Romans 9:3. Exodus 32:30–35 begins a new day with Moses' opening statement to his kinsmen, that "you have sinned a great sin . . . perhaps I can make atonement for your sin" (v. 30). Moses then turns to YHWH to intercede for forgiveness of Israel's sin of the golden calf (v. 31). He requests God to forgive his people, otherwise he wishes to be erased from τῆς βίβλου σου ἧς ἔγραψας (your book that you have written, v. 32).[58] However, YHWH refuses Moses' intercession, saying, "Whoever sinned against me, I will erase him from my book" (v. 33). This statement is followed by the theme of YHWH's punishment of Israel's sin of the calf (vv. 34–35). In other words, Moses' martyr-like sacrificial intercession for his kinsmen failed.

---

55. For example, break the covenant tablets, destroy the calf, and show judgments on Israel.
56. See also Dozeman, *Exodus*, 701.
57. The restoration part can be seen clearly in the following two chapters (Exod 33–34). In Rom 9–11, Paul indicates and criticizes the rebellions of Israel of their unbelief, but then also shows God's final restoration of Israel: Israel failed in obtaining God's righteousness (9:31), and they were ignorant of God's righteousness (10:3). With the voice of Isaiah, Paul criticizes Israel as disobedient and contrary people. However, for Paul, this is not the final fate of Israel, he already knows the mystery of the salvation of Israel in the eschatological future (11:26). Therefore, part of the discourse procession is captured by the pattern of discourse in Exod 32.
58. We use the LXX as a comparison with Paul here, since we assume that Paul had access to LXX and used the Greek translations available to him. Note that LXX here refers to the Old Greek texts of Scriptures. For further discussions of Paul's Greek Bible, see Stanley E. Porter, "Paul and His Bible: His Education and Access to the Scriptures of Israel," in *As It Is Written: Studying Paul's Use of Scripture*, ed. Stanley E. Porter and Christopher D. Stanley (Atlanta: SBL, 2008), 34–40. The book perhaps refers to some sort of written record, perhaps "a scroll of fate or a table of genealogies, in which names may be written or erased. In the New Testament, this becomes the 'book of life' of those destined for Heaven (Luke 10:20; Phil 4:3; Rev 3:5; 13:8, etc.). The Mesopotamians similarly held that the gods kept a 'tablet of destiny' and also inscribed fate in sheep entrails and in the stars." See William Henry Propp, *Exodus 19–40: A New Translation with Introduction and Commentary.* AB 2A (New York: Doubleday, 2006), 564–565.

It is significant to examine the connections between Moses' intercession in Exodus 32 and Paul's intercession in Romans 9:3. We have discussed that Paul is evoking Moses' intercession for Israel here. However, in Romans 9, Paul does not mention Moses until 9:15. Although Paul has Moses in view, instead of using Moses' voice, Paul declares with his own voice his willingness to be cursed for the sake of his kinsmen. Now let us compare Moses' intercession with Paul's. First, in Exodus 32, Moses asks God to forgive Israel's sin of the golden calf based on his sacrifice of being blotted out from the book.[59] In Romans 9, Paul implicitly allies himself with the prophet Moses through his martyr-like sacrifice of intercession for his kinsmen in being separated from Christ. In Exodus 32, Israel's sin – the construction of the golden calf – is obviously stated (32:1–6) before Moses' intercession; however, in Romans 9:1–5, there is no indication of the sin of Paul's kinsmen. We can infer, however, that Paul views his kinsmen to be aligned with the ancient Israelites, who were embroiled in idolatry with the golden calf. In other words, Paul sees the sin of his Jewish contemporaries as similar to the ancients' sin of idolatry. If we read the following text of Romans 9–11, it shows that Paul's voice here hints that his kinsmen committed the sin of idolatry through their unbelief in the mediator of the New Covenant, Jesus Christ.[60] Second, both intercessions have recourse to the heritage of Israel, particularly the patriarchs: Paul lists a series of aspects of Israel's heritage, including the patriarchs that God has provided for them; Moses implores God not to destroy Israel and asks God to remember the patriarchs – Abraham, Isaac, and Jacob/Israel (cf. Rom 9:4–5; Exod 32:13, 33:1). Third, their views of the curses are different from each other: for Paul, being separated from Christ is the curse that matters for

---

59. What does blotted out from the book mean here? Some argue that it may refer to the book of life (see Stuart, *Exodus*, 684–689). Stuart parallels Moses' words in Exod 32:32 with Ps 69:28, "May they be blotted out of book of life and not be listed with the righteous." Others say it refers to a special relationship with God. According to John Durham, having one's name in the book refers to a special relationship with Yahweh. See Durham, *Exodus*, 433: "Moses asks Yahweh to forgive Israel or to erase his own name from the book Yahweh has written, a reference apparently to a register of those loyal to Yahweh and thereby deserving his special blessing."

60. Cf. Abasciano, *Paul's Use of the Old Testament in Romans 9:1–9*, 101–102.

one's life and death; for Moses, one's name being erased from the book is the curse that matters.

3.2.3 Thematic-organizational Meaning

Throughout Romans 9:1–5, Paul brings Christ into all his argumentation. Paul labors to value positively his kinsmen and part of their traditions by creatively Allying Jewish tradition with the viewpoints of his early Christian community: his lament over Israel is within the sphere of Christ and the Holy Spirit; his martyr-like intercession for Israel is on the basis of Christ; and Christ is seen as part of the Israelites' heritage. In this way, Paul re-contextualizes the traditional Jewish discourse patterns of [Lament over Israel], [Martyr-like Intercession for Israel], and [Heritage of Israel] by allying them with the element of Christ*ness*.

Regarding the relationships of the three ITFs in Romans 9:1–5, the peak point of the ITFs is [Martyr-like Intercession for Israel: Paul] (Henceforth [Intercession: Paul]); and the other two ITFs are in Complementary relationships with it. As we have mentioned, the thematic items "curse" and "sin" contained in [Intercession: Paul] have been represented in nuanced relations:

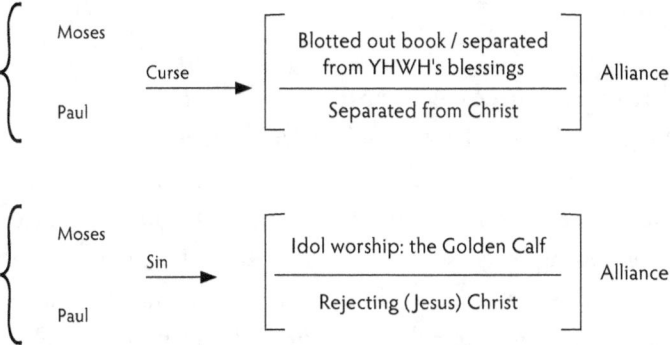

In Romans 9:1–5, Paul implicitly allies the curse of separation from Christ (Christian language) with the curse in the voice of Moses; and the sin of rejecting Christ as the same as the sin of idol worship in Moses' time.

Paul's [Lament over Israel] expresses the fact that Paul, like other prophets, is concerned for Israel and has something important to speak to them; however, both grammatically and structurally, Paul's martyr-like intercession for Israel is the most prominent element. It evokes the idea that Paul, like Moses, would die for his kinsmen, Israel. After Paul implicitly establishes his identity as a Mosaic prophetic figure, he begins to enumerate the advantages of God's people, Israel. Actually, the heritage of Israel is embedded in Paul's intercession for Israel in Christ. In some ways, he allies with the conservative voice of Israel's heritage. However, the one key item, "Christ," does not appear in most literature related to the heritage of Israel. The sense of "Christ" as used by Paul in the text refers to the Messiah, Jesus Christ; however, the concept of Messiah in early Judaism mostly refers to the political realm in which God provides the ideal Davidic ruler for Israel. There is no designation for any future redeemer, like Jesus Christ as the Messiah.[61] What can justify Paul's effort to base the Jewish*ness* element on the Christ*ness* discourse? Paul's identity as a Mosaic prophet justifies the fact that his words are from God and are therefore valuable. Moses has traced back YHWH's promise to the patriarchs when he intercedes for Israel (Exod 32:13, 33:1); the pattern is similar here, Paul's martyr-like intercession for Israel is followed by the statement of Israel's heritage in Romans 9:1–5.

3.2.4 Multiple Voices: Viewpoints of Paul's Jewish Contemporaries on Intercession for Israel

A fuller intertextual analysis of heteroglossia is possible if we look at some other texts from alternative social voices.[62] We shall not do a detailed analysis of the following texts as we did for Romans 9:1–5, but we can take a synoptic view of intertextual relations to discern several relevant thematic patterns. Cultures are internally differentiated and systematically related among different social groups.[63] The way to understand these differences

---

61. B. Witherington, "Christ," in *Dictionary of Paul and His Letters*, ed. Gerald F. Hawthorne, Ralph P. Martin and Daniel G. Reid (Downers Grove: InterVarsity Press, 1993), 95.
62. Cf. Lemke, "Discourses in Conflict," 43.
63. Lemke, "Intertextuality and Text Semantics," 87.

is to analyze the pairings of thematic combinations.[64] We have seen the thematic patterns of Romans 9:1–5. Now let us turn to some other Jewish literature to discuss their way of (dis)associating these thematic formations.

It is helpful to engage in a synoptic view of the intertextual reading of *4 Ezra* in what follows, for some of its thematic combinations resemble Romans 9:1–5 (e.g. Ezra's lament over Israel and his intercession for Israel). According to most scholars, *4 Ezra* was composed around AD 100 and is known as a Jewish document.[65] Metzger has rightly indicated that the main body of the book (chs. 3–14) was written by a Jewish author, and the first two chapters of introduction and a kind of appendix of chapters 15 and 16 may be later expansions by a Christian.[66] The first two chapters which constitute the Christian introduction depict Ezra as a proclaimer of the law of God to the Gentiles after being rejected by Israel (2:33–41), as one who reproves "the Jewish people for their waywardness despite God's repeated mercies (1:4–2:32)."[67] From chapter 14, it can be seen that Ezra was "revered as a figure of great status, equal to that of Moses."[68] Also, through the main body (chs. 3–14), the role of Ezra has been cast by the author as that of a prophet[69] "who expresses the religious problematic of the community and who refers the community's dilemma to the community's god."[70] Therefore, there exist shared similarities between Ezra and Paul in terms of their roles and missions. Therefore, it will be interesting to investigate the thematic patterns of part of *4 Ezra* in a synoptic view with Romans 9:1–5.

---

64. Ibid.
65. B. M. Metzger, "The Fourth Book of Ezra: A New Translation and Introduction," in *The Old Testament Pseudepigrapha*, ed. James H. Charlesworth (Peabody: Hendrickson, 2011), 520.
66. Ibid., 517–518.
67. Ibid., 517.
68. Michael E. Stone, *Fourth Ezra: A Commentary on the Book of Fourth Ezra*. Hermeneia. (Minneapolis: Fortress, 1990), 37.
69. "The book opens with Ezra the prophet in great distress over the desolation of Zion and the wealth of her enemies (3:1b–2)." See E. Breech, "These Fragments I Have Shored against My Ruins: The Form and Function of 4 Ezra," *JBL* 92 (1973), 270.
70. Breech, "These Fragments," 272.

The book of *4 Ezra* is a Jew's "reflections after the destruction of Jerusalem in 70 CE – an event which left the Jewish 'religion' never the same again."[71] Consisting of seven visions, the particular pathos of the book is that the author wrestles with the question: Why has God delivered his people into the hands of their enemies?[72] In other words, it is a book questioning God's faithfulness.[73] The first three visions contain dialogues between Ezra and the angel Uriel;[74] the last four visions do not follow the dialogue pattern, but express Ezra's consolation,[75] reassuring the community in the midst of their despair.[76] The third vision (6:35–9:25) offers an extremely long dialogue between Ezra and Uriel, which contributes to demonstrating the position Ezra takes in terms of the question with which he is struggling. It is instructive to do a synoptic reading of *4 Ezra* (6:35–9:25), in which the prophet Ezra intercedes for his community,[77] along with Paul's intercession for his kinsmen in Romans 9:1–5.

The third vision starts with Ezra's sorrow or distress over Israel's situation (6:35–37): "I *wept* again and fasted seven days as before, . . . *my heart was troubled* within me again, and I began to speak in the presence of the Most High. For *my spirit was greatly aroused*, and *my soul was in distress*."[78]

---

71. Bruce W. Longenecker, *Eschatology and the Covenant: A Comparison of 4 Ezra and Romans 1–11*. JSNTSup 57. (Sheffield: JSOT Press, 1991), 40.
72. Metzger, "Fourth Book of Ezra," 521.
73. Longenecker, *Eschatology and the Covenant*, 40.
74. As Longenecker has observed, "Although the two characters are actively engaged in dialogical exchange throughout, there is no proposition which both characters formally agree upon in the end. No conclusion appears in the dialogues; they simply come to an end. . . . The author sets up a curious tension between these characters without an explicit indication of where he himself stands." (See Longenecker, *Eschatology and the Covenant*, 41) Therefore, there have been various efforts to find out the author's viewpoint through the dialogues, that is, whether the author allies with Ezra or Uriel. We will not attempt to find out what the viewpoint of the author of *4 Ezra* is, but will focus on Ezra's voice in the text.
75. Breech, "These Fragments," 172.
76. Cf. Longenecker, *Eschatology and the Covenant*, 45. Regarding the structure of the last four visions, Stone has appropriately identified "one vision that is part dialogue and part waking experience (vision 4), two symbolic dreams and their interpretations (visions 5 and 6), and a final narrative about the receipt of a revelation (vision 7)." See Stone, *Fourth Ezra*, 28.
77. Breech, "These Fragments," 271.
78. The translation is from Stone, *Fourth Ezra*, 176. Italics mine.

Ezra expresses his sorrow in the presence of the Most High, which can be compared with Paul's lament before Christ concerning Israel. On one hand, both of them demonstrate their sorrow and love toward Israel; on the other hand, although both of them appeal in their speeches to the divine being, Paul speaks in the sphere of Christ (Rom 9:1), Ezra in the presence of the Most High.

After opening with an expression of Ezra's sorrow, there follows the address of Ezra's complaint about God, which is embedded in a statement of the special role of Israel (6:38–59).[79] Ezra indicates in the address that (1) the world is created for Israel; (2) Israel is God's people, first-born, only begotten and zealous for God; and (3) Israel shall possess the world as an inheritance (6:55–59). In contrast, Ezra describes the nations as nothing, for "they are like spittle" and "their abundance like a drip from a bucket." Therefore, Ezra emphasizes the privilege of Israel as God's people over the nations. Reading this with Romans 9:4–5, we can see that Paul refers to the privileges/heritage of Israel as God's people as well. However, Paul, contrary to Ezra, does not prioritize the privilege of Israel so as to press down the nations.

One striking feature in the third vision is Ezra's intercession for the ungodly (7:102–111). The ungodly here refers to the ungodly Israelites who do not observe the law.[80] After Uriel kept rejecting Ezra's intercession for the ungodly, Ezra turns to implore God to show mercy to his people (8:4–36):

> I will speak about *your people*, for whom I am grieved, and about *your inheritance*, for whom I lament, and about *Israel*, for whom I am sad, and about *the seed of Jacob*, for whom I am troubled. Therefore I will pray before you for myself and for them, for I see the failings of us who dwell in the land, and

---

79. It can be divided into two sections: God's creation in the six days (6:38–54); and the special role of Israel (i.e. the creation is for Israel).

80. When Ezra intercedes for the ungodly, he gives domestic examples of fathers (who intercede) for sons, or sons for parents . . . relatives for their kinsmen, or friends for those who are most dear (7:102–103); also after Uriel rejects Ezra's intercession, he turns to examples like Moses for our fathers in the desert, Joshua for Israel in the days of Achan, Samuel in the days of Saul.

> I have heard of the swiftness of the judgment that is to come. Therefore hear my voice, and understand my words, and I will speak before you (8:15–19).[81]

In Ezra's prayer toward God, he asks for God to have mercy on the ungodly of Israel on the basis of those righteous Israelites:

> O look not upon the sins of your people, but at those who have served you in truth. Regard not the endeavors of those who act wickedly, but the endeavors of those who have kept your covenants amid afflictions. . . . Let it not be your will to destroy those who have had the ways of cattle; but regard those who have gloriously taught your Law . . . (8:26–30)

From the above demonstration, it can be inferred that the thematic patterns of the third vision in *4 Ezra* resemble those of Paul's thematic patterns in Romans 9:1–5: Ezra's lament over Israel in the presence of the Most High, the special privilege of Israel, and Ezra's intercession for ungodly Israel on the basis of the righteous.

However, in examining specific parts of these two texts (*4 Ezra* 6:35–9:25, Rom 9:1–5), we see that they contrast with each other. Paul's sorrow is partially because of Israel's rejection of Jesus Christ[82] and their refusal of the inclusion of the Gentiles in Paul's view of salvation.[83] What Paul wishes is his people's acceptance of Jesus as Christ and their acceptance of the Gentiles into their community, but Ezra's sorrow is due to Israel's

---

81. Italics mine.
82. In Romans 9:3, Paul demonstrates that his anguish is that God's people have failed to recognize their Messiah, Jesus Christ. See Dunn, *Romans 9–16*, 525. Wright also views Paul's unceasing grief as based on the Jew's refusal to believe in Jesus; but Reasoner indicates that Paul may also be concerned with the way the Roman political world was threatening Jewish identity in the world in Romans 9. See Mark Reasoner, "Romans 9–11 Moves from Margin to Center, from Rejection to Salvation: Four Grids for Recent English-Language Exegesis," in *Between Gospel and Election: Explorations in the Interpretation of Romans 9–11*, ed. Florian Wilk, J. Ross Wagner and Frank Schleritt (Tübingen: Mohr Siebeck, 2010), 81. However, Reasoner's reading is less reasonable in the context.
83. Later on, Paul will argue for inclusion of the Gentiles in God's salvific plan (Rom 10:11–13; 11:11–15).

suffering caused by the Gentiles, and he prays God to destroy the Gentiles. What Ezra wishes is that God would grant favor to Israel over against the Gentiles. Therefore, Paul's intercession for Israel is in conflict with Ezra's intercession for ungodly Israel. In sum, Paul attempts to align with his Jewish contemporaries by expressing his concerns, but at the core of his stance on the relationship between the Israelites and the Gentiles, he seems to have been in conflict with many of them.

3.3 Romans 9:6–13

3.3.1 Presentational Meaning: God's Promise and Who are God's People

As we have mentioned, the presentational meaning refers to the discourse's construction of "the way the world is,"[84] which corresponds to Halliday's ideational meaning. In the following, we will investigate the participants of the process first, and then examine the phrasal and clausal structures and the relationships of the clause complexes in Romans 9:6–13, so that the presentational meaning of the thematic formations can be established under this close scrutiny.

From chart 2 in appendix 3, two kinds of participants can be observed: the word and the people. The word refers to the divine word of God (God's word, God's promise, and God's purpose) in c4A, c7A and c8E (vv. 6, 8, 12). The people, referring to Israel or Abraham's descendants/children, can be categorized into two kinds of groups: the individual and the corporate. The former – such as Abraham, Rebecca, Isaac, the elder, the younger, Jacob, and Esau – are related to the successive Israelite generations. The latter can be further divided into two contrasting groups: the children of flesh and the children of God/promise. This probably indicates that the main issue of this discourse unit has something to do with the interaction between God's word and the Israelites. We can label this sort of discourse as [God's Promise to the Patriarchs].

---

84. Lemke, *Textual Politics*, 33.

Chart 2 shows that the dominant type of clause is relational, for this section focuses on the relationships of God and his people – Israel according to promise. Therefore, these relational clauses of identity aid in explaining Paul's idea about what it means to be God's children (what Israel's identity means). Similar to the previous passage (Rom 9:1–5), the dominant verbal aspects are imperfective (present tense), which may indicate that Paul considers the status of being God's people to be significant even in Paul's days. Interestingly, all the tense forms appearing in the Scriptures about the promise are future (Gen 18:10, 14; 21:12; 25:23). Most future forms are located in the promise to Abraham and Sarah, with the exception of one to Rebecca (Rom 9:12; Gen 25:23), which suggests the significant role of the promises.[85] The significance of Paul's employment of Scriptures of promise may be that it reveals the faithfulness of God's word.

In the following, a detailed analysis of clausal structures will be provided. The first clause οὐχ οἷον . . . ὅτι (not . . . such as that) in c4A (v. 6a) is a negation-expression.[86] It denies the ὅτι clause that the word of God has failed, which is dialogic in that it invokes itself as responding to the claim that the word of God has failed.[87] Obviously, Paul indicates disagreement with the view that God's word has failed in any way. This clause sets the keynote for the whole section (vv. 6b–13), signaling Paul's position as the stance of denial of this accusation of God. With a γάρ in c5A (v. 6b), the subsequent clauses (c5A–c8Hb, vv. 6b–13) justify the statement of c4A (v. 6a). In c5A (v. 6b), Paul draws a distinction between πάντες οἱ ἐξ Ἰσραηλ

---

85. These future tense forms do not signal a time in the future. Actually, the promises had been realized when Paul wrote the letter.

86. BAGD considers the phrase as a mixture of οὐχ οἷον (by no means) and οὐχ ὅτι (not as if). So do many commentators, e.g. Cranfield, *Romans*, 472; Moo, *The Epistle to the Romans*, 572, n. 12; Dunn, *Romans 9–16*, 538. Basically, οἷον is appositional to the ὅτι clause. The adverb οὐχ denies οἷον which refers to the ὅτι clause.

87. There are at least two understandings of the phrase "the word of God": first, it might refer specifically to the gospel, since Paul uses it to depict the message of the gospel in 1 Cor 14:36; 2 Cor 2:17; 4:2; Col 1:25; 1 Thess 1:8; 2:13; 1 Tim 4:5; 2 Tim 2:9; Tit 2:5 (see Moo, *The Epistle to the Romans*, 572 and n.14; also Dunn, *Romans 9–16*, 538–39); and second, it might refer to God's scriptural words, particularly, God's promises to Israel about their privileges just listed. Most scholars would agree with the second option in this context. See Moo, *The Epistle to the Romans*, 573; Cranfield, *Romans*, 472–73; Dunn, *Romans 9–16*, 539; Brendan Byrne, *Romans*. SP 6. (Collegeville: Liturgical Press, 1996), 293, etc. Due to their arguments, it is the second meaning that I prefer here.

and οὗτοι ᾽Ισραὴλ,[88] the comprehensive Israel and the elected Israel (οὗτοι Israel).[89] The following clauses bear a pattern of antithesis, negation, and affirmation (οὐδέ/οὐ . . . ἀλλά) to confirm the distinction. These two sets of nominal groups can be illustrated as follows:

The Comprehensive Israel	The Elected Israel
πάντες οἱ ἐξ ᾽Ισραὴλ (all those from Israel);	οὗτοι ᾽Ισραὴλ (these [are] Israel);
πάντες τέκνα (all children);	σπέρμα ᾽Αβραάμ (the seed of Abraham);
τὰ τέκνα τῆς σαρκός (children of flesh): (Ishmael + Isaac)	τέκνα τοῦ θεοῦ (the children of God);
	τὰ τέκνα τῆς ἐπαγγελίας (the children of promise);
	ἐν ᾽Ισαὰκ . . . σοι σπέρμα (in Isaac – the seed)

Therefore, Paul sets out two antithetical Israels: one Israel existing within the other comprehensive Israel. By doing so, Paul confirms that the way for Israel to be God's people is based on God's promise rather than on human flesh. In verse 7, Paul distinguishes σπέρμα ᾽Αβραάμ from πάντες τέκνα, confirmed by directly quoting Genesis 21:12b without any introductory formulas, "through Isaac shall your seed be named."[90] Paul seems to blend the voice of God in Genesis 21:12 into his. The phrase, τοῦτ᾽ ἔστιν, "that is," in verse 8, introduces a note of clarification.[91] Paul further clarifies the

---

88. There exists an alternative understanding of these two phrases, but election within Israel fits the context better. For an alternative explanation, see John M. G. Barclay, "Paul's Story: Theology as Testimony," in *Narrative Dynamics in Paul: A Critical Assessment*, edited by Bruce W. Longenecker, (Louisville: Westminster John Knox, 2002), 149. He argues against the concept of election within Israel. As he says, "It is clear that God's grace is not a matter of selection within Israel but of a leveling of all (on the stone of offence, 9:32–33), so that 'there is no distinction between Jew and Greek.'"
89. Cranfield, *Romans*, 473.
90. It sounds like that the children of the flesh (Ishmael, son of Hagar) are not children of God, but the children of the promise (Isaac, son of Sarah) are counted as the true descendants. We will discuss this further in the intertextual section on the Genesis texts.
91. Dunn, *Romans 9–16*, 541. Cf. Matt 27:46; Mark 7:2; Acts 1:19; 19:4; Rom 7:18; 10:6, 8; Phlm 12; 1 Pet 3:20.

distinction of "the children of the promise" (or "the children of God") from the children of the flesh.[92] Therefore, it sounds like, for Paul, the children of flesh (Ishmael, the son of Hagar) are not children of God, but the children of the promise (Isaac, the son of Sarah) are counted as the true seed. However, we should note that Isaac was Abraham's child of the flesh as was Ishmael; the decisive idea is not whether Isaac was born by the flesh or by the spirit, but the fact that he was the carrier of the divine promise.[93] With a γὰρ in c7A (v. 9), the promise that Paul has just mentioned is explained and emphasized.[94] By quoting Genesis 18: 14 (10),[95] Paul seems to explain that Isaac, the son of Sarah, becomes the son of promise, "About this time I will return and Sarah shall have a son." The introductory projection, "this is the word of the promise" (c7A, v, 9a), attributes the quotation to the voice of the divine, with which voice Paul aligns.

The transitional phrase οὐ μόνον ... ἀλλὰ καὶ (not only ... but also) in c8A and c8B① (v. 10) makes clear that verses 10–13 take the argument of verses 7–9 one step further.[96] The following subordinate clauses (c8C~c8E) provide the circumstance for the promise given to Rebecca. After

---

92. Cranfield, *Romans*, 475.
93. Ibid., 475–76. As Moo also points out, for Paul, what counts is grace, not race. This principle implies that "he includes within those covenantal blessings the new life experienced by believers in Christ." See Moo, *The Epistle to the Romans*, 577.
94. With Sanday and Headlam, Cranfield states that ἐπαγγελίας "must be the predicate of the sentence thrown forward in order to give emphasis and to show where the point of the argument lies." See Sanday and Headlam, *Romans*, 242; Cranfield, *Romans*, 476.
95. Actually, the quoted verse seems to be an amalgam of LXX Gen 18:10 and 18:14. See Dunn, *Romans 9–16*, 541.
96. According to Moo, Paul, in vv. 10–13, moves down one patriarchal generation to develop the distinction between the comprehensive Israel (children of flesh) and the elected Israel (children of promise) (see Moo, *The Epistle to the Romans*, 578–580). The case of Isaac and Ishmael might not be enough to support the truth of the statement in v. 8 that it is the promise of God that matters in making Abraham's children to be God's children. Although both Isaac and Ishmael were children of Abraham's begetting, their mothers were different; Ishmael's mother was Sarah's handmaid, and this difference could possibly explain why Abraham's seed should be reckoned through Isaac and not through Ishmael. This might be the reason that Paul goes on to cite a second and clearer example of Jacob and Esau who shared the same father as well as the same mother, which excludes the factor of birthright as the basis for being God's children. See Cranfield, *Romans*, 476. See also Moo, *The Epistle to the Romans*, 579–80: "It is worth noting that Isaac's rival was but a half-brother, the son of a different woman, while Jacob's rival was his own twin. It would demonstrate Paul's argument for the lack of natural distinguishing characteristics separating Jacob and Esau."

introducing the fact that Rebecca will conceive children from Isaac in verse 10, Paul parallels a series of antithetical oppositions:

γεννηθέντων,πραξάντων τι ἀγαθὸν ἢ φαῦλον	ἡ κατ' ἐκλογὴν πρόθεσις τοῦ θεοῦ
ἐξ ἔργων	ἐκ τοῦ καλοῦντος
ὁ μείζων	ὁ ἐλάσσων
τὸν Ἠσαῦ ἐμίσησα	τὸν Ἰακὼβ ἠγάπησα

Therefore, Paul sets up an antithesis between two persons: Esau, the elder whom I hated; Jacob, the younger whom I loved. They correspond to the two chains of phrases: "doing," "from works" in contrast to, "God's purpose of election," "from calling." By reading the following text in Romans 9–11, we discover that Paul establishes a contrasting pair of thematic formations: [Human's Doing] vs. [God's Calling].[97] Through these antithetical Oppositions, the point has been made: God's calling and promise determine the true heirs of Jacob (the true Israel). In other words, these subordinated statements demonstrate that the divine distinguishing between Jacob and Esau preceded their birth, and thus excludes the possibility of its being in any way dependent on works.[98]

The phrase οὐκ ἐξ ἔργων ἀλλ' ἐκ τοῦ καλοῦντος, which is a key theme in Romans 10, functions as the manner (one of the circumstantial attributive categories for a relational process) of God's purpose of election. It points out that God's own calling establishes the basis for determining who are identified as his people. In Moo's words, "There was nothing within the person of Jacob and Esau that could have been the basis for God's choice of the one over the other."[99] Therefore, it becomes apparent that God's purpose of election is wholly dependent on God himself who calls.[100] The exact

---

97. Paul's Jewish contemporaries would not agree with this Opposing contrast.
98. Cranfield, *Romans*, 478. According to Cranfield, the meaning of ἔργων refers to God's requirement (see Cranfield, *Romans*, 198); however, Dunn considers ἐξ ἔργων as the usual "ἐξ ἔργων formulation," that is, works of the law (see Dunn, *Romans 9–16*, 543).
99. Moo, *The Epistle to the Romans*, 580.
100. Cranfield, *Romans*, 478.

quotation of the last part of LXX Genesis 25:23 – ὁ μείζων δουλεύσει τῷ ἐλάσσονι (the elder shall serve the younger) in c8F (v. 12b) supports Paul's argument of God's purpose according to election. The comparative clause καθὼς γέγραπται[101] in c8G (v. 13) conjoining verse 13 to verses 11–12 describes similar scriptural voices regarding God's purpose of election.[102] Also, the clause καθὼς γέγραπται is a generalized projection modifying the voice of the prophet Malachi into a normative statement from God:[103] τὸν Ἰακὼβ ἠγάπησα, τὸν δὲ Ἠσαῦ ἐμίσησα ("Jacob I loved, but Esau I hated"). Therefore, the quotation of Malachi 1:2–3 in Romans 9:13 has been attached to verse 12,[104] so as to emphasize the point that God's promise was prior to the birth of Rebecca's twins.[105] One question needs to be raised here: why does Paul suddenly quote Malachi in the midst of the quotations from Genesis and Exodus?[106] Chilton rightly observes that Paul implicitly claims that his analogy has prophetic warrant and shows that he is in line with the prophets.[107] Paul intentionally quotes Malachi 1:2–3 here;[108] the

---

101. According to Porter, "A comparative clause describes items between which similarities are being drawn." Also καθὼς γέγραπται (as it is written) is a fairly common comparative phrase found in the NT. See Porter, *Idioms of the Greek New Testament*, 242–243.

102. There is some controversy about why God hates Esau. Some suggest that Paul means only that God loved Esau less than he loved Jacob, since he blessed both, but Jacob was used in a more positive and basic way in the furtherance of God's plans. Although God left Esau and Edom outside the relationship, they are still the object of God's merciful care, according to the testimony of the Scriptures. See Cranfield, *Romans*, 480. Moo argues that "hate" should be understood as "reject." "Love" and "hate" are not emotions that God feels but actions that he carries out. See Moo, *The Epistle to the Romans*, 589–590; Sanday and Headlam, *Romans*, 247–248.

103. According to Watson, the standard formula καθὼς γέγραπται "presents a citation as a completed utterance that is definitive and permanently valid." See Watson, *Paul and the Hermeneutics of Faith*, 45.

104. The only variation for the LXX text is in the order of the first three words (cf. Cranfield, *Romans*, 479).

105. Cf. Waetjen, *Romans*, 237.

106. Rom 9: 13 quotes Mal 1: 2–3. The only variation for the LXX text is in the order of the first three words. See Cranfield, *Romans*, 479.

107. Chilton, "Romans 9–11," 29.

108. Mal 1: 2–3 is located within the small unit of vv. 2–5, which concerns Yahweh's love for Israel. The prophet, in v. 2a, sets out the parameters of the issue to be addressed: "I have loved you, says the Lord." Verses 2b–5 then provide the prophet's argument that Yahweh does indeed love the people, Israel (see Marvin A. Sweeney et al., *The Twelve Prophets*, v. 2:716, [Collegeville: Liturgical, 2000], 722–23). According to Abasciano, Malachi is "addressed to an apostate Israel that challenged the covenant faithfulness and

quoted statement reiterates the role reversal and emotions of the Genesis narrative.[109]

In conclusion, the above investigations of [God's Promise to the Patriarchs] indicate that elected Israel is God's people based on God's promise (vv. 8–13).[110] The focus of this discourse section is about true descent from Abraham, the identity of the people of God. Paul brings in the stories of the Patriarchs – Abraham and Isaac (Ishmael) – to argue that it is the children of promise rather than the children of flesh that are the true seed of Abraham and who belong to God's people. Moreover, the preference of [God's Calling] over [Human's Doing] further corroborates God's sovereign role in deciding who his people are through excluding the factor of birthright. Therefore, it is God's calling that establishes the basis for who are his people. In addition, Paul allies the normative scriptural voice from Malachi with [God's Calling], which strengthens his viewpoint that it is God's calling that determines who God's people are. However, if we bring in examples of Jewish literature concerning [God's Calling] and [Human's Doing], it can be seen that according to this tradition God calls Jacob over Esau because he knows that Esau is evil and Jacob will do good deeds.[111] In other words, Paul allies [God's Promise to the Patriarchs] and [God's Calling] with the generalized scriptural voice of God's sovereignty in election, which establishes his and his community's viewpoint about who God's people are.

---

justice of God." Also, "The prophet refutes and rebukes these blasphemous attitudes and assures Israel of God's covenant love and faithfulness." Abasciano, *Paul's Use of the Old Testament in Romans 9:1–9*, 65.

109. Sweeney et al., *The Twelve Prophets*, v. 2:724. It is interesting to ask whether Paul means to give some hints on the reversed roles of Israel and the Gentiles as indicated in Romans 9:30 31: "Gentiles . . . have attained it . . . but Israel . . . did not succeed in fulfilling that law."

110. Verses 6b–9 state that the child of flesh opposes the child of promise. The way of Paul's use of the Scriptures indicates that "Isaac was the child of promise, and not born κατὰ σάρκα; his birth therefore depends upon the promise which was in fact the efficient cause of it, and not the promise upon his birth." Sanday and Headlam, *Romans*, 242. Cf. Cranfield, *Romans*, 476; Moo, *The Epistle to the Romans*, 577–578.

111. See the detailed analysis of the related Jewish literature in the section below.

3.3.2 Scriptural Voices

The Scriptures that have been utilized in Romans 9:6–13 are from Genesis and Malachi: Genesis 18:10, 14; 21:12; 25:23; and Malachi 1:2. In the following, we will examine these scriptural texts in their own co-texts first, and then demonstrate Paul's viewpoint toward these scriptural texts as well.

Starting in Genesis 18, the Scripture narrates the fact that Sarah's bearing of Isaac was promised by God (Gen 18:10, 14), and in Genesis 21:1–7, Sarah gives birth to Isaac, confirming that God's promise has been realized. Between Genesis 18:17 and 20:18, there are several narrative accounts concerning the destruction of Sodom, the rescue of Lot, the sin of Lot, and the issue between Abraham and Abimelech. We will focus on the texts concerning the birth of Isaac, that is, Genesis 18:9–16, which narrates the promise of Isaac's birth, and Genesis 21:1–21, which narrates the realization of God's promise. According to the narration of Genesis 18:9–16, after Abraham showed his hospitality to the three men,[112] YHWH promised him that Sarah would have a son in due season (18:10). Verse 9 mentions "they," the three men who spoke to Abraham about Sarah; then the third person singular is used of the person speaking in the projection clause (he said, cf. Gen 18:10a). It seems that "he" refers to YHWH, since "he" turns to "I" in the projected clause of locution, "I will return to you about this time next year" (18:10b). The one who returns to Abraham later is YHWH. In verses 13–14, the name of YHWH is stressed as the speaker who repeats the promise that he will visit again and that Sarah will have a son in due time. Chapter 21 opens with a response to the promise, "Then the LORD took note of Sarah as he had said, and the LORD did for Sarah as he had promised" (NAS). Then the narrator describes Sarah's pregnancy, the birth of Isaac, Isaac's circumcision, and the joy of Sarah, etc. (vv. 1–7). These are followed by the account of Abraham's domestic conflict involving Sarah and Hagar and the exclusion of Hagar and their son, Ishmael (vv. 8–21). Sarah asks Abraham to expel Ishmael when she sees Ishmael mocking her son Isaac (v. 8). Abraham is grieved when YHWH appears and proclaims to him that he should listen to what Sarah has asked, because "in Isaac shall

---

112. Fruchtenbaum indicates that one of these three men is "God in visible form, and the other two are angels. In rabbinic tradition, all three are angels." See Arnold G. Fruchtenbaum, *The Book of Genesis* (San Antonio: Ariel Ministries, 2009), 309.

your seed be called." That is, Isaac was to be the son of the inheritance. Then YHWH continues to reveal Ishmael's future to Abraham, "And of the son of the maid I will make a nation also, because he is your seed" (v. 13). Therefore, Ishmael's role as Abraham's seed was not denied by YHWH, although he was not able to obtain the promised heritage. However, Paul attributes a new meaning to Abraham's seed, that is, the inherited descendants, who are the children of God.

After providing the list of the sons of Ishmael (25:12–18), the birth of Esau and Jacob in 25:19 signals a transition back to the sons of Isaac, "Now these are the generations of Isaac, Abraham's son." Isaac's wife Rebecca is depicted as barren, just as Sarah (25:21), but after Isaac's intercession for her, YHWH answered him and thus Rebecca conceives. In other words, the twins born by Rebecca are due to God's grace, just as Isaac's birth is based on God's promise. Because of the twin sons struggling within her, Rebecca turns to inquire of YHWH, and YHWH replies with an oracle, "Two nations are in your womb; and two peoples shall be separated from your body; and one people shall be stronger than the other; and the older shall serve the younger" (25:23). After recording the birth of the twin sons in verses 24–26, the narrator recounts Esau's selling of his birthright to Jacob (vv. 27–34), including the comment, "So Esau despised his birthright" (v. 34). Therefore, the triumph of Jacob over Esau was first predicted by YHWH before they were born, and subsequently, Esau's own action of selling the birthright confirms his loss of his status. Note that some other expressions of first century Christian literature comment on Esau, "that there be no immoral or godless person like Esau, who sold his own birthright for a single meal" (Heb 12:16, NAS). In other words, Esau's selling his birthright was an evil, godless action.

An investigation of Paul's way of using of Genesis 25:23 offers us his viewpoint on why Jacob is the seed of Abraham. Prior to his quoting, "the elder will serve the younger," Paul demonstrates a series of contrasts between Human's doing and God's calling: neither doing good or bad, but God's purpose of election; not by works, but by the calling. Therefore, Paul's viewpoint on the triumph of Jacob rests on the basis of God's purpose or God's doing. That is why he particularly allies with the prophetic voice, "Jacob I loved, but Esau I hated," in order to make this voice more convincing.

The prophetic text, Malachi 1:2–3, is within the first oracle of the book (1:2–5), which takes the form of prophetic dispute.[113] In verse 1, the text identifies the receivers of Malachi's prophecy: Israel. The first oracle concerns YHWH's love toward Israel. After the statement "I have loved you (1:2a)," the prophet immediately receives the disputation, "How have you loved us? (1:2b)." The prophet responds with a restatement of his premise: "I have loved Jacob but I have hated Esau," following up with evidence concerning the disaster that YHWH poured upon Edom (vv. 3–4). Obviously, the reference to Jacob and Esau concerns the nations descended from them; "It is these nations to which the prophet really refers."[114] However, Paul's use of Malachi 1:2b emphasizes the individuals Jacob and Esau so as to confirm his viewpoint that the formation of God's children is based only on God's promise or God's calling. That is, God is the center.

In sum, the account of the promise and birth of Isaac in Genesis 18 and 21 corroborates Paul's voice that the formation of God's people is through promise, not through physical heirship, for it is through Isaac that offspring shall be named after Abraham (Gen 21:12c). He quotes precisely the last part of LXX Genesis 21:12 in verse 7 (ἐν Ἰσαὰκ κληθήσεταί σοι σπέρμα). Regarding the next generation, the author of Genesis did not provide an explicit reason in the narration of the story of Jacob and Esau in Genesis 25 as to why Esau would serve Jacob, although he does give the story of Esau's selling his birthright for a dish of pottage. Paul makes it apparent

---

113. Ralph L. Smith, *Micah-Malachi*. WBC 32. (Waco: Word Books, 1984), 304; Terry Eddinger, *Malachi: A Handbook on the Hebrew Text* (Waco: Baylor University Press, 2012), 9. "There are many prophetic disputes in the OT. Some of them are disputes with other prophets (cf. Mic 2:6–11; Jer 28:1–17), and some are disputes with lay persons (Isa 40:27–28; Ezek 12:21–28). The style is often called the question-and-answer or 'catechetical' style. Some have called it 'Socratic' after the style of the Greek philosopher. The structure of this pericope is simple. The prophet first states a truth, then his disputants state their objections by asking a question. Finally the prophet restates his premise and supports it with hard evidence." See Smith, *Micah-Malachi*, 304. Also, Glazier-McDonald indicates, "The question and answer schema embodies the essence of prophecy and enables us to see the prophetic process at work." See Beth Glazier-McDonald, *Malachi, the Divine Messenger* (Atlanta: Scholars Press, 1987), 19–23 (23).
114. Glazier-McDonald, *Malachi*, 34.

that, even before the birth of Jacob and Esau and without regard to their actions, God's calling and purpose had been manifest through his love of Jacob over Esau. The voice of the prophet Malachi has been generalized to strengthen Paul's viewpoint on the superiority of God's authority.

3.3.3 Thematic-organizational Meaning

Throughout Romans 9:6–13, the carrying thematic formations are about God's word: [God's Promise] and [God's Calling]. The use of the story of Abraham and Isaac focuses on God's promise as the basis of defining God's people (the true seed of Abraham). A series of scriptural persons – Abraham, Sarah, Isaac, Rebecca, Jacob and Esau – has been brought forward to show that God's promises to his people have been realized in history, and that all these happened because of God's purpose in election. The two ITFs here indicate a distinguishing within the children of Abraham, with those who are called or elected based on the promise of God demarcated as the ones who properly belong to the true seed of Abraham. God's faithfulness has been demonstrated in the realization of his promise to the patriarchs. Along with God's faithfulness, the identity of God's people is established according to the promise. In other words, the character of God is intertwined with the identity of God's people. That is, he who is God decides who his people are. Regarding the relationships of the two ITFs, it can be inferred that they ally with each other in Paul. Both of them argue that the formation of God's people is based on God's words.

Besides the carrier formations of God's word, another intertextual thematic relation that Paul constructed should not be neglected. Paul sets [God's Calling] in an Opposition relationship with [Human's Doing]. Although in Paul's day some Jews believed that a person's destiny was already determined by God's choice,[115] most of Paul's Jewish contemporaries would ally the two formations [God's Calling] and [Human's Doing] coherently.

---

115. David B. Capes, Rodney Reeves and E. Randolph Richards, *Rediscovering Paul: An Introduction to His World, Letters, and Theology* (Downers Grove: IVP Academic, 2007), 25. See other texts like 1 Cor 7:17: "Let each of you lead the life that the Lord has assigned, to which God called you. This is my rule in all the churches." Also, Paul believes that God could change the destiny of a person's birth (Eph 2:11–13). See Capes, Reeves, and Richards, *Rediscovering Paul*, 26.

3.3.4 Multiple Voices: Viewpoints of Paul's Jewish Contemporaries on God's Word and Human's Doing

In Romans 9:6–13, Paul uses the story of the patriarchs to defend God's authority in deciding who his people are. The following analysis investigates the book of *Jubilees* and selections from Philo's works to see how Paul converged with and diverged from his Jewish contemporaries in the Second Temple Period.

The book of *Jubilees* is considered to be written between the years 170 and 150 BC.[116] The author, as a Jew, "belongs within the Hasidic or Essene tradition"; or "probably belongs to a priestly family."[117]

Jubilees 16:1–4 rewrites Genesis 18:1–15, the second announcement of Isaac's birth; and *Jub.* 17:1–14 rewrites Genesis 21:8–21, the expulsion of Hagar and Ishmael.[118] Nevertheless, similar thematic patterns remain in *Jub.* 16–17 and Genesis 18–21. The following provides a synoptic reading of *Jub.* 16–17 in order to determine what the author of Jubilees' understanding of Isaac was as Abraham's inherited descendant. *Jubilees* 16:1–4 briefly recounts the announcement of the birth of Isaac.[119] With the exception of the discourse of Abraham's hospitality in *Jub.* 16–17, the

---

116. James C. VanderKam, *The Book of Jubilees: A Critical Text* (Leuven: Peeters, 1989), vi; see also O. S. Wintermute, "Jubilees: A New Translation and Introduction," in *the Old Testament Pseudepigrapha*, ed. James H. Charlesworth (Peabody: Hendrickson, 2011), 44. According to Wintermute, the struggle of the author's group plays a significant role in the struggles of the Maccabean age. As he says, "The author's strict interpretation of the Law, his appeal to a distinct set of traditions which reported the cultic life and piety of the patriarchs, his hostility to surrounding nations, his abhorrence of gentile practices, his insistent demand for obedience to God's commands in a time of apostasy, his belief that God was about to create a new spirit within his people which would make possible a proper relationship between God and Israel, and his preoccupation with adherence to a calendar of 364 days are some of the characteristics which identify him as part of a zealous, conservative, pious segment of Judaism which was bound together by its own set of traditions, expectations, and practices. It is well known that such groups played a significant role in the struggles of the Maccabean age." See Wintermute, "Jubilees," 45.

117. Wintermute, "Jubilees," 44–45.

118. Jacques T. A. G. M. van Ruiten, *Abraham in Jubilees: The Rewriting of Genesis 11:26–25:10 in the Book of Jubilees 11:14–23:8*. SJSJ. (Leiden: Brill, 2012), 169–170.

119. This is the translation by Wintermute: "And on the new moon of the fourth month we appeared unto Abraham, at the oak of Mamre, and we talked with him, and we announced to him that a son would be given to him by Sarah his wife. And Sarah laughed, for she heard that we had spoken these words with Abraham, and we admonished her, and she became afraid, and denied that she had laughed on account of the words. And we told her the name of her son, as his name is ordained and written

announcement is not from YHWH himself, but from the angels (first person plural: "we"). Also, it is these angels that will return to Sarah at a specific time when Sarah will be pregnant (*Jub.* 16:4). The announcement of the birth of Isaac is followed by the judgment on Sodom (*Jub.* 16:5–6) and the sin of Lot with his daughters (*Jub.* 16:7–9). The text then turns to the birth of Isaac at verse 12, "The Lord visited Sarah and did for her as he had said."[120] Verses 3–4 describe Sarah's pregnancy, the birth of Isaac, and his circumcision on the eighth day. There are two additions to *Jub.* 16–30, where the corresponding parts cannot be found in Genesis. The first addition is the flashback to the visit of the angels (16:15–19) and the second one is the description of the joyful festival of tabernacles (16:20–31).[121] In the first addition, the message of the angels indicates the election of one of Isaac's sons (Israel) out of all the nations.[122] After the discourse of Isaac's birth and the two additions, *Jub.* 17:1–14 begins to rewrite Genesis 21:8–21, which concerns Isaac's weaning and the expulsion of Hagar and Ishmael. The thematic patterns of these two texts (*Jub.* 17:1–14 and Gen 21:8–21) are similar.[123] In *Jub.* 17:6, it is YHWH (cf. the angels) who tells Abraham to listen to Sarah concerning the expulsion of Hagar and Ishmael, "because [it is] through Isaac that a name and seed

---

in the heavenly tablets (i.e. Isaac). And (that) when we returned to her at a set time, she would have conceived a son." See Wintermute, "Jubilees," 87–88.

120. VanderKam, *Jubilees*, 96.

121. Ruiten, *Abraham in Jubilees*, 189–195.

122. *Jub.* 16:16–18: "We blessed him [Abraham] . . . that he would not yet die until he became the father of six sons and (that) he would see (them) before he died; but (that) through Isaac he would have a reputation and descendants. All the descendants of his sons would become nations and be numbered with the nations. But one of Isaac's sons would become a holy progeny and would not be numbered among the nations, for he would become the share of the Most High. All his descendants had fallen into that (share) which God owns so that they would become a people whom the Lord possesses out of all the nations; and that they would become a kingdom, a priesthood, and a holy people." See VanderKam, *Jubilees*, 97–98.

123. The descriptions of the reason that Sarah asks Abraham to expel Ishmael are a bit different. In *Jubilees*, Sarah saw Ishmael playing and dancing, and Abraham being extremely happy; it is Sarah's jealousy of Ishmael that triggers her to do it. In Gen 21, Sarah saw Ishmael mocking their son, so it is probably her anger with Ishmael's inappropriate behavior that makes her want to expel Ishmael. However, this small difference does not affect their similarities in the overall thematic patterns.

will be named for you."[124] Consequently, the author of *Jubilees* allies with Genesis to view Jacob as the descendent who inherits. However, note that Ishmael is not denied as Abraham's seed, "I will make him into a great nation because he [Ishmael] is from your seed" (*Jub.* 17:7).[125] Therefore, the author of *Jubilees* views Isaac as YHWH's inherited descendant on the basis of God's promise. This is not so different from Paul's viewpoint on Isaac's role as the inheriting descendant.[126] However, Paul explicitly separates the children of the flesh from the children of the promise (Rom 9:8). Although both Isaac and Ishmael are children of the flesh, Isaac is additionally the child of the promise; therefore, Isaac will be the seed of Abraham. The author of *Jubilees*, on the other hand, views both Isaac and Ishmael as the seed of Abraham, but Isaac as the seed that will carry the name of Abraham.

The report of the birth of Jacob and Esau in *Jub.* 19:13–14 is a rewriting of Genesis 25:21–27.[127] Several parts of Genesis 25:21–27 are omitted, including "the infertility of Rebecca, the intercession of Isaac for her, and God answering this prayer, after which Rebecca became pregnant."[128] Also, *Jubilees* does not mention the struggle between the children in the womb, nor "the image of each brother as a nation."[129] It is mentioned later that Esau sells his right as the firstborn because of the pottage (*Jub.* 24:2–7), with the concluding comment, "so Jacob became the older one, but Esau was lowered from his prominent position" (*Jub.* 24:7; cf. Gen 25:34).[130] In

---

124. Wintermute, "Jubilees," 90.
125. Ibid.
126. However, Philo has different voice: Philo also repeatedly refers to Isaac's birth story and provides his view of the story. In *Leg. All.* 3.219, as Abasciano correctly states, "Philo emphasizes Isaac's supernatural birth as one begotten of God. In line with his name, Isaac represents joy and laughter." (see Abasciano, *Paul's Use of the Old Testament in Romans 9:1–9*, 174). Philo emphasizes Ishmael's inferiority to Isaac, and Isaac is perfect in virtue in *Sobr.*8ff and *Cher.* 3–10 (see Cf. Abasciano, *Paul's Use of the Old Testament in Romans 9:1–9*, 174). These texts from the Second Temple Period provide evidence of how some Jews reflected on the stories of Isaac's birth and Ishmael's expulsion. Abasciano, *Paul's Use of the Old Testament in Romans 9:1–9*, 175.
127. Ruiten, *Abraham in Jubilees*, 239.
128. Ibid., 241.
129. Ibid.
130. Ibid.

Genesis 25, there is no explicit comment on Jacob and Esau;[131] however, *Jub.* 19:13–14 clearly states that "Jacob was perfect and upright, while Esau was a harsh, rustic, and hairy man." The author of *Jubilees* also expands on the affirmation of Rebecca's (and Abraham's) preferential love for Jacob over Esau in *Jub.* 19:16–31.[132] The reasons for the preference have been provided in *Jub.* 35:13–14: the deeds of Jacob are right, but Esau has made his deeds evil. This viewpoint becomes apparent in Philo's work. For instance, Philo's account of the birth of Jacob and Esau contradicts Paul's:

> Again, they say that Jacob and Esau, the former being the ruler, and governor, and master, and Esau being the subject and the slave, had their several estates appointed to them while they were still in the womb. For *God, the creator of all living things, is thoroughly acquainted with all his works*, and before he has completely finished them he comprehends the faculties with which they will hereafter be endowed, and altogether *he foreknows all their actions [τὰ ἔργα] and passions*. For when Rebecca, that is the patient soul, proceeds to ask an oracle from God, the answers are, "Two nations are in thy womb, and two people shall come forth from the bowels, and one people shall be stronger than the other people, and the elder shall serve the younger."[133]

Philo tends to argue that good and evil were foreknown by God even when Jacob and Esau were not yet born.[134] A similar viewpoint can be found in some other Jewish texts. For example, we see this in Pseudo-Philo 32:5–6,

---

131. Note that there is an implicit comment on Esau's selling of his birthright, "Esau despised his birthright" in Gen 25:34, which is not the explicit ethical comment we find in *Jubilees*.

132. Wintermute, "Jubilees," 92.

133. *Leg. All.* 3.88. Italics mine. See Philo, *The Works of Philo: Complete and Unabridged*, trans. Charles Duke Yonge (Peabody: Hendrickson, 1993), 60. Also see Moo's translation, Moo, *The Epistle to the Romans*, 583, n. 60.

134. Philo has argued elsewhere that Rebecca conceived the two natures of good and evil. See Philo, *Sacr.* 4. See also Philo, *Works of Philo*, 94: "And this will be more evidently shown by the oracle which was given to Perseverance, that is to Rebecca; for she also, having conceived the two inconsistent natures of good and evil. . . . And he[God]

in the hymn of Deborah.¹³⁵ This hymn proclaims that God loved Jacob, but he hated Esau because of his deeds. Again this is found in the Jewish work of *4 Ezra* which refers to the election of Jacob over Esau (3:15–19).¹³⁶

Paul in Romans 9, however, opposes this kind of Jewish viewpoint that considers Jacob's election to be based on God's foreknowledge of his works or his wicked deeds,¹³⁷ emphasizing that what really counts is God's purpose of election and his own calling (vv.11b and 12b). Note that Paul actually aligns with some of his Jewish contemporaries about the election/rejection of the heirs of Abraham, but he opposes the reason they give for this rejection: failure to perform good works. Therefore, in the story of Jacob and Esau,¹³⁸ Paul disagrees with his fellow Jews, who hold the view that they are chosen because of their works of obedience to the law. Paul's viewpoint on the true seed of Abraham is stated explicitly: that God's purpose of election remains, "not because of works but because of his call" (Rom 9:11–12).¹³⁹

Therefore, many Jewish people would align with Paul in believing that not all of the physical heirs of Abraham are elect. The reasons that they restrict the range of the elect of Israel are different from Paul's, although a voice that rejects the advantage of mere physical descent from Abraham

---

answered her inquiry, and told her, 'Two nations are in thy womb.' This calamity is the birth of good and evil."

135. It reads, "He [God] gave Isaac two sons, both also from a womb that was closed up. And their mother was then in the third year of her marriage; and it will not happen in this way to any woman, nor will any female so boast. But when her husband approached her in the third year, to him there were born two sons, Jacob and Esau. And God *loved Jacob, but he hated Esau* because of his deeds. And in their father's old age Isaac blessed Jacob and sent him into Mesopotamia, and there he became the father of twelve sons. And they went down into Egypt and dwelt there." See D. J. Harrington, "Pseudo-Philo: A New Translation and Introduction," in *The Old Testament Pseudepigrapha*, ed. James H. Charlesworth (Peabody: Hendrickson, 2011), 346. Emphasis original.

136. See Metzger, "Fourth Book of Ezra," 528–529.

137. As Abasciano points out that, "Even Qumran evidences belief in election based on foreknowledge of righteous and moral character and reprobation based on wicked deeds." Abasciano, *Paul's Use of the Old Testament in Romans 9:10–18*, 57; Abasciano, *Paul's Use of the Old Testament in Romans 9:1–9*, 57, n. 89.

138. In this story, Paul moves down one patriarchal generation to develop further his distinction between an ethnic and a selective Israel. Cf. Moo, *The Epistle to the Romans*, 578.

139. Cf. Gal 3:29, "If you belong to Christ, then you are Abraham's seed, heirs according to the promise."

can be heard in the Jewish literature. *Jubilees* 15:30–32[140] suggests a conditional election/rejection, arguing that despite their descent from Abraham, Ishmael and Esau are non-elect, because the Lord knew their character to be wicked.[141] A similar emphasis on the ethical reasons of rejection (Esau is evil in his deeds) can be found in Philo's treatment of Jacob and Esau, which depicts Esau as "the companion of wickedness," who threatens over Jacob.[142]

These examples, from *Jubilees* and Philo, demonstrate the fact that they share a similar viewpoint on the election of Jacob. The reason for God's choice of Jacob over Esau, though both births are from God's promise, is that the latter is inferior to the former. Paul, however, stresses that Jacob's election arises from God's purpose and calling, instead of any human's doing. Therefore, these examples in the Jewish tradition hold to viewpoints on Abraham's true seed that differ significantly from Paul's.[143]

3.4 Romans 9:14–29

3.4.1 Presentational Meaning: God's Authority, God's Mercy and God's People

After alternately discussing God's words and who belongs to God's people according to the stories of the patriarchs, Paul continues to speak of God

---

140. It reads, "For the Lord did not draw Ishmael and his sons and his brothers and Esau near to himself, and he did not elect them because they are the sons of Abraham, for he knew them. But he chose Israel that they might be a people for him. And he sanctified them and gathered them from all of the sons of man because many nations and many people, and they all belong to him, but over all of them he caused spirits to rule so that they might lead them astray from following him. But over Israel he did not cause any angel or spirit to rule because he alone is their ruler and he will protect them and he will seek for them at the hand of his angels and at the hand of his spirits and at the hand of all of his authorities so that he might guard them and bless them and they might be his and he might be theirs henceforth and forever" (See Wintermute, "Jubilees," 87).
141. Wintermute, "Jubilees," 87. Cf. Abasciano, *Paul's Use of the Old Testament in Romans 9:1–9*, 173.
142. *Det. Pot. Ins.* 45–46. See Philo, *Works of Philo*, 117.
143. The author of *Jubilees* demonstrates that Ishmael and Esau were led astray away from following God by angels or spirits (See *Jub.* 15:30–32). Philo holds that Ishmael is inferior to Isaac, and Isaac is perfect in virtue (see *Leg. All.* 3.219; *Sobr.*8ff and *Cher.* 3–10).

and his people by tracing Israel's history of exodus and exile as presented in the books of Exodus and Isaiah. In other words, the renewed identity of God's people and their relationship with God will be brought into view in verses 14–29.

God's nature, particularly his authority and mercy, is the argumentative center for this section. Verses 14–18 provide a disputation speech formulation, which depicts Paul arguing against the accusation of God's injustice. A disputation speech begins with a series of rhetorical questions, embedded with a voice of refutation from the word of God, and Paul's answer, which includes a rebuttal of the refutation with an explanation.[144] Verse 14 consists of three clauses in a relationship of paratactic extension with one another.[145] The first primary clause – τί οὖν ἐροῦμεν (c9A) – is typical of questions Paul uses to advance his argument.[146] The implied participant reference "we" is the sayer. It includes Paul and his interlocutor. So, Paul identifies himself with his interlocutor by offering a question. The subsequent paratactic clause c9B (v. 14b) raises specifically a yes or no interrogative question about God – the potential accusation of God that his interlocutor would make: μὴ ἀδικία παρὰ τῷ θεῷ; (is there injustice with God?). With the third paratactic clause c9C (v. 14c), Paul dismisses the accusation with the emphatic answer μὴ γένοιτο ("By no means"). The subsequent verses 15–18 explain Paul's rebuttal. Therefore, the discourse pattern of verses 14–18 basically follows a disputation speech: two rhetorical questions (c9A, c9B, v. 14ab) which implied the refutation of God's justice; Paul's answer of rebuttal: μὴ γένοιτο; and further explanation of God's authority and mercy in verses 15–18. There is a lexical chain concerning God's mercy – ἐλεέω^{x3}, οἰκτίρω^{x2}, and ἐλεάω^{x1} – which belongs to the thematic formation [God's Mercy].[147] Also, a group of phrases – τὴν δύναμίν μου, τὸ ὄνομά μου, and θέλει^{x2} – belong to the thematic formation

---

144. Claus Westermann, *Basic Forms of Prophetic Speech* (Louisville, KY: Westminster John Knox, 1991), 201; Andrew E. Hill, *Malachi: A New Translation with Introduction and Commentary* (New York: Doubleday, 1998), 34; Eddinger, *Malachi*, 9.
145. See chart 2 of appendix 4.
146. See Rom 3:5; 6:1; 7:7. Cf. Moo, *The Epistle to the Romans*, 591.
147. The thematic formation [God's Mercy] spreads throughout Israel's Scripture and Second Temple Jewish literature (Exod 34:6–9; Num 14:18; Neh 9:1; Pss 86:15; 103:8; 145:8; Joel 2:13; Jonah 4:2; Nah 1:3; Deut 7:9–10; 2 Kgs 13:23; Isa 30:18; Jer 32:18; *Sir*

[God's Power].[148] That is, God's justice is realized in these two aspects of the description of God, his power and mercy. In the following, a detailed clause-by-clause analysis will be carried out.

In verses 15–17, Paul provides scriptural evidence to deny the accusation of the injustice of God (c9B). With a γὰρ, c10A (v. 15a) provides a scriptural voice for his emphatic denial. Among most projecting introduction with speaking formulas, the sayers would be (general or specific) Scriptures, however, the sayer here is "God," the implied participant reference, which is demonstrated in the finite verb λέγει. The receiver of the verbal clause (λέγει) is Moses (τῷ Μωϋσεῖ), the grammaticalized participant reference. It is worthy of noticing that Moses is referred to not as a way of identifying the quotation, but as an example of God's mercy to Israel.[149] The wording is an exact quotation of Scripture – Exodus 33:19 LXX (v. 15) – for they agree with each other precisely.[150] The designation of Moses suggests that Paul preserves the voice of YHWH in Exodus 33:19. In other words, instead of generalizing the voice of YHWH into his current situation, Paul keeps the quoted text Exodus 33:19 within its own co-text: after Israel's sin with the calf, the tension within Israel and YHWH became intense. At this point of the co-text, Moses pleads for mercy, and YHWH resolves the tension by promising to show mercy to Israel.[151] The section of Exodus that Paul employs here "provides the theological center of Israel's struggle to belong to Yahweh."[152] Therefore, God's mercy to Israel is highly related to Israel's identity as God's people. Moreover, God himself is a merciful God. Cranfield has mentioned that Paul most likely thought of the clause (Exod 33:19) parallel to Exodus 3:14,[153] where God's innermost

---

2:11; *Wisd Sol* 3:9; 4:15; 15:1; *Pss. Sol.* 9:8–11; *T. Jud.* 19:3; *T. Zeb* 9:7; *Jos. As.* 11:10; *Ps. Philo* 13:1; 35:3; *4 Ezra* 7:3,3 etc.). Cf. Dunn, *Romans 9–16*, 552.

148. Note that the desirative mental verb states that God can have mercy or harden whoever he wills. This suggests God's superior power or authority.

149. Cf. Dunn, *Romans 9–16*, 551–552.

150. Dunn, *Romans 9–16*, 552.

151. Durham, *Exodus*, 445–446.

152. Ibid., 446.

153. Cf. Dunn, *Romans 9–16*, 552: Dunn sees "an intended link with the repetition and development of Exod 33:19 in 34:6."

nature has been revealed.[154] Piper argues that "Paul saw in Exodus 33:19 a paraphrase of God's 'name.'"[155] Therefore, God's mercy to Israel expresses who he is. Interestingly, Paul's argument alternates between the argumentation of the identity of God's people based on his promise (vv. 6–13) and the nature of God (his faithfulness and justice [v. 6 and v. 14]). This follows from the fact that who can be God's people depends on who God is. As Johnson rightly states, "God elects because of who God is, not because of who people are."[156] With οὖν (therefore), an inference drawn from the quotation has been provided in c11A (v. 16). This clause is made from the three genitive phrases, in which their subjects are blurred,[157] and states that God's mercy does not depend on human willingness or activity, but God's being merciful.[158] The γάρ in c12A (v.17a) introduces a second explanation for the denial of the accusation.[159] Again, the Scripture is the sayer of the verbal process. Abasciano is correct to say that "by referring to Scripture as the speaker, Paul buttresses his argument as coming from the authoritative word of God."[160] The receiver of the verbal process, τῷ Φαραώ, as grammaticalized participant reference, is marked. In contrast to Moses, Pharaoh is introduced as one of those who resist God[161] with wording is quoted from Exodus 9:16.[162] Dunn is right to point out, "In drawing this conclusion from Exodus 9:16 Paul shows very clearly that he is conscious of its

---

154. Cranfield, *Romans*, 483. Cranfield emphasizes the point that God's free will in mercy is not the freedom of an unqualified will of God. The words of Exodus "clearly do testify to the freedom of God's mercy, to the fact that His mercy is something which man can neither earn nor in any way control." See Cranfield, *Romans*, 483.
155. Piper, *Justification of God*, 67.
156. Johnson, *Function of Apocalyptic*, 139.
157. There are different suggestions on the subject, such as "the choice," "mercy," "the matter generally," etc. See Cranfield, *Romans*, 484, and Moo, *The Epistle to the Romans*, 592–593.
158. Moo, *The Epistle to the Romans*, 593; Cranfield, *Romans*, 484–485.
159. Dunn, *Romans 9–16*, 553.
160. Abasciano, *Paul's Use of the Old Testament in Romans 9:10–18*, 195. In Rom 9:15, Paul introduces the quotation of Exod 33:19b with God himself as the implicit speaker to similar effect.
161. Cranfield, *Romans*, 485.
162. This quotation is significantly different from the LXX. Paul may be translating from a Hebrew text. See Dunn, *Romans 9–16*, 563; Christopher D. Stanley, *Paul and the Language of Scripture: Citation Technique in the Pauline Epistles and Contemporary Literature*. SNTSMS 69. (Cambridge: Cambridge University Press, 1992), 106–109.

co-text, since that word (harden) is particularly prominent in that section of the Exodus narrative (Exod 4:21; 7:3, 22; 8:15; 9:12, 35; 10:1, 20, 27; 11:10; 13:15; 14:4, 8, 17)."[163] In other words, God's hardening of the heart of Pharaoh is in view in the quotation in verse 17. God is the actor of the material verb ἐξήγειρα (raise), and you (Pharaoh) functions as the recipient in c12B (v.17b).[164] In c12Ca (v. 17c), God remains as the actor in the material verb ἐνδείξωμαι in order to demonstrate his powers. Also God's name is the goal of the verbal process of διαγγελῇ (proclaim) with the whole world as the space circumstance (c12Cb, v. 17d). The verb διαγγελῇ is in the passive voice, and the goal, the name of God, is mapped on to the subject, so it is assigned modal responsibility.[165] In other words, God's action and the delivery of his name proceeds from his own will. Then with οὖν, Paul arrives at the conclusion in verse 18 that ὃν θέλει ἐλεεῖ, ὃν δὲ θέλει σκληρύνει ("He has mercy on whom he will, and he hardens whom he will").[166] God is the senser of the desiderative mental verb θέλει (will) in verse 18 (cc13AB). God again is the senser of the mental verb ἐλεεῖ (have mercy) and the actor of the material verb σκληρύνει (harden).[167] So far, God's power in his action is the climax of the co-text. Note that the implied reference changes to the third person singular in verse 18: from "I will have mercy on whom I have mercy . . ." to "He has mercy upon whomever he wills . . ." This suggests that the voice of God in Exodus turns to a normative message

---

163. Dunn, *Romans 9–16*, 554.

164. It is a material process of transitivity. According to Halliday, "Material clauses construe figures of 'doing-&-happening.' They express the notion that some entity 'does' something." This type of clause represents a configuration of Actor + Process+ Goal. Halliday and Matthiessen, *An Introduction to Functional Grammar*, 179–180.

165. See Halliday and Matthiessen, *An Introduction to Functional Grammar*, 182.

166. Most scholars argue that the structure of vv. 17–18 parallels vv. 15–16, a scriptural introduction with a quotation being followed by a conclusion, which indicates that vv. 17–18 contain a second reason to reject the accusation that God is unjust (cf. Moo, *The Epistle to the Romans*, 594). However, if v.16 is a conclusion drawn from v. 15, obviously, v. 18 does not arrive at its conclusion only from v. 17, but from vv. 15–17. Therefore, vv. 17–18 do not function as a parallel to vv. 15–16.

167. According to BDAG, when God is subject, it refers to hardening the heart of someone; with a human subject, it refers to one's heart being hardened, e.g. Heb 3:8, 15; 4:7. See BDAG, "σκληρύνω," 930. According to Moo, σκληρύνω occurs 23 times in the LXX. Thirteen refer to a spiritual condition that leads people to fail to revere God, obey his laws, and the like. Moo, *The Epistle to the Romans*, 596–597, n. 47.

concerning God: his mercy (vv. 15–16) and his power (including proclaiming his name and hardening people's hearts [v. 17]).

Verses 19–21 center on the authority of God. After arguing that God exercises his free will in mercy and hardening (v. 18), a question of refutation from the human perspective arises – τί ἔτι μέμφεται; (v. 19). Paul nullifies this objection by highlighting the fundamental inadequacy of the human position of opposition and accusation of God.[168] Then he explains it by invoking the metaphor of the molded object and the molder (v. 20b), and the second metaphor of the potter and vessel (v. 21) to enhance his statement of God's decisive authority over human beings. Again, the disputation speech becomes clear at this point. In c14A (v. 19a), Paul probably quotes his interlocutors (who are the objectors) – Ἐρεῖς μοι οὖν – and their objections – τί . . . ἔτι μέμφεται; τῷ γὰρ βουλήματι αὐτοῦ τίς ἀνθέστηκεν; ("how can he [God] blame [a person], for who can resist his intention?"). This objection responds to Paul's teaching of God's justice based on his sovereign act in verse 18. If God "hardens whom he wills," how can it be fair for one (e.g. Pharaoh) to be blamed, since he cannot resist God's intention or will.[169] Therefore, the question "is there injustice with God?" is still pertinent. The voice of the objection here may be from a Pharisaic Jew who criticizes Paul's argument for not leaving enough room for human free will.[170] Paul's sharp response to the objection is introduced with nominal direct address ὦ ἄνθρωπε (v. 20). The interjection ὦ here expresses a deep emotion.[171] As Jewett observes, there is a tone of grief and warning in these opening words.[172] The adversative μενοῦνγε (on the contrary) contrasts with the objection in verse 19, which conveys the same tone and prepares for the sharp response with a series of rhetorical questions.[173] The first denunciation serves Paul's following argumentation. The relational

---

168. Cf. Belli, *Argumentation and Use of Scripture in Romans 9–11*, 97.
169. See Jewett, *Romans*, 591; Moo, *The Epistle to the Romans*, 600–1. Dunn states, "The question is a legitimate one, and Paul's response indicates that he does not dispute its logic." See Dunn, *Romans 9–16*, 555.
170. Moo, *The Epistle to the Romans*, 600, n. 60.
171. BDAG, "ὦ," 1a, 1101. See also Moo, *The Epistle to the Romans*, 601.
172. Jewett, *Romans*, 592.
173. Ibid.

clause of c15A (v. 20a) conveys the subordinate status of "you" (human beings) to God.[174] Actually, the two fundamental participants, God and men, are found in contrast to one another.[175] This contrast is signaled in a few semantic items: ἀνθέστηκεν (oppose), ἀνταποκρινόμενος (answer back), and μενοῦνγε (on the contrary). The participant references change from focusing on Moses, Pharaoh, and God to "you" or "men" (the interlocutors) and God in verses 19–21.

The subsequent metaphors of the molded/molder and the vessel/potter, which are offered to answer the rebukes, emphasize the gulf between human beings and God, the creature and the creator (v. 20b, v. 21).[176] The former is from the perspective of the molded to the molder, that is, the molded has no right to question the molder; and the latter is reversed, from the potter to the vessel, that is, the potter has authority to make the vessel of honor or of dishonor. In sum, the lexical chains that related to God and men – e.g. βούλημα and ἐξουσίαν, ἀνθίστημι and ἀνταποκρίνομαι – and the series of contrasting pairs – ἄνθρωπε and θεῷ, τὸ πλάσμα and τῷ πλάσαντι, ὁ κεραμεὺς τοῦ πηλοῦ and φυράματος – denote a sort of discourse [God's Authority].[177] If Dunn is right to point out that the potter with his clay was a popular image for God as Creator in Jewish thought,[178] then we can label this ITF as [God's Authority: Creation]. Note that "the

---

174. Note that "you," the object, has been emphasized by placing it before the predicate.
175. Cf. Belli, *Argumentation and Use of Scripture in Romans 9–11*, 95.
176. It was popular in Jewish thought to use a potter with his clay as an image of God as Creator: Ps 2:9; Isa 29:16; 41:25; 45:9; Jer 18:1–6; *Sir* 33:13; *T. Naph.* 2: 2, 4; 1 QS 11:22; Wis 15:7, etc. See Dunn, *Romans 9–16*, 557, and Moo, *The Epistle to the Romans*, 602.
177. It was not rare to use the metaphor of a potter and vessel to talk about God's authority in the Second Temple Period literature. 1QS 11:20–22 contrasts the wonderful deeds of God to the lowliness of humans with the image of the molded and molder also. (It reads, "Who can endure Thy glory, and what is the son of man in the midst of Thy wonderful deeds? What shall one born of woman be accounted before Thee? Kneaded from the dust, his abode is the nourishment of worms. He is but a shape, but moulded clay, and inclines towards dust. What shall hand-moulded clay reply? What counsel shall it understand?" See Géza Vermès, *The Complete Dead Sea Scrolls in English* [New York: Allen Lane, 1997], 117). This theme can also be found in Job 10:9; 38:14; Isa 29:16; 41:25; 45:9–10; Jer 18:1–6; *T. Naph* 2:2, Wis 15:7–19, *Sir* 33:7–15 etc.
178. Dunn, *Romans 9–16*, 557.

hermeneutic of the true prophet primarily stressed God's role as creator."[179] Also, the clay and potter motif is also a popular prophetic theme.[180] In other words, Paul has the concept of true prophecy in mind when using these metaphors.

Verses 22–29 focus on God's mercy, seen in his patient endurance of the vessels of his wrath. The participial clause in verse 22 (cc18AB) is in a concession relation to the primary clause, c18①②. It indicates that God has the ability to make the vessels of wrath into destruction, but he chooses to patiently endure them. Therefore, God's mercy has been expressed. The ἵνα clause in verse 23 stands in a purpose relation to c18①②.[181] That is, the purpose of God's enduring the vessels of wrath is to make known the riches of his mercy. In this way, Paul has articulated God's authority to deal either positively or negatively with human beings according to his own purpose.[182] The main flow of Paul's view can be shown in the dual usages of language: σκεύη ὀργῆς (the vessel of wrath) vs. σκεύη ἐλέους (the vessel of mercy); ἐνδείξασθαι τὴν ὀργὴν (to show his wrath) vs. γνωρίσαι τὸ δυνατὸν αὐτοῦ (to make known his power); κατηρτισμένα εἰς ἀπώλειαν (to prepare for destruction) vs. ἃ προητοίμασεν εἰς δόξαν (which he had made ready for glory). This dual usage of language recalls the above scriptural examples: Moses (v. 15), Pharaoh (v. 17), and the "potter/vessel" image (vv. 20b–21).[183] As Byrne has observed, "Paul speaks of God's (negative) intentions with respect to 'vessels of wrath,' on one hand (v. 22), and (positive) intentions with respect to 'vessels of mercy,' on the other (v. 23)."[184] On the whole, Paul attempts to highlight God's authority to deal with human beings according to his own free will, as part of his nature or character. That is, human being has no right to question God's justice.

---

179. C. A. Evans, "Paul and the Hermeneutics of 'True Prophecy': A Study of Romans 9–11," *Bib* 65 (1984): 561.

180. Cf. Jer 18:1–10.

181. See chart 1 of appendix 4 regarding the clause numbers.

182. Byrne, *Romans*, 301.

183. See also Byrne, *Romans*, 301.

184. Ibid.

Verses 23b–24 begin to bring in the receivers of God's mercy, who are God's people (cf. ἐκάλεσεν in v. 24),[185] and Paul cites a catena of texts to explain that God has mercy on both the Gentiles and Israel (vv. 25–29).[186] The joining phrase σκεύη ἐλέους (c18C, v. 23) can be linked with οὓς in verse 24, and οὓς stands in apposition to ἡμᾶς, which refers to those being called from the Jews and the Gentiles.[187] Verses 25–29 confirm the theme of God's mercy toward his people. They explain who belongs to the vessels of mercy: God's people, including the Gentiles and Israel. In a word, the relative pronoun οὓς in c18E parallels ἃ, which refers to σκεύη ἐλέους (the vessel of mercy). Therefore, the relative clause ἃ προητοίμασεν εἰς δόξαν (c18D, v. 23b) indicates that God has prepared the vessel of mercy beforehand for glory; and the relative clause οὓς καὶ ἐκάλεσεν ἡμᾶς οὐ μόνον ἐξ Ἰουδαίων ἀλλὰ καὶ ἐξ ἐθνῶν (c18E, v. 24) illustrates further that who God has called (both from the Jews and the Gentiles) belong to the vessels of mercy. In other words, the fact that the identity of God's people can be realized is based on God's mercy. In sum, the scriptural catena (vv. 25–29) provides explanations for the fact that both the Gentiles and the Jews are under mercy. Now let us turn to the catena of scriptural texts.

Romans 9:25–26 quotes Hosea 2:25 and 2:1 (LXX) with the introductory projecting formula ὡς καὶ ἐν τῷ Ὡσηὲ λέγει (c19A, v. 25). The phrase ὡς καὶ suggests its linkage with the claim in verse 24 concerning the call of God.[188] Thus, the verb λέγει corresponds to ἐκάλεσεν in verse 24,[189] belonging to verbal verb. Therefore, the third person singular form of the verb λέγει should refer to YHWH. In other words, the scriptural voice in the texts of Hosea is the oracle of YHWH. It is God's voice that confirms

---

185. Cf. vv. 6–13. It is God's promise or his calling that makes people God's people.
186. This point will be further developed in Rom 11. Note that the combination of the catena texts is unlikely to have already been in existence before Paul, in other words, the combination and the changes to the texts is by Paul himself. See Moo, *The Epistle to the Romans*, 612.
187. Dunn, *Romans 9–16*, 570; Jewett, *Romans*, 598; see also Moo, *The Epistle to the Romans*, 611; Cranfield, *Romans*, 498.
188. Jewett, *Romans*, 599.
189. Ibid.

who are his people.¹⁹⁰ Let us examine the following Hosea texts in Romans 9:25–26. The first quotation differs noticeably from the LXX text.

Hosea 2:25 ἐλεήσω τὴν Οὐκ-ἠλεημένην καὶ ἐρῶ τῷ Οὐ λαῷ μου λαός μου

Romans 9:25 καλέσω τὸν οὐ λαόν μου λαόν μου καὶ τὴν οὐκ ἠγαπημένην ἠγαπημένην

Paul reverses the order of the clauses, with a καλέσω clause substituted for that of ἐρῶ and the verb ἠγαπημένην replacing that of ἠλεημένην.¹⁹¹ The substitution of καλέσω for ἐρῶ establishes a verbal link between verse 25 and verse 24 and to the earlier discussion of "calling" in the promise section (cf. vv. 7 & 12).¹⁹² The second quotation repeats verbatim the phrase in Hosea 2:1. The linking word καλέω also makes a linkage of verses 25 and 26 (καλέσω vs. κληθήσονται): "I will call not my people my people" vs. "They (not-my-people) will be called 'sons of the living God.'" Another linking phrase is οὐ λαός μου, while in verse 26 οὐ λαός μου has been reversed to υἱοὶ θεοῦ ζῶντος. Consequently, God's people have further been described as "sons of the living God."¹⁹³ Paul thus combines the two Hosea

---

190. Within Rom 9–11, only in Rom 9 does Paul use the voice of God in the projection introductory formula, which corroborates the idea that the main focus of Rom 9 is God.

191. It is not very clear why Paul changes from ἐλεέω to ἀγαπάω here. It is suggested that the change provides a verbal connection between v. 25 and Paul's earlier discussion of Jacob and Esau, the loved/hated contrast of vv. 10–13, where ἀγαπάω belongs to a cluster of terms within the semantic field of election. Wagner further points out that, "By echoing the earlier allusion to the Jacob/Esau story in this way, Hosea's words intimate a reversal of the divine exclusion of Esau." See Wagner, *Heralds of the Good News*, 82. Cf. David Ian Starling, *Not My People: Gentiles as Exiles in Pauline Hermeneutics*. BZNW 184. (Berlin: de Gruyter, 2011), 112.

192. Starling, *Not My People*, 112.

193. In the Second Temple Period, Hosea's description of restored Israel as "son of the living God" was applied to "a restored future Israel," or "to Gentile proselytes who become 'sons of the living God' through their conversion and embrace of the Mosaic law" (See Starling, *Not My People*, 128). For instance, in *Jub.* 1:25, "sons of the living God" refers to ethnic Israel. It is in the context of divine speech to Moses, which states the promise of future restoration to a repentant Israel (*Jub.* 1:22–25). The author of *Jubilees* demonstrates that the hope of restoration is for all Israel, and to return to God is to return to his commandments (See Wintermute, "Jubilees," 129).

texts into one whole piece, because both texts speak of the reversed identity of the northern kingdom of Israel.[194]

The introductory projecting formula Ἡσαΐας δὲ κράζει ὑπὲρ τοῦ Ἰσραὴλ (Isaiah cries out concerning Israel) in verse 27 is followed by the combined scriptural quotations from Hosea and Isaiah texts. So, Paul preserves Isaiah's own voice, which suggests that Paul has the co-text of the employing texts in mind. The quotation of Romans 9:27 here is an amalgam of Hosea 1:10 (LXX) and Isaiah 10:22; Romans 9:28 quotes from Isaiah 10:22–23, which brings in the remnant motif that some of the Jews will be saved.[195] The way that Paul combines and changes the scriptural texts can be found in chart 4 of appendix 4. The proverbial expression of ἡ ἄμμος τῆς θαλάσσης (sand of the sea), employed by both Hosea 1:10 and Isaiah 10:22, has been associated with God's promised blessing to Abraham and Jacob's descendants many times in Scripture (cf. Gen 22:17; 32:13; 41:49; Josh 11:4; Judg 7:12; 1 Sam 13:5; 1 Kgs 4:20).[196] It "describes the blessing enjoyed by Israel before their rebellion and God's judgment on the nation."[197] The second half of the Scripture comes from Isaiah 10:22, with the alternating of the synonymous pair from κατάλειμμα to ὑπόλειμμα. The remnant theme in

---

A different application of the expression "sons of the living God" is found in *Jos. Asen* 19.8, in which it refers to Gentile converts. Cf. Starling, *Not My People*, 129. The date and authorship of *Joseph and Aseneth* is controversial. Some argue for late antiquity with a Christian composer; but it is more likely that it is the work of a Jewish author writing in the Second Temple Period. See J. J. Collins, "Joseph and Aseneth: Jewish or Christian?" *JSP* 14 (2005): 97–112; George W. E. Nickelsburg, *Jewish Literature between the Bible and the Mishnah: A Historical and Literary Introduction* (Minneapolis: Fortress, 2005), 332–338; and Starling, *Not My People*, 130.

194. Cf. Stanley, *Paul and the Language of Scripture*, 109–113. Paul may make some changes if P[46], the Syriac Peshitta, and a string of Western text-type manuscripts have been adapted. See the discussions in Starling, *Not My People*, 113–114.

195. It has been said that Paul contradicted himself by saying that only a remnant of the Jews will be saved and "all Israel will be saved" in Romans 11:26. L. Gaston holds the opinion that the remnant "is the same as the 'all Israel' which is to be saved in 11:26." See Lloyd Gaston, *Paul and the Torah* (Vancouver: University of British Columbia Press, 1987), 140. Heil holds the position that v. 27 promises that "a remnant of presently unbelieving Israel will come to believe and be saved." See J. P. Heil, "From Remnant to Seed of Hope for Israel: Romans 9:27–29," *CBQ* 64 (2002): 705; also Gadenz, *Called from the Jews and from the Gentiles*, 121, n. 157. We will investigate further the meaning of τὸ ὑπόλειμμα σωθήσεται later.

196. J. Andrew Dearman, *The Book of Hosea*. NICOT 29. (Grand Rapids: Eerdmans, 2010), 104. Dearman, *The Book of Hosea*, 104.

197. Wagner, *Heralds of the Good News*, 91.

Romans 9:27–29 accords with the Isaianic passage.[198] It shows that God spared a portion of Israel (9:27c). Some scholars emphasize the positive dimension of the remnant concept here by arguing that the salvation of the remnant becomes a sign of the salvation of Israel as a whole.[199] It is not certain whether the text implies the extension of salvation from a remnant to the whole of Israel in Romans 9:27–29, but it is crucial that the salvation of the remnant is based on God's mercy (cf. 9:29), because the word of judgment will be executed on the earth (v. 28). In verse 28, Paul conflates Isaiah 10:22–23 and 28:22 to demonstrate that this word of judgment will be executed completely and decisively on the earth.[200]

The introductory projecting clause (c21A) in Romans 9:29 continues to preserve Isaiah's voice as the sayer. In other words, Paul quotes Isaiah 1:9 without alteration, which corroborates the theme of God's mercy through his keeping of the remnant. That is, Isaiah 1:9 signifies YHWH's merciful act and faithfulness to the Israelites.[201] But note that the remnant theme is not about continuity of ethnic descent but of the faithfulness of God.[202]

---

198. The use of Isaiah in Rom 9:27–29 concerns the remnant theme. The ITF [the Remnant] can be found in the Scriptures and Second Temple Period literature. For instance: 2 Kgs 21:14; Ezek 5:10; Mic 4:7; 5:7–8; *Sir* 44:17; 47:22; 1 Macc 3:35; 1QS 4:14; 5:13; CD 1:4–5; 2:6–7; 1QM 1:6; 4:2; 13:8; 14:5–9; 1 QH 6:32; 6:8; and 7:22, etc.). Cf. Dunn, *Romans 9–16*, 573.

199. Gadenz, *Called from the Jews and from the Gentiles*, 123.

200. The participle συντελῶν is difficult to understand, since this is the only occurrence in the New Testament. According to BDAG, the verb means "cut short, limit, shorten." Cf. Gadenz, *Called from the Jews and from the Gentiles*, 127–130; Shum, *Paul's Use of Isaiah in Romans*, 209.

201. Shum, *Paul's Use of Isaiah in Romans*, 212. Also, as Barclay states, "It is God's grace and God's word that is constant, even in the midst of total unfaithfulness." See Barclay, "Paul's Story," 152.

202. Note that the remnant can refer to different groups of people in ancient Jewish literature. It can refer to the people who did not go into Noah's ark, that is, "a remnant was left to the earth when the flood came" (*Sir* 44:17). It can refer to the Assyrians (1 QM 1:6 Assyrian shall come to an end, leaving no remnant). However, most of the time, it refers to a remnant of Israel (CD 1:4–5; 2:6–7; 1QM 13:8; 14:5–9; *Sir* 47:22 etc). Regarding the remnant of Israel, as we have noticed, the ITF [the Remnant] can be viewed both negatively as well as positively in some Jewish literature: on the one hand, Israel was punished for having forsaken Yahweh (e.g., Isa 1) so the remnant of Israel is under judgment; on the other hand, the remnant motif can denote a hope of deliverance by Yahweh (e.g. Isa 10:22).

The view of [the Remnant] in the gospels allies with Paul's in Rom 9. For instance, [the Remnant] in Matthew 22:1–14, is also related to the inclusion of the Gentiles in the salvific plan of God. The conclusion from this parable from the wedding banquet: πολλοί

Neither should one fail to notice that the term σπέρμα resumes the topic of the true seed within Israel in verses 6–9; in this section the main argument is that God's word has not failed because "not all Israel are Israel." In verses 25–29, through the catenaic employment of the Scriptures, Paul asserts that despite Israel's lack of faithfulness (which is implied in v. 29) God remains faithful to his word and remains merciful to Israel by saving a remnant of them.

In sum, verses 14–18 focuses on God's nature: his authority and his mercy to buttress divine election as arising out of God's willing, not out of anyone's wishing or doing (v. 16). Verses 19–29 continue to discuss God's nature and the identity of his people. Paul expands on the idea that God's justice is dependent on who God is – his authority over human beings (vv. 19–21) and his mercy to his people (vv. 22–23) – although these people deserve wrath and destruction. The catenaic scriptural employments from Hosea and Isaiah (vv. 25–29) utilize the voices of God and the prophet Isaiah to illustrate (1) the oracle that the Gentiles can be included as God's people (vv. 25–26), and (2) God's mercy towards Israel in preserving a remnant of them (vv. 27–29). Therefore, Paul's use of the voice of God's people, including not only Jews but also Gentiles, is endorsed by the divine oracle in Hosea 2:25 and 1:10. Also, Paul allies with the voice of Isaiah to reinforce the theme of God's mercy to Israel. Note that the theme of God's nature alternates with the concept of the identity of his people throughout Romans 9:6–29.

3.4.2 Scriptural Voices

In Romans 9:14–29, Paul uses several Mosaic texts and prophetic texts: Exodus 33:19; 9:16, Hosea 2:1; 2:25; Isaiah 10:22–23 (28:22?) and 1:9. Important insights arise from examining these scriptural texts in their

---

γάρ εἰσιν κλητοί, ὀλίγοι δὲ ἐκλεκτοί (for many are called, but few are chosen) is pertinent to the remnant theme in Rom 9. "Many" and "few" indicate that all Israel was called by God but only some were actually chosen for the messianic banquet. This parable is located in the third of the triad of parables about the themes of "God's gracious invitation to the guests, their refusal to respond, the king's judgment that fell on them as a result, and the extension of the invitation to others." See Grant R. Osborne, *Matthew*. ZECNT (Grand Rapids: Zondervan, 2010), 795, 803.

own co-texts first and then assessing what Paul's voice is toward them in Romans 9:14–29.

After the sin of the golden calf (Exod 32), the Israelites lost the presence of God (Exod 33:1–6). Moses went into the tent of meeting (33:7–11) and interceded for Israel (33:12–23). There are two stages to Moses' intercessory prayer in the tent: first, Moses' intercession for God's guidance of his people (vv. 12–17), and then his request to see God's glory (vv. 18–23).[203] In this second intercessory prayer, when Moses asks to see God's glory (v. 18), God's speech becomes dominant. First, as Dozeman observes, Moses' request for God's glory "moves the prayer from the earlier petition for guidance to the desire for a new level of enlightenment into the very character of God."[204] Then in verse 19, God reveals his divine name to Moses and expresses his intention to bestow mercy to whomever he sees fit.[205] Note YHWH's response to Moses: he will cause all goodness to pass in front of Moses. According to Durham, "goodness" here is taken as the "beauty" of YHWH, which suggests a theophany.[206] Many commentators notice that YHWH reveals his divine name here, sharing a similar pattern with that of Exodus 3:14, YHWH's first appearance to Moses.[207] In other words, YHWH's announcement about bestowing his divine mercy on the people of his choosing (33:19) reveals his character: he who he is. Finally, verses 20–23 conclude the intercessory prayer of Moses "with divine instructions for theophany in response to Moses' request to see the divine glory."[208] In addition, YHWH's gracious character is reasserted in Exodus 34:1–9, in which YHWH instructs Moses to reissue the broken tablets of the covenant. Therefore, Exodus 33:19 in its co-text reveals God's character of mercy. Paul corroborates this divine voice when he preserves the voice of God in verse 15 (τῷ Μωϋσεῖ γὰρ λέγει).

---

203. Cf. Dozeman, *Exodus*, 725.
204. Ibid., 729.
205. Ibid., 730.
206. Durham, *Exodus*, 452.
207. Carol L. Meyers, *Exodus*. NCamBC. (Cambridge: Cambridge University Press, 2005), 264. אֶהְיֶה אֲשֶׁר אֶהְיֶה (I am who I am) vs. וְחַנֹּתִי אֶת־אֲשֶׁר אָחֹן וְרִחַמְתִּי אֶת־אֲשֶׁר אֲרַחֵם ("I will be gracious to whom I will be gracious, and will show mercy on whom I will show mercy"). See also Dozeman, *Exodus*, 730.
208. Dozeman, *Exodus*, 730.

After employing the passage concerning God's merciful character in Exodus 33:19, Paul continues to quote Exodus 9:16 in Romans 9:17 ("I have raised you up for the very purpose of showing my power in you, so that my name may be proclaimed in all the earth"). Examining Exodus 9:16 in its own co-text provides insights. Exodus 9:13–35 recounts one of the ten plagues: it first announces the plague of hail (vv. 13–21), then the event occurs (vv. 22–26), and, finally, Pharaoh's response is given (vv. 27–35).[209] There are several important features to be noted about the plague of hail. First, Moses is presented as YHWH's prophetic messenger: "Thus said YHWH" (v. 13). Next, the conflict is prolonged by demonstrating the power of YHWH in verses 15–16: thus the name of YHWH will be proclaimed through all the land of Egypt (v. 16). Finally, after Moses executes the plague, Pharaoh confesses his sin, but when the plague ceases, Pharaoh hardens his heart refusing to release the Israelites (vv. 34–35).[210] This hardening theme occurs in Pharaoh's response to God after the cessation of the plague.

In sum, Exodus 33:19 and 9:13–35 demonstrate respectively God's merciful character and his power in hardening whomever he wills. In Romans 9:14–18, we see that Paul intentionally points out the names of Moses and Pharaoh in the introductory projection formulas, which suggests that Paul is attempting to keep the scriptural voices of the texts of Exodus. From the above analysis of the co-texts of Exodus 9:16 and 33:19, it can be inferred that Paul has the co-text of Exodus 9 and 33 in mind when he quotes parts of them. He then generalizes the voices of these two texts into a normative message while turning the first person singular ("I will have mercy on whom I have mercy, and I will have compassion on whom I have compassion") into the third person singular, "He has mercy upon whomever he wills, and he hardens the heart of whomever he wills" (Rom 9:18). Consequently, Paul's use of the two Exodus texts stresses the fact that God's merciful character and his authority is consistent from the past until the present.

---

209. Ibid., 234.
210. Ibid., 236–238.

Paul then moves to the prophetic texts in his use of Scripture, the books of Hosea and Isaiah in Romans 9:24–29. The first three chapters of the prophetic book Hosea "are primarily concerned with Hosea's marriage and family as the metaphorical means to understand the relationship between YHWH and Israel."[211] An outline of these chapters, provided by Dearman, can aid our understanding of Hosea 1–3 as a whole unit:[212]

I. Superscription	1:1
II. Hosea's Family	1:2–3:5
A. Marriage, Children, and *Judgment* on Israel	1:2–9
B. *Reversal* of the Judgment and *Restoration* of Israel and Judah	1:10–2:1
C. *Charge* against the Mother as a Sign of the Case against Israel	2:2–13
D. *Reversal* of the Judgment against Israel and Its Transformation	2:14–23
E. *Love Her Again* as a Sign that YHWH Loves Israel and Judah	3:1–5

From the above outline, we can perceive a pattern of alternation between judgment and reversal of the judgment (restoration),[213] followed by an expression of YHWH's love of Israel and Judah that concludes the section. The Hosea texts (2:23 and 1:10) employed by Paul are from the sections (1:10–2:1; 2:14–2:23) that concern reversal of the judgment and restoration of Israel and Judah.

The historical context of Hosea is located in the mid and latter parts of the eighth century BC (Hos 1:1) during the period that Israel struggled to preserve her identity under the oppression of foreign forces.[214] Hosea 1:10–2:1 [MT 2:1–3] is a reversal of the judgment of Israel, and expands

---

211. The rest chapters (chs. 4–14) "are made up of prophetic speeches addressed to Israel and Judah." See Dearman, *The Book of Hosea*, 16.
212. Dearman, *The Book of Hosea*, 17. Italics mine. Ben Zvi has a similar structure. See Ehud Ben Zvi, *Hosea*, FOTL 21A, (Grand Rapids: Eerdmans, 2005), 4, 35.
213. Dearman, *The Book of Hosea*, 17.
214. Ibid., 3.

to "include Judah in God's future saving restoration."[215] In Hosea 1:10 (MT 2:1), there are several expressions that are important to consider. The phrase "sand of the sea" associates God's promised blessing with the patriarchs, e.g. Abraham and Jacob: "Their descendants will be like the sand of the sea."[216] The other phrase, υἱοὶ θεοῦ ζῶντος (children of the living God), "is a corporate reversal of the name of Not-My-People"[217] and is a new name for the reconstituted people of God.[218] The two negative names of Hosea's children, Lo-ammi (1:9) and Lo-ruhamah (1:6), are reversed into positive forms in 2:1, that is, Ammi (my people), and Ruhamah (mercy). Therefore, it is YHWH's intention to save and "to overcome his people's failure."[219] Note that in Hosea's day, the division between Israel and Judah had already lasted for two hundred years,[220] so verse 11 depicts the Israelites and the Judahites gathering and appointing for themselves one head, which may suggest a union of the Israelites and the Judahites as God's children.

Hosea 2:23 (MT 2:25) is located in the second part (2:14–23) of chapter 2 – a promised future restoration for Israel – which reverses the judgmental language used for idolatrous Israel in 2:2–13, just as the judgmental language of 1:2–9 is reversed in 1:10–2:1. Verse 23 reverses the names of the two children of Hosea: Lo-ammi (not my people) to my people and Lo-ruhamah (no mercy) to mercy. The renewal of the relationship between Israel and YHWH is dependent on God's merciful salvation to deliver them from their failures.[221]

---

215. Ibid., 103. Regarding the structure of Hos 1:2–2:1, see Ben Zvi, *Hosea*, 45.
216. Gen 22:17; 32:12, cf. Gen 15:5; 26:4; Exod 32:13; Deut 1:10; 10:22; 1 Chr 27:23. See also Dearman, *The Book of Hosea*, 104.
217. Dearman, *The Book of Hosea*, 104. Cf. יֹאמַר לָהֶם בְּנֵי אֵל־חָי vs. יֵאָמֵר לָהֶם לֹא־עַמִּי אַתֶּם
218. Dearman, *The Book of Hosea*, 104. Also, according to Goodwin, "Hosea's description of restored Israel as 'sons of the living God' was taken up and applied variously to postexilic Israel in the writer's own time, to a restored future Israel, and to Gentile proselytes who become 'sons of the living God' through their conversion and embrace of the Mosaic law." See Starling, *Not My People*, 128; Mark Goodwin, *Apostle of the Living God: Kerygma and Conversion in 2 Corinthians* (Harrisburg: Trinity Press International, 2001), 42–64. However, Starling considers this understanding to be unconvincing. See Starling, *Not My People*, 128–131.
219. Dearman, *The Book of Hosea*, 106.
220. Ibid., 105.
221. Cf. Dearman, *The Book of Hosea*, 131.

Paul must have this co-text of Hosea in view, for he intentionally points out Hosea as the recipient of God's oracle (He [God] says to Hosea) in Romans 9:25. The focus in employing these two Hosea texts is on renewing the relationship between God and his people. It is God himself who resolves and overcomes the failures of the ten northern tribes of Israel, so that he can reconstitute or redefine the name of his people.[222] Notice that Paul most likely applies "not-my-people" to the Gentiles;[223] in other words, Paul views the apostate Israel as having the same status as the Gentiles. Just as God graciously reversed the status of apostate Israel, the position of the Gentiles, who are not God's people, will be reversed by God's gracious calling of them to be the children of God.

In Romans 9:27, 29, Paul allies with the voice of the prophet Isaiah to testify of God's mercy in preserving the remnant of Israel.[224] The point has been made by Isaiah that the remnant can be saved, because they rely on God, not on arms or foreign forces, in the co-text of Isaiah 10:20–23.[225] Helpful in understanding Paul's use of these texts is the following

---

222. Some scholars argue that the original context of the Hosea texts is the promised restoration of the ten northern tribes of Israel, not the inclusion of Gentiles, because "not-my-people" in Hos 1:10 refers to the ten northern tribes of Israel, so they are the Israelites, not the Gentiles. See Gadenz, *Called from the Jews and from the Gentiles*, 108–109. See also Chilton, "Romans 9–11," 27–37; Starling, *Not My People*, 118. Some would argue that Paul does not disregard the original context by reading "not-my-people" in Hos 1:10 as the Gentiles, because the texts from Hosea can refer not only to the northern tribes of Israel, but also to Hosea's children by Gomer, who were viewed as not belonging to the people of Israel (see Gadenz, *Called from the Jews and from the Gentiles*, 107). Sterling argues that Paul's convictions regarding Christ and his own identity as a Gentile apostle made him expand the reference of the original context to the Gentiles (see Starling, *Not My People*, 121). However, the reason that Paul uses the text of Hosea does not concern whether it refers to the Gentiles or not; it concerns the renewing or redefining of the meaning of God's people.

223. From a Christian point of view, Paul's reading of the inclusion of Gentiles can be analogous with 1 Pet 2:9–10 ("Once you were not a people, but now you are God's people; once you had not received mercy, but now you have received mercy"). Cf. Hays, *Echoes of Scripture in the Letters of Paul*, 67.

224. The historical setting, denoted by "that day," refers to the Assyrian invasion, which was from 733 to 721 BC. See John D. W. Watts, *Isaiah 1–33* (Waco: Word, 1985), 191.

225. King Hezekiah distanced himself from Assyria, but "sought affiliation with the Philistines, Phoenicians, and Babylonians in opposing Assyria. In consequence the Assyrian king Sennacherib took military action and Hezekiah had to surrender and pay heavy tribute." See S. H. Widyapranawa, *Lord Is Savior: Faith in National Crisis: A Commentary on the Book of Isaiah 1–39*. ITC. (Grand Rapids: Eerdmans, 1990), 62.

examination of Isaiah 10:20–23 in its own co-text. Isaiah 10:5–34 is a complete section of the prophetic oracle that concerns Assyria and Israel,[226] which can in turn be divided into three sub sections: destruction of the proud Assyria (vv. 5–19);[227] the salvation of a remnant of Israel (vv. 20–27a), and the climax of the righteous rule of God in his time (vv. 27b–34).[228] The issue of the remnant in verses 20–27 is worth further notice. Although "the people of Israel will be as the sand of the sea" is the promise that God gave to Abraham (Gen 22:17, 32:13; cf. Hos 2:1), there is then a restriction that "only a remnant of them will return" (v. 22), which implies a judgmental tone within this remnant theme.[229] Similarly, Romans 9:29 quotes Isaiah 1:9 without alteration, which corroborates the remnant motif; Isaiah 1 is essentially judgmental in tone.[230] However, at the end of this threatening woe-oracle, the prophet develops a gleam of hope in verse 9, where, according to Childs, the prophet hints at the remnant theme: "a few survivors"

---

226. In the co-text of Isa 10:20–23, the remnant of the house of Jacob in v. 20 refers to the people of northern Israel. See, Watts, *Isaiah 1–33*, 191.

227. The role of Assyria is positive at first when it is the executor of God's judgment against Israel, but then it becomes boastful and arrogant about its power. God thus destructs it, with wildfire sweeping it. See Brevard S. Childs, *Isaiah* (Louisville: Westminster John Knox, 2001), 93.

228. This division is common among scholars. See Childs, *Isaiah*, 90–97 and Widyapranawa, *Lord Is Savior*, 59–66. This third sub section is difficult to understand. However, with the great variety of images, it most likely indicates that God's righteous rule, as Childs has observed, will "establish divine sovereignty over all human pretenses of world power." See Childs, *Isaiah*, 97. Also, in 10:32, "this very day" suggests that this is the day that the "LORD puts a halt to the invasion," and "interferes and renders the Assyrians powerless." See Widyapranawa, *Lord Is Savior*, 66.

229. The remnant theme in the scriptural tradition contains a bi-polar reference: a negative judgmental notion and a positive notion of the survival of a remnant. For instance, in Ezek 5, Ezekiel denounces the evil of Israel in that they rebelled against God's ordinances and statues, and proclaims that God will execute judgment on Israel, scattering the remnant to all the winds. In Mic 4–5, the remnant theme expresses a salvific scene, "Your [God] hand shall be lifted up over your adversaries, and all your enemies shall be cut off" (Mic 5:9). The remnant theme in Isaianic tradition is particularly twofold: on the one hand, Israel was punished for having forsaken Yahweh (e.g. Isa 1), so the remnant of Israel is under judgment tone; on the other hand, the remnant motif also denotes a hope of deliverance by Yahweh. Hasel even states that Isa 10:22–23 contains the dual polarity of Isaiah's remnant motif. See Gerhard F. Hasel, *The Remnant: The History and Theology of the Remnant Idea from Genesis to Isaiah* (Berrien Springs: Andrews University Press, 1974), 318. See also Shum, *Paul's Use of Isaiah in Romans*, 209–210.

230. In vv. 4–9, "Israel was directly confronted and rebuked for having forsaken Yahweh, and was then promised Yahweh's relentless punishment." Shum, *Paul's Use of Isaiah in Romans*, 212.

prevent Zion from being utterly destroyed like Sodom and Gomorrah.[231] In other words, the element of judgment is present, but "it is not final since the seed provides hope for the future."[232] This signifies Yahweh's merciful actions and faithfulness towards the Israelites.[233]

In sum, Paul uses the Hosea text, which expresses God's mercy in reversing the failure of idolatrous Israel, to develop the idea of God's mercy in including the Gentiles into his people. He then allies the two Isaianic texts together to testify about the mercy of God, although both of the Isaianic texts bear a judgmental tone toward Israel. In other words, Paul recontextualizes the prophetic scriptural co-texts by bringing the Hosea text together with the Isainic texts. The new discourse patterns of the prophetic co-text demonstrate God's merciful character to both Gentiles and Israel.

3.4.3 Thematic-organizational Meaning

The above analysis of presentational meaning shows that the interweaving thematic formations in Romans 9:14–29 are [God's Authority], [God's Mercy], and [God's People]. It is important to enter into a discussion about the relationships of these ITFs in Romans 9:14–29. The ITFs [God's Mercy], [God's Authority], and [God's people] stand in Alliance with one another to justify God's justice. The first two ITFs concern God's nature: the merciful God is also the powerful God of creation, who has the authority to determine who can be his people. According to the promise, the descendants of Jacob became the people of God (vv. 6–13). The employing of Exodus 33:19, which hints at Israel's sin with the golden calf, refers to God's mercy towards rebellious Israel. In other words, if the descendants of Jacob want to remain as God's people, they need God's mercy to gain forgiveness for their rebellion. Verses 22–23 particularly point out that although God can show his wrath and make known his power, he chooses to endure with patience, so that "he can make known the riches of his glory for the vessels of mercy," whom he called not only from the Jews but also from the Gentiles. At this point, [God's Mercy] is allied with [God's

---

231. Childs, *Isaiah*, 19.
232. Gadenz, *Called from the Jews and from the Gentiles*, 133.
233. Shum, *Paul's Use of Isaiah in Romans*, 212.

People]. Later on, the ITF [God's People] is expanded. The prophetic passages from Hosea and Isaiah have been integrated by Paul to show that, as God's mercy has been poured out on the ten tribes of Israel in history, it can also be extended to the Gentiles in Paul's contemporary time. With the Isaianic texts, Paul reveals God's mercy toward failed Israel, who faithlessly relied on human alliances to protect them. Therefore, the Mosaic text, Exodus, and the prophetic passage have all worked together to show Israel's rebellion in history (from Moses' time to the time of Isaiah). However, throughout the text, [God's Mercy] is like a "carrier wave" to which other thematic formations are linked, binding Romans 9:14–29 together as a meaningful whole.

3.4.4 Multiple Voices: Paul's Jewish Contemporaries' Viewpoints on God's Nature and God's People

In Romans 9:14–29, God's justice/righteousness is associated with his mercy and authority, and the way to become God's people is based on God's mercy. In the following, we will bring in related Second Temple Jewish literature concerning similar themes. We will not be able to examine all the related literature exhaustively, but will choose some representative books, including such works as *Wisdom of Ben Sira* and *Wisdom of Solomon*, to present Paul's Jewish contemporaries' viewpoints on the relationship of God's mercy, authority, and the establishment of his people.

The Apocryphal book *Wisdom of Ben Sira* (henceforth, *Sir*) was likely compiled sometime in the first quarter of the second century BC, which is "before the Maccabean crisis under Antiochus IV."[234] The Greek translation was subsequently made by his grandson, probably around 132 BC.[235] Ben Sira himself was a professional scribe,[236] adept in the study of wis-

---

234. Martin Goodman, *The Apocrypha* (Oxford: Oxford University Press, 2012), 69; Maurice Gilbert, "Methodological and Hermeneutical Trends in Modern Exegesis on the Book of Ben Sira," in *The Wisdom of Ben Sira: Studies on Tradition, Redaction, and Theology*, ed. Angelo Passaro and Giuseppe Bellia (Berlin: Walter de Gruyter, 2008), 7. See also Alexander A. Di Lella and Patrick W. Skehan, *The Wisdom of Ben Sira: A New Translation with Notes*. AB 39. (Garden City: Doubleday, 1987), 9.
235. Di Lella and Skehan, *Sirah*, 8.
236. According to Desilva, "Yeshua Ben Sira, a scribe living and teaching in Jerusalem, brought the wisdom tradition of Israel squarely in line with the core value of Torah

dom.²³⁷ In the prologue written by his grandson, the author is portrayed as a devotee of the Hebrew writings, a pursuer of Israelite wisdom: "My grandfather, who had devoted himself for a long time to the study of the Law, the Prophets, and the other books of our ancestors, and developed a thorough familiarity with them, was prompted to write something himself in the nature of instruction and wisdom" (v. 3).²³⁸ Although the teaching of Ben Sira, as a series of aphorisms and reflections on Israel's Scriptures, is not systematic,²³⁹ it covers broad subjects concerning the Scriptures: God, the election of Israel, retribution, repentance, faith, good works, fear of the Lord.²⁴⁰ Therefore, some themes of the teaching are related to Paul's teaching in Romans 9, particularly concerning the subject of God and the election of Israel (18:1–14; 33:7–15). These related texts in *Sir* will be examined.

Sira 18:1–14 represents the fourth poem of the section (16:24–18:14), "divine wisdom and mercy as seen in the creation of humankind."²⁴¹ The poem extols the Lord as the just and merciful God, who has mercy for every human being. The first two verses (18:1–2) proclaim that God, as the creator of the whole world, is the judge of all alike. In the presence of God's utter transcendence, human beings are not able to measure his majestic power or to recount his mercies (vv. 4–8). Therefore, the first eight verses fully depict God's superiority and authority over human beings; however, God is "patient with them" and he "pours out his mercy upon them," (v. 11) because he knows and sees their miserable end (vv. 12–13a). In other words, God's authoritative and merciful nature is allied in *Sir* 18:1–14. Also, God's mercy is associated with the miserable fate of human beings. It sounds as if God's mercy is for all, not just Israel; however, this "all" is restricted to those "who accept his [God's] guidance, who are diligent in his

---

observance." See David Arthur DeSilva, *Introducing the Apocrypha: Message, Context, and Significance* (Grand Rapids: Baker Academic, 2002), 153.
237. Di Lella and Skehan, *Sirah*, 10; Gilbert, "Methodological and Hermeneutical Trends," 7.
238. The translations are from Di Lella and Skehan, *Sirah*, 131.
239. Di Lella and Skehan, *Sirah*, 75.
240. Ibid.
241. The section title is from Di Lella and Skehan, *Sirah*, 176.

precepts" (v. 14).²⁴² In other words, Ben Sira probably considers those who can have God's mercy to be law-observers. Consequently, the particular role of Israel is in view here. Moreover, in the last poem (*Sir* 17:1–32), *Ben Sira* intentionally states the particular role of Israel: "Over every nation he places a ruler, but the Lord's own portion is Israel" (17:17). Therefore, for Ben Sira, God's authority and merciful nature is allied with his own people, the Israelites.

Sira 33:7–15 argues for the justice of God (theodicy),²⁴³ which resembles Paul's formation of God's authority in creation (Rom 9:20–21). Ben Sira indicates that God controls and appoints different ways for human beings:²⁴⁴

> All men are from the ground, and Adam was created of the dust. In the fullness of his knowledge the Lord distinguished them and appointed their different ways; some of them he blessed and exalted, and some of them he made holy and brought near to himself; but some of them he cursed and brought low, and he turned them out of their place. As clay in the hand of the potter – for all his ways are as he pleases – so men are in the hand of him who made them, to give them as he decides (*Sir* 33:10–13 RSV).

At first glance, this passage shows that divine authority rules over humanity, which is created out of earth (33:10). Also, God has authority to bless some and curse others (*Sir* 33:12), that is, "God makes people walk in their different paths."²⁴⁵ It illustrates the contrast between the election of Israel (the blessed and exalted) and the dispossession of the Canaanites (the cursed).²⁴⁶ In many ways, *Sir* 33: 10–13 expresses similar themes to Paul's. It not only employs the identity issue (the blessed Israel and the cursed Canaanites), but also the metaphor of potter and clay to buttress the idea

---

242. The translation of v. 14 is from Di Lella and Skehan, *Sirah*, 279.
243. Goodman, *The Apocrypha*, 97.
244. Cf. Goodman, *The Apocrypha*, 98.
245. Ibid.
246. Ibid.

that "human beings [are] in the hands of their Maker, to be dealt with as he decides (κατὰ τὴν κρίσιν αὐτοῦ)" (33:13). Therefore, Paul's thematic formation [God's Authority: Creation] shares similarities with Ben Sira's idea of God's authority in creation.

However, when associating God's authority and mercy with his people, Paul's and Ben Sira's views diverge. From the expanded co-text of this discourse unit (Rom 9:14–29), it can be seen that, for Paul, God has authority over the decision regarding who can be elected, that is, not only people from the Jews, but also from the Gentiles (v. 24). A close investigation of *Sir* 33:7–15 shows that it argues that God has authority to bless those who fear the Lord and study the law (*Sir* 32:14–15), and curse those who are do the opposite, that is, the evil and ungodly. According to Di Lella, *Sir* 33:7–15 opposes Jewish Hellenizers who questioned Israel's divine election.[247] In other words, *Sir* teaches that those people whom the Lord blesses (33:12a) refers to the call and blessing of Abraham and his descendants, the Israelites. Others whom the Lord curses and removes from their place (33:12b–c) refers to the Gentiles in general who were not chosen.[248] The particular role of Israel is manifest in 17:17 as well: "Over every nation he places a ruler, but the Lord's own portion is Israel." In sum, when Paul deals with divine authority over human deeds or choices, he argues for God's authority in including the nations (Gentiles) in the election. However, Ben Sira argues for God's authority to exclude the Gentiles from election, to remove the ungodly away from their place. In other words, Paul says something substantially different from what his contemporaries say.[249]

Another important related text concerning God's mercy and his people is *Wisdom of Solomon*. Although it is difficult to determine an exact date for *Wisdom of Solomon*,[250] the scholarly consensus is to place it "in Alexandria somewhere between 220 BCE and 50 CE."[251] In particular, a date contem-

---

247. Di Lella and Skehan, *Sirah*, 400.
248. Particularly, the Gentiles refer to the Canaanites, "who the Lord had expelled 'from their place.'" Di Lella and Skehan, *Sirah*, 400.
249. Cf. Johnson, *Function of Apocalyptic*, 150.
250. Ernest G Clarke, *The Wisdom of Solomon: Commentary* (Cambridge: University Press, 1973), 1.
251. Jonathan A. Linebaugh, *God, Grace, and Righteousness in Wisdom of Solomon and Paul's Letter to the Romans: Texts in Conversation* (Leiden: Brill, 2013), 28.

porary with Philo of Alexandria is adopted by current scholars, that is, a date around Caligula's principate (AD 37–41).[252] In other words, *Wisdom of Solomon* can be dated to the time of Paul. The following focuses on the part of the book concerning God's mercy to his people.

The ITF [God's Mercy] in Wis 3:8–12 is also about God's mercy toward his chosen people, but it occurs in the co-text of comparing God's cursing to the nations. The following is the translation of Wis 3:8–12:

> The godly will judge nations and hold power over peoples, even as the Lord will rule over them forever. Those who trust in the Lord will know the truth. Those who are faithful will always be with him in love. *Favor and mercy belong to the holy ones. God watches over God's chosen ones.* The ungodly will get what their evil thinking deserves. They had no regard for the one who did what was right, and instead, they rose up against the Lord. Those who have contempt for wisdom and instruction will be miserable. People like this have no hope. Their work won't amount to anything. Their actions will be worthless. They will marry foolish people. Their children will be wicked. Their whole family line will be cursed (CEB).[253]

God's mercy and gracious visitation is directed toward his chosen people, but the godless receive punishment because they were careless about justice and rebelled against the Lord. Note that this passage holds a high view of godly people, whereas the ungodly, referring to the nations or peoples (the Gentiles), are cursed. So ITF [God's mercy] associates with [God's people], that is, God's mercy is for his people and his curse is for the ungodly, the Gentiles. Therefore, God's people, those whom God has chosen, consist

---

252. Goodman, *The Apocrypha*, 48; Linebaugh, *God, Grace, and Righteousness*, 28–29; David Winston, *The Wisdom of Solomon: A New Translation*. AB 43. (Garden City: Doubleday, 1979), 3, etc. Winston even argues that Wisdom was deeply influenced by Philo, due to a number of striking linguistic parallels and a considerable degree of similarity in literary and religious themes. See Winston, *Wisdom*, 59–63.
253. Italics mine.

of physical Israel according to the viewpoint of the author of *Wisdom of Solomon*.

Both *Ben Sira* and the author of *Wisdom of Solomon* consider that God's mercy pertains to his chosen people only, in contrast to his curse on the nations (cf. Wis 3:8–12). Ben Sira praises God's authoritative nature in creation and his mercy toward human beings, but he is concerned with the fate of his ethnic nation, arguing for God's authority to exclude the Gentiles from election. Therefore, Paul's voice on the relationship between God's nature and his elected people is substantially different from that of his Jewish contemporaries. Paul deviates from his Jewish contemporaries in that he includes the Gentiles as vessels of mercy. Moreover, Paul's view of the relationship between God's authority and the formation of his people would ally in important ways with that of the early Christian community represented in Matthew's gospel. For instance, the words of John the Baptist in Matthew 3:9 are remarkable in regards to God's authority over God's people. John says to the Pharisees and Sadducees, "Do not imagine you can say, 'We have Abraham as our father'; for I tell you, God is able from these stones to raise up children to Abraham." So, in Matthew, God has power to decide who his children are, whether they are the descendants of Abraham or not.

Returning to the concept of the remnant, it should be noted that ancient Jewish literature can refer to different groups of people by that term. It could refer to the people who did not go into Noah's ark, that is, "a remnant was left to the earth when the flood came" (*Sir* 44:17). It could refer to the Assyrian (1 QM 1:6 Assyrian shall come to an end, leaving no remnant). However, most of the time, it refers to a remnant of Israel (CD 1:4–5; 2:6–7; 1 QM 13:8; 14:5–9; *Sir* 47:22). As we have noticed regarding the remnant of Israel, the ITF [the Remnant] can be viewed both negatively as well as positively in Jewish literature: on the one hand, when Israel is punished for having forsaken YHWH (e.g. Isa 1), the remnant of Israel is under a judgmental tone; on the other hand, the remnant motif denotes a hope of deliverance by YHWH (e.g. Isa 10:22).

The view of [the Remnant] found in some early Christian literature, such as the book of Matthew, allies with Paul's in Romans 9. For instance, [the Remnant] in Matthew 22:1–14 is also related to the inclusion of the

Gentiles in the salvific plan of God. The conclusion from this parable about the wedding banquet – πολλοὶ γάρ εἰσιν κλητοί, ὀλίγοι δὲ ἐκλεκτοί ("for many are called, but few are chosen" – is pertinent to the remnant theme in Romans 9.[254] "Many" and "few" indicate that all Israel was called by God but only some were actually chosen for the messianic banquet.[255] Therefore, Paul's view of the remnant can be identified with the views produced by certain members of the early Christian community, such as those represented by Matthew's gospel. Also, in Romans 9:27–29, the ITF [the Remnant] promotes a positive view of salvation for the remnant due to God's mercy towards his people. Paul also continues to express his concern over ethnic Israel through the voice of Isaiah.

3.5 Conclusion

In Romans 9, Paul focuses initially on God himself (theocentric).[256] This is evidenced in the fact that the carrying thematic formation focuses on the nature of God – God's faithfulness (based on the realizations of his promises), his righteousness, his mercy, and his authority. The identities of God and God's people are developed by Paul in Romans 9. Therefore, the pattern of Paul's speeches resembles prophecy, since the words that Paul proclaims come from God, who fills him to overflowing with words about the people of God. Particularly, Paul presents himself as a Mosaic figure in his Martyr-like intercession for Israel (vv. 1–3).

The carrying thematic formation in Romans 9:6–13 is [God's Promise], which serves as the basis for deciding who belongs to God's children. The identity of God's people is argued, interweaving with [God's Promise], in verses 6–13. The realization of God's promises to the Patriarchs substantiates the faithfulness of God's word. The thematic formation which is

---

254. This parable is located in the third of the triad of parables about the themes of "God's gracious invitation to the guests, their refusal to respond, the king's judgment that fell on them as a result, and the extension of the invitation to others." Osborne, *Matthew*, 795. Emphasis mine.

255. Osborne, *Matthew*, 803.

256. Evans, "Paul and the Prophets," 120; James A. Sanders, *From Sacred Story to Sacred Text: Canon as Paradigm* (Philadelphia: Fortress, 1987), 87–105.

established in verses 14–29 is [God's Nature], specifically, [God's Mercy]. Other thematic formations surround it and are linked to it. Within the ITF [God's Mercy], the sub-thematic formation, [God's People], is developed; in this section, [God's People] is extended to the Gentiles. Interestingly, both sections involve [God's Nature] as the carrying thematic formation and [God's People] as the corresponding formation which is interwoven with it. In sum, [God's Nature] – including his promise, his mercy, and his authority – represents the carrier formation and is the focal formation that binds Romans 9:6–29 together. In other words, this chapter is theocentric. Since Paul identifies himself as a Mosaic prophet when he speaks to God's people in verses 1–5, he considers his speech to be true prophecy; as Evans has indicated, true prophecy is theocentric, not ethnocentric.[257]

Paul's overall usage of the Scriptures yields significant findings. Regarding the nature of God, Paul allies the promise passage in Genesis (Gen 18:10, 14; 21:12) with the passage on God's mercy and authority in Exodus and also with some texts of Hosea and Isaiah. Moreover, [God's Promise] in Genesis serves as the originating story about God's relationship with the Patriarchs, who are mentioned in Exodus repeatedly when God reveals himself to Moses (Cf. Exod 3:13–21). The surrounding co-text of [God's Nature] in Exodus 32–34 is about renewing relationship between Israel and God, since the sin with the calf is the very first rebellion spoken of in Exodus. This is the first marked point in the relationship between God and Israel in terms of Israel's rebellion against God. The employing of prophetic texts from Hosea and Isaiah develops the ITFs [God's People] and [God's Mercy]. It is worth noting that the historical background behind the employed prophetic texts is the exile of Northern Israel; this is another marked stage in Israel's history. Therefore, Paul's argument for "who God is" and "who can belong to God" is based on the salvific history of Israel. This is the unchanging God, and he decides who his people are. Therefore, Paul converges the Mosaic tradition with one tradition of prophetic literature.

From the above analysis of Romans 9:1–29, it can be concluded that Paul presents himself as a Moses-like prophet, who is delivering an authoritative message from God to God's people – including his Jewish

---

257. Evans, "Paul and the Prophets," 120.

contemporaries and Gentile believers – in a new age. The interweaving thematic formations of [God's Nature] and [God's People] resemble the prophetic tradition of true prophecy. Paul demonstrates that God is faithful in fulfilling the promises that he made to the Patriarchs, and in how God decides who his people are. Later on, God's justice/righteousness is shown in both his mercy and his authority. By God's mercy and authority, the Gentiles have been included within the arena of his people. Through the interweaving of thematic formations in the text, the Scriptures have been employed to establish Paul's comprehension of the salvific history of Israel and to reveal his prophetic identity as a Moses-like prophet. Moreover, the comparative reading of Romans 9:1–29 with Paul's contemporary Jewish literature, such as *4 Ezra*, *Wisdom of Ben Sira*, *Wisdom of Solomon*, the book of *Jubilees*, and the works of Philo, demonstrates that although Paul shares similar concerns with his Jewish contemporaries, the core of his viewpoint (for instance, God's promise and God's People) diverges from them.

CHAPTER FOUR

Paul's Critique of Israel: An Intertextual Thematic Analysis of Romans 9:30–10:21

4.1 Introduction

After the preceding discussion of the significant issues of the nature of God and who God's people are, this chapter turns to focus on Paul's argument for the relationship of faith, righteousness, law, Christ, and the inclusion of the Gentiles. This section therefore recalls Paul's earlier argument in Romans 1–8.[1]

Most commentators would agree that Romans 9:30–10:21 can be grouped together as a large complete section after Romans 9:1–29. There are several features that demonstrate the unity of this section. The beginning and ending parts of this section are examined in the following chart:[2]

---

1. Douglas Carl Mohrmann, "Semantic Collisions at the Intertextual Crossroads: A Diachronic and Synchronic Study of Romans 9:30–10:13," (Unpublished PhD Thesis, Durham University, 2001), 14; Dunn, *Romans 9–16*, 576–577.
2. Single underlining denotes the words of the verbal process; double underlining denotes the semantic domains of the verbs that relate to seeking and finding; the words with thick underlining refer to Israel; and with dotted underlining refer to the Gentiles.

⁹:³⁰ Τί οὖν <u>ἐροῦμεν</u>; ὅτι <u>ἔθνη</u> τὰ μὴ <u>διώκοντα</u> δικαιοσύνην <u>κατέλαβεν</u> δικαιοσύνην, δικαιοσύνην δὲ τὴν ἐκ πίστεως,
³¹ Ἰσραὴλ δὲ <u>διώκων</u> νόμον δικαιοσύνης εἰς νόμον οὐκ <u>ἔφθασεν</u>.
. . .
¹⁰:¹⁹ ἀλλὰ <u>λέγω</u>, μὴ Ἰσραὴλ οὐκ ἔγνω; πρῶτος Μωϋσῆς <u>λέγει</u>· ἐγὼ παραζηλώσω <u>ὑμᾶς</u> ἐπ' <u>οὐκ ἔθνει</u>, ἐπ' <u>ἔθνει</u> ἀσυνέτῳ παροργιῶ <u>ὑμᾶς</u>.
²⁰ Ἠσαΐας δὲ ἀποτολμᾷ καὶ <u>λέγει</u>· εὑρέθην [ἐν] τοῖς ἐμὲ μὴ <u>ζητοῦσιν</u>, ἐμφανὴς ἐγενόμην τοῖς ἐμὲ μὴ <u>ἐπερωτῶσιν</u>.
²¹ πρὸς δὲ τὸν Ἰσραὴλ <u>λέγει</u>· ὅλην τὴν ἡμέραν <u>ἐξεπέτασα</u> τὰς χεῖράς μου πρὸς <u>λαὸν ἀπειθοῦντα καὶ ἀντιλέγοντα</u>.

The chart shows the correspondence between Romans 9:30–31 and 10:19–21. In the first place, the main human participant references in both parts are Israel and the Gentiles. In other words, the final part recapitulates the theme introduced in 9:30–31.[3] Belli has rightly observed the repeated themes between the two:[4]

9:30 Gentiles (do not pursue)	10:20 Gentiles (do not seek, do not ask)
9:31 Israel (pursues law-righteousness)	10:21 Israel (disobedient and rebellious)

Second, repeated verbal processes appear in both parts (ἐροῦμεν vs. λέγω/λέγει). This suggests that this section may be about the author's speech concerning Israel and the Gentiles. Third, there are eight verbs possessing similar semantic domains that relate to seeking and finding, four words in each part. Therefore, these two corresponding parts serve to tie together Romans 9:30–10:21, thus showing that it consists of one whole, coherent unit. This section shows that Paul values the Gentiles who did not seek God in law-righteousness, and he regards his Jewish contemporaries' pursuit of law-righteousness as disobedience and rebellion against God.

---

3. Belli, *Argumentation and Use of Scripture in Romans 9–11*, 321.
4. Ibid., 320–321.

The thematic formations of this section must be identified and examined. The expression τί οὖν ἐροῦμεν (9:30) signals the new section. Some new subjects have been introduced: righteousness, faith, law, Christ (9:30–10:4), the Gentiles, and Israel. It should be noted that through the Opposing contrast between the righteousness of law and that of faith, Paul's critique of Israel, for their failure to attain righteousness, has already been implied. Since 10:5, the contrast between the righteousness of law and of faith has been further elaborated (10:5–8). Verses 9–13 (key terms πιστεύεται, καρδία, στόματι) explains the universal scope of salvation in Christ through the alliance of Paul's voice with the prophetic voices. On this basis, prophetic criticism has been brought in to condemn Israel's rebellion (vv. 14–21) in not listening to God's gospel and the idea of its extension to the Gentiles. As we have mentioned, Israel and the Gentiles have been reintroduced in the last part to correspond with the initial discussion of the two groups of people (vv. 19–21). In sum, Romans 9:30–10:21 is a coherent whole with three subdivisions: Israel, who has been shown to have failed in law-righteousness by the Opposing contrast of law and faith righteousness (9:30–10:4); the core message of the gospel for Israel, which is faith righteousness and the universal scope of God's people (10:5–13); and Israel, who has failed to acknowledge the Gentiles as part of God's people (10:14–21). This tidy thematic topic pattern indicates that 9:30–10:21 is a complete and coherent section. In the following, we will investigate text semantics of each of the three sections. In each section, presentational meaning will be provided first, followed by scriptural voices, thematic-organizational meaning, and then multiple voices.

4.2 Romans 9:30–10:4

4.2.1 Presentational Meaning: Israel's Failure to Attain Righteousness

The τί-interrogative question τί οὖν ἐροῦμεν;[5] ("What shall we say?") focuses our attention on a transition to a new topic – the relationship of law and faith in terms of righteousness. The conjunction ὅτι brings in the projected clauses, which orient our attention to two groups of people (the Gentiles and Israel) in regard to faith and law:[6] The two contrasting pairs of lexical items, ἔθνη and Ἰσραήλ, are realized by the same process pattern (material: action [Actor-Process-Goal]). The Gentiles have been described as those who did not pursue righteousness (i.e. of law) by the device of embedded elaboration.[7] In contrast, in c2 (v. 31), Israel has been described as those who pursue the righteousness of law by the same elaborative device.[8] Ironically, instead of Israel, the Gentiles are those who attained (καταλαμβάνομαι) righteousness. Israel did not attain (φθάνω) the (righteousness of) law (c2A, v. 31). In other words, two contrasting voices of righteousness are represented in verses 30–31 (c1-c2).

---

5. It is Paul's patterned use of οὖν together with rhetorical questions, which produce paragraph boundaries. See Cynthia Long Westfall, *A Discourse Analysis of the Letter to the Hebrews: The Relationship between Form and Meaning* (London: T & T Clark, 2005), 47.
6. There are numerous discussions about Paul's view of the law. In Romans, Paul's statements of the law are diverse, and some even seem contradictory. For instance, sometimes Paul speaks positively about the law: Christians uphold the law through faith (Rom 3:31); the law is holy and the commandment is holy and just and good (Rom 7:12); the law is spiritual (Rom 7:14); the law is good (Rom 7:16); I serve the law of God with my mind (7:25); the just requirement of the law might be fulfilled in us who walking according to the Spirit (Rom 8:4); the one who loves another has fulfilled the law (Rom 13:8), etc. Sometimes, Paul makes negative statements about the law: no human being will be justified in his sight by deeds prescribed by the law, for through the law comes the knowledge of sin (Rom 3:20); the promise to Abraham was not through the law (Rom 4:13); the law brings wrath (Rom 4:15); the law came in, with the result that the trespass multiplied (Rom 5:20); our sinful passions aroused by the law (Rom 7:5), etc. For detailed discussions, see E. P. Sanders, *Paul, the Law, and the Jewish People* (Philadelphia: Fortress, 1983); James Dunn, *Paul and the Mosaic Law* (Grand Rapids: Eerdmans, 2001); Heikki Räisänen, *Paul and the Law*. WUNT 29. (Tübingen: Mohr, 1987); A. Andrew Das, *Paul, the Law, and the Covenant*. Peabody: Hendrickson Publishers, 2001. This dissertation regards the law Paul was talking about in Romans 9–11 to be the Mosaic Torah.
7. See appendix 5, chart 1.
8. See appendix 5, chart 1.

Similar to the pattern of c1-c2, c3A-c3B comprises a τ-interrogative question (διὰ τί; c3A, v. 32a) with an answer (c3B, v. 32b), and the conjunction ὅτι brings in two contrasting projected clauses οὐκ ἐκ πίστεως (c3Ba) and ὡς ἐξ ἔργων (c3Bb). Conjunctive particle ἀλλά retains an adversative sense. In other words, the semantic meaning of the prepositional phrases ἐκ πίστεως and ἐξ ἔργων is in an Opposition with each other in this co-text. Regarding the relationships of c1-c2 and c3A-c3B, they are structurally parallel to each other, and they are semantically related to each other, for the rhetorical question διὰ τί (c3A) is designed to clarify the statement that Israel did not obtain the righteousness of law (c2). Therefore, c3 is in a clarification relationship with c2. So far, the text indicates that obedience to the law and belief in faith are both ways to attain righteousness, but Paul's voice suggests that the right way to attain righteousness is from faith. This is because Paul demonstrates his critique of Israel, who chooses the wrong way to attain righteousness through works. He holds a negative value toward law-righteousness in some sense.[9] But why does Paul resist allying law/works with righteousness?[10] In the following part (cc4A–D, v. 32c–33), the text brings forward a new thematic topic – the stumbling stone – to strengthen his contention for faith-righteousness.

Although there is a lexical link πίστις/πιστεύω with the previous righteousness discourse, the semantic meaning in this portion (c4; vv. 32c–33) is different: the lexical items – δικαιοσύνην, νόμος, and ἔργον – are totally absent in verses 32c–33 (c4). The rhetorical structure changes from a

---

9. In what sense does Paul view law-righteousness negatively? Does Paul consider the law or the observance of law as a bad thing per se? If not, then under what conditions is it that Paul opposes law-righteousness? We will come back to this point in a later analysis. We should note that in Jewish orthodoxy of the Pharisaic community, obedience to the law is the right way of fulfilling what God demands. The phrase νόμον δικαιοσύνης appears to depict the essence of Jewish piety (Wis 2:10–11): "Let us overpower the poor righteous man, let us not spare a widow, nor reverence the old grey hairs of the aged. Let our strength be a law of righteousness, for that which is weak proves useless." According to Jewett, "The expression 'law of righteousness' appears to be employed in this passage to depict what a propagandist would understand to be the essence of Jewish piety, which the rulers planned to replace by brute strength." Jewett, *Romans*, 610. Moreover, Wis 1:16 and 4:20 depict the ungodly men's lawless deeds as convicting them to their face.

10. What is the root/reason for Paul to ally "righteousness" with "faith"? According to Watson, the seed of Pauline doctrine of righteousness by faith grows from Hab 2:4. Cf. Watson, *Paul and the Hermeneutics of Faith*, 151–158.

question-answer pattern to a correspondence between quotation and antecedent.[11] The antecedent states Israel's stumbling over the stone (c4A, v. 32c), which is supported by a combined scriptural text (Isa 8:14, 28:16; cc4B–D). In other words, the scriptural voice provides evidence to support the statement in verse 32c (c4A) that they (Israel) stumbled over the stumbling stone. The projecting clause καθὼς γέγραπται[12] (c4B, v. 33a) signals a generalized scriptural voice that will be presented.[13] The two projected clauses (cc4C–D, v. 33b) come from the conflation of Isaiah 28:16 and 8:14.[14] The situational contexts of these two texts are not directly related to each other, so Paul's use of the generalized projecting formula may intend to eliminate the specific original contexts and treat the stumbling stone text as a generally valid text in his time. Lexicogrammatically, the new lexical terms, πρόσκομμα and its verbal form προσκόπτω, repeatedly appear in the projected clauses. If included in the same semantic domain[15] as the term πρόσκομμα ("stumbling"), it appears five times in verses 32c–33 (c4). Moreover, the nominal groups that connect to πρόσκομμα have been repeated three times: τῷ λίθῳ τοῦ προσκόμματος (c4A), λίθον προσκόμματος and πέτραν σκανδάλου (c4C). This would be recognizable as a formation of [Stumbling Stone] to the first Christian communities (cf. Matt 21:42, Mk 12:10–11; Luke 20:17–18; Acts 4:11; *Barn* 6:2–4). Note that one key thematic item πιστεύω in verse 33b (c4D) belongs to the preceding formation of [Faith-Righteousness]. With the standard introductory formula, καθὼς

---

11. This correspondence entails a degree of repetition, which occurs at both the lexical and semantic levels.

12. It should be noted that the standard introductory formula, καθὼς γέγραπται with minor variations, occurs 16 times in Romans (1:17; 2:24; 3:4, 10; 4:17; 8:36; 9:13, 33; 10:15; 11:8, 26; 12:19; 14:11; 15:3, 9, 21). This formula is traditional in Jewish and Christian literature, like Josh 9:2b (LXX); 2 Kgs 14:6; 2 Chr 23:18; 4Q 174 1.i.12; Test. Levi 5:4; Mark 1:2; Luke 2:23; Acts 7:42, 15:15 etc. Cf. Watson, *Paul and the Hermeneutics of Faith*, 43–46, and its note 32.

13. In Watson's words, the standard formula (as it is written) "presents a citation as a completed utterance that is definitive and *permanently valid.*" Italics mine. See Watson, *Paul and the Hermeneutics of Faith*, 45.

14. In Isa 28:16, Isaiah called for faith in Yahweh at the time of the Assyrian crisis, and in Isa 8:14 warned that Israel would find Yahweh to be "a stone which causes stumbling, a rock which brings about a fall." See Dunn, *Romans 9–16*, 593.

15. πρόσκομμα, προσκόπτω, σκάνδαλον, and καταισχύνω all belong to domain 25 P: offend, be offended. See J. P. Louw and Eugene A. Nida, *Greek-English Lexicon of the New Testament: Based on Semantic Domains* (New York: UBS, 1989), 308–309.

γέγραπται, the author allies his formation of [Faith-Righteousness] with [Stumbling Stone]. The main purpose of this Alliance for Paul is probably to point out the missing point of [Law-Righteousness], so as to support his negative evaluation of Israel's law-righteousness. In sum, Romans 9:30–33 set [Faith-Righteousness] against [Law-Righteousness]; and the reason for this Opposition implied in the thematic formation [Stumbling-Stone].

It is helpful to examine Romans 10:1 (c5). The nominative of address ἀδελφοί shifts us from an argumentative tone to an intimate personal call. The personal tone is enhanced by the semantic domains of emotions and psychological faculties (εὐδοκία τῆς ἐμῆς καρδίας) in c5Ba (v. 1) and the lexical items δέησις and θεόν in c5Bb (v. 1), which indicate a personal religious intercession expression. The phrase ἡ δέησις πρὸς τὸν θεόν (c5Bb) expands as an extension to that in c5Ba. Both psychological intimacy (εὐδοκία τῆς ἐμῆς καρδίας) and religious intercession (ἡ δέησις πρὸς τὸν θεόν) expressions work together for religious salvation (c5Bc). The phrase εἰς σωτηρίαν probably refers back to Romans 1:16–17, the theme verses of Romans,[16] and Paul's desire for the goodness of Israel can be summed up in this phrase.[17] This sort of intercession discourse pattern (Relational: Identifying) occurs in Romans 9:1–3 when Paul portrays himself as a Mosaic figure interceding for Israel,[18] and in some other prophetic Jewish texts as well.[19] Through this intercession discourse formation, Paul identifies himself with the non-believing Jewish people with a sense of brotherhood. In other words, he is one of them according to the flesh. Therefore, Paul stands in the noble tradition of Israel: praying for his own people.[20] In sum, Paul's attitude toward the Jewish people (probably his accusers) is

---

16. Cf. Dunn, *Romans 9–16*, 586.

17. The semantics of salvation in the tradition of the intercessor usually refers to deliverance from oppression. Cf. Dunn, *Romans 9–16*, 594.

18. Moses prayed to God because of Israel's betrayal of God in favor of idol worship, in order to save the Israelites from God's wrath; otherwise, God would have consumed all the people (Exod 32:9–14; Deut 9:18–20).

19. For instance, one case is Samuel's prayer to save the people of Israel from the hand of the Philistines, after they turned away from the Baals and the Astartes (1 Sam 7: 5–11). The other case is Jeremiah's prayer to God for the remnant of Israel, so that God could save them from the king of Babylon, when the remnant promises to obey the voice of God (Jer 42:2–4, 19–22). See also Ps 99:6; Ezek 11:13.

20. Dunn, *Romans 9–16*, 586.

empathy. In some sense, Paul allies with them here. As we have mentioned, this alliance has occurred in 9:1–3, in which Paul expresses his good will and continual prayer for Israel's salvation.[21]

After indicating a personal prayer for Israel, which demonstrates Paul's concern for his kinsmen, the negative evaluation of Israel follows (c6–c7, vv. 2–3). Clause 7 (v. 3) clarifies further the statement in c6 (v. 2) that Israel's zeal for God is not according to knowledge. The projecting clause μαρτυρῶ . . . αὐτοῖς (c6A) places us in the realm of meta-discourse. The actor of the verbal process (μαρτυρῶ) in the projecting clause is neither "we" (Rom 9:30–32b) nor "they" (Rom 9:32c), but "I" (implied in the verb μαρτυρῶ, referring to Paul himself). In other words Paul allies himself with the Jewish people. With the projected clause ζῆλον θεοῦ ἔχουσιν (Relational: Attribution), we may orient ourselves to the discourse of Israel's religious zeal, a feature which has been attributed to Israel by Paul.[22] So far, Paul's voice seems to confirm Jewish religious piety. However, the textual meaning makes a very important move with the adversative conjunction ἀλλά in c6Bb (c6Ba and c6Bb in a relation of Adversative, v. 2). Paul comments that their zeal for God is οὐ κατ' ἐπίγνωσιν ("not according to knowledge"). The knowledge here relates particularly to religious knowledge. In other words, Paul criticizes Israel for their inappropriate zeal for God. With an inferential conjunctive word γὰρ in c7, the text lists the reasons for the critique. One key reason lies in the main sentence in c7B (v. 3), that is, Israelites have not submitted to the righteousness of God (τῇ δικαιοσύνῃ τοῦ θεοῦ οὐχ ὑπετάγησαν). The two participial clauses, ἀγνοοῦντες . . . τὴν τοῦ θεοῦ δικαιοσύνην (c7Aa) and τὴν ἰδίαν [δικαιοσύνην] ζητοῦντες στῆσαι (c7Ab), elaborate why Israel did not subject themselves to God's righteousness.[23] Here again righteousness language appears, as in Romans 9:30–32ab. The lexical term δικαιοσύνην now links with – instead of faith and law – θεοῦ and ἰδίαν, which constructs a pair of opposing contrasts: τοῦ θεοῦ δικαιοσύνην vs. τὴν ἰδίαν δικαιοσύνην. So, the text directly

---

21. Byrne, *Romans*, 311.
22. What does "Israel's religious zeal" mean? How does other Second Temple Jewish literature evaluate religious zeal? All related discourses will be provided in the section of multiple voices.
23. Schreiner, *Romans*, 543.

contrasts God's righteousness with Israel's own righteousness. An intertextual comparison to another Pauline text (Phil 3:6–9) evinces an example where Paul contrasts "God's righteousness" to a righteousness of "one's own."[24] From these examples, we can see that Paul contrasts Israel's own righteousness through zeal for the law with the righteousness from God on the basis of faith. Paul argues that Israel failed to submit to God's righteousness, because they wrongly focused on God's righteousness in connection with their zeal of the law;[25] and the role of law is not to establish a system of righteousness on its own terms, but to lead solely to the means of righteousness constituted by Christ.[26] The effect of the law, as Paul mentioned earlier in the letter, was not to constitute a means of righteousness, but "to multiply transgression" (Rom 3:20; 4:15; 5:20a; 6:15; 7:15, 13; cf. Gal 3:23–24).[27] In other words, this text expresses that it is faith-righteousness that allies with God's righteousness,[28] but Israel's law-righteousness misses the real point of God's saving righteousness. A case in view is Paul himself, who had zeal for the law before his Damascus encounter with Jesus.

In sum, the righteousness language pairs in 10:1–3 (c5~c7) parallel with the previous contrast of faith-righteousness and law-righteousness

---

24. Moo, *The Epistle to the Romans*, 635. Phil 3:9 reads, μὴ ἔχων ἐμὴν δικαιοσύνην τὴν ἐκ νόμου ἀλλὰ τὴν διὰ πίστεως Χριστοῦ, τὴν ἐκ θεοῦ δικαιοσύνην ἐπὶ τῇ πίστει.

25. Moo, *The Epistle to the Romans*, 636. Sanders would argue that, according to Paul, Israel failed to submit to God's righteousness, because they ignored the fact that membership in the body of those who will be saved is based on faith in Jesus Christ, not on the obedience of the law. For Sanders, one's own righteousness is not one's merit-seeking self-righteousness. Torah-observance is not about merit, but maintenance of the status. See Sanders, *Paul, the Law, and the Jewish People*, 42–45, 140. Thus Paul's charge is directed against a nationalism and ethnocentrism that excludes Gentiles by erecting boundary markers (e.g. circumcision, Sabbath, and food laws), seeking to maintain righteousness as something distinctive to the Jews. See Dunn, *Romans 9–16*, 587–588. Schreiner argues against this New Perspective of Paul, and suggests, "the reason . . . that the Jews did not subject themselves to the saving righteousness of God is because they were ignorant of the fact that righteousness was a gift of God's grace and they mistakenly thought they could secure their own righteousness by observing the Torah." See Schreiner, *Romans*, 543–544. However, both views point out that Israel failed in pursing God's righteousness, because they do not understand the significance of the Christ event.

26. Byrne, *Romans*, 312.

27. Byrne, *Romans*, 312.

28. Moo, *The Epistle to the Romans*, 75. In Romans the stem δικαιο- coincides with πιστ- in 1:17; 3:2–5, 33, 25, 26; 4:3, 5, 9, 11, 13, 20, 22; and also 9:33; 10:4, 9, 10, 11. See Douglas Atchison Campbell, *The Deliverance of God: An Apocalyptic Rereading of Justification in Paul* (Grand Rapids: Eerdmans, 2009), 768.

in 9:30–32b (c1–c3). That is, God's righteousness has a similar semantic meaning as faith-righteousness, and Israel's own righteousness as law-righteousness.[29] Through the contrast of these pairs of righteousness language, Paul points out Israel's failure in attaining faith-righteousness, God's righteousness. It seems that Paul replaces the role of the law with faith in Jesus Christ.[30] However, it is worthy of noting that Paul's comments on Israel's failure proceed from his being concerned for them (10:1), like a prophet's speech to God's people for the sake of those people. In other words, the formation of [Intercession: Paul] (c5, v. 1) frames our understanding of Paul's critique – Israel's being ignorant of God's righteousness (c6–c7, vv. 2–3). That is, this soft tone of critique is proceeding from Paul's heartfelt concern for them (c5, v. 1; cf. 10:21).[31]

After the prophetic and heartfelt critique of Israel through discourse about righteousness, a relational-identifying statement is introduced (c8A, 10:4a). With the prepositional phrase εἰς δικαιοσύνην and the dative phrase παντὶ τῷ πιστεύοντι ("for everyone who believes"), righteousness, faith/belief, law, and Christ have been brought together. In c8A, two lexical items – νόμος and Χριστὸς[32] – are in a relationship in which each interprets the other: Χριστὸς is identified as the τέλος of law. It must have been innovative to connect νόμος with Χριστὸς in the first-century non-believing Jewish communities. The clause does not only carry the concept of the relationship between Christ and the law, but also explains why pursuing righteousness through the law did not work; it is because Christ is the τέλος of the law. The interpretation of τέλος in verse 4 has been very controversial.[33] The two dominant views are to translate it either as "goal" or

---

29. Campbell has a similar opinion. See Campbell, *Deliverance of God*, 784.
30. Campbell has observed that for Paul, Israel's failure is due to their ignoring Christ as Messiah and pursuing God's saving righteousness based on righteous activity informed by the law. Campbell, *Deliverance of God*, 786.
31. Paul's critique of Israel in 9:30–10:4 is implied in his rational statements of the right way for righteousness. The tone of the argument in Romans 9:30–10:4 is not antagonistic.
32. Χριστός has appeared in Rom 9:4. This is the second time the term appears in Rom 9–11. However, in this section (Rom 9:30–10:21) it is the first time it appears.
33. For the history of interpretation, see Robert Badenas, *Christ the End of the Law: Romans 10:4 in Pauline Perspective*, JSNTSup 7, (Sheffield: JSOT Press, 1985), 7–37; Thomas R. Schreiner, "Paul's View of the Law in Romans 10:4–5," *WTJ* 55 (1993):113–135; Schreiner, *Romans*, 544–48; Dunn, *Romans 9–16*, 589–591, etc.

"end."³⁴ However, there is not much difference between the two. In this co-text, based on verses 10:5–8, the term τέλος can be understood as "goal" or "end" (cf. Rom 6:21–22; 2 Cor 3:13; 1 Tim 1:5).³⁵ For the sake of brevity, we will refer to it as "goal." However, what does "Christ is the goal of the law" mean? For Paul, the goal of the commandments was to promise life (Rom 7: 10b); however, it resulted in death (Rom 7:10c). Instead, it is Jesus Christ who will bring life to all the believers (Rom 6:5–11, "We will certainly be united with him in a resurrection like his . . . so you must consider yourselves dead to sin and alive to God in Christ Jesus"). In other words, Christ is the goal to which the law pointed.³⁶

In conclusion, Paul sets an Opposition of law-righteousness and faith-righteousness, and argues that Israel was failing in regard to faith/God's righteousness, for they pursued righteousness according to their own works, and they did not see that Christ was the goal of the law. However, all these critiques come from Paul's heartfelt concern for his Jewish contemporaries, his kinsmen.

---

34. Most current scholars interpret τέλος as "end."
a. It could mean that Christ has replaced Torah as the mark of community membership (see Terence L. Donaldson, *Paul and the Gentiles: Remapping the Apostle's Convictional World* [Minneapolis: Fortress, 1997], 215).
b. Kim argues that "it is no longer Torah but Christ" refers to the fact that Christ has superseded the Torah as the revelation of God (see Seyoon Kim, *The Origin of Paul's Gospel* [Tübingen: Mohr, 1984], 274).
c. Bell states that "the law comes to an end not because of its failure but rather because the law has a time-limited function to condemn until the revelation of Christ (Gal 3:15–4:7)." (see Richard H. Bell, *The Irrevocable Call of God: An Inquiry into Paul's Theology of Israel*, WUNT 184, [Tübingen: Mohr Siebeck, 2005], 42. Bell continues to state that the condemning function of the law still applies to those who do not believe in Christ, but it does not apply for the people who have faith in Christ).
d. Dunn argues that Christ is the end of "the law as a means to righteousness." For a detailed explanations, see James Dunn, "Righteousness from the Law and Righteousness from Faith: Paul's Interpretation of Scripture in Romans 10:1–10," in *Tradition and Interpretation in the New Testament*, ed. Earle E. Ellis and Gerald F. Hawthorne (Grand Rapids: Eerdmans, 1987), 222. See also Schreiner, "Paul's View of the Law in Romans 10:4–5," 121–123.
35. Schreiner, "Paul's View of the Law in Romans 10:4–5," 117; also see the book, Badenas, *Christ: the End of the Law*, 1985.
36. Schreiner, *Romans*, 545. According to R. Badenas, Paul's hermeneutics of the Scripture or Torah is different from that of his contemporaries since it is based upon a new fact that traditional Judaism and the OT itself did not know: the Christ event. Now Paul reads the Torah in the light of Christ. Badenas, *Christ the End of the Law*, 149.

4.2.2 Scriptural Voices

Two famous stone-texts have been integrated together in Romans 9:32b–33, where phrases from Isaiah 8:14 (λίθον προσκόμματος καὶ πέτραν σκανδάλου) are placed in the middle of a section taken from Isaiah 28:16.[37] This middle section – a costly stone, a choice, a precious cornerstone for the foundation (λίθον πολυτελῆ ἐκλεκτὸν ἀκρογωνιαῖον ἔντιμον εἰς τὰ θεμέλια αὐτῆς) – portrays the (corner) stone positively; however, this is omitted and replaced by a negative image of a stone of stumbling from Isaiah 8:14.[38]

Before discussing how Paul uses the prophetic Scriptures to support his stance, an examination of the texts in their own co-texts is in order. The historical setting of Isaiah 8:11–15, in which the literary unit 8:14 is set,[39] falls in the period of the Syro-Ephraimite war.[40] The divine warning to the prophet Isaiah is directed against both houses of Israel, who arrange a conspiracy because they are in fear of the foreign political powers (2 Kgs 15:25–17:4). YHWH will become a trap and snare for them (Isa 8:14–15) if they depend on human conspiracy and efforts to attain salvation. Therefore, the prophet is warned not to follow the way of Israel and not to undertake a conspiracy (Isa 8:11–12); he is called upon to direct attention to the real source of power and awe, God, because the future does

---

37. There is a slight revision of these two phrases. According to Stanley, "Paul could have (1) extracted the phrases λίθου προσκόμματι and πέτρας πτώματι from their separate locations in Isa 8:14, and then (2) replaced the unusual πτῶμα (found nowhere in Paul) with the typically Pauline σκανδάλου (cf. Rom 11:9, 14:13, 16:17; 1 Cor 1:23; Gal 5:11), (3) modified the cases of every word to fit the new context, and (4) inserted a connective καὶ to complete the new construction." See Stanley, *Paul and the Language of Scripture*, 123.

38. It is not very clear what the cornerstone refers to in Isa 28:16. Scholars have suggested: (1) the law of God revealed on Zion, (2) Solomon's temple, (3) Jerusalem, (4) David's archetypal monarchy, (5) the remnant, (6) YHWH's relationship with his people, (7) Zion, the eschatological kingdom, (8) the Messiah, (9) the future remnant, or YHWH's promise to be with those who trust him (See Mohrmann, "Semantic Collisions," 65). No matter what the cornerstone refers to, it is considered to be a positive image in Isa 28:16. The stumbling stone in Isa 8:14 probably refers to YHWH. The context of Isa 8:14 implies that YHWH is the sanctuary of his people, and he can protect them from destruction. When Judah did not trust or obey God's words through Isaiah, or they rejected an alliance with YHWH, then YHWH's judgment would come upon them like a trap and a snare for the inhabitants of Jerusalem. In this sense, YHWH became a stumbling stone for Judah. Cf. Mohrmann, "Semantic Collisions," 46–47.

39. Childs, *Isaiah*, 70.

40. Ibid., 71.

not lie in the throes of power politics and clever human machinations, but lies with God, the Holy One of Israel.⁴¹ Consequently, YHWH's proclamation is double-edged: "to the people who trust in him, he is a sanctuary, but conversely, he has become 'a trap and snare' to Israel on which they will stumble and be broken."⁴² It should be noted, that in this Isaianic co-text, trust in God depends on learning the νόμος (vv. 16, 20). In other words, those who trust in God have been given the law as a help (v. 19), so that they will not seek out other means.⁴³

Traditionally, Isaiah 28–33 is grouped together as a series of prophetic woe oracles (28:1; 29:1, 15; 30:1; 31:1; 33:1). The oracles in these chapters date from a period before the fall of the Northern Kingdom and extend up to the Assyrian invasion of 701 BC, in contrast to the earlier chapters 2–11, which focus on the Syro-Ephraimite war.⁴⁴ Isaiah 28:1–4 introduces a new corpus of oracles that are largely set at a subsequent period in Judah's history after the Syro-Ephraimite crisis.⁴⁵ Verses 5–6 are marked grammatically by the introduction of an eschatological formula (τῇ ἡμέρᾳ ἐκείνῃ).⁴⁶ Aernie states that these two verses provide "a positive contrast to the notion of judgment, describing the eschatological exaltation of the Lord and the corresponding restoration of a faithful remnant."⁴⁷ This distinction between judgment and hope provides a framework for the following sections of Isaiah 28 and the larger section of Isaiah 28–33.⁴⁸ After the oracle containing the judgment on the Northern Kingdom, the analogy is drawn between Israel's destruction and Judah's.⁴⁹ The collection of oracles (chs. 28–33) focuses on "the foolishness of trusting in alliances with foreign

---

41. Ibid., 74–75.
42. Childs, *Isaiah*, 75. Cf. Mohrmann, "Semantic Collisions," 46–47.
43. Wagner, *Heralds of the Good News*, 141.
44. Childs, *Isaiah*, 197.
45. Ibid., 206.
46. Childs, *Isaiah*, 205; Jeffrey W. Aernie, *Is Paul also among the Prophets?: An Examination of the Relationship between Paul and the Old Testament Prophetic Tradition in 2 Corinthians*, LNTS 467, (New York: T & T Clark, 2012), 95.
47. Aernie, *Paul among the Prophets*, 95.
48. Ibid.
49. Childs, *Isaiah*, 206.

nations when only in God's wisdom and purpose is there true salvation."[50] Isaiah 28:16 is set within the immediate literary co-text of verses 14–22: After a word of judgment directed against the scoffers of Jerusalem, the leaders of the people, who plan with "clever machinations" for their protection through alliance with Egypt ("a covenant with death") and its chthonian gods ("a pact with Sheol"), will be swept away (vv. 14–15, 17–19), but the oracle of promise to the people who trust in God, embedded in verse 16, leaves the people with hope.[51]

Therefore, the stumbling stone in Isaiah 8:14 and 28:16 has different connotations: the former is negative and the latter is positive. This may be why in Romans 9:33 there is no attribution to Isaiah and no demarcation between the two cited texts. Paul blurs the original situations in the two texts and tries to apply the stumbling text in a new situation.[52] Paul may ally behaviors related to zeal for the law with Israel's pursuing help from foreign nations in Isaiah's day. By doing so, he expresses his viewpoints on Israel, who is zealous for the law, but does not truly understand God's plan for them by sending Jesus as their Messiah.

In addition, Paul's viewpoint on the stone-texts is similar to the way that the stone-texts have been used to refer to Jesus Christ in early Christian communities. The same two texts from Isaiah also appear together in 1 Peter 2:6–8.[53] Here, the reference to the stumbling stone may be drawing upon an early Christian apologetic text. In some texts (Matt 21:42; Mark 12:10–11; Luke 20:17–18; Acts 4:11; *Barn* 6:2–4), the "stone" has

---

50. Ibid..

51. Childs, *Isaiah*, 207–8; Aernie, *Paul among the Prophets*, 96–97.

52. Regarding who the stumbling stone refers to, there are various discussions. See Shum, *Paul's Use of Isaiah in Romans*, 221. Some say the stone refers to YHWH, Zion, the Davidic Monarchy, faith by which salvation is granted, or even "the whole complex of ideas relating to the Lord's revelation of his faithfulness and the call to reciprocate with the same kind of faithfulness toward him." Regardless of whether the stone refers to God or not, the combination of these two stone texts indicates that, as Israel in Isaiah's day had relied on their own efforts and political alliances with foreign nations, so also Paul's Jewish contemporaries strove to pursue righteousness by their own device of zeal for the law. Cf. Shum, *Paul's Use of Isaiah in Romans*, 217.

53. See Byrne, *Romans*, 314; Dunn, *Romans 9–16*, 583–584; Moo, *The Epistle to the Romans*, 629.

been understood messianically with respect to Jesus.[54] In these cases, the authorial stance allies with that of early Christian communities. In verse 33b (c4D), a significant thematic item is the phrase ὁ πιστεύων ἐπ' αὐτῷ ("one who believes in him"), in which "him" is commonly applied to Jesus Christ. Therefore, Paul generalizes the scriptural voice of Isaiah, which has been allied with the first Christians' voice regarding the stone-text. By doing so, Paul provides a significant way for his audience to understand why he sets faith-righteousness and law-righteousness in an incompatible position. The reason becomes explicit in Romans 10:4, when Paul evaluates law, faith, and righteousness in terms of Christ. For Paul, the true goal of the law is to point to Christ. This facet will be developed in the subsequent text. Actually, the relation of Christ and law (v. 4) represents a culminating point which serves to carry forward the new information into Romans 10:5–8.

4.2.3 Thematic-organizational Meaning

From the above analysis, it can be seen that Romans 9:30–10:4 repeatedly sets [Faith-Righteousness] against [Law-Righteousness], and other thematic formations are surrounding or are subordinated in order to support this Opposition. The relationship of the law and Christ represented in c8 (v. 4) provides the basis or reasons for the other two parts regarding the issue of righteousness (c1-c4 and c5-c7). In the first part, Paul contrasts [Faith-Righteousness] with [Law-Righteousness] and points out that Israel fails to attain [Faith-Righteousness]. Paul employs the stumbling-stone text as a reason in support of his argument – Christ is implicitly referred to here.

Paul's prayer for the salvation of Israel (10:1) provides the circumstance for his negative statement that Israel is ignorant of God's righteousness (vv. 2–3), in which Paul criticizes Israel's zeal for God, pursued without knowledge. However, Paul's prayer prepares us to understand that the critique derives from his concern for his Jewish community. Romans 10:2–4,

---

54. See Byrne, *Romans*, 314; Dunn, *Romans 9–16*, 583–584. It is worth noting that some Jews before Paul's day were already apparently identifying the stone with the Messiah (1QH 6:26–27; 1QS 8:7 etc.). See Moo, *The Epistle to the Romans*, 629. However, the stumbling stone has been applied to Jesus Christ in Christian communities. For instance, 1 Cor 1:23 – "we proclaim Christ crucified, a stumbling block to Jews" – makes clear that that the "stone" refers to "Christ." See also 1 Cor 10:14.

again, sets the thematic formation [God's Righteousness] against [One's Own Righteousness]. There exist correspondences to the righteousness formations in Romans 9:30–33 and 10:2–4. That is, God's righteousness has a similar semantic meaning to faith-righteousness, and Israel's own righteousness to law-righteousness. Also, [Stumbling Stone] and the text-specific formation of [Christ and Law] in verse 4 are in a relation of Alignment, since parts of them correspond with each other: ὁ πιστεύων ἐπ' αὐτῷ οὐ καταισχυνθήσεται ("He who believes in him will not be put to shame") vs. εἰς δικαιοσύνην παντὶ τῷ πιστεύοντι ("That everyone who believes *shall attain* righteousness"). Also, these two formations are used to explain the reasons for the choice of faith/God's righteousness over law/Israel's righteousness. Thus, the reasons focus on Christ, because Christ is the τέλος of the law. This focus will be elaborated in the following verses (vv. 5–13).

Based on the above analysis, the following chart demonstrates the intertextual relations among these thematic formations:[55]

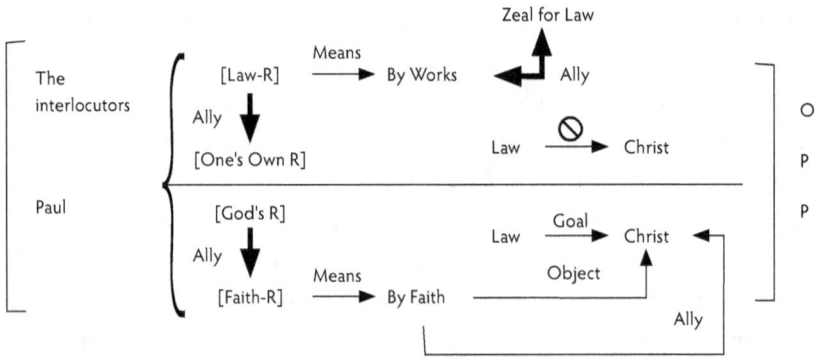

4.2.4 Multiple Voices: Paul's Jewish Contemporaries Viewpoints on Law, Righteousness, and Faith

We have seen the two contrasting types of righteousness that Paul constructs, which have been accumulated in two phrase-chains: for the Gentile: δικαιοσύνην δὲ τὴν ἐκ πίστεως (c1Cb), ἐκ πίστεως (c3Ba), τὴν τοῦ θεοῦ

---

55. "R" stands for "Righteousness"; "Opp" stands for "Opposition."

δικαιοσύνην (c7Aa); and for Israel: νόμον δικαιοσύνης (c2B), ἐξ ἔργων (c3Bb), τὴν ἰδίαν [δικαιοσύνην] (c7Ab). This contrast shows that Paul sees an incompatibility between faith-righteousness and law-righteousness (Opposition). However, a Qumran pesherist would rather ally "law observance" with "faithfulness." In 1QpHab viii.1–3,[56] "the righteous" is identified with "all those who observe the law among the Jews," whereas "by faith" refers to "their faith in the Teacher of Righteousness."[57] Therefore, their righteousness (that is, law observance) is parallel with faithfulness.[58] However, Paul disconnects the bonds of "righteousness" and "law observance" and allies "righteousness" with "faith" in Romans 9:30–32ab. The fusion of righteousness with faith for Paul may rely on his reading of Habakkuk 2:4.[59] Therefore, Paul's voice of faith-righteousness allies with the prophet Habakkuk, but is different from some Qumran sects.

It is obvious that Paul holds negative opinions about law-righteousness and distinguishes it from God's righteousness. However, connectedness among righteousness, law, and God is quite common in some Jewish literature. For instance, Ezekiel 18:5–9, 21–22 finds that one who follows the decrees and faithfully keeps the laws is righteous. It states:

> If a man is *righteous* and does what is *lawful and right* . . .
> walks in my statutes, and is careful to observe my ordinances,
> he is righteous, he shall surely live, says the Lord GOD. . . .
> But if a wicked man turns away from all his sins which he has

---

56. The book of Habakkuk was delivered in the sixth century BC, when Israel was threatened by two forces, the Babylonians (under Nebuchadnezzar) and internal religious strife between the pious worshipers of the Lord and the ungodly. The Qumran commentary on Habakkuk is written around the first century BC, when Israel is again threatened by a foreign power, probably the Romans, and Israel is also suffering from "internal strife between the wicked and the pious, exemplified by the conflict between the Teacher of Righteousness and his opponents, the Man of the Lie and the Wicked Priest." See Michael Owen Wise, Martin G. Abegg, and Edward M. Cook, *The Dead Sea Scrolls: A New Translation* (London: Harper Collins, 2005), 80.
57. Wise, Abegg, and Cook, *Dead Sea Scrolls*, 85; Watson, *Paul and the Hermeneutics of Faith*, 159.
58. Contra to Watson, who sees a distinction between righteousness with faith here. See Watson, *Paul and the Hermeneutics of Faith*, 159. Cf. Wise, Abegg, and Cook, *Dead Sea Scrolls*, 84–85.
59. Watson, *Paul and the Hermeneutics of Faith*, 151–158.

committed and keeps all my statutes and does *righteousness and mercy*, he shall surely live; he shall not die. None of the transgressions which he has committed shall be remembered against him; for the *righteousness* which he has done he shall live.[60]

Apparently, the author of Ezekiel allies righteousness, which is from God, with lawfully obedient behaviors; and a righteous person is one who keeps God's ordinances and statutes and does righteousness, which will lead him/her into life.[61] As a matter of fact, it is not uncommon in the Jewish tradition to ally righteousness with commandments or law.[62] In the Pharisaic community, a form of Judaism for laypeople, obedience to the law is the right way of fulfilling what God demands; the righteousness of law (νόμον δικαιοσύνης) appears to depict the essence of Jewish piety. In other words, Paul disconnects the bond between law-righteousness and God's righteousness, and replaces the latter with faith righteousness. In what sense is Paul opposed to law-righteousness? Surely, Paul does not oppose lawful behavior, since Paul very likely still observed the law (Acts 21:20–26).[63] Then what is Paul hoping to achieve by downplaying the value of law-righteousness? The answer can be seen from his alliance of

---

60. The translation is from the RSV with a few revisions of mine. Italics mine.
61. Watson, *Paul and the Hermeneutics of Faith*, 159.
62. It is common that "righteousness" is paralleled with "law." For instance, Prov 3:16 (LXX): ἐκ τοῦ στόματος αὐτῆς ἐκπορεύεται δικαιοσύνη νόμον δὲ καὶ ἔλεον ἐπὶ γλώσσης φορεῖ (out of her mouth proceeds righteousness and she carries law and mercy upon her tongue; *Pss. Sol.* 14:1–2: πιστὸς κύριος τοῖς ἀγαπῶσιν αὐτὸν ἐν ἀληθείᾳ τοῖς ὑπομένουσιν παιδείαν αὐτοῦ, τοῖς πορευομένοις ἐν δικαιοσύνῃ προσταγμάτων αὐτοῦ ἐν νόμῳ ᾧ ἐνετείλατο ἡμῖν εἰς ζωὴν ἡμῶν (The Lord is faithful to those who love him in truth, to those who endure his discipline; to those who live in the righteousness of his commandments, in the law, which he has commanded to us for our life [LXE]); Susanna 1:3: καὶ οἱ γονεῖς αὐτῆς δίκαιοι καὶ ἐδίδαξαν τὴν θυγατέρα αὐτῶν κατὰ τὸν νόμον Μωυσῆ (Her parents were righteous, and had taught their daughter according to the law of Moses [RSV]). Wis 2:10–11 reads, "Let us overpower the poor righteous man, let us not spare a widow, nor reverence the old grey hairs of the aged. Let our strength be a law of righteousness, for that which is weak proves useless." According to R. Jewett, "The expression 'law of righteousness' appears to be employed in this passage to depict what a propagandist would understand to be the essence of Jewish piety, which the rulers planned to replace by brute strength." Jewett, *Romans*, 610. Moreover, Wis 1:16 and 4:20 depicts that the ungodly men's lawless deeds will convict them to their face.
63. Cf. Phil 3:5–6; Gal 1:14.

law-righteousness with Israel's own righteousness, which is opposed to God's righteousness (10:2–3).

In the contrast of the thematic formations [God's Righteousness] and [One's Own Righteousness], Paul comments that Israel has a zeal for God but not according to knowledge (οὐ κατ' ἐπίγνωσιν or ἀγνοοῦντες). A similar thematic formation can be evinced in Philippians 3:6, in which ζῆλος and δικαιοσύνην τὴν ἐν νόμῳ have been placed together. Paul, as an example of zeal for God, is depicted in Philippians 3:6 as a persecutor of the church. It is highly possible that, for Paul, persecution of the churches was one of the typical representations of "zeal for God" in his time. In Galatians 1:13–14, Paul describes his earlier life in Judaism as violent persecution of the church of God and he sees this as a zeal for the traditions of Israel; he says, "[For in] my earlier life in Judaism, I was violently persecuting the church of God and was trying to destroy it. I advanced in Judaism beyond many among my people of the same age, for I was far more zealous for the traditions of my ancestors." Likewise, in Acts 22:3–5, Paul is depicted as an Israelite who is zealous for God in persecuting the first Christians. Therefore, zeal for God in Romans 10:2–3 may refer to zealous violence, and Paul probably opposes those whose extreme zeal for God is expressed by taking up arms or becoming violent, as he did.

However, there are many popular Jewish texts that depict Israel's passionate and consuming zeal for God. A typical representative of such zeal for God is Phinehas. He intervened to work against the Israelites' participation in Moabite worship of the "Baal of Peor."[64] He violently killed the Israelite, Zimri, and the Midianite women, Cozbi, with a spear for their illegal sexual intercourse (Num 25:6–8). This action called off God's anger, and the plague was stopped. Phinehas's zeal for God (ἐζήλωσεν τῷ θεῷ αὐτοῦ) caused him to make atonement for the sons of Israel, and as a grandson of Aaron the priest, he was appointed to an eternal priesthood (Num 25:10–13).[65] Phinehas's zealous action entitled him to be reckoned as righ-

---

64. Cf. Watson, *Paul and the Hermeneutics of Faith*, 174.

65. Watson rightly points out that "his [Phinehas'] action recalls the Levites' slaughter of worshippers of the golden calf (Exod 32:25–29), and the non-violent atoning interventions of Aaron (Num 16:46–48) and Moses (Num 21:8–9). Phinehas' spear, Aaron's censer, and Moses' bronze serpent all serve to halt the spread of a plague among

teous (Ps 106:28–31). That is, the story of Phinehas has been illustrated with the formation of the themes of "zeal of God" and "righteousness" in Psalm 106:28–31.[66] This zealous story has been repeatedly retold in the Jewish literature in a way that related it to the issue of "righteousness" (e.g. *Sir* 45:23–24; *1 Macc.* 2:50–54; *4 Macc.* 18:12; *Leg. All.* iii.242 [Philo]).

From the above intertextual analysis, it can be inferred that Paul's negative comments on Israel's law-righteousness, its being ignorant of God's righteousness, and its attempt to establish its own righteousness actually tell against Israel's zeal for the law, particularly their zealous actions against the first Christians. As with the pre-converted Paul,[67] there may be a group of Jews who are against the faith of the first Christians, especially their proclamation of the crucified Jesus as their Lord, the Messiah. The zeal for the law characteristic of this group of Jews may be displayed in their zealous actions against the first Christians' faith and practice, likely related to the Jesus-followers' religious practice of Christ devotion. According to Capes, "Early Christians worshiped the crucified Jesus. This was an offense to Israel's God, on a par with idolatry."[68] In other words, the opposing voices of the pre-converted Paul and his like advocate zeal for the law as a way of righteousness since, for them, the Jesus-focused messianic movement jeopardizes their way of life in "Judaism."[69]

In sum, Paul's discourse pattern of righteousness is to set law-righteousness and faith-righteousness in an incompatible contrast. He disconnects the relations of law with faith, and law-righteousness with God-righteousness,

---

the people. Just as the Levites' action is their ordination for YHWH's service (Exod 32:29), so Phinehas is appointed to an eternal priesthood." Watson, *Paul and the Hermeneutics of Faith*, 175.

66. The language in Ps 106:28–31 is close to Num 25, which asserts that Phinehas' zeal has been reckoned to him as righteousness. Watson compares Phinehas's and Abraham's righteousness, asserting that in both cases, righteousness is constituted by a single action – Phinehas "intervened," Abraham "believed God"; however, their actions oppose each other: one possesses a heroic quality, and the other not. See Watson, *Paul and the Hermeneutics of Faith*, 176–181. Also see J. A. Ziesler, *The Meaning of Righteousness in Paul: A Linguistic and Theological Enquiry* (Cambridge: University Press, 1972).

67. The use of "converted" is not in the sense of conversion to a new religion (i.e. from Judaism to Christianity). At Paul's time, there was no religion called "Christianity" yet.

68. Capes, Reeves, and Richards, *Rediscovering Paul*, 85. See also, Martin Hengel, *The Pre-Christian Paul*, *The Pre-Christian Paul* (London: SCM, 1991), 83.

69. S. A. Cummins, "Divine Life and Corporate Christology," 196.

holding a different view of righteousness than his non-believing Jewish contemporaries' communities. Paul opposes his own previous attitude of being zealous for the law and opposes those who would be in the same camp. In Romans 9:30–10:4, Paul generalizes the scriptural voice of Isaiah to dismiss the value of zeal for the law and to confirm Jesus as their expected Messiah.

4.3 Romans 10:5–13

We have indicated the possible meaning of the term τέλος in 10:4: Christ is the goal of the law – the promise of life. In other words, the goal/purpose of the law is fulfilled by Christ. We should keep in mind that Paul has already pointed out, "The very commandment that promised life proved to be death to me" (7:10).[70] Two points can be observed: first, the purpose of the commandment is to give life; and second, the commandment fails in its goal. The reason that the law fails in fulfilling its goal is because of sin, the culprit that has used the law as a bridgehead to produce death.[71] In Romans 7:7–25, Paul affirms that the law is "holy," "just," and "good" (7:12), but the power of sin makes it impossible for human beings to fulfill the law and so attain the promised life.[72] When the law allies with the power of sin, its purpose to fulfill the promise of life cannot become a reality. Eventually, this promise is accomplished by Jesus Christ (8:3).[73] In other words, the goal of the law to promise life did not succeed until Jesus

---

70. Watson suggests a direct allusion to Lev 18:5 here: "In speaking of the law as being 'unto life' (Rom 7:10), he alludes in the first instance to Lev 18:5." See Watson, *Paul and the Hermeneutics of Faith*, 506.

71. According to Schreiner, "Sin subverts the Torah to advance its purposes and actually stimulates and provokes the desire to sin through the Torah! This is not to deny that the law promises life to those who keep it, nor does it lead to the conclusion that the law is evil. The law and the commandments are good and a revelation of God's will." Schreiner, *Romans*, 359; see also Moo, *The Epistle to the Romans*, 423.

72. Moo, *The Epistle to the Romans*, 439.

73. As Schreiner has observed, "Christ's work on the cross provides the basis for the deliverance of believers from condemnation, while the Holy Spirit supplies the power for conquering sin so that the law can now be kept (8:1–4)." Schreiner, *Romans*, 395.

Christ came.⁷⁴ In this sense, the Christ event fulfills the goal of the law – to promise a new life, which Paul also illustrates in 10:6–8.⁷⁵

If the former half of Romans 10:4 has been supported by 10:5–8, the latter half of 10:4 is illustrated by 10:11–13: the universal scope of salvation is implied in the phrase, εἰς δικαιοσύνην παντὶ τῷ πιστεύοντι (v. 4b, c8B).⁷⁶ The lexical chains πᾶς, δικαιοσύνη, πιστεύω, καταισχύνω, ἐπικαλέομαι, and σῴζω, in verse 4b and verses 11–13, share collocational ties, for they recurrently appear in the same typical semantic relations to one another in many texts. We can recognize that they probably belong to a specific sort of discourse, which we shall call [Salvation in Christ] here.

4.3.1 Presentational Meaning

In Romans 10:5–8, a Pentateuchal text (Lev 18:5 and Deut 30:11–14) has been employed after each projecting clause. The projecting clause, "Moses writes . . ." (v. 5a, c9A), directs us to the quotation (Lev 18:5).⁷⁷ Here the voice of Moses is explicitly invoked. It suggests that the situational context of Leviticus 18:5 should be in view when Paul quotes it. The projected clause (v. 5b, c9B) is a quotation from Leviticus 18:5 with a few

---

74. Cf. Gal 3:23–24: Πρὸ τοῦ δὲ ἐλθεῖν τὴν πίστιν ὑπὸ νόμον ἐφρουρούμεθα συγκλειόμενοι εἰς τὴν μέλλουσαν πίστιν ἀποκαλυφθῆναι, ὥστε ὁ νόμος παιδαγωγὸς ἡμῶν γέγονεν εἰς Χριστόν, ἵνα ἐκ πίστεως δικαιωθῶμεν· "Before faith came, we were guarded under the law, being enclosed until the coming faith to be revealed. Therefore, the law is our guardian to *lead* us into Christ, so that we might be justified by faith."
75. Paul's use of the two texts Lev 18:5 (in v. 5) and Deut 30:11–14 (in vv. 6–8) has been the subject of considerable debate. In this passage one sees Paul's understanding of the relationships between Christ and the Mosaic law and also his basic approach to the scriptural texts. Paul seems to set these two quoted texts (both from the Pentateuch) antithetically against each other, and the way he uses Deut 30:11–14 seems to disregard the Deuteronomic context. In order to solve this problem, some scholars deny any contrast between the two quoted texts. Other scholars argue for a positive salvation-historical contrast. Still other scholars perceive the contrast in terms of the tension between literacy (the written Torah) and orality (the oral gospel). This dissertation, however, will explain that Paul uses the two quotations complementarily.
76. Italics mine.
77. The meaning of the phrase τὴν δικαιοσύνην τὴν ἐκ [τοῦ] νόμου in the projecting clause (Μωϋσῆς . . . γράφει τὴν δικαιοσύνην τὴν ἐκ [τοῦ] νόμου) is synonymous with the previous phrases νόμον δικαιοσύνης (9:31, c2B), ἐξ ἔργων (9:32, c3Bb), and τὴν ἰδίαν δικαιοσύνην (v. 3, c7Ab).

adjustments.⁷⁸ With a particle δέ,⁷⁹ a second projecting clause is introduced: "The righteousness from faith says thus . . ." (v. 6a, c10A).⁸⁰ Paul does not introduce Moses in this second introductory formula; instead he personalizes the righteousness from faith itself as a speaker. It is possible that Paul intends to blur the situational context of Deuteronomy 30:12–14 and make it generalized or normative. The projected clause (vv. 6b–8, c10B–c11Cb) does not quote verbatim from Deuteronomy 30:12–14. The scriptural text interweaves with Paul's interpretation of law. In a certain sense, the two projecting clauses set a pattern of a contrasted pair consisting of law-righteousness and faith-righteousness as occurred in 9:30–10:4. However, do the elements of this righteousness pair contrast with each other in the same way as those in 9:30–10:4? The answer is, probably not. We should note that there are some novelties in this second contrast. The first projecting clause traces law-righteousness back to Moses, and employs a text from Leviticus; the second projecting clause uses a personalized voice of faith-righteousness to speak for the Deuteronomic text. Although the two Pentateuchal texts are employed in different styles (one points to a specific situational context, the other is in a generalized tone), the two

---

78. Lev 18:5 reads: ἃ ποιήσας ἄνθρωπος ζήσεται ἐν αὐτοῖς. For occurrences of alterations, see Stanley, *Paul and the Language of Scripture*, 126–128. Leviticus 18:5 is an oft-quoted text in the Hebrew Scriptures: Ezek 20:11, 13, 21; and Neh 9:29. In Ezekiel, it describes Israel's rebellion against God, but God responds with grace, giving them law to observe, so that everyone shall live. Badenas indicates that the law is God's great gift of life to Israel (Badenas, *Christ the End of the Law*, 120). In Neh 9:29, "Lev 18:5 is quoted as a reference to the covenant relationship of Yahweh with his people, and the promise of life which he gives to his children" (Badenas, *Christ the End of the Law*, 120). For more quotations of Lev 18:5 in Jewish writings, see Preston M. Sprinkle, *Law and Life: The Interpretation of Leviticus 18:5 in Early Judaism and in Paul*. WUNT 241. (Tübingen: Mohr Siebeck, 2008), 25–130.

79. The conjunctive δέ can function as adversative and connective as well. See Porter, *Idioms of the Greek New Testament*, 208. Most scholars interpret it as "adversative." However, it is much more likely to be understood as a "connective" δέ in this co-text. We will give further explanation subsequently. For more discussion about δέ, see Stephanie Black, *Sentence Conjunction in the Gospel of Matthew: καί, δέ, τότε, γάρ, οὖν and Asyndeton in Narrative Discourse*, JSNTSup 216, (London: Sheffield Academic, 2002), 142–178. Black views δέ as low-to mid-level discontinuity in Matthew.

80. It can be noted that the phrase ἡ . . . ἐκ πίστεως δικαιοσύνη is synonymous with the previous ones δικαιοσύνην δὲ τὴν ἐκ πίστεως (9:30, c1Cb), ἐκ πίστεως (9:32, c3Ba), and τὴν τοῦ θεοῦ δικαιοσύνην (v. 3, c7Aa).

projected clauses are not antithetically against each other, as some scholars claim.[81] Actually, the elements of the righteousness pair in 10:5–8 are compatible with each other, particularly after Paul indicates the relation of Christ and the law in 10:4. First, it is possible to understand the particle δέ grammatically as a connective.[82] Second, to put the concept of Christ as the goal of the law (i.e. the promised life) into perspective, the righteousness from the law which points to life in Leviticus 18:5 is further elaborated by the righteousness of faith in Romans 10:6–8. Therefore, the contrast of law and faith is much more probable in a compatible Dialogical relation. Let us investigate the two scriptural passages briefly first, for we will examine the Scriptures in more detail in the section of Scriptural Voices.

Obviously, Paul resorts to the origin of law-righteousness by employing Leviticus 18:5. As Dunn has observed, "Lev18:5 is the first statement in the Jewish Scriptures of what was evidently a typical expression of Israel's sense of obligation under the covenant – 'do and thus live.'"[83] Leviticus 18:1–5 emphasizes that the Lord is Israel's God, and their obedience to God's commandments shall lead to life. From the typical viewpoint of Israel, God's righteous saving action requires Israel's religious piety toward God to be demonstrated through their conformity to the law, and then, through this means of obedience, Israel can be rescued from suppression by foreign powers (e.g. Egypt, Canaan).

The second projected clause uses Deuteronomy 30:12–14. Careful investigation of Romans 10:6–8 shows that Paul has deleted all the expressions of Deuteronomy 30:12–14 which refer directly to the observance of the law, and replaced them with the phrases related to believing/trusting in Christ.[84] Wagner has appropriately observed that, by doing so, Paul demonstrates exegetically that doing the law that leads to life is none other than believing/trusting in Christ.[85] Let us examine Romans 10:6–8 in detail.

---

81. For instance, Ernst Käsemann, *Commentary on Romans* (Grand Rapids: Eerdmans, 1980), 283–292; Moo, *The Epistle to the Romans*, 646.
82. Cf. Porter, *Idioms of the Greek New Testament*, 208. Black, *Sentence Conjunction*, 142–178.
83. See Dunn, "Righteousness," 223. For this detailed text-critical issue in Rom 10:5, see Sprinkle, *Law and Life*, 166–167, n. 2.
84. Wagner, *Heralds of the Good News*, 162; Badenas, *Christ the End of the Law*, 125.
85. Wagner, *Heralds of the Good News*, 164.

Rom 10:6–8	Deut 30:12–14 LXX	Notes
ἡ δὲ ἐκ πίστεως δικαιοσύνη οὕτως λέγει		Paul's referring to faith-righteousness
μὴ εἴπῃς ἐν τῇ καρδίᾳ σου	μὴ εἴπῃς ἐν τῇ καρδίᾳ σου	Deut 8:17 & 9:4
τίς ἀναβήσεται εἰς τὸν οὐρανόν	οὐκ ἐν τῷ οὐρανῷ ἄνω ἐστὶν λέγων τίς ἀναβήσεται ἡμῖν εἰς τὸν οὐρανὸν καὶ λήμψεται αὐτὴν ἡμῖν καὶ ἀκούσαντες αὐτὴν ποιήσομεν	Deut 30:12
τοῦτ' ἔστιν Χριστὸν καταγαγεῖν		Paul's interpretive note
ἤ· τίς καταβήσεται εἰς τὴν ἄβυσσον;	οὐδὲ πέραν τῆς θαλάσσης ἐστὶν λέγων τίς διαπεράσει ἡμῖν εἰς τὸ πέραν τῆς θαλάσσης καὶ λήμψεται ἡμῖν αὐτήν καὶ ἀκουστὴν ἡμῖν ποιήσει αὐτήν καὶ ποιήσομεν	Deut 30:13
τοῦτ' ἔστιν Χριστὸν ἐκ νεκρῶν ἀναγαγεῖν		A further Pauline note
ἀλλὰ τί λέγει;		The projection
ἐγγύς σου τὸ ῥῆμά ἐστιν ἐν τῷ στόματί σου καὶ ἐν τῇ καρδίᾳ σου	ἔστιν σου ἐγγὺς τὸ ῥῆμα σφόδρα ἐν τῷ στόματί σου καὶ ἐν τῇ καρδίᾳ σου καὶ ἐν ταῖς χερσίν σου αὐτὸ ποιεῖν	Deut 30:14
τοῦτ' ἔστιν τὸ ῥῆμα τῆς πίστεως ὃ κηρύσσομεν		A further Pauline note

From the above chart, several things can be observed: First, it is worthy of note that Paul replaces the clause ἡ ἐντολὴ αὕτη ἣν ἐγὼ ἐντέλλομαί σοι σήμερον (Deut 30:11) with μὴ εἴπῃς ἐν τῇ καρδίᾳ σου, a phrase which appears in the beginning of both Deuteronomy 8:17 and 9:4. One of the reasons for the employment of this latter phrase may be because of its nesting word καρδία ("heart"), which repeatedly appears in Paul's illustration of his view of righteousness that follows (Rom 10:8–10).[86] The second important reason is that, as mentioned above, Deuteronomy 8–9 corresponds to 29–30 in some way, particularly in the remembering of God's grace in leading them out of Egypt and the mentioning of the "heart" and "test" themes. Third and most importantly, the theme of the literary co-text around these two passages is that "the people of Israel are warned against viewing Yahweh's mighty acts of deliverance as an affirmation of their own righteous conduct."[87] Therefore, Paul uses Deuteronomy 8:17/9:4 and Deuteronomy 30:12–14 to make his points emphasizing faith-righteousness: to be righteous is to love God with all your heart and all your soul; and the love of God, in the era after the Messiah Jesus came, is about the establishment of a relationship with Christ just as their observance of God's law was in the past.[88]

The second thing we should note is that Paul seems to eliminate everything about observing the commandments of God and replaces this material with expressions referring to Christ's exaltation and resurrection.[89] Paul

---

86. Paul repeats καρδία three times in these three verses. Interestingly, McConville sees that the similarity between Deuteronomy and the prophets lies in the theology of the "heart": "In the former [Deuteronomy] this is best known in the exhortation called the 'Shema' (after its first word in Hebrew): 'Hear, Israel! . . . You shall love the LORD your God with all your heart, with all your soul and with all your might' (6:4; cf. 10:12), but it occurs more widely and in key places. The metaphor of a circumcision of the heart (10:16; 30:6) has an expressed echo in Jer 4:4, and in general comes close to the strong prophetic rejection of ritual actions that have no genuine corresponding devotion to God (e.g. Isa 1:10–17; Amos 5:21–24). In Deut 30:1–10, in fact, the emphasis on obedience from the heart together with the need for the grace of God in restoring the covenantal relationship puts Deuteronomy close to the new-covenant theology of Jer 31:31–34." See J. G. McConville, *Deuteronomy*. AOTC 5. (Downers Grove: InterVarsity, 2002), 20–21.

87. Stanley, *Paul and the Language of Scripture*, 130.

88. Note that this does not mean Israel should cease to obey their law and decrees, but it points out that the way to be righteous is no longer through their conformity to the commandment.

89. Stanley has written, "Paul has eliminated everything that pertains to the original passage – that the law can and should be fulfilled – is clearly at odds with Paul's own efforts to wean his Gentile converts from the notion that they need to accept the yoke of Torah in order to assure their participation in the covenant of Yahweh. On another level, the changes give voice to a far-reaching hermeneutical judgment: the same "word" (τὸ ῥῆμα, Rom 10:8 = Deut 30:14) that Moses described as being "near" in the law has now come to full expression and become available to all in Christ. The numerous omissions that mark Paul's handling of Deut 30:11–14 are thus firmly grounded in his own Christian theology." Stanley, *Paul and the Language of Scripture*, 130.

deftly replaces Deuteronomy's reference to "doing the commandment" and substitutes αὐτήν (referring to the commandment) with Christ.[90] He understands "the two questions in the quotation as references to bringing Christ down from heaven or up from among the dead."[91] Also, one striking feature of Paul's citation of Deuteronomy 30:14 is that he drops the last phrase ἐν ταῖς χερσίν σου αὐτὸ ποιεῖν ("do it by your hands"), but keeps "the word is near you, in your mouth and in your heart."[92] That is, the word (referring to the law, the commandment) in Deuteronomy has been identified with the word of faith that Paul's community has proclaimed (v. 8, c11C). Interestingly, the phrase τὸ ῥῆμα τῆς πίστεως does not appear in Deuteronomy. Instead, the phrases τὰ ῥήματα τοῦ νόμου τούτου and τοὺς λόγους τοῦ νόμου τούτου appear repeatedly (Deut 27:3, 26; 28:58; 29:28; 31:24, etc.). This confirms that Paul is attempting to identify the word(s) of the law with the word of faith; and "doing the law" with "a relationship with Christ." By doing so, Paul demonstrates that Christ is the goal to which the law has pointed, "a matter of what God has done in the resurrection and exaltation of Christ."[93] Therefore, it is evident that Paul's voice does not place Leviticus 18:5 against Deuteronomy 30:12–14. Paul attempts to make clear that the "doing" that leads to "life" is finally fulfilled in Jesus Christ. Therefore, Paul makes the Mosaic Scriptures ally with his voicing of the compatible contrast of faith and law-righteousness in terms of the purpose of the law: the alliance shows that the law pointed towards life, the manifestation of God's righteousness in Christ.[94] We can label this type of compatible contrast based on scriptural proof as [Righteousness: Law to Christ].

Now let us turn to the early Christian proclamation in verses 9–10. The discourse pattern of verses 9–10 is different from verses 5–8, and its subject

---

90. Some scholars have a similar idea. See J. Ross Wagner, "The Heralds of Isaiah and the Mission of Paul: An Investigation of Paul's Use of Isaiah 51–55 in Romans," in *Jesus and the Suffering Servant*, ed. W. H. Bellinger and William Reuben Farmer (Harrisburg: Trinity Press International, 1998), 164; Badenas, *Christ the End of the Law*, 130; Johnson, *Function of Apocalyptic*, 158.
91. Wagner, *Heralds of the Good News*, 164.
92. Cf. Dunn, *Romans 9–16*, 613.
93. Wagner, *Heralds of the Good News*, 164.
94. Badenas, *Christ the End of the Law*, 131.

matter changes from the previous contrast of law/faith-righteousness to an early Christian proclamation. Verse 9 consists of two conditional protases ("if you confess . . ." and "if you believe . . .") and one apodosis ("you will be saved"); and verse 10, with two paratactic clauses, confirms the proclamation. If we read verse 9 and verse 10 as interweaving, then it can be seen that the confession "God raised Jesus from the dead" will bring us into righteousness (Rom 4:25), and that the belief in "Jesus as Lord" will bring us into salvation. Here no difference should be supposed between the meaning of "righteousness" and "salvation."[95] "Each expresses in a general way the new relationship with God that is the result of believing 'with the heart' and confessing 'with the mouth.'"[96]

How does Paul relate the proclamation of [Salvation in Christ] with Paul's generalized voice of the Deuteronomic text? Paul constructs them in a harmonious relation. The conjunctive ὅτι in verse 9 can denote a causal clause.[97] This ὅτι clause is in a causal relation to the antecedent, ἐγγύς σου τὸ ῥῆμά ("the word is near you"). The nearness of the word is suggested in the manner that one may get saved: to confess with your lips and to believe in your heart the proclamation. In this sense, Paul makes the formation [Salvation in Christ] to be in Alliance with the voice of Deuteronomy 30:12–14.

The other relation of these two parts of the texts is displayed in the lexical chain: mouth and heart. Verses 9–10 use the words "mouth" and "heart"[98] to link with Deuteronomy 30:14 (or Rom 10:8) to express the

---

95. Moo, *The Epistle to the Romans*, 659.
96. Ibid.
97. It could also denote a content clause, that is, this ὅτι clause is a clarification of the antecedent, τὸ ῥῆμα τῆς πίστεως ὃ κηρύσσομεν ("the word of faith that we proclaim"). It is said that the content of this proclamation is that Jesus as Lord (v. 9a, c12A) and that God raised Jesus from the dead (v. 9b, c12B), a subject which is common in early Christian literature (See Rom 4:24–25; 8:11; Gal 1:1; 1 Cor 6:14; 15:4, 12, 20; 2 Cor 4:14; 1 Thess 1:10; Col 2:12; Eph 1:20; Acts 3:15; 4:10; 10:40; 1 Pet 1:21). Cf. Moo, *The Epistle to the Romans*, 658, n. 59.
98. In Paul's use of Deut 30:12–14, we can see that he focuses on the "heart" text in this passage. One of the reasons that Paul merges Deut 8:17 and 9:4 with Deut 30:11–12 may be because of its intertextual thematic node καρδία ("heart"), which repeatedly appears in Paul's following illustration of his view of righteousness (Rom 10:8–10). Paul's repeated reference "heart" text can hardly be accidental. Actually, Paul has repeated this point earlier. As Dunn rightly observes, "Paul underlines the fact that faith operates from the

significance of the confession of Jesus' lordship, and belief in his resurrection, in terms of righteousness and salvation. Dunn has rightly observed that "to talk of the 'heart' is to talk of faith; faith operates at and from the level of the heart. To talk of the 'mouth' is to talk of confession; confession is the primary and essential outward manifestation corresponding to faith."[99] Therefore, Paul continues to emphasize faith in one's heart as the way of being righteous (πιστεύσῃς ἐν τῇ καρδίᾳ σου, καρδίᾳ . . . πιστεύεται εἰς δικαιοσύνην). The implied participant references become the unspecified individual reference "you" (v. 9) and "he" (v. 10). This type of reference leads to the following theme of the universal scope of salvation (vv. 11–13).

With the projecting clause "the Scripture says" (v. 11, c14A), Paul reintroduces a universal note by returning to part of the thematic formation of the "stone-text" (Isa 28:16; cf. 9:33). It can be noted that Paul does not invoke the voice of Isaiah here; instead he uses the whole Scripture to speak for the prophetic voice, which makes the quoted prophetic texts generalized or normative. The addition of πᾶς in verse 11 enables it to parallel with verse 13, which is a quotation from Joel 3:5 (LXX). It is very likely that the scriptural introductory formula (the clause of locution projection) in verse 11 is valid for the quotation of verse 13 as well. The clausal pattern of the two quotations resemble each other: the subject πᾶς has been elaborated by a verbal clause.

πᾶς	ὁ πιστεύων ἐπ' αὐτῷ	οὐ καταισχυνθήσεται	v. 11
πᾶς	ὃς ἂν ἐπικαλέσηται τὸ ὄνομα κυρίου	σωθήσεται	v. 13
a	=b (expansion: hypotactic elaboration)[100]		

---

level of the heart. In view of his repeated emphasis earlier that the real business of the law is 'in the heart' (2:15), that the circumcision God wants is 'of the heart' (2:29), that the obedience God calls for is "from the heart" (6:17)." See Dunn, *Romans 9–16*, 614.

99. Dunn, *Romans 9–16*, 616.

100. There are three types of expansion: elaborating, extending and enhancing. For elaboration, it can be divided into paratactic elaboration and hypotactic elaboration. See Halliday and Matthiessen, *An Introduction to Functional Grammar*, 395–399.

In the above chart, the two main verbs (καταισχυνθήσεται and σωθήσεται) are both in the emphatic form (future tense) and semantically both are oriented in the direction of salvation. Similarly, ὁ πιστεύων ἐπ' αὐτῷ ("whoever believes in him") resembles ὃς ἂν ἐπικαλέσηται τὸ ὄνομα κυρίου ("whoever calls on the name of the Lord"). This parallel pattern has appeared in verse 10, the second part of [Salvation in Christ]: πιστεύεται καρδίᾳ εἰς δικαιοσύνην vs. ὁμολογεῖται στόματι εἰς σωτηρίαν. If we read these two formations as interweaving, then not only do they both proclaim the need to believe in him (or to believe in one's heart), but also to "confess in one's mouth" says something similar to "call on the name of Lord" (both actions lead toward the result of salvation). In this sense, the formation [Salvation in Christ] and the prophetic Scripture (Isa 28:16 and Joel 3:5) say the same thing about salvation but with different emphases: the former stresses the way of salvation, the latter the scope of salvation. If we label the prophetic Scripture regarding the scope of salvation as [Unification of Jews and Nations], then [Salvation in Christ] is in a Dialogical relation with [Unification].

The scope of salvation has been emphasized in [Unification]. First, the key lexical term πᾶς runs through verses 11–13 (c14Ba, c15Ba, c15Bb, c16A), and denotes the universal scope of salvation; second, the parallel structure of verses 11 and 13 frames verse 12 in the middle, which particularly explains what πᾶς means. That is, it includes Ἰουδαίου τε καὶ Ἕλληνος (both Jews and Gentiles).

Paul therefore allies the scriptural voice of the scope of salvation with early Christian proclamation [Salvation in Christ]. He sees that "one who confesses with his mouth (Jesus is Lord) will be saved" (v. 10) has a similar meaning to the prophetic saying, "everyone who calls upon the name of the Lord will be saved" (v. 13). The thematic item "Call upon the Lord" is quite common in the LXX and Jewish literature, and is used to ask God for help or intervention.[101] "Call upon the Lord" was also used by the early Christians with reference both to God the Father and to Christ.[102] Paul takes

---

101. E.g. Deut 4:7; Isa 55:6; 2 Macc 3:22; Judg 16:2; see also Moo, *The Epistle to the Romans*, 660.
102. E.g. Acts 9:14, 22:16; 2 Tim 2:22; 1 Pet 1:17 and 1 Cor 1:2; see also Moo, *The Epistle to the Romans*, 660.

"the Lord" as Jesus Christ here in order to indicate that one is righteous by having faith in Jesus Christ/calling upon his name. In his citation of Joel 3:5 in 10:13, Paul brings together two crucial terms, "everyone" (cf. vv. 4, 11, 12) and "salvation" (cf. vv. 1, 9, 10). Again, in the Jewish Scriptures, the one on whom people called for salvation was YHWH; Paul identifies this one with Jesus Christ, the Lord, as does the early church.[103] Therefore, Paul's voice in this final passage brings a universal scale to salvation, instead of limiting it to Israel.

4.3.2 Scriptural Voices

We have shown that Paul has combined two Pentateuchal texts to explain that Christ is the goal of the law, and he also allies the Pentateuchal texts with two prophetic texts on the basis of the early Christian proclamation in order to demonstrate the scriptural prophetic confirmation of the universal scope of salvation. However, what does each scriptural text mean in its own co-text? And how do they relate to each other? In Romans 10:5–13, Paul has used four scriptural texts, Leviticus 18:5, Deuteronomy 30:11–34, Isaiah 28:16 and Joel 3:5. Let us examine these scriptural texts in their own co-texts first.

Leviticus 18 is YHWH's speech to Moses about the legislation of sexual laws (vv. 6–23), which is framed by parenetic material (vv. 2b–5; 24–30) in order to instruct Israel not to follow the practices of Egyptians and Canaanites and to call them to be a holy people.[104] Two formulae of YHWH's self-introduction, "I am YHWH, your God" (vv. 2–4) and "I am YHWH" (v. 5), occur repeatedly in the first parenetic section (vv. 2b–5).[105]

---

103. Moo, *The Epistle to the Romans*, 660.
104. John E. Hartley, *Leviticus* (Dallas: Word Books, 1992), 286. The law is authoritative instruction for Israel's life, since it derives from God himself. See McConville, *Deuteronomy*, 43.
105. They are also scattered through other parts of the Pentateuch (e.g. Lev 18–26) and the Prophets (e.g. Isa 40–55, and Ezekiel). See Hartley, *Leviticus*, 291. Note that God calls himself "your God" in the formula (I am YHWH, your God) to identify himself with Israel, just as he did with the patriarchs, Abraham, Isaac, and Jacob (e.g. Exod 3:6, 15). This formula also reminds Israel of God's providing the Decalogue to them through Moses at Mount Sinai, so that they are made aware of the need to observe the laws because of the holy character of the God they worship. See Hartley, *Leviticus*, 291.

The formulae usually come after a law or at the end of a group of laws.¹⁰⁶ In other words, in obeying these laws the Israelites express their faithfulness towards YHWH. The main verbs ποιέω, φυλάσσω, and πορεύομαι which occur in verses 4–5 are repeated throughout the speech (ποιέω²ˣ, φυλάσσω⁵ˣ, πορεύομαι²ˣ), and point to the way of life for Israel.¹⁰⁷ Therefore, the role of the formulae and their combination with a group of laws in Leviticus 18 is to teach Israel, as the people of YHWH, their distinctive way of life. Further, verse 5 denotes that the keeping of God's statues and ordinances bears the promise of life. Consequently, God has opened a way to life through keeping God's word, his statues, and ordinances.¹⁰⁸ In the context of the parenesis (vv. 24–30), the life here refers to "a secure, healthy life with sufficient goods in the Promised Land as God's people."¹⁰⁹ Therefore, the law is God's guidance for Israel about how to live in a pagan world.

Let us now turn to Deuteronomy. Deuteronomy 30:12–14 is within Moses' final covenant address in Deuteronomy 29–30, which explores Israel's acceptance of the terms of the covenant, whether curse or blessing.¹¹⁰ After the historical review of YHWH's acts of deliverance in bringing Israel out of Egypt (29:2–9)¹¹¹ and confirmation of Israel's commitment to God's covenant (vv. 10–15), the curse – the bitter future – is applied to those whose hearts have turned away from YHWH (vv. 16–28).¹¹² Deuteronomy 30 starts from a future time when Israel would be scattered among the

---

106. They are also scattered through other parts of the Pentateuch (e.g. Lev 18–26) and the Prophets (e.g. Isa 40–55, and Ezekiel). See Hartley, *Leviticus*, 291.
107. Hartley, *Leviticus*, 290.
108. Ibid., 293.
109. Ibid., 293.
110. McConville, *Deuteronomy*, 413.
111. It should be noted that vv. 4–5 strike a note that recalls 8:2–5. Both passages mention clothes and shoes that did not wear out for forty years in the wilderness (8:4; 29:5). Also, the familiar language of "heart" and "test" confirms their similarity. "There [8:2–5] YHWH tested them to know what was 'in their heart,' and exhorted them to 'understand/know in their hearts' (8:5). Here [29:2–9], he has not yet given them 'hearts to understand/know . . . The same moral issue is broached as was found in 9:4–6." (See McConville, *Deuteronomy*, 414.) If this is right, then there is a close connection between chs. 8–9 and chs. 29–30.
112. The address first attributes Israel's exile to their dull hearts and deaf ears (29:3–4). It then proceeds to describe the bitter future that awaits them, since their hearts turned away from God (29:16–28).

nations (30:1 διασκορπίζω/נדח: scatter, exile). It addresses the fact that if Israel and its children return to YHWH, they will be restored. This chapter can be grouped into three sub-sections: verses 1–10, verses 11–14, and verses 15–20.

It is interesting to note that the formula יְהוָה אֱלֹהֶיךָ (YHWH, your God) appears 15 times throughout Deuteronomy 30, and occurs intensively in the first section (12 times in vv. 1–10). The formula functions as the subject of verbs such as "restore," "gather," "circumcise," and "give," and as the object of the verbs "turn" or "return." That is, when Israel turns to God and obeys his commandments with all their heart and all their soul, God will restore them and have compassion on them (30:1–10). Therefore, YHWH remains as initiator in Israel's restoration, and he enables his people to be renewed (Deut 30:8).[113] Also, however, Israel shares the obligation to turn to YHWH.[114] The dramatic new thing of the address to Israel occurs in verse 6, that is, the "circumcision of the heart." Why? We know that this first part (vv. 1–10) deals with the problem of the broken covenant. "That problem could not be solved by a mere turning back of the clock; a new thing had to be done to deal effectively with Israel's sinful disposition. And the answer lay in Yahweh's acting in a completely new way in order to make covenant life with him possible."[115] Therefore, the circumcision of the heart is connected with the call for Israel's love for God (the term "heart" occurs frequently in this passage), which in turn leads them to life. It is significant that to love God, thus to live, in Moses' description, means to obey God and observe all his commandments (30:8).[116]

---

113. McConville, *Deuteronomy*, 43. McConville has shown the similarity between Deut 30:1–10 and Jer 31:31–34. Both passages relate to the new covenant and in both places YHWH enables the renewed people to be faithful.

114. According to McConville, the verb ἐπιστρέφω[ἰάομαι]/שוב (return) is crucially important in vv. 1–10, they express the obligation on Israel to change completely. See McConville, *Deuteronomy*, 426.

115. Ibid., 427.

116. McConville has observed the relationships of faithfulness and observance of the law in Deuteronomy. As he said, "faithfulness involves the keeping of Torah, or commandments (Deut 30:8; Jer 31:33). Torah is therefore not in tension with promise or forgiveness. . . . As for individual piety, the devotion of Israelites, both as a community and as individuals, is the aim of the book's exhortations to love the LORD from the heart." See McConville, *Deuteronomy*, 43.

After Moses emphatically addresses the easy availability of the commandment (30:11–14),[117] a section which is employed by Paul in Romans 10:6–8, the address ends with Moses' exhortation to Israel to choose life and blessings rather than death and the curse (30:15–20).[118] The dominant theme of the third part is "life" (terms related to life occur six times), an extension from 30:6.[119] This "life" theme culminates in verses 19–20 with a strong appeal to "choose life" (v. 19b). The prospect of "life" will fulfill the ancient promise to Abraham, Isaac, and Jacob in the final verse.

In a word, the idea of "do the law (or return to God) and thus live" has been brought to the fore in Deuteronomy 30. The climax of the exhortation occurs in the final verse (v. 20): you should be "loving the LORD your God, obeying his voice, and cleaving to him; for that means life to you and length of days, that you may dwell in the land which the LORD swore to your fathers, to Abraham, to Isaac, and to Jacob, to give them" (RSV). Therefore, the life promised to the three patriarchs will be fulfilled in the people also if they return to God's words of commandment. In paralleling Leviticus 18 and Deuteronomy 30, it can be seen that the two important elements for Israel's sense of identity as God's people have been repeated again and again in both texts: (1) "(I am) YHWH, your God"; and (2) the expressions: "do the law" or "love YHWH, your God with all your heart and all your soul," so that you shall live.

Therefore, both the holy code of Leviticus 18 and the exhortation to the Israelites in Deuteronomy 30 express the idea that the goal of the law is to point to the promise of life. First, both texts emphasize Israel's identity as God's people ("I am YHWH, your God"); second, the settings of both texts occur at a time when Israel will enter/reenter into their Promised Land (Deut 30:1–10 concerns Israel's restoration and reentering into the Promised Land after their exile); third, both texts show that Israel's obedience to the word of God/the law will bring them into the promised life. Therefore, Paul wisely allies the two Pentateuchal texts in order to illustrate that the goal of the law is the promised life. Paul, however, emphasizes

---

117. Watson, *Paul and the Hermeneutics of Faith*, 438.
118. Ibid.
119. McConville, *Deuteronomy*, 430.

that this life is in Christ. In other words, the goal of the law is fulfilled in Christ. As he argues in Galatians and elsewhere in Romans, the law was our παιδαγωγὸς (guardian) εἰς Χριστόν (into Christ), for "God has done what the law, weakened by the flesh, could not do: sending his own Son . . . in order that the just requirement of the law (τὸ δικαίωμα τοῦ νόμου) might be fulfilled in us . . ." (Rom 8:3–4). Therefore, in Romans 10:5–10, Paul makes an effort to show that Christ will fulfill the role of the law, that is, the promise of life. Paul does not use the two Pentateuch texts antithetically against each other, but he interweaves the early Christian proclamation with his reading of Scripture. Like Leviticus 18, Deuteronomy 30 associates the "heart" phrases with phrases of observance of the law,[120] and Paul uses the "heart" text to link with Jesus Christ. It seems that Paul uses Deuteronomy 30:12–14 and Leviticus 18:5 to illustrate the identity of God's people in the era of Christ, which consists of being in a relationship with him.

After indicating the nearness of God's word in verse 8 and the proclamation of the early Christians' faith in Jesus Christ in verses 9–10, the two prophetic texts are brought in to support the universal scope of God's salvation to all who believe in Jesus Christ (cf. Rom 10:4b). In the following, we will examine the two prophetic texts in their co-texts first.

Isaiah 28:16 appears in Romans 9:33 (the stone-texts that implicitly point to Jesus Christ), and we have discussed how the literary co-text around this verse establishes a contrast between a reliance on human conspiracy and a trust in God, in order to entreat the Jews to return to God. The final part of Isaiah 28:16 ([πᾶς] ὁ πιστεύων ἐπ' αὐτῷ οὐ καταισχυνθήσεται) offers the audience a gleam of hope.[121] Paul adds πᾶς to express the Isaianic saying's scope of applicability.[122] However, "those who believe in him" does not refer to both the Jews and the nations in Isaiah 28, but only the Jewish people in this co-text.

---

120. It should be remembered that the original voice of Deut 30 cried to ally the Israelites' obedience of the commandments with their love toward God.
121. Shum, *Paul's Use of Isaiah in Romans*, 220.
122. Ibid., 221.

The book of Joel consists of seventy-three verses and has been divided into three or four chapters.[123] Joel 3:1–5 is closely related to Joel 2:18–27, so that Jerome included them together as chapter 2 in the Vulgate.[124] According to Crenshaw, the structure of the text can be outlined as follows: (1) Calamity in Judah and its Reversal (1:1—2:27); (2) Signs and Blessings (3:1–5); and (3) Judgments of the Foreign Nations (4:1–21).[125] The immediate co-text of Joel 3:1–5 is about the restoration of Judah and divine judgment on the nations: there is a prophetic call to turn to YHWH with the heart (2:12–17), and YHWH becomes zealous for his land and has mercy on his people so as to execute judgment on the nations (2:18–27). Joel 3:1–5 is a message of signs and blessings,[126] which looks forward to a new age in which all of God's people (young and old, male and female) will have all they need of God's Spirit (3:1).[127] In this new age, there is a new way of living, in which everybody can possess the Spirit.[128] Afterward, Joel 4 focuses once again on the judgment of the nations.[129]

Interestingly, πᾶς in Joel 3:5 LXX is exclusively regarded as the Jewish people, those who adhere to the Jewish religion. As Belli has noted,

> This [πᾶς as all the Jewish people] is confirmed by the second part of Joel 3:5, where the place of salvation is specified as Zion and Jerusalem, and even more so by chapter 4 that follows, which describes, in parallel with the return of the survivors of Judah and Jerusalem, the judgment of the nations in the terrible valley of Jehoshaphat (4:1–2).[130]

---

123. Most English versions of Bible, except the Jewish Publication Society version and the New American Bible, adopt a tripartite division. The Hebrew text (BHS) and the Greek version (LXX) indicate four chapters: Joel 3:1–5 (LXX) equals 2:28–32 in English translations, and 4:1–21 (LXX) equals 3:1–21. See James L. Crenshaw, *Joel: A New Translation with Introduction and Commentary* (London: Doubleday, 1995), 11.
124. Douglas K. Stuart, *Hosea-Jonah* (Dallas: Word, 1998), 257.
125. Crenshaw, *Joel*, 12–13.
126. Stuart, *Hosea-Jonah*, 262.
127. According to Stuart, "The old era was characterized by the Spirit's selective, limited influence on *some* individuals: certain prophets, kings, etc." See Stuart, *Hosea-Jonah*, 261.
128. Stuart, *Hosea-Jonah*, 262.
129. Crenshaw, *Joel*, 12–13.
130. Belli, *Argumentation and Use of Scripture in Romans 9–11*, 287.

In other words, there is no universal announcement of salvation for all (that is, both the Jews and the Gentiles) in Isaiah 28:16 and Joel 3:5; instead, the two prophetic passages focus on exclusive salvation for the Jewish people.[131] The question can then be raised: how then was Paul able to read into the text a universal announcement for all without distinction? It would be too convenient to say that Paul's reading of the Scripture is based on his christological thought. The reasons why Paul uses these two prophetic Scriptures are complex, and we can note at least several as follows: (1) the co-texts of both Isaiah 28:16 and Joel 3:5 point to a gleam of hope of a new life, for YHWH will intervene in their existence, and for Paul, the coming of Jesus Christ is God's way to step into Israel's history. (2) The discourse pattern of early Christian proclamation resembles these two prophetic texts: compare πᾶς ὁ πιστεύων . . . κύριον Ἰησοῦν, σωθήσῃ (cf. 10:4b, vv. 9–10) to πᾶς ὁ πιστεύων/ ἐπικαλούμενος αὐτόν . . . οὐ καταισχυνθήσεται/ σωθήσεται (cf. vv. 11–13). We should note that "to call on the Lord" is quite common in the Jewish tradition and the one on whom the Jews called for salvation was YHWH (e.g. Deut 4:7; 1 Sam 12:17–18; 2 Sam 22:4, 7; Pss 4:1; 14:4; 18:3, 6; Isa 55:6; Lam 3:57; Judg 6:21; 8:17; 9:14; *2 Macc.* 3:22, 31; 4:37; 7:37; 8:2; 12:6; *Pss. Sol.* 2:36; 9:6).[132] The pattern of calling on the Lord is also common in the early Christian community; however, here "the Lord" can both refer to God the Father and to Christ (Acts 9:14; 2 Tim 2:22; 1 Pet 1:17; Acts 9:21; 22:16; 1 Cor 1:2).[133] Here, the name that people called upon has been identified with Jesus Christ, the Lord. Therefore, Paul's hermeneutical principle is based on the coming of Jesus Christ, whose arrival denotes a new epoch. (3) It is not unusual to express the universal scope of salvation as including both Israel and the nations, for example, in Isaiah 2:2–4, 56–66; Micah 4:1–4; and Zechariah 8:18–23.[134] In other words, Paul's viewpoint on the universal

---

131. Belli responds that the new hermeneutical principle comes to Paul from the experience of the event of grace in Christ Jesus. Cf. Belli, *Argumentation and Use of Scripture in Romans 9–11*, 288.

132. Cf. Dunn, *Romans 9–16*, 610.

133. Moo, *The Epistle to the Romans*, 660.

134. See Aaron Sherwood, *Paul and the Restoration of Humanity in Light of Ancient Jewish Traditions*. AJEC. (Leiden: Brill 2013), 29–147.

scope of salvation is not without prophetic scriptural proofs. Therefore, the early Christian proclamation allies with the discourse of universal salvation implied in the two prophetic texts.

4.3.3 Thematic-organizational Meaning

From the above analysis, we can see that the three thematic formations interweave with one another: [Righteousness: Law to Christ] is further explained by [Salvation in Christ] in compatible relation; and [Salvation in Christ] is in a Dialogical relation with [Unification of Jews and Nations]: they speak of the same thing in different ways. The thesis statement in verse 4 is further demonstrated in verses 5–13. The clause τέλος ... νόμου Χριστὸς has been explained in verses 5–10: the goal of the Mosaic law is fulfilled in Christ, who will bring salvation to all that have faith in him. The clause εἰς δικαιοσύνην παντὶ τῷ πιστεύοντι has been illustrated in verses 11–13. The early Christians' proclamation [Salvation in Christ] is in alliance with [Righteousness: Law to Christ]. Therefore, Paul allies Pentateuchal texts of the law with the early Christians' proclamation of [Salvation in Christ], and also with the scriptural prophetic voice. Therefore, Paul's approach to the relationship of the law and Christ is to ally them together, and he attempts to display the fact that the alliance relies on the continuity of the Pentateuchal and prophetic texts.[135]

4.3.4 Multiple Voices: Paul's Jewish Contemporaries' Viewpoints on the Scope of Salvation

In this section, the book of Baruch and a Philonic text (*On the Virtues*), will be considered in order to perform an intertextual comparative analysis so that these Jewish texts can shed light on Paul's view of the scope of salvation in Romans 10:5–13.

Baruch is composed of three main sections: after an introduction (1:1–14), a confession of Israel's guilt and an acknowledgement of God's righteousness are described in the first main part (1:15–3:8); the second part, a poem, praises wisdom as God's special gift to Israel, and denies that

---
135. Contra Watson, who considers the antithesis between the law and the prophets, and even the law itself exists in a state of self-contradiction. See Watson, *Paul and the Hermeneutics of Faith*, 54–77.

other nations have found the key to wisdom (3:9–4:4); and the last section is a prophetic consolation, an assurance of Israel's restoration, and deliverance oracles (4:5–5:9).[136] It is known that these three parts were composed at different times, during the Second Temple Period, after the second century BC but before AD 70.[137] Our concern, however, is with the book's final form, which was completed about the time of Paul.

For the sake of space, the Baruch text appears in appendix 7, but the textual analysis is performed here, followed by an intertextual comparative reading with Romans 10:5–13. The thematic structure of the first main part of Bar 1:15–3:8, which deals with confession of sin, shares the Deuteronomic sin-exile-repentance-return pattern.[138] It starts with a contrast of God's righteousness with the shame of Israel's dispersion (1:15). It then gives the reason for Israel's failure: because they sin against God in their disobedience to the voice of God and his commandments (1:17–21). The curse then comes upon them as Moses has declared (cf. Deut 27:26; 29:20–28; 30:15–20). Interestingly, the author later on allies the voice of God with the prophet's command to serve the king of Babylon (cf. 2: 21, 24).[139] In other words, in terms of Baruch, Israel's failure relies not only on their ancestors' disobedience to the commandment of Moses in the times past, but also on their present disobedience to God's voice through the prophets. The final speech in the first section (Bar 2:27–35) expresses hope for a future beyond the curse, a passage which is like a pastiche of biblical citations from Deuteronomy, Leviticus, Ezekiel, and Jeremiah:[140] (1) the renewed relationship with God (Deut 30:1–2, 6; Lev 26:40–41; Ezek 36:11);[141] (2) the return to the Promised Land according to the promise

---

136. DeSilva, *Introducing the Apocrypha*, 198–99; see also, Watson, *Paul and the Hermeneutics of Faith*, 454–473.

137. Alison Salvesen, "Baruch," in *The Apocrypha*, ed. Martin Goodman, John Barton and John Muddiman (Oxford: Oxford University press, 2012), 113.

138. Per Jarle Bekken, *The Word Is near You: A Study of Deuteronomy 30:12–14 in Paul's Letter to the Romans in a Jewish Context*, BZNW 144, (New York: Walter de Gruyter, 2007), 171.

139. The first part is set against the background of the exiles in Babylon.

140. See Watson, *Paul and the Hermeneutics of Faith*, 461–462.

141. Bar 2:31–33: "They will know that I am the Lord their God. I will give them a heart that obeys and ears that hear; and they will praise me in the land of their exile, and will

to the patriarchs (Lev 26:42–43; Jer 30:3);[142] (3) an increase in numbers of people (Deut 30:5);[143] and (4) an everlasting covenant (Jer 31:33; Ezek 36:28).[144] This feature of Baruch's usage of Scripture is similar to Paul's style: both of them use prophetic material to reinforce "what has already been said through Moses" (cf. Rom 3:9–20, 10:5–21).[145]

The second section of Baruch (3:9–4:5) is a wisdom poem, which identifies the law with personalized Wisdom.[146] In this section the reason that Israel is exiled to the nations is because they have forsaken the fountain of wisdom (3:12). "Walking in the way of God" refers to "learning where there is wisdom, where there is strength, where there is understanding." It is this wisdom and understanding that can lead one into length of days and life (3:13–14). In other words, according to Baruch, the life that God promised through obedience to the Mosaic Torah can be fulfilled by holding to wisdom. As he indicates, "She is the book of the commandments of God, and the law that endures forever. All who hold her fast will live, and those who forsake her will die" (4:1–2). Therefore, the second feature shared between Baruch and Paul is that both of them identify the Mosaic law with something else: one with wisdom, one with Jesus Christ.[147]

The later part of the second section of Baruch (3:36–4:4) continues with the theme of wisdom, focusing on the scope of the availability of wisdom. It states that wisdom is given to "Jacob his servant and to Israel,

---

remember my name, and will turn from their stubbornness and their wicked deeds; for they will remember the ways of their fathers, who sinned before the Lord."

142. Bar 2:34a: "I will bring them again into the land which I swore to give to their fathers, to Abraham and to Isaac and to Jacob, and they will rule over it." Cf. Lev 26:42–43.

143. Bar 2:34b: "I will increase them, and they will not be diminished."

144. Bar 2:35: "I will make an everlasting covenant with them to be their God and they shall be my people; and I will never again remove my people Israel from the land which I have given them."

145. Watson, *Paul and the Hermeneutics of Faith*, 462.

146. For instance, when employing Deut 30:12–13 in Bar 3:29–30, in which the law language is replaced by the wisdom language, as Paul does with Christ in Rom 10:6–8.

147. Suggs even argues that the view that Torah is the embodiment of Wisdom paves the way for the view that Christ=Wisdom=Torah (see M. Jack. Suggs, "The Word Is near You: Romans 10:6–10 within the Purpose of the Letter," in *Christian History and Interpretation: Studies Presented to John Knox*, ed. John Knox, William Reuben Farmer and C. F. D. Moule [Cambridge: University Press, 1967]:299–312). However, it is not necessary that Paul had the book of Baruch in mind when he wrote Romans.

whom he loved" (3:37–38), and exhorts Israel to seize wisdom – "do not give your glory to another, or your advantage to an alien people (ἔθνει)" – in 4:2–4. Therefore, in Baruch, wisdom is given to Israel alone, not to the other nations. Regarding the scope of salvation (or wisdom), Baruch and Paul oppose each other.

Now let us do an intertextual comparative reading between Bar 1:15–4:4 and Romans 10:5–13. On the one hand, the two texts share similar thematic patterns. First, both of them ally law with a personalized figure (Wisdom vs. Christ); second, both texts affirm the Deuteronomic tradition of the goal of the law which points to life; third, both texts use the prophetic material to reinforce their view of the Mosaic text; and fourth, they both use a mediator to explain the law so as to show the scope of God's people. However, Paul traces back to the promise to Abraham to confirm that the Christ event will bring the Gentiles into the scope of God's people, while on the contrary, in Baruch, Wisdom is uniquely for Israel, "on the basis of the law which was given to Israel alone unlike the other nations."[148]

Therefore, Paul's opinion as to who are God's people is divergent from this example of his Jewish contemporaries' views, based on his understanding of the Christ-event (Gal 1:16: Christ revealed him to be an apostle to the Gentiles). Having examined the voice of Baruch, let us consider another Jew of the Diaspora, Philo, whose writing can also shed light on Paul's argumentation.

Philo, a Greek-speaking Jew, lived from about 20 BC to AD 50.[149] According to Scholer, "He is one of the most important Jewish authors of the Second Temple period of Judaism and was a contemporary of both Jesus and Paul."[150] Because of this, Philo's work is significant for Pauline studies. One part of Philo's works focuses on the exegesis of Moses' Pentateuch, which can be seen in the treatises *On the Creation, On Abraham, On Joseph, The Decalogue, The Special Laws, On the Virtues (Virt.)* and *On Rewards and Punishments (Praem.)*. Some passages of *Virt.* show its close connection with Romans 10:5–13. We will do some textual analysis of these Philonic

---

148. Bekken, *The Word Is near You*, 171.
149. David M. Scholer, "Forward," in *The Works of Philo: Complete and Unabridged* (Peabody: Hendrickson, 1993), ix.
150. Ibid.

passages so as to aid in our intertextual comparative reading. Helpful in this regard is a synoptic view of *Virt.* in order to discern the relevant ITFs on the basis of Romans 10:5–13.

Four virtues – courage (1–50), humanity (51–174), repentance (175–186) and nobility (187–227) – are illustrated by Philo on the basis of the Pentateuch.[151] Themes such as law-obedience, the way to join the Jewish community, the true people of God, the elaboration of Deuteronomy 30:12–14, and the pursuit of the virtue of justice (δικαιοσύνη), are closely related to the themes in Romans 10:5–13. In particular, the discourse on repentance (μετάνοια) allies the theme of Moses' law with the theme of the scope of God's people.

Philo depicts Moses' virtues of piety and righteousness through his exhorting "all people everywhere" to join the fellowship of πολιτείας.[152]

> (175) Being fond of virtue, fond of goodness, and above all fond of humanity, the most holy Moses urges all people everywhere to become followers of piety and justice, setting before those who repent (μετάνοια), as before the victorious, the great prizes of fellowship in the best of polities (πολιτείας) and enjoyment of everything in it, both great and small.[153]

This section of *On Repentance* starts with Moses' exhortation of all people to join the (Jewish) community. But who are these "all people" and in what way can they join the community? The key term μετάνοια sheds light on the answers. The word μετάνοια indicates a change or turning of some

---

151. Cf. Num 25 and 30; Deut 20, 22, and 28 (courage); Num 27 and various laws in Exodus, Leviticus, and Deuteronomy (humanity); Deuteronomy 26, 30 (repentance); and Genesis (nobility). See Bekken, *The Word Is near You*, 29, n.18.

152. According to BDAG, the term πολιτεία can contain the meanings as follow: (1) the right to be a member of a sociopolitical entity, citizenship (e.g. Act 22:28); (2) a sociopolitical unit or body of citizens, state, people, body politic (Eph 2:12); (3) behavior in accordance with standards expected of a respectable citizen, way of life, conduct. In the co-text of *On Repentance*, πολιτεία most possibly refers to a way of life. That is, Philo exhorts all people to join the Jewish community, their way of life.

153. The translation is from Walter T. Wilson, *On Virtues: Introduction, Translation, and Commentary*. PAC. (Leiden: Brill, 2011), 79.

kind.[154] In the current co-text, it is used to describe the conversion of both repentant Jews away from transgressions against the law and non-Jews towards Judaism.[155] The first and essential form of repentance is "from the worst of bad polities, ochlocracy, to that polity which is most well-ordered, democracy" (*Virt.* 180). *On the Virtues* 180–182 continues to "deal with the national and ethical conversion of the proselytes from pagan mob-rule and immorality to Jewish morality with the Jewish πολιτείας."[156] In this part, Philo provides a list of moral ethics for the proselytes who are turning from pagan society to the Jewish πολιτείας. Philo has specifically described the proselytes as "having forsaken their family by blood, their homeland, their customs, the temples and images of their gods and the gifts and honors offered to them" (*Virt.* 102). In other words, in the Philonic era, non-Jews should break with their old ways in order to convert to the Jewish community.[157] It should be noted that the opportunity for the proselytes to repent is provided only through the grace and forethought of God.[158]

On the Virtues 183–184 indicates that conversion is a change ἐξ ἀναρμοστίας εἰς ἀμείνω (from discord to harmony) by a rendering and exposition of Deuteronomy 30:11–14.

> (183) Moreover, Moses delivers to us very beautiful exhortations to repentance, by which he teaches us to alter our way of life, changing from an irregular and disorderly course into a better line of conduct; for he says that *this task is not one of any excessive difficulty, nor one removed far out of our reach, being neither above us in the air nor on the extreme borders of the sea, so that we are unable to take hold of it; but it is near us, abiding, in fact, in three portions of us, namely, in our mouths, and our hearts, and our hands; by symbols, that is to say, in our*

---

154. Wilson, *On Virtues*, 359.
155. Ibid., 359–360. Bekken observes, "It (μετάνοια) can be applied both to repenting Jews and to Gentiles who became proselytes." Bekken, *The Word Is near You*, 90.
156. Bekken, *The Word Is near You*, 91.
157. Cf. Wilson, *On Virtues*, 257–48. *Joseph and Aseneth* depicts Aseneth as repudiating not only idolatry, but also all ties and commitments associated with her previous life.
158. Wilson, *On Virtues*, 375.

words, and counsels, and actions; for the mouth is the symbol of speech, and the heart of counsels, and the hands of actions, and in these happiness consists. (184) For when such as the words are, such also is the mind; and when such as the counsels are, such likewise are the actions; then life is praiseworthy and perfect. But when these things are all at variance with one another life is imperfect and blameable, unless someone who is at the same time a lover of God and beloved by God takes it in hand and produces this harmony. For which reason this oracular declaration was given with great propriety, and in perfect accordance with what has been said above, "Thou hast this day chosen the Lord to be thy God, and the Lord has this day chosen thee to be his people."[159]

Philo allies Moses' law with the virtues: "God's command and law is that we be just, kind, beneficent, temperate, high-minded, superior to toils, superior to pleasures, free of all envy and malice."[160] When employing Deuteronomy 30:11–14, Philo changes the subject of the discourse, "this commandment," into τὸ πρᾶγμα (the thing), "so that what is now 'near' is not the law per se, but the proselyte's opportunity to convert and follow the law. Elsewhere, he takes "this commandment" as a reference to the good (*Praem.* 80; cf. *Praem.* 81) or to virtue (*Prob.* 68)."[161] Therefore, like Paul and Baruch, Philo also identifies the law with something else – the virtues, the good. For Philo, Moses' law can lead the Jews and the proselytes into the virtues.

In conclusion, like Paul in Romans 10:5–10, Philo uses Deuteronomy 30:11–14 to reinterpret who are the true people of God. However, Philo applies Deuteronomy 30:11–14 to "the conversion of Gentiles who become proselytes and join the Jewish community, i.e. the commonwealth of people living according to the laws and constitution of Moses."[162]

---

159. The italic part is Philo's adaptation of Deut 30:11–14. The translation is from http://www.earlychristianwritings.com/yonge/book31.html (accessed 14 Feb 2014).
160. Wilson, *On Virtues*, 371.
161. Wilson, *On Virtues*, 372.
162. Bekken, *The Word is Near You*, 113.

4.3.5 Conclusion

Romans 10:5–13 further elaborates the thesis statement that τέλος γὰρ νόμου Χριστὸς εἰς δικαιοσύνην παντὶ τῷ πιστεύοντι (Christ is the goal of the law for righteousness to everyone who has faith). As discussed earlier, Paul first invokes Moses' voice in Leviticus to witness that the purpose of the law is for the promise of life. And then he makes Moses' voice normative in reinterpreting Deuteronomy 30:12–14 to mean that the purpose of law for life is fulfilled in Christ. The alliance of Moses' voice with the early Christian proclamation of [Salvation in Christ] strengthens Paul's argument that Christ is the goal of the law in 10:4. With the generalized voice of the prophets Isaiah and Joel, Paul brings in another significant Christian element – the scope of salvation. Blending with the prophetic voice, Paul's own argument for the universal scope of salvation (both the Jews and the Gentiles) has been manifest in Romans 10:11–13. We also can note that the literature of Paul's Jewish contemporaries, like *Baruch* and Philo, opposes Paul's voice on the universal scope of salvation by their way of reading the Scripture. In sum, Paul marries the Mosaic texts with the prophetic texts to witness his voice on salvation, and his viewpoint on the scope of salvation is somewhat unique among his Jewish contemporaries.

4.4 Romans 10:14–21

In Romans 10:5–13, Paul allies his voice with Moses, and with the prophets Isaiah and Joel in order to illustrate that Christ is the true goal (τέλος) of the law, and that all who have faith will attain righteousness (10:4). In doing so, not only does Paul point out that the gospel he and his community proclaimed was announced beforehand in the Scriptures,[163] but he also implies a critique of his Jewish contemporaries' not accepting God's words. In this section, Paul step by step depicts his fellow Jews' resistance to the gospel as fulfilling what has been said in Deuteronomy and Isaiah about Israel's rejection of God's message. Paul finally invokes Isaiah's voice

---

163. Wagner, *Heralds of the Good News*, 180.

to sharply criticize his fellow Jews: "All day long I have held out my hands to a disobedient and contrary people" (10:21; cf. Isa 65:2).

4.4.1 Presentational Meaning

Romans 10:14–21 starts with a set of questions and answers in the form of scriptural utterance. There is a set of four parallel rhetorical questions in verses 14–15a (c17A–c17D), each beginning with the interrogative πῶς and repeating the verb from the end of one question at the start of the next.[164] The questions culminate in the necessity of sending out preachers of the good news (v. 15a, c17D). The final question in the series is supported by a scriptural formulaic projecting clause (καθὼς γέγραπται, c17Ea) with a projected clause, which is a quotation from Isaiah 52:7 (v. 15b, c17Eb): ὡς ὡραῖοι οἱ πόδες τῶν εὐαγγελιζομένων [τὰ] ἀγαθά ("How beautiful are the feet of those who preach good news"). Paul allies with the voice of Isaiah to confirm that the preachers have been sent. With an adversative conjunction, ἀλλά, he provides a statement that not "all" listen to (ὑπήκουσαν) the gospel (v. 16, c18A),[165] which again is supported by the voice of Isaiah, signaled by γάρ in the scriptural formulaic projecting clause (Ἠσαΐας γὰρ λέγει). The projected clause is a quotation from Isaiah 53:1, which is used to confirm that not all Israel believes the gospel.[166] It should be noted that the lexical chain of "preach" (εὐαγγελιζομένων), "hear" (ὑπήκουσαν), and "believe" (ἐπίστευσεν) has been repeated in reverse in verses 15b–16, corresponding to the middle part of the series of the rhetorical questions (call – **believe – hear – preach** – send).[167] Finally, signaled by ἄρα,[168] the clause-complexes (ἡ πίστις ἐξ ἀκοῆς ἡ δὲ ἀκοὴ διὰ ῥήματος Χριστοῦ) in verse 17 are in a Result relation with the previous clause-complexes (vv. 14–16). In other words, verse 17 highlights the central points of Paul's arguments (**faith – hearing – gospel**).[169] Interestingly, it also elaborates Isaiah's voice in verse 16 (τίς ἐπίστευσεν τῇ ἀκοῇ ἡμῶν;

---

164. Cf. Moo, *The Epistle to the Romans*, 663.
165. We will discuss who this "all" refers to later.
166. Cf. Dunn, *Romans 9–16*, 622–23.
167. Emphasis mine.
168. Louw 89.46, "a marker of result as an inference from what has preceded."
169. Emphasis mine.

c18Bb): the first nominal clause ἡ πίστις ἐξ ἀκοῆς (c19A, v. 17a) recapitulates the Isaianic voice of "believe what we heard"; the second paratactic extensive clause ἡ . . . ἀκοὴ διὰ ῥήματος Χριστοῦ (c19B, v. 17b) further explains the message that "we heard," that is, the word of Christ. Therefore, verse 17 is a recapitulation and also a corroboration of the Isaianic voice in verse 16. Throughout verse 14 to verse 17, one key word ἀκούω has shown up repeatedly in different forms (ἀκούω in v. 14^{x2}; ὑπακούω in v. 16a; ἀκοή in vv. 16b, 17ab). Also ἀκούω has been picked up immediately in verse 18 (c20B, ἤκουσαν). Consequently, "hear" is an interlocking point, thus a culminating concern, in verses 14–17,[170] for the key lexical term extensively introduced is about "hearing."[171] We should note that the key term has been tied together with other lexical terms regarding "belief,"[172] "gospel," or "the words of Christ"[173] In other words, Paul groups together "belief" and "gospel" in order to relate them with "hearing." This nominal group denotes christological language.[174]

[16]Ἀλλ' οὐ πάντες ὑπήκουσαν τῷ εὐαγγελίῳ. Ἡσαΐας γὰρ λέγει· κύριε, τίς ἐπίστευσεν τῇ ἀκοῇ ἡμῶν;

[17] ἄρα ἡ πίστις ἐξ ἀκοῆς, ἡ δὲ ἀκοὴ διὰ ῥήματος Χριστοῦ.

We know that "belief in the gospel" or "have faith in the gospel or the word of Christ" is a very common discourse in Christian proclamation. Here, gospel is the object of the actions (e.g. preach, believe, hear, receive, etc.). Therefore, in the lexical chain of "hearing," "belief," and "gospel," it is "belief" that corresponds to "hearing" in the sense of governing their object, "gospel." If "hearing" is a culminating concern in verses 14–17, its correspondent part, "belief," should be the corresponding culminating concern in these verses as well. This is shown by the repeated combinations

---

170. Contra Wagner, *Heralds of the Good News*, 170. Wagner sets the culminating point in preaching, "culminating in the necessity for preachers to be sent out with the good news."
171. "Hearing" is denoted by double underlining in the following chart.
172. "Belief" is signaled by single underlining.
173. They are denoted by thick underlining.
174. Cf. Belli, *Argumentation and Use of Scripture in Romans 9–11*, 291.

of these throughout verses 14–17: πῶς . . . πιστεύσωσιν οὗ οὐκ ἤκουσαν; (v. 14), τίς ἐπίστευσεν τῇ ἀκοῇ ἡμῶν; (v. 16), ἡ πίστις ἐξ ἀκοῆς (v. 17).[175]

Therefore, the main concern of verses 14–17 is that Paul exhorts Israel to *hear* the message of the gospel of Christ, which implies that this message is a prophetic message from God.[176] However, the Israelites refuse to accept it, because they do not believe the gospel.[177] We will label this thematic formation as [Disbelief of the Gospel]. The structural pattern of the thematic formation is: a set continuity of rhetorical questions (vv. 14–15a) + Isaianic Scripture (v. 15b) + a statement of Israel's disobedience (v. 16a) + Isaianic Scripture (v. 16b) + a further interpretation note (v. 17). The second half of this semantic pattern is similar to Paul's application of Deuteronomy 30:11–14 in Romans 10:6–8, particularly Deuteronomy 30:14 in Romans 10:8; both of them quote a piece of Scripture and then provide a further explanation by adding the christological message to the key word. This is demonstrated in the subsequent chart:[178]

Verse no.	The scriptural texts	Pauline note
10:16b–17	Ἡσαΐας γὰρ λέγει· κύριε, τίς ἐπίστευσεν τῇ ἀκοῇ ἡμῶν;	ἄρα ἡ πίστις ἐξ ἀκοῆς, ἡ δὲ ἀκοὴ διὰ ῥήματος Χριστοῦ
10:8	ἀλλὰ τί λέγει; ἐγγύς σου τὸ ῥῆμά ἐστιν ἐν τῷ στόματί σου καὶ ἐν τῇ καρδίᾳ σου,	τοῦτ' ἔστιν τὸ ῥῆμα τῆς πίστεως ὃ κηρύσσομεν

Another item to note is the participant references in this formation. The verbal forms in the texts (vv. 14–17) are all third person plural. In

---

175. Italics mine. It seems that Paul exhorts Israel to hear, because this is the word of the Lord. Cf. Deut 6:4–5: "Hear, O Israel: the Lord our God, the Lord is one. You shall love the Lord your God with all your heart and with all your soul and with all your might." (ESV)

176. Italics mine.

177. In the later intertextual part, we will show that the author of *Wisdom* exhorts the pagan kings (who are representative of the Gentiles) to hear Wisdom or Jewish law (cf. *Wisdom*, chs. 1 and 6).

178. The double underlining and single underlining denote the repeating elements in the scriptural texts and Pauline note; the italics in 10:17 and 8 shows the shared christological message, which appears in Pauline note of 10:8 as well.

other words, the main participant references have been implied as a "they," but to whom does "they" refer? Some scholars consider "they" to have a general reference, including Israel and the Gentiles;[179] other scholars argue that it refers solely to Israel.[180] It is more likely that "they" refers to an indeterminate people, including the Jews and Greeks (cf. v. 12). There are at least two reasons for this. First, the catchword ἐπικαλέομαι in verse 14 is a point of contact with the previous verse, verse 13, which quotes Joel 3:5 and in which πᾶς is understood by Paul as both Jews and Greeks. In other words, it is more likely that "they" refers to the Jews and the Gentiles in the mind of Paul.[181] Second, Paul's modifications of Isaiah 52:7 demonstrate his viewpoint that the subject here includes Jews as well as Gentiles. As Wagner rightly observes, "He [Paul] omits the phrase 'on the mountains,' a specific reference to the area surrounding Jerusalem. Paul's elimination of any reference to Zion allows him to apply the quotation to the broader geographical scope of Christian proclamation, which includes Gentiles as well as Jews."[182] However, with the adversative conjunction ἀλλά in verse 16, the participant reference seems to narrow down to Israel. This suggests that the gospel has been proclaimed to both Israel and the Gentiles, but not all of them have accepted the gospel. Those who did not accept the gospel probably refers to Israel (v. 16). In other words, Paul criticizes his Jewish contemporaries who refuse to believe the gospel that he and the first Christians proclaimed. However, to put Paul's prayer for his kinsmen early on (10:1) into perspective, it should be noted that, "if Paul sharply criticizes his fellow Jews, he does so not as an outsider slinging mud, but as a prophet, wounding that he may heal."[183]

---

179. Belli, *Argumentation and Use of Scripture in Romans 9–11*, 96–97. Belli takes the third person plural subjects of the verbs in this part as indeterminate, including Jews and Greek, Israel and Gentiles.

180. Cf. Moo, *The Epistle to the Romans*, 662; Cranfield, *Romans*, 553, etc.

181. Moo has argued that the last use of the third person plural verbs is in 10:2–3, where Paul indicts Israel for their ignorance of God's righteousness; vv. 14–21 continue that indictment, "as Paul removes any possible excuse that the Jews might have for their failure to respond to God's offer of righteousness in Christ." See Moo, *The Epistle to the Romans*, 662. However, Paul's critique of Israel's unbelief starts with v. 16; in vv. 14–15, he analyzes the conditions for people to call upon the Lord.

182. For more modifications, see Wagner, *Heralds of the Good News*, 173.

183. Wagner, *Heralds of the Good News*, 178.

It is worthy of note that the image of the preachers that has been given in verse 15 may refer to Paul and the first Jewish Christian preachers. The catchword κηρύσσω in verse 15 makes it connect with verse 8, τὸ ῥῆμα τῆς πίστεως ὃ κηρύσσομεν (the "we" here refers to Paul and the first Christians). Also, the word ἀποστέλλω (v. 15) could link with Paul's self-identification as ἀπόστολος ἀφωρισμένος εἰς εὐαγγέλιον θεου in Romans 1:1. Paul is attempting to identify the εὐαγγελιζόμενος ἀγαθά in Isaiah 52:7 with the εὐαγγέλιον θεου, that is, ῥήματος Χριστοῦ (the word of Christ) in verse 16. In other words, Paul sees his proclamation of the gospel prefigured in Isaiah 52:7.[184] As Evans observes, "Paul's understanding of the apostolic obligation to proclaim the gospel is informed by the prophetic voice of Second Isaiah: "And how can men preach unless they are sent? As it is written, 'How beautiful are the feet of those who preach good news' " (Rom 10:14–17; cf. Isa 52:7; 53:1).[185]

If in verses 14–17, Paul constructs a thematic formation of [Disbelief of Gospel: Israel], then he continues to display Israel's refusal of God's word in the pair of negative rhetorical questions (v. 18 and v. 19): ἀλλὰ λέγω + negative rhetorical question + scriptural quotation.[186] Both verse 18 and verse 19 share this similar composition with each other. The parallel projecting introductory formulas (ἀλλὰ λέγω) bring in the parallel negative rhetorical questions (μὴ οὐκ ἤκουσαν; and μὴ Ἰσραὴλ οὐκ ἔγνω;). That is, they heard (ἤκουσαν) the words of Christ and they know (Ἰσραὴλ ἔγνω) God's plan for the Gentiles, but they still disobeyed the messages. It should be noted that the first person singular "I," referring to Paul himself, has been added as one of the main participant references in verses 18–19. In light of the new participant references and the specific pattern of the negative rhetorical question in verses 18–21, we can view this part as a new thematic formation, which can be labeled as [Israel's Disobedience: Refusal even Having Heard and Known] (henceforth [Disobedience]).

The first part of [Disobedience] addresses the idea that Israel has already heard of the word (of the gospel) by juxtaposing the voice of the psalmist

---

184. See Wagner, *Heralds of the Good News*, 173–174. Cf. John 12:37–38.
185. Evans, "Paul and the Prophets," 120.
186. Cf. Belli, *Argumentation and Use of Scripture in Romans 9–11*, 308.

in Psalm 18:5 (LXX) to prove that Israel has heard (v. 18). The catchword ῥήματα in Psalm 18:5 would refer to the word of the law. However, Paul reconnects Psalm 18:5 with the Christian proclamation; the two occurrences of the nominal phrases (ὁ φθόγγος αὐτῶν and τὰ ῥήματα αὐτῶν), in Paul's mind, share similar semantic meanings with that of τὸ ῥῆμα τῆς πίστεως (v. 8), εὐαγγελιζομένων (v. 15b), εὐαγγέλιον (v. 16a), and ῥήματος Χριστοῦ (v. 17).[187] The second part of [Disobedience] concentrates on the fact that Israel already knows that the scope of salvation extends to the nations, supported by the voices of Moses and Isaiah (vv. 19–20). Resuming the projecting clause ἀλλὰ λέγω as in verse 18, Paul goes a step further to ask whether Israel ἔγνω, since they had already heard the word of the gospel. The negative rhetorical question itself implies a positive answer that Israel has "known." Paul then speaks through the voices of Moses and Isaiah to testify that the inclusion of the nations has been part of God's plan. The use of πρῶτος suggests that Moses is the first or the early witness, and thus the δὲ in verse 20 marks an Additive relation, suggesting Isaiah is also the witness. Paul has a tendency to ally the voices of Moses and Isaiah to testify with his voice against Israel (Rom 10:6–13, 11:8; cf. Rom 3: 21: μαρτυρουμένη ὑπὸ τοῦ νόμου καὶ τῶν προφητῶν),[188] for it is vital for him that the gospel he preaches has been embraced by the prominent figures, Moses and Isaiah. It should be noted that Moses has been identified as the greatest of the prophets in Deuteronomy: "Moses is both model for any future prophet (18:15, 18) and the greatest of all prophets (34:10–12)."[189] Paul probably considers both Moses and Isaiah as key representatives of the prophetic role in the history of Israel and identifies himself with them. *Tg. Neof.* (Deut 32:1) considers "the role of Moses and Isaiah as witnesses against Israel: Two prophets arose to testify against Israel, Moses the

---

187. Belli, *Argumentation and Use of Scripture in Romans 9–11*, 311, Wagner, *Heralds of the Good News*, 185.

188. This alliance has further been strengthened in Rom 11:8, where Paul conflates the voices of Deut 29:3 and Isa 29:10 without any comment. See also Michel Quesnel, "La figure de Moïse en Romains 9–11," *NTS* 49 (2003):331–333. Quesnel sees different roles that Moses has taken; and he argues that in Rom 10:19–21, Moses takes a prophetic role as Isaiah.

189. Patrick Miller, "'Moses My Servant': The Deuteronomic Portrait of Moses," *Int* 41 (1987):248.

prophet and Isaiah the prophet. . . . And the two of them, because they feared the holy Name, arose to testify against Israel."[190] Therefore, Paul's voice against Israel has been foretold, not only in Moses, but also in Isaiah, who bears witness to the same truth in regard to Israel. The final part of [Disobedience] (v. 21) is Paul's explicit critique of Israel's disobedience through the voice of the prophet Isaiah in Isaiah 65:2, "All day long I have held out my hands to a disobedient and contrary people." Here Israel is modified by two verbal participles containing a negative tone of value – ἀπειθοῦντα καὶ ἀντιλέγοντα.[191]

In sum, Paul criticizes Israel's unbelief of the gospel that "Jesus is Lord and has been raised from the dead" (cf. Rom 10:9–10) and their disobedience to God in refusing to believe that the scope of salvation includes the Gentiles as well. Paul's critiques are based on the voices of Isaiah, the psalmist, and Moses. In particular, he allies the voices of Moses and Isaiah to argue against Israel's disobedience. Paul probably considers himself to be in the same prophetic tradition as Moses and Isaiah in sending God's message to Israel.

4.4.2 Scriptural Voices

In Romans 10:14–21, several scriptural texts have been employed: Isaiah 52:7; 53:1; Psalm 18:5; Deuteronomy 32:21; and Isaiah 65:1–2. Let us investigate them in their own co-texts and then consider how Paul's voice interacts with these other scriptural voices.

The first text is from Isaiah 52:7,[192] whose co-text, Isaiah 52:1–12, is about God's promise to restore the Holy City, Jerusalem. Isaiah 52:1–6 is YHWH's promise to Israel that once Israel has been oppressed and exploited by foreigners, they will be redeemed.[193] Isaiah 52:7–10 is a proc-

---

190. For the translations see Wagner, *Heralds of the Good News*, 189, n. 206.
191. The term ἀπειθέω has a key role in Paul's analysis of Israel's failure as the opposite of ὑποτάσσω (10:3) and ὑπακούω (10:16), and it stands in opposition to the πιστεύω and ὁμολογέω which the word of faith evokes (10:8–10:14). See Dunn, *Romans 9–16*, 627.
192. Paul quotes them in reference to the proclamation of the gospel. See Aernie, *Paul among the Prophets*, 137.
193. Isa 52:1, the uncircumcised and the unclean will not be allowed in the Holy City, Jerusalem; vv. 3–6, YHWH said that Israel shall be redeemed and in a purified city; Israel will come to know its God.

lamation that "God has forgiven his people and announces his imminent salvation to the exiles languishing in Babylonian captivity."[194] The good news in verse 7 refers to God's breaking into history to bring Israel back to Jerusalem, that is, God's sovereign rule.[195] Watts has similar comments on the content of the good news: "Peace, goodness, and salvation, Your God reigns! In historical context this means that Darius, Yahweh's protégé, has firmly grasped the reins of power. Peace has returned to the empire and so to Jerusalem."[196] Verse 8 is a call to joy because of the return of YHWH to Zion. Verses 9–10 "invite all Jerusalem to sing a song of praise because God has comforted his people (cf. 40:1) and all the world will see his salvation."[197] Therefore, the good news in Isaiah 52:7 consists of God's salvation of the captive Jerusalem. However, in Romans 10:15, Paul leaves out the phrases ἐπὶ τῶν ὀρέων ("on the mountain") and εὐαγγελιζομένου ἀκοὴν εἰρήνης "(preaching the gospel of peace")", elements which indicate the specific situation of Israel on the mountain of Jerusalem at the time of the Babylonian captivity. By omitting the situational elements of the proclamation of good news in its Isaianic co-text, the tone of the projected clause has been transformed into a more generalized one. This is also evinced in the general formulaic introduction, the projecting clause καθὼς γέγραπται ("as it is written").[198] Therefore, Paul's voice reframes the prophetic voice of Isaiah so as to emphasize the general truth – the normative truth – that the good news has been preached.

The second quoted text, Isaiah 53:1, is part of the fourth servant song (Isa 52:13–53:12).[199] The two divine speeches (52:13–15 and 53:11b–12) frame the confession speech of the "we" in the middle.[200] According to Childs, "the confessing 'we' of the Old Testament is always Israel and not

---

194. Childs, *Isaiah*, 406.
195. Ibid.
196. John D. W. Watts, *Isaiah 34–66* (Waco: Word, 1987), 217.
197. Childs, *Isaiah*, 406.
198. We should note that Paul does not use a formulaic introduction here, such as "Isaiah says."
199. Isa 53:1, those messengers ("we") probably refers back the same messengers in 52:7–10, since "the arm of YHWH" has appeared in both texts. See Watts, *Isaiah 34–66*, 230.
200. Childs, *Isaiah*, 411.

the nations (Hos 6:1ff; Jer 3:21ff; Dan 9:4ff, etc.)."[201] The divine speech in 52:13 begins with the servant's exaltation and then "describes the astonishment and confusion that the figure of the servant evokes."[202] Verse 15 particularly points out that, because of this figure, many nations and kings will see and understand: "What they were not told, they will see, and what they have not heard, they will understand" (52:15). Then Isaiah 53:1 is oriented towards Israel, "Who has believed what we have heard? And to whom has the arm of the LORD been revealed?" Two groups within Israel are implied in this rhetorical question: one represents those who hear and proclaim the divine revelation; the other consists of those who do not believe the proclamation. Childs has observed, "The response to the servant would divide the people of Israel into two groups, those who believe and those who oppose."[203] Therefore, Isaiah 52:15—53:1 constructs a pair of contrasts: the seeing and understanding of nations and kings in contrast with the unbelief of Israel.[204] Also, Isaiah 53:2–11 is the narrative of the suffering servant, which was applied to Jesus Christ in the early Christian community (cf. Acts 8:32–36).[205] Actually, this formation is similar to Paul's formation of righteousness: Gentiles who did not pursue righteousness have attained it, and Israel who pursued righteousness failed to attain it (Rom 9:30–31). Their failure is because they stumbled over the stumbling stone, Jesus Christ, the suffering servant.

Therefore, the co-text of Isaiah 53:1 corresponds with Paul's discussion of Israel's unbelief in Romans 10. Lexicogrammatically, the projecting formulaic introductory in Romans 10:16 preserves the prophet's name Isaiah (Ἠσαΐας . . . λέγει), allowing Isaiah to speak in his own voice.[206] It suggests that Paul allies with Isaiah's voice in his critique of Israel's unbelief. At this

---

201. Ibid., 413.
202. Ibid., 412.
203. Ibid., 414.
204. It contrasts with *Wisdom*'s view of the nations and the kings. *Wisdom* 1 and 6 appeal to the kings of the nations to hear and understand Wisdom or the law, but those pagan kings failed.
205. The discussion of Isaiah 53 in the New Testament is complicated. See all the articles in the book, Bernd Janowski and Peter Stuhlmacher, eds., *The Suffering Servant: Isaiah 53 in Jewish and Christian Sources* (Grand Rapids: Eerdmans, 2004).
206. Wagner, *Heralds of the Good News*, 179.

point, Isaiah's voice is Paul's voice; Paul's voice about contemporary Israel does not differ from Isaiah's about his contemporaries.

It is beneficial to turn to Psalm 18:5 LXX. Psalm 18 can be divided into four sections: "space and time (vv. 1–5a); the sun (vv. 5b–7); the law (vv. 8–11); and an examination of conscience and the final request (vv. 12–15)."[207] The first two sections are about God's created natural world (part one), and the last two about the human rational and moral life (part two). In part one, the inanimate beings – like the heavens, day, or light – have been personified in order that they can tell, proclaim, declare, pour forth speech, and declare knowledge, etc. In this co-text, their voice and their words (18:5a) refer to the voices of the inanimate beings, not Christian preachers. In part 2, YHWH's teaching refers to the law (the Torah), for the following four near-synonyms can all embrace the meaning of the teaching as YHWH's instruction (vv. 18:8–10): ὁ νόμος τοῦ κυρίου (v. 8), τὰ δικαιώματα κυρίου (v. 9), ἡ ἐντολὴ κυρίου (v. 9), and τὰ κρίματα κυρίου (v. 10).[208] The psalmist allies the creation of the world with the revelation of the law. The law as the guiding principle in life harmonizes with the order of the universe.[209] Therefore, the psalmist's voice of proclamation is concerned with God's created world. However, Paul reconnects them with the Christian proclamation of Christ. The two occurrences of nominal phrases, ὁ φθόγγος αὐτῶν and τὰ ῥήματα αὐτῶν, refer to the Christian proclamation: that of the εὐαγγελιζομένων (Rom 10:15b), the εὐαγγέλιον (v. 16a), the ἀκοή ἡμῶν (v. 16b), and the ῥῆμα Χριστοῦ (v. 17).[210] Therefore, Paul hijacks the psalmist's voice to make it his own.[211] It is interesting that this quotation enters without any projecting formulaic introductory (e.g. "David says"). This may suggest that Paul attempts to

---

207. Konrad Schaefer and David W. Cotter, *Psalms* (Collegeville: Liturgical, 2001), 45.
208. Cf. John Goldingay, *Psalms*, 3 vols. (Grand Rapids: Baker Academic, 2006), 1:290–291.
209. Schaefer and Cotter, *Psalms*, 46–47.
210. Belli, *Argumentation and Use of Scripture in Romans 9–11*, 311; Wagner, *Heralds of the Good News*, 185.
211. Contra Wagner, *Heralds of the Good News*, 185. Wagner considers that Ps 18:5 (God as creator) grounds Paul's affirmation "both of the inscrutable wisdom of God's plan to redeem his people and of the incomparable power of God to effect their deliverance."

blur the psalmist's voice with his own by intentionally leaving out the projecting formulaic introductory clause.

A brief investigation of Deuteronomy 32:21 and Isaiah 65:1–2, which Paul employs in Romans 10:19–21, offers important insights. Deuteronomy 32:1–43, the Song of Moses, is like a summary of Israel's history.[212] Here are the stanzas for the song, which show the relationship of YHWH and Israel throughout history:[213]

1–3	Opening declaration, call of witnesses
4–9	YHWH's faithfulness, Israel's unfaithfulness
10–14	Elaboration of YHWH's care for Israel
15–18	Israel's apostasy
19–25	YHWH's decision to judge them
26–35	He relents, because of their folly
36–43	He will finally vindicate himself, and save his people

The above structure briefly summarizes the history of YHWH and Israel: God's faithfulness and care for Israel, Israel's apostasy, God's judgment or punishment of Israel, and finally God's restoration of them because of his mercy. Deuteronomy 32:21 is in the co-text of Israel's apostasy and God's punishment. Verse 21ab indicates Israel's apostasy in terms of their idol-worship that angers God (αὐτοὶ παρεζήλωσάν με ἐπ' οὐ θεῷ παρώργισάν με ἐν τοῖς εἰδώλοις αὐτῶν; "they provoked me with no-god and angered me with their idols"). Verse 21cd, the part that Romans 10:19 quotes, is God's corresponding response to them, God's punishment of Israel (cf. Deut 32:21c–25): they are provoked to jealousy through their defeat by "no-nation" (the Gentiles). Then in the next section (v. 26ff), the theme turns to the judgment of Israel's enemies and salvation for Israel.

In Romans 10:19, Paul explicitly identifies the voice of Moses in the projecting formulaic introductory clause (Μωϋσῆς λέγει) and follows the

---

212. Herbert W. Basser, *Midrashic Interpretations of the Song of Moses*, American University Studies 2, (New York: Peter Lang, 1984), 4.
213. The divisions are from McConville. See McConville, *Deuteronomy*, 451.

wording of Deuteronomy 32:21cd closely, except the change of the person pronoun from αὐτοὺς to ὑμᾶς. It suggests that Paul allies his voice with that of Moses; their voices concerning the salvation of Israel do not differ from each other. However, Paul particularly emphasizes the role of the no-nation in the salvation of Israel by their provoking God's people to jealousy. Therefore, he considers the catch word "no-nation" a prophecy of the mission to the Gentiles: "The inclusion of Gentiles in the new people of God stimulates the Jews to jealousy and causes Israel to respond in wrath against this movement in salvation history."[214] We should note that the expression of a no-nation recalls Romans 9:25–26, where Paul quotes the Hosea prophecy about those "not my people" becoming the people of God.

The prophet Isaiah's voice, marrying with that of Moses, witnesses to the appropriateness of Paul's critique of Israel's disobedience. Isaiah 65 basically can be divided into two parts: the first section concerns the fact that although YHWH is available for Israel, their unresponsiveness brings judgment, the judgment on the apostates (vv. 1–16); and the second part "announces a radically new vision of the future," that is, "a new world order different in kind from the past."[215] Isaiah 65:1 indicates that God lets himself be available for unresponsive Israel. God is there, waiting to be found by those who do not seek him; he is present to be called upon. While the prophet stresses God's faithfulness to his disobedient people, Israel, he criticizes Israel's refusal to seek God and instead to choose to pursue foreign cults. This critique is obvious in verses 2–5 which depicts Israel "walking in evil ways, provoking me continually, sacrificing in gardens, burning incense on tiles, sitting in tombs, spending the night in secret places, and eating swine's flesh."[216] According to Childs, "These forbidden practices often reflect illicit cultic rules known from Ugarit, Babylon, and elsewhere."[217] God's judgment on these apostates follows, "I will repay into their bosom," and "I will measure full recompense into their bosoms for their former deeds" (vv. 6–7). In verses 8–16, the description turns to the

---

214. Moo, *The Epistle to the Romans*, 668.
215. Childs, *Isaiah*, 537.
216. Ibid., 535.
217. Ibid.

contrast between the apostates and the servants. After a divine oracle in verse 8 ("Thus says the Lord"), the speech turns to the servants first (vv. 8–10), who are "offspring from Jacob," "heirs to my mountains," and "my chosen people." The servants are God's people who seek him (evoking v. 1), and God assures them of salvation ("not destroy," "inherit the mountain," "dwell there," "a place to lie down," etc.). Verses 11–12 pick up the theme of the apostates, who forsook rather than sought YHWH.[218] This is followed by the sharp contrast of blessings and curses which are allocated to the faithful servants and the apostates.[219] After judgment on unresponsive Israel (vv. 1–7), and the blessings and cursing of the servants and the apostates (vv. 8–16), there comes a new order for the new world in part two (vv. 17–25). Verse 23 summarizes the eschatological hope: "They shall be offspring blessed by the Lord and their descendants as well." Verse 24 once again invokes verse 1 by the repetition of the theme of God's accessibility to those who call and speak. Therefore, the overall thematic patterns of Isaiah 65 somewhat repeat Deuteronomy 32: Israel's apostasy, God's blessing on the seeker and judgment on the apostates, and God's restoration of them to a new order of the world.[220]

In Romans 10: 20–21, Paul bisects the quotation of Isaiah 65:1–2 into two parts with two projecting introductory formulas at the beginning of each verse. The explicit pointing out of the voice of Isaiah (Ἡσαΐας δὲ ἀποτολμᾷ . . . λέγει, v. 20) indicates that Paul allows Isaiah to speak through his own voice. The projected clauses in verses 20–21 are quoted from part of Isaiah 65:1–2, and the quotations are close to Isaiah's own wording, except for the positions of some words, as indicated in the following chart:[221]

---

218. Childs, *Isaiah*, 536; Walter Brueggemann, *Isaiah 40–66*. 2 vols. WestBC. (Louisville: Westminster John Knox, 1998), 2:242–243.
219. See also Childs, *Isaiah*, 536–537.
220. Besides the thematic connections between Deut 32 and Isa 65, there are also lexical links between them, particularly on the theme of Israel's idol-worship. For example, ὁ λαὸς οὗτος ὁ παροξύνων με ("this people who provoke me"); θυσιάζουσιν . . . τοῖς δαιμονίοις ("sacrifice to the demon"); ἃ οὐκ ἔστιν ("who is not God"); see also Deut 32:16, 19, 21. Cf. Wagner, *Heralds of the Good News*, 202.
221. The underlined parts in both columns show the wordings they share; the italicized and the bolded phrases indicate positions which have been moved. We should note that Paul at first leaves out the clause that related to the term ἔθνος in Isa 65:1 (I said, Behold, I am here, to *a nation*, who called not on my name), in which context it is synonymous

Isaiah 65:1–2 LXX	Romans 10:20–21
¹ **ἐμφανὴς ἐγενόμην** τοῖς ἐμὲ μὴ ζητοῦσιν εὑρέθην τοῖς ἐμὲ μὴ ἐπερωτῶσιν εἶπα ἰδού εἰμι τῷ ἔθνει οἳ οὐκ ἐκάλεσάν μου τὸ ὄνομα ² ἐξεπέτασα τὰς χεῖράς μου **ὅλην τὴν ἡμέραν** πρὸς λαὸν ἀπειθοῦντα καὶ ἀντιλέγοντα οἳ οὐκ ἐπορεύθησαν ὁδῷ ἀληθινῇ ἀλλ' ὀπίσω τῶν ἁμαρτιῶν αὐτῶν	²⁰ εὑρέθην [ἐν] τοῖς ἐμὲ μὴ ζητοῦσιν, **ἐμφανὴς ἐγενόμην** τοῖς ἐμὲ μὴ ἐπερωτῶσιν. ²¹ **ὅλην τὴν ἡμέραν** ἐξεπέτασα τὰς χεῖράς μου πρὸς λαὸν ἀπειθοῦντα καὶ ἀντιλέγοντα.

These suggest that Paul is attempting to preserve Isaiah's voice and its situational context in Isaiah 65. If we briefly look at Romans 11 together with Romans 10, we can see that the thematic patterns in Romans 10–11 resemble those of Isaiah 65: the critique of Israel's sin (Rom 10:18–21); the contrast of two groups in Israel (the chosen and the remaining, cf. Romans 11:7), which corresponds to the two groups in Isaiah 65 (the servants/chosen and the apostates); the judgment on the remaining (Rom 11:8–10); and finally the restoration of the whole, both Israel and the Gentiles. Moreover, Isaiah 65:1–7 speaks of Israel's sin of unresponsiveness to God, which, for Paul, is the same sin committed by his contemporaries; they hear and they know, but they do not respond to or accept the gospel (Rom 10:18–21). Therefore, in general, Paul allies with the voice of Isaiah in terms of the process of salvation.

However, there are some nuances in Paul's application of Isaiah 65:1. The prophet blames those in Israel who do not seek God and praises people who seek God for the promise of rewards (Isa 65:1, 10). On the contrary, Paul values these people who did not seek God through the law, and associates these people (identified with Israel in Isaiah 65:1) with the Gentiles.[222] In other words, Paul identifies Israel's current sin of not including the Gentiles in God's plan of salvation with Israel's past sin of not seeking or

---

with the term λαός – Israel. Cf. Wagner has a similar chart, see Wagner, *Heralds of the Good News*, 207.

222. Wagner has rightly pointed out that Paul transforms 65:1 from a declaration of condemnation for Israel into a proclamation of salvation for Gentiles. See Wagner, *Heralds of the Good News*, 211.

answering God's calling. This type of identification, linking Israel's sin of exclusiveness with Israel's disobedience to God, was an alien concept to non-Christian Jews in the early first century of Jewish society, but Paul repeats this semantic relation through Romans 9–11. Therefore, Paul and his community's voice in understanding Israel's sin to be their belief in the exclusion of the Gentiles from salvation was unique. In addition, Paul marries Moses' voice in Deuteronomy 32 with Isaiah's in Isaiah 65:1 as he mixes these two prophets' voices together in Romans 11:8. In other words, Paul carries the voice of Moses into Isaiah's in Romans 10:20, which identifies those who did not seek God as the Gentiles instead of Israel.

In sum, several scriptural voices exist together with Paul's dominant voice concerning the Jews, the Gentiles, and their sin in Romans 10:14–21. These are the explicit voices of Moses and Isaiah, which Paul indicates ally with his own voice concerning Israel's apostasy. However, Paul identifies Israel's apostasy as idolatry, based on their exclusion of the Gentiles from the economy of salvation. This perception of Israel's sin was new in first-century Jewish communities. From the above analysis, it can be seen that Paul allies himself as a prophet in line with the prototypical prophet, Moses, who testifies against Israel's sin.

4.4.3 Thematic-organizational Meaning

From the previous presentational analysis, we can see that there are two specific-text thematic formations: [Disbelief] and [Disobedience] in Romans 10:14–21. They are in a Complementarity relationship in order to express two aspects of Israel's failure in receiving God's message to them. In [Disbelief], Paul points out that, although Israel has heard the message of the gospel, they have not believed it; then Paul further indicates that Israel refuses to acknowledge that the scope of salvation shall be extended to the Gentiles, as has already been prophesied in Moses and Isaiah. These two aspects actually correspond to the previous section, verses 9–13, which also focuses on the early Christian proclamation (vv. 9–10) and the scope of salvation (vv. 11–13).

However, how does Paul arrive at the confirmation of Israel's disbelief and disobedience? This may be viewed through his way of reading the

Scriptures. Here are the intertextual links that Paul has made in Romans 10:14–21:

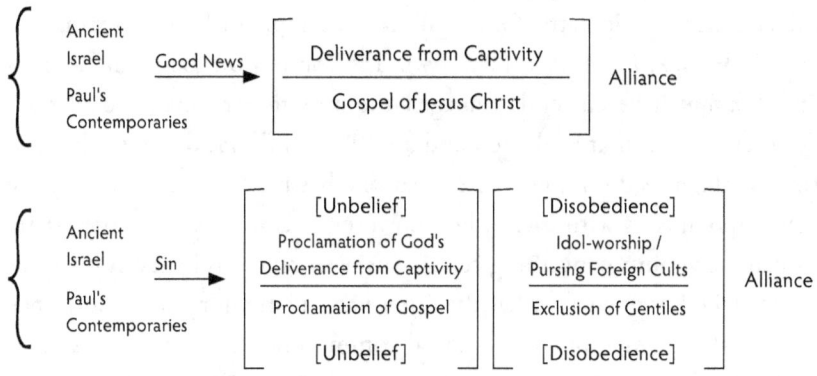

In sum, Paul re-contextualizes the Scriptures and allies the good news of deliverance from captivity as the good news of Jesus Christ. He also links ancient Israel's disbelief of the proclamation of deliverance with the proclamation of the gospel. Moreover, ancient Israel's idol-worship is again allied with Paul's Jewish contemporaries' exclusion of the Gentiles as people of God. This new pattern of constructing the discourse relations suggests a new meaning-making practice in first-century Jewish society.

4.4.4 Multiple Voices: Paul's Jewish Contemporaries' Viewpoints Concerning Israel's Sin in Relation to the Gentiles

Paul's voice in Romans 10:14–21 attempts to point out the disobedience or apostasy of Israel in the domain of Jewish-Gentile relationships. Paul indicates that Israel has heard the message of the gospel, but they have not believed it (vv. 14–17); they hear and know that God has extended the scope of salvation to the Gentiles, but they refuse to acknowledge this. Therefore, Paul allies himself with the voices of Moses and Isaiah in order to criticize Israel's sin of disbelief and disobedience to God's word. As we have mentioned, Moses' and Isaiah's critiques of Israel are due to Israel's idol-worship of no-gods in the pagan world; therefore, from Paul's viewpoint, Israel's disbelief and disobedience to the gospel is the same sin as their idolatry in the past.

Now let us consider Paul's Jewish contemporaries' viewpoints on Israel, the Gentiles, and idolatry. One significant example of Jewish literature in view is *Wisdom of Solomon* (*Wisdom*). The connections between Romans and *Wisdom* have currently engaged the attention of many scholars.[223] Some even argue that Paul knew and used *Wisdom*.[224] However, the linguistic resemblances do not guarantee that one has used the other. If they are contemporaneous with each other, however, it is possible that they share similar viewpoints concerning certain social or religious issues. It does not matter whether one writer has the other particularly in mind or not; since they lived in contemporaneous social communities, their ideas on similar topics can be considered within an intertextual reading in order to demonstrate social heteroglossic voices. We will employ the relevant parts of *Wisdom* in a synoptic reading with Romans 10:14–21 so as to consider the heteroglossic thematic relations in the two texts and their attitudes toward the issue of Israel in the context of other nations and their cultic culture. Before we do an intertextual reading of Romans 10:14–21 and *Wisdom*, let us divide the structure of *Wisdom* first. There is some disagreement about

---

223. John M. G. Barclay, "Unnerving Grace: Approaching Romans 9–11 from the Wisdom of Solomon," in *Between Gospel and Election: Explorations in the Interpretation of Romans 9–11*, edited by Florian Wilk, J. Ross Wagner and Frank Schleritt, (Tübingen: Mohr Siebeck, 2010), 91–109; Linebaugh (Barclay's doctoral student), *God, Grace, and Righteousness*; Campbell, *Deliverance of God*, 360–362; Watson, *Paul and the Hermeneutics of Faith*, 380–411; B. R. Gaventa, "The Rhetoric of Death in the Wisdom of Solomon and the Letters of Paul," in *The Listening Heart: Essays in Wisdom and the Psalms in Honor of Roland E. Murphy*, ed. Kenneth G. Hoglund and Roland E. Murphy (Sheffield: JSOT Press, 1987), 127–145. Some commentaries, e.g. Sanday and Headlam, *Romans*, 268–269; Anders Nygren, *Commentary on Romans*, trans. Carl C. Rasmussen (London: SCM, 1952), 114–116; Moo, *The Epistle to the Romans*, 133, etc. Note that Eduard Grafe is one of the earliest scholars who noticed the overlapping between *Wisdom* and parts of the Pauline letters. See E. Grafe, "Das Verhältniss der paulinischen Schriften zur Sapientia Salmonis," in *Theologische Abhandlungen*, ed. Adolf von Harnack (Freiburg: J. C. B. Mohr, 1892).

224. The corresponding parts between Romans and *Wisdom* have been argued as follows: Rom 1:18–32 and Wis 13–14 (Grafe, Sanday and Headlam, Nygren, Campbell); Rom 2 and Wis 11–15 (Nygren argues that Paul in Rom 2 attacks *Wisdom*'s presumption that the divine wrath is restricted to Gentiles because they are idolatrous and immoral, see Nygren and Rasmussen, *Commentary on Romans*, 115–16); Rom 9:5–29 with Wis 12:2, 3–18, and 15:7 (Campbell); Rom 7:7–11 and Wis 16–19 (Watson); Rom 9–11 and *Wisdom* (Barclay, "Unnerving Grace," 91–109).

where to locate breaks. For example, chapters 6 and 10 serve as contact points in "rounding off one section as they introduce the next."[225] However, a general consensus of the structure is as follows:

> Chs. 1–5/6: The role of wisdom in human destiny, comparing the fate of the righteous and the ungodly;
>
> Chs. 6–9/10: Discussion of the nature and the origin of wisdom;
>
> Chs. 10–19: History of the chosen people in Exodus, inserted with a part to discuss idolatry in chapters 13–15.[226]

The readers to whom *Wisdom* was addressed involve three groups of people: first, those fellow Jews who had abandoned their Jewish way of life and been attracted to the cultural life of the Greeks (2:12–16);[227] second, those faithful Jews, the godly; and third, Gentile readers, the Egyptians (the ungodly).[228]

Wisdom of Solomon speaks of the Gentiles intermingling with Israel. The author not only exhorts the pagan kings to seek wisdom, but also shows God's mercy toward the Gentiles by giving them space for repentance. The first part of *Wisdom* begins with an exhortation to the pagan kings of the earth (1:1: "Love justice, you who rule the earth") and encloses in *Wisdom* 6 an exhortation to the kings to seek for wisdom (6:1: "Hear then, you kings"). In other words, this *inclusio* around the first part of *Wisdom* indicates the universal scope of the addressees (cf. 1:7 τὴν οἰκουμένην, the whole world). The author of *Wisdom* has the Gentiles particularly in mind. Interestingly, the pairings of the righteous and the ungodly in *Wisdom* 2–5 focus on these two types of the Jewish people. Therefore, like Paul in Romans 10:18–21, the author of *Wisdom* speaks of the Gentiles and Israel

---

225. Linebaugh, *God, Grace, and Righteousness*, 29.
226. Clarke, *Wisdom*, 3–4; Linebaugh, *God, Grace, and Righteousness*, 30.
227. The author's purpose was to rekindle in those Jewish people a genuine zeal for God and their law. See Clarke, *Wisdom*, 4–5.
228. Ibid.

interacting so as to evaluate Israel in relation to the Gentiles. Also, both authors consider that the Gentiles are those who did not seek God/Wisdom. In *Wisdom* 1:1, the author exhorts the pagan rulers to seek the Lord with a sincere heart (ἐν ἁπλότητι καρδίας ζητήσατε αὐτόν). He implies that the pagan rulers are those who did not seek the Lord. The ὅτι clause in *Wisdom* 1:2 indicates the easy accessibility of the Lord as Isaiah 65:1 has depicted (ὅτι εὑρίσκεται τοῖς μὴ πειράζουσιν αὐτόν ἐμφανίζεται δὲ τοῖς μὴ ἀπιστοῦσιν αὐτῷ). Both texts demonstrate that God took the initiative to manifest himself. Moreover, in *Wisdom* 6:12, the idea of wisdom's easy accessibility is repeated again (ἡ σοφία . . . εὐχερῶς θεωρεῖται ὑπὸ τῶν ἀγαπώντων αὐτὴν καὶ εὑρίσκεται ὑπὸ τῶν ζητούντων αὐτήν). In other words, the author of *Wisdom* exhorts the Gentiles to seek wisdom, that is, he appeals to them to convert to the Jewish way of life (cf. 6:17–18, loving wisdom means the keeping of her laws). Moreover, *Wisdom*, to a certain degree, shows God's mercy to the Gentiles. After the middle section speaks of the nature and origin of *Wisdom* (chs. 6–9), the third section is concerned about the history and the divine economy during the Exodus (chs. 11–19). Before the insertion of the idolatry section (chs. 13–15), the author of *Wisdom* shows us God's mercy toward the Egyptians and the Canaanites. Although the Egyptians "were misled into worshiping brute reptiles and worthless beasts," (11:15) and God has power to scatter them by a single breath (11:20), God still has compassion over all, and will overlook their sins with a view to their repentance (11:23). As with the Canaanites, God gave them space for repentance (12:3–10).

Now a question must be raised: Why did the author attempt to demonstrate that God has mercy toward the Gentiles? Is he trying to show that God is merciful to all people, both Jews and Greeks, without any bias? It seems not. All of God's mercy toward the Gentiles, in the viewpoint of *Wisdom*'s author, is for the sake of God's own people: "For if your children's enemies, who deserved to die, you punished with such care and indulgence allowing them time and space to work free from their wickedness, how conscientiously did you pass judgment on your sons, to whose fathers you gave sworn covenants full of good promise?" (Wis 12:20–21). In chapters 13–15, the author of *Wisdom* even exonerates the idolatry of Israel and identifies the sin of idolatry with the Egyptians. Finally, a concluding doxology is provided, that is, God is on the side of Israel: κατὰ πάντα γάρ κύριε ἐμεγάλυνας τὸν λαόν σου καὶ ἐδόξασας καὶ οὐχ ὑπερεῖδες ἐν παντὶ καιρῷ καὶ τόπῳ παριστάμενος ("For in every way, O Lord, you exalted and glorified your people, and did not neglect to assist them in every time and place"). Therefore, *Wisdom* places the relationship of God and Israel in the context of the pagan world. Although the author acknowledges God's mercy toward the Gentiles, its ultimate purpose is for the sake of Israel, who, as God's chosen people, will be exalted and glorified by God. On the contrary, the Gentiles are those unresponsive people who sin against God by idol-worship.

In conclusion, both Paul and the author of *Wisdom* are concerned about the fate of Israel against the backdrop of God's relationships with the Gentiles. However, they oppose each other in their ideas about Israel, the Gentiles, and idolatry. First, *Wisdom* asks for the Gentiles to seek Jewish wisdom so as to follow the Jewish way of life. Paul, through use of the prophetic Scripture, criticizes Israel's disobedience due to their exclusion of the Gentiles from the scope of God's people. Second, *Wisdom* criticizes the Gentiles' idolatry and their not-seeking of Israel's wisdom. Paul considers Israel's sin of idolatry to be the same as their belief in the exclusion of the Gentiles. In other words, Paul, considering the role of the Gentiles in God's salvific plan, demonstrates that Israel has been considered disobedient to God's word, which can be regarded as the sin of idolatry. However, *Wisdom* argues for God's favoring Israel. For the author of *Wisdom*, it is the Gentiles (the Egyptians or the Canaanites) who practice idolatry and sin against God, not Israel. The author of *Wisdom* tries to exonerate Israel's sin of idolatry and states that God will exalt and glorify Israel in the eschatological future. Although Paul has a similar view that all Israel will be saved in the eschatological future (Rom 11:25–26),[229] his insistence on including the Gentiles into the scope of salvation makes his stance different from that of his Jewish contemporaries.

---

229. The term "all Israel" shall refer to all of ethnic Israel, which we will investigate in the next chapter.

4.4.5 Conclusion

In Romans 10:14–21, Paul criticizes Israel's disbelief and disobedience to the word of the gospel and the prophetic announcement of the inclusion of the Gentiles in God's salvific plan for his people. He allies with the voices of Moses and Isaiah in critiquing Israel's apostasy in terms of their idolatry. He deftly identifies Israel's exclusion of the Gentiles with the sin of idol worship, which was the new semantic pattern of discourse in Paul's time. This novelty in Paul's voice may come from God's revelation of the message to Paul, which indicates Paul's prophetic role in delivering God's words to Israel. It would be common to place Israel in the context of a pagan world in the first-century context, but Paul's voice is distinguished from his contemporaries, particularly, the voice of *Wisdom*, in that the scope of salvation will extend to the Gentiles in terms of the words of Christ.

4.5 Conclusion

Paul addresses numerous crucial issues, such as righteousness, faith, law, Christ, the gospel, and the inclusion of the Gentiles in God's salvific plan in Romans 9:30–10:21. He establishes the relationship between faith and righteousness, and dissects the bond between law and righteousness on the basis of Christ. Paul criticizes Israel's pursuit of righteousness on the basis of law (works) and their zeal for God that is without knowledge (which may refer to their persecutions of the first Christians). However, Paul frames this critique within his heartfelt concern for his kinsmen's salvation. Allying with the Mosaic voice and some prophetic voices, Paul explains that Christ is the goal of the law for the promise of life to all who believe in Christ, including Israel and the Gentiles. Also, Paul generalizes the voices of Moses and Isaiah so as to sharply criticize Israel's rebellion in refusing this gospel, as well as to proclaim the revelation of the inclusion of the Gentiles in the scope of salvation. Paul allies himself with the prophetic tradition of Moses and Isaiah in order to testify against Israel's rebellion – the idol-worship shown in their exclusion of the Gentiles from the scope of salvation. We have also considered some of Paul's contemporary Jewish literature, which shares similar thematic patterns with Romans 9:30–10:21, for instance, 1QpHab, Baruch, Philo's *On Virtue*, and *Wisdom of Solomon*. The intertextual comparative reading of Romans 9:30–10:21 with related Jewish literature indicates that Paul's viewpoints about righteousness, faith, law, and the scope of salvation are divergent from his Jewish contemporaries, which makes Paul's voice unique in his time. All these factors suggest that Paul considers himself as a prophet in delivering the word of God, which testifies against Israel with his heartfelt concern about God's people.

CHAPTER FIVE

Paul's Warning to the Gentiles and the Salvation of All God's People: An Intertextual Analysis of Romans 11

5.1 Introduction

The last chapter demonstrated that in Paul's prophetic critique of Israel's rebellion in turning away from God's word concerning the gospel of Christ and the universal scope of salvation, Paul identified himself with a prophetic voice in line with the prophets Moses and Isaiah. He testifies against Israel by generalizing these prophetic voices into a single normative voice. By means of an intertextual reading of Paul alongside contemporary Jewish literature, we have also shown that, like a prophet, Paul's message about God's salvific plan is unique among his Jewish contemporaries. In Romans 11, Paul continues to invoke scriptural voices (e.g. 1 Kgs, Deut, and Isa) to enhance his message of God's salvific plan for Israel and the Gentiles. As Belli correctly observes, "In 11:3–4 we find two texts from 1 Kings 19 combined; in Romans 11:8–10, Paul instead conflates Deuteronomy 29:3 with Isaiah 29:10 and right afterward cites Psalm 69 [68]:23–24; then in verses 26b–27, Isaiah 59:20–21 is conflated with Isaiah 27:9."[1]

How does Paul see these different scriptural voices? In what way does he dis/associate himself from/with their voices? How should we understand the role and the relationships of all these Scriptures in Paul's arguments for

---

1. Belli, *Argumentation and Use of Scripture in Romans 9–11*, 344.

God's salvific plan for Israel and the Gentiles? Does Paul have a particular way of articulating the discourse pattern of this salvific plan? In the following, we will attempt to provide answers to all these questions.

Romans 11 can be divided into three sections: verses 1–10, verses 11–32, and verses 33–36.[2] We will investigate both the textual and intertextual analysis of the first two main sections; and in each section, presentational meaning will be provided first, followed by scriptural voices, thematic-organizational meaning, and then Paul's Jewish contemporaries' viewpoints on the topics.

5.2 Romans 11:1–10

5.2.1 Presentational Meaning: The Remnant of Israel

The major types of clauses are material, verbal, and relational, which suggests that the passage (vv. 1–10) concerns more about outer world experiences (doing or speaking things) among different participants, rather than about inner psychological display or reflection (note that there are only two mental clauses in this passage).[3] The relationship of the main clause complexes in Romans 11:1–10 is paratactic taxis (18 paratactic taxis vs. 5 hypotactic taxis).[4] The six paratactic projections and one hypotactic projection govern the interaction of the main speeches, which constitute the main information flow in verses 1–10. The sayers of the six projection locutions are Paul^{x2} (v. 1 and v. 7), Elijah (v. 2), God (v. 4), the Scripture

---

2. There is a common agreement regarding the structure of Romans 11. Most commentators (Käsemann, Munck, Cranfield, Sanday and Headlam, Barrett etc.) provide the outline as follows: 1–10, 11–24, 25–32, and 33–36, based on "the rhetorical question in v. 11 and the introductory formula in v. 25, and the clear break after v. 32." See Dan G. Johnson, "The Structure and Meaning of Romans 11," *CBQ* 46 (1984):91. We prefer to separate into three sections: 1–10, 11–32, and 33–36, not only because of the similar introductory formulae "therefore, I say" followed by a question μὴ γένοιτο; but also because the whole section of vv. 11–32 focuses on Paul's speech to the Gentile Christians in the Roman church (see the later discussions on vv. 11–32). See also Moo, *The Epistle to the Romans*, 671. In addition, vv. 33–36 are a doxology to God. We will not investigate this with regard to the four aspects of meaning, but we will give a brief explanation of vv. 33–36 to see what its role is in Rom 9–11.

3. See appendix 9.

4. Ibid.

(blending the voices of Moses and Isaiah, v. 8), and David (v. 9). Therefore there are several voices that interact with each other. It can be seen that the six verbal aspects in the paratactic projecting clauses are imperfective and stative aspects,[5] which denote the prominent roles of the sayers and their speaking processes in the information flow. In the following, we will investigate the presentational meaning in detail.

The conjunction οὖν shows an inferential sense in relation to the previous discussions.[6] As we have discussed in regard to Romans 10, particularly verses 14–21, Paul sharply criticizes Israel's rebellious refusal of God's word. Paul's negative evaluation of Israel culminates in the voice of Isaiah, "All day long I have held out my hands to a disobedient and contrary people" (10:21). Therefore, the question could be raised as to whether God would reject his people due to their rebellion. Paul actually has anticipated this question; thus, through the projecting clause λέγω οὖν, he raises the rhetorical question, μὴ ἀπώσατο ὁ θεὸς τὸν λαὸν αὐτοῦ;[7] (has God rejected his people?), which contains an implicit denial as the answer.

Moreover, the following three main independent clauses (c1B, c2, c3, vv. 1b–2a) provide Paul's three confirmations of the denial. In other words, the answer for the question includes three parts: the directly strong negative response to the question (c1B, v. 1b), Paul's self-introduction of his Jewish identity (c2, v. 1c) in the center, and the final confirmation, whose wording corresponds to the question ("God has not rejected his people whom he foreknew").[8] The first response is a strong negative phrase μὴ γένοιτο (by no means), by which phrase Paul rejects the accusation of God's

---

5. Four verbal processes (λέγω or λέγει) are with imperfective aspects, one action process (γέγραπται) and one mental process (οἴδατε) with stative aspects.
6. The combination of λέγω . . . μὴ also hints at its relationship with Rom 10:18–19, where Paul twice combines the verbal process verb and the negative particle (λέγω . . . μὴ) to indicate that Israel has heard and known about the gospel. Note that the combination of λέγω . . . μὴ introduces a question expecting a negative answer. Cf. Cranfield, *Romans*, 543.
7. There is a textual variation for τὸν λαὸν αὐτοῦ. According to P[46], F G b; Ambrosiaster, Pelagius, and the Gothic, there exists a word κληρονομίαν. Wagner thinks the latter is a better reading, for it brings into clearer focus both the identity of Paul's scriptural precursors and the significance for Paul's larger argument in Rom 9–11 concerning God's faithfulness to Israel. Cf. Wagner, *Heralds of the Good News*, 221–222.
8. Some commentators consider that these wordings reflect Ps 94:14 and 1 Sam 12:22. See Moo, *The Epistle to the Romans*, 674.

injustice in 9:14. With the conjunctive particle καὶ, Paul refers to his own Jewish identity as a case study which denies the notion that God has rejected Israel as his people.[9] We should note that Paul identifies himself with the Jewish people as far back as Abraham and the patriarchal period (the tribe of Benjamin). This description of Paul's solidarity with the Jewish people explains his concern about Israel in Romans 9:2–3 and 10:1.[10] The third response to the question is a positive assertion of God's non-abandonment of Israel with a scriptural text – οὐκ ἀπώσατο ὁ θεὸς τὸν λαὸν αὐτοῦ (God has not rejected his people). The wording of verse 2a resembles Psalm 94:14 and 1 Samuel 12:22.[11] The relative clause, ὃν προέγνω (whom he foreknew), defines the antecedent λαός, which refers to who "his people" are.[12] It is ethnic Israel of which Paul speaks, as he identifies himself as one of them. The statement "God has not rejected his people" allies with that of "God's word has not failed" in Romans 9:6. Both of them assert God's faithfulness, but from different perspectives. One considers that

---

9. The logic here is as follows: if God has rejected his people, then Paul himself as an Israelite would have been rejected already. See Cranfield, *Romans*, 544. I found Käsemann's view unconvincing in contending against Paul's intention to present himself in v. 1 as evidence of God's acceptance of his people, only because it is difficult to differentiate the destiny of the people from that of the individual. See Käsemann, *Commentary on Romans*, 299. Dunn argues that Paul's self-definition as an Israelite expresses an authentically Jewish viewpoint. See Dunn, *Romans 9–16*, 635.

10. Both Rom 9:2–3 and 10:1 show Paul's concern about Israel, his kinsmen.

11. Cf. Moo, *The Epistle to the Romans*, 674; Belli, *Argumentation and Use of Scripture in Romans 9–11*, 364; Jewett, *Romans*, 654. According to Moo, "He [Paul] changes the future ἀπώσεται to the aorist ἀπώσατο because he is thinking of the situation of Israel's rejection of Christ that he has just depicted. (The shift from κύριος to θεὸς may reflect Paul's general preference to use κύριος of Jesus.) Paul may have had his attention drawn to Ps 94:14 [93:14 LXX] partly by the 'echo' of his remnant theme created by the use of ἐγκαταλείπω in the second lime of the Psalm verse." Similar arguments occur in Belli and Dunn, see Belli, *Argumentation and Use of Scripture in Romans 9–11*, 365–366; Dunn, *Romans 9–16*, 636. However, it is not necessary that Paul's change of tense signals time transition (see Porter, *Verbal Aspect*, 17–109). For further discussion of Paul's use of Ps 94:14 and 1 Sam 12:22, see Bruce N. Fisk, "Paul among the Storytellers: Reading Romans 11 in the Context of Rewritten Bible," in *Paul and Scripture: Extending the Conversation*, ed. Christopher D. Stanley (Atlanta: Society of Biblical Literature, 2012), 55–94.

12. Some scholars consider the relative clause restrictive, so that "Paul would be asserting only that God had not rejected a certain body of elect persons from within Israel." See Moo, *The Epistle to the Romans*, 674, Cranfield, *Romans*, 545. However, those scholars' interpretations are affected by their reformed theological thinking. We should investigate the text closely to determine the function of the clause. In the following argument, we will see that Paul here is speaking of God's people as a whole national entity.

God's particular salvific plan toward Israel remains unchanged (11:2a), and the other emphasizes that God's promise to the patriarchs (from Abraham to Jacob, whose other name is "Israel") holds true. In this sense, the two Pauline statements in 9:6 and 11:1–2 contain similar value orientations: God is faithful to Israel. We will label God's non-abandonment of Israel as [God's Faithfulness: Non-abandonment].

The two main participants, God and I (Paul), in the first rhetorical question and answers (vv. 1–2a), shift to you, the Scripture, Elijah and Israel in verses 2b–4.[13] The mental projecting clause ἢ οὐκ οἴδατε provides a new thematic meaning by means of the subsequent projected clause – ἐν Ἠλίᾳ τί λέγει ἡ γραφή (c4Ba, v. 2b). This orients us to Scripture that relates to Elijah, which also implies that Paul assumes that his audience is familiar with Scripture.[14] The clause ὡς ἐντυγχάνει τῷ θεῷ κατὰ τοῦ Ἰσραήλ (c4Bb, v. 2c) keeps us grammatically within the projection, and provides a temporal circumstance to its primary clause concerning what the Scripture says of Elijah (c4Ba, v. 2b). The Scripture that Paul employs refers to Elijah's accusation of Israel (c4C, v. 3), in which he enumerates the sins of Israel: killing the prophets, demolishing God's altars, and now seeking the life of the only prophet left, Elijah himself. It is obvious that the Scripture here refers to the story of King Ahab's attack on the prophets (1 Kgs 19:1–18). Paul employs the part recounting "Elijah's lament about being left alone after the slaughter of the prophets (1 Kgs 19:10b/14b)" here.[15] So far, according to the voice of Elijah, Israel's sins are their idol-worship and their killing of prophets.

The contrastive conjunction ἀλλά introduces another verbal projecting clause with the divine oracle as the sayer (ἀλλὰ τί λέγει αὐτῷ ὁ χρηματισμός; c4D, v. 4) in a rhetorical question format, which constructs an antithesis to the prophet Elijah's voice in his accusation (cc4B–C) with the divine voice (c4D). This can be seen from their projecting introductory clauses: ἐν Ἠλίᾳ τί λέγει ἡ γραφή ὡς ἐντυγχάνει τῷ θεῷ κατὰ τοῦ Ἰσραήλ

---

13. See appendix 9.
14. See Moo, *The Epistle to the Romans*, 675.
15. Later, Paul will employ the Lord's concluding reassurance to Elijah (1 Kgs 19:18b). See Moo, *The Epistle to the Romans*, 676.

(c4B, v. 2bc) vs. τί λέγει αὐτῷ ὁ χρηματισμός (c4D, v. 4a).[16] The contrast of ἐντυγχάνει τῷ θεῷ (he appeals to God: "He" refers to Elijah, cf. ἐν Ἠλίᾳ ... ἡ γραφή) with αὐτῷ ὁ χρηματισμός (divine oracle to him) indicates the distinction between human appealing (ἐντυγχάνω) and the divine word of God. Also, the two corresponding complements (τῷ θεῷ and αὐτῷ) suggest the interaction between God and Elijah: Elijah appeals to God; and God responds to him through a divine oracle. Elijah accuses Israel of the sin of killing prophets, demolishing altars, and especially seeking Elijah's life. However, God's response foregrounds Israel's sin of *idol worship*: κατέλιπον ἐμαυτῷ ἑπτακισχιλίους ἄνδρας, οἵτινες οὐκ ἔκαμψαν γόνυ τῇ Βάαλ.[17] In other words, Israel's sin of killing prophets and demolishing God's altars is actually the sin of idol worship from the divine perspective. It can be seen that "bowed the knee to Baal" belongs to the idolatry discourse of the Israelite people, which can be labeled as [Israel's Sin: Idolatry]. Therefore, we can see that the clause complexes – the two main projecting clauses (λέγω οὖν and ἢ οὐκ οἴδατε) with each of their combining clauses – integrate tightly with the semantic meaning of Romans 11:1–4 in that it indicates God's non-abandonment of Israel (11:1–2a), and hints at Israel's sin of idolatry (vv. 2b–3), and God's grace for the remnant (v. 4).[18]

The thematic formation [Remnant] runs through the interaction between the voices of Elijah and God. We should note that there are two main verbs which correspond to each other in the Scripture: ὑπολείπω and καταλείπω. Both are in the aorist passive form, indicating that the receivers are left because of divine grace. The former states that the prophet himself is the only remnant and the latter replies to him with the fact of

---

16. Here ἐν Ἠλίᾳ does not mean that there were scriptural texts written by Elijah. See Moo, *The Epistle to the Romans*, 675; Jewett, *Romans*, 655; Cranfield, *Romans*, 545–555; Byrne, *Romans*, 333, etc.

17. Italics mine.

18. It states in v. 4 that there are "seven thousand men who have not bowed the knee to Baal." For a discussion of "Remnant," see Paul E. Dinter, "The Remnant of Israel and the Stone of Stumbling According to Paul (Romans 9–11)," Unpublished D Phil Thesis, Union Theological Seminary in New York, 1979; Ronald E. Clement, "'A Remant Chosen by Grace' (Romans 11:5): The Old Testament Background and Origin of the Remnant Concept," in *Pauline Studies: Essays Presented to Professor F.F. Bruce on His 70th Birthday*, ed. Donald Alfred Hagner and Murray J. Harris (Exeter: Paternoster, 1980), 106–121.

the remnant of 7,000.[19] This text-specific thematic formation [Remnant] is further expanded in verse 5. The fact that verse 5 (c5) as a simplex (contrast with the previous clause-complexes) serves to foreground its pivotal role in succeeding to the previous [Remnant] by picking up the key word λεῖμμα; it explains explicitly God's gracious election. Grammatically speaking, the adverb οὕτως (so, in this manner) and the particle οὖν (accordingly, therefore) draw an inference from the preceding arguments.[20] As I have mentioned earlier, the key word λεῖμμα is cognate with ὑπολείπω and καταλείπω, the two main verbs from the previously cited Scriptures (vv. 3–4). As God had left (καταλείπω) for himself a body of 7,000 worshipers in Elijah's time, so at the present time (ἐν τῷ νῦν καιρῷ: c5, v. 5), which refers to Paul's time, God has brought into existence a remnant (λεῖμμα), too.[21] The preposition κατά denotes the relationship between the "remnant" and "the gracious election" (ἐκλογὴν χάριτος).[22] That is, the existence of the remnant is grounded on God's gracious election. With the particle δέ, the following conditional clause complex (c6, v. 6) elaborates the term χάρις. The apodosis of the conditional clause brings in an antithesis of χάρις and ἐξ ἔργων: if by grace, no longer by works. Note that the lexical-semantic relation between "by grace" and "by works" is similar to the pair "by faith" and "by works" in Romans 9:32. With a conjunctive particle ἐπεί, a paratactic causal-conditional clause – ἐπεὶ ἡ χάρις οὐκέτι γίνεται χάρις (otherwise grace is no longer grace) – evaluates "(chosen) by works" negatively. So far, the lexical allocation of χάρις (grace [x4]) and ἐκλογή (election [x1]) can be considered to belong to the thematic formation [Gracious Election], while the wording ἔργον here plays a key role in the thematic formation [Law-righteousness] (cf. 9:32). This succinct antithesis co-patterns with that of 9:11–12 (ἐκλογή, καλέω vs. πράσσω, ἔργον) and 9:32 (πίστις vs. ἔργον).[23] It indicates that there are certain thematic ties among the following lexical

---

19. Actually, the theme of remnant appears in Rom 9:27 when Isaiah cries out to Israel that the remnant will be saved.
20. The phrase οὕτως οὖν occurs in Matt 6:9 and Luke 14:33. See Jewett, *Romans*, 658, n.73.
21. Cf. Moo, *The Epistle to the Romans*, 677.
22. See Louw and Nida, "κατά," 777.
23. Cf. Romans 3:20, 27–28; 4:2.

items – ἐκλογή, καλέω, πίστις and χάρις,[24] and that they are antithetical to the collocational ties between ἔργον and πράσσω. In other words, the thematic formation [Gracious Election] stands in opposition to [Law-righteousness]: "Standing by grace and standing on the basis of one's own works – these are mutually exclusive."[25] Also, the antithetical contrast of these two formations is repeated throughout Romans 9–11, and even the whole letter. Note the two prominent verbal aspects – stative and imperfective (γέγονεν and γίνεται – in verses 5–6, which emphasize the opposing relationship of the two thematic formations [Gracious Election] and [Law-righteousness] in Paul's voice. This may suggest that his proposed thematic opposition may represent something new and unacceptable to most of Paul's Jewish contemporaries, since most Jewish people considered that their law-righteousness was based on their position as God's elected people. For example, as we have shown in the last chapter, a Qumran pesherist would ally "law observance" with "faithfulness" (see the section 4.2.4). Therefore, Paul's voice setting the antithetical contrast between these two formations would not be acceptable by most of his Jewish contemporaries. He might even be persecuted because of this "alien" voice.

The theme of the Jews' persecution of the prophets was not uncommon in the first-century Christian communities (e.g. Matt 23:29–30; Mark 12:1–9).[26] It seems that Paul in some way sees himself as resembling a persecuted prophet. His prophetic self-understanding shows in the use of the example of Elijah: he compares himself with Elijah, who felt alone and threatened.[27] In addition, Paul usually relied upon the Jewish social markers of his day when he was in trouble. For instance, when Paul was accused by the Jews in Jerusalem of defiling the holy place, he resorted to his Jewish identity: "I am a Jew, born in Tarsus in Cilicia, but brought up in this city at the feet of Gamaliel (Acts 21:39; cf. Rom 11:1c)."[28] In other words,

---

24. It means that some of them usually appear together in certain types of discourse through multivariate structure.
25. Cranfield, *Romans*, 548.
26. Bell, *Irrevocable Call*, 68.
27. Evans, "Paul and the Prophets," 120.
28. Capes, Reeves, and Richards, *Rediscovering Paul*, 27.

Paul probably encountered some trouble in delivering the gospel that he believed was revealed to him by Christ to his Jewish contemporaries.

The rhetorical question τί οὖν suggests that the following thematic meaning indicates that a conclusion will be given from what has been said in verses 1–6.[29] Its thematic meaning starts from c7Ba (v. 7b) – ὃ ἐπιζητεῖ Ἰσραήλ, τοῦτο οὐκ ἐπέτυχεν – which is about Israel's seeking and gaining. The semantic meaning of verse 7 and its grammatical structure are similar to those of Romans 9:30–31, which says that Israel did not attain righteousness from faith by pursing law-righteousness. Paul probably has this previous passage in mind here; that is, what Israel failed to obtain is righteousness from faith:[30]

Romans 11:7	Romans 9:30–31
Τί οὖν;	Τί οὖν ἐροῦμεν;
ὃ ἐπιζητεῖ Ἰσραήλ, τοῦτο οὐκ ἐπέτυχεν	Ἰσραὴλ δὲ διώκων νόμον δικαιοσύνης εἰς νόμον οὐκ ἔφθασεν
ἡ δὲ ἐκλογὴ ἐπέτυχεν	ἔθνη τὰ μὴ διώκοντα δικαιοσύνην κατέλαβεν δικαιοσύνην, δικαιοσύνην δὲ τὴν ἐκ πίστεως
οἱ δὲ λοιποὶ ἐπωρώθησαν	

From the above chart, it can be seen that what Israel sought (the lexical term ἐπιζητέω shares a similar semantic domain with διώκω) was law-righteousness, but they failed to obtain it (Louw's description of the lexical-semantic meaning of the term ἐπιτυγχάνω is similar to that of φθάνω.)[31] In contrast, the elected (the Jewish Christians) and the Gentiles (Gentile

---

29. Cranfield, *Romans*, 548.
30. Cf. Wagner, *Heralds of the Good News*, 239, in which figure 4.2 compares these two passages. Also see Jewett, *Romans*, 661. Note that the parallel entities in Rom 9:30–31 are the Israel and the Gentiles, but here the two groups are within Israel.
31. According to Louw, the semantic domains of the term ἐπιτυγχάνω are: to acquire or gain what is sought after – "to acquire, to obtain, to attain" (57.60), and the term φθάνω: to attain or arrive at a particular state – "to come to be, to attain, to achieve"(13.16). See Louw and Nida, "ἐπιτυγχάνω," 564; "φθάνω," 150.

Christians) obtain (the semantic domain of the term ἐπιτυγχάνω is synonymous with that of καταλαμβάνω)[32] it – the righteousness from faith. Compared to Romans 9:30–31, there is a new element, that is, the hardening of the rest (c7Bc, v. 7c),[33] which is the key point of the voice in the following scriptural texts (vv. 8–10). If Romans 9:30–31 points out Israel's failure in attaining God's Righteousness, then in 11:7, Paul further articulates the reason for their failure, that is, they are hardened (ἐπωρώθησαν).[34] Actually, there are three actors in verse 7: Ἰσραήλ, ἡ ἐκλογὴ and οἱ λοιποί. The corporate term Ἰσραήλ refers very likely to οἱ λοιποί of Israel, for they are located respectively in the two Complementizing ITFs:[35] [Israel's failure] and [Israel's hardening]. As we have indicated, these Israelites fail to obtain what they are seeking, because they are hardened (ἐπωρώθησαν); so failed Israel refers to Israel which is hardened. Therefore, the two distinct groups that concern Paul are the chosen (or the remnant) and the rest (οἱ λοιποί) within Israel.[36] The contact point between Paul's voice about Israel and the scriptural voices is the theme of Israel's hardening.[37] The first projecting introductory clause in verses 8–10 – καθὼς γέγραπται – suggests a generalized scriptural voice concerning the hardening. The projected clauses quote the conflated Scriptures, Deuteronomy 29:3 LXX and Isaiah 29:10. This combination of the Mosaic voice in Deuteronomy and the prophetic voice in Isaiah occurred in Romans 10:19–21 too. It seems

---

32. Both terms belong to the semantic domain 57G, "Take, obtain, gain, and lose." See Louw and Nida, "ἐπιτυγχάνω," 565, "καταλαμβάνω," 564.

33. It is worthy of note that the hardening theme occurs in Rom 9:18 and 11:25 as well.

34. The hardness usually refers to a stubbornness that refuses to listen to God or to obey him. See A. E. Steinmann, "Hardness of Heart," in *Dictionary of the Old Testament: Pentateuch*, ed. T. Desmond Alexander and David W. Baker (Downers Grove: InterVarsity, 2003), 381.

35. Both ITFs denote a negative side of Israel. See Lemke, "Discourses in Conflict," 48, and Lemke, "Intertextuality and Text Semantics," 100.

36. Moo, *The Epistle to the Romans*, 679–680; Jewett, *Romans*, 661. Some have assumed that the chosen also refers to Gentile Christians, for example, Dunn, *Romans 9–16*, 648.

37. What caused the hardening? According to the following Scriptures, God gave them a spirit of stupor, so that they cannot see and hear (c8, v. 8). Therefore, it is a divine hardening. But why does God harden the rest? First, Paul mentioned Israel's disobedience to God by Baal worship in vv. 2–4. It is highly possible that Paul hints that God hardened the rest of Israel because of their idolatrous worship here. Second, the quoted Scriptures also contribute to explaining this divine hardening.

that Paul tends to unite the voices of the prophet Moses and the prophet Isaiah and generalizes their voices, without distinguishing between the past and the current situation. The Mosaic curse in Deuteronomy 29 (v. 4, vv. 17–20, vv. 25–26) is the discourse in which Moses warns Israel not to worship pagan deities. Isaiah 29:10 is located in a co-text that claims that Israel, instead of trusting in God, relies on human forces (like Egypt) for protection (Isa 30:1–7). Thus the prophet condemns them because "these people draw near with their mouths and honor me (YHWH) with their lips, while their hearts are far from me, and their worship of me is a human commandment learned by rote" (Isa 29:13). Again, Paul allies idolatrous worship (Deut 29:3 LXX) with Israel's disbelief in God and reliance on human strength in battle (Isa 29:10). By using the general projecting clause (καθὼς γέγραπται), Paul makes his voice about Israel's sin claim that their current disbelief of God's word is no different from their idol worship in the past. Therefore, Israel's disbelief or idol-worship in the past has been applied to the unbelief of Paul's Jewish contemporaries.[38]

With the second projecting introductory clause – καὶ Δαυὶδ λέγει – Psalm 68:23–24 LXX has also been included to speak about the theme of hardening. Why does Paul incorporate these references together? At the surface linguistic level, there is a linkage within them created by the phrase ὀφθαλμοὺς τοῦ μὴ βλέπειν/οἱ ὀφθαλμοὶ αὐτῶν τοῦ μὴ βλέπειν.[39] Also, worthy of note is the use of passages from all three section of the Scripture in verses 8–10 – Torah (Deut 29:3 [LXX], Prophets (Isa 29:10), and the writings (Ps 68:22–23 LXX) – in line with Jewish hermeneutics.[40] In addition, it is of importance to note that Paul preserves the voice of the psalmist, David (the projecting introductory clause Δαυὶδ λέγει).[41] In

---

38. See Meadors' analysis: Meadors, *Idolatry and the Hardening of the Heart: A Study in Biblical Theology* (London: T&T Clark, 2006), 142–144.
39. According to later rabbinic tradition, this rhetoric has been referred as *Gezera Shawa*, which means "inference from similar words." It belongs to one of Hillel's seven rules of interpretation, but it could be derived from rules of Hellenistic rhetoric current in Alexandria in the first century BC. See E. Earle Ellis, *The Old Testament in Early Christianity: Canon and Interpretation in the Light of Modern Research* (Grand Rapids: Baker, 1991), 87–91.
40. Dunn, *Romans 9–16*, 634; Moo, *The Epistle to the Romans*, 681.
41. It is worth noticing that Ps 68 LXX is widely used in a prophetic description of Jesus' ministry in the New Testament. See Matt 27:34, 48 (Ps 68:21 LXX); Mark 3:21 (Ps

other words, the statement of the curse over the persecutors is attributed to David himself. Therefore, Paul keeps his distance from the psalmist's voice cursing the persecutors (for Paul, the heart-hardened Israel).[42] Why does Paul employ the voice of the psalmist here? The answer to this follows in detail in the next section of scriptural voices.

In sum, Paul first confirms that God has not abandoned his people through three confirmations of the denial (vv. 1b–2a), while at the same time he employs the voices of Elijah and the divine oracle in order to demonstrate Israel's sin of idolatrous worship and the existence of the remnant that has been kept by God (vv. 2b–4). Then Paul's voice stresses God's gracious election is not on the basis of works. Next, the comparison of the elect and the rest who had been hardened corresponds to the contrast of faith-righteousness and law-righteousness in 9:30–32a. Israel's hardening plays a pivotal role in the following scriptural voices. Through the generalized scriptural voice, which blurs Isaiah and Moses, Paul demonstrates that Israel has failed from the past up to the time of Paul's contemporaries. However, Paul employs the voice of the psalmist to point out that although hearted-hardened Israel deserves dark cursing, he still wants to limit the psalmist's cursing to a specific context, not establish it as a generally valid fact that can be applied into his Jewish contemporaries. By doing so, Paul's voice makes the grace of God's election prominent. This paves a way for the following argument concerning Israel's salvation.

5.2.2 Scriptural Voices

It is helpful to examine the scriptural voices (1 Kgs 19:10, 14; Deut 29:4, Isa 29:10; and Ps 68:23 LXX) in their own co-texts first, and then explore how Paul's voice relates to these scriptural voices. The Scriptures being used

---

68:6–7 LXX); 15:23, 36 (Ps 68:21 LXX); Luke 23:36 (Ps 68:21 LXX); John 2:17 (Ps 68:9 LXX); 15:25 (Ps 68:4 LXX); 19:29 (Ps 68:21 LXX); Acts 1:20 (Ps 68:25 LXX); Rom 15:3 (Ps 68:9 LXX); cf. Phil 4:3 (Ps 68: 28 LXX); Rev 3:5 (Ps 68: 28 LXX). However, it is not necessary that Paul sees messianic connotation in this co-text. Contra Wagner (see *Heralds of the Good News*, 261–265).

42. Cf. Stanley: "Direct quotations serve to insulate the quoting author from negative reactions to a particular statement or viewpoint. . . . The remainder (the quoted part) is implicitly charged to the original source." See Christopher D. Stanley, *Arguing with Scripture: The Rhetoric of Quotations in the Letters of Paul* (New York: T&T Clark International, 2004), 31.

by Paul in Romans 11:3–4 belong to the story of King Ahab's attack on the prophet, Elijah (1 Kgs 19:1–18). The whole Elijah story is constructed in 1 Kings 17–19. These three chapters place Elijah in three settings: a private setting of ordinary people in daily life (ch. 17), a public or political setting (ch. 18), and the setting of an encounter with God (ch. 20). The settings comprehensively present the life of a prophet who stands before God to whom God speaks directly.[43] Chapter 19 focuses on the interactions between the prophet Elijah and YHWH. This is the thematic flow of this chapter:

> 19:1–3 Introduction: Due to Jezebel's threat, Elijah flees to Beer-sheba
>
> 19:4–8 Elijah's interaction with the messenger in the dessert
>
> 19:9–18 Elijah's encounter with YHWH at Mount Horeb
>
> 19:19–21 Elijah finding Elisha after leaving Horeb

The introduction of chapter 19 links to chapter 18 by informing Jezebel what happened at Mount Carmel. The core linking part is in 1 Kings 18:20–40 where Elijah and the prophets of Baal contend for the loyalties of the people of Israel.[44] Elijah's purpose for the contest is to force the people of Israel to choose YHWH over Baal as their God: "O Lord, God of Abraham, Isaac, and Israel, let it be known this day that you are God in Israel" (1 Kgs 18:36). Besides the theme of Israel's idolatrous worship of Baal, another implicit theme should be given attention, that is, God's

---

43. Walsh has provided a good picture of these settings: in private life, Elijah bears a divine word for the faithful; in public, "he is Yahweh's representative before king and people, condemning and punishing unfaithfulness, calling to conversion and offering hope, finally praying for and receiving the display of divine power in fire and rain"; in encounter with God, he is one who God speaks and appears to. See Jerome T. Walsh, *1 Kings* (Collegeville: Liturgical, 1996), 284.

44. Walsh, *1 Kings*, 244; Walter Brueggemann, *1 & 2 Kings*. SHBC. (Macon: Smyth & Helwys, 2000), 223–227.

supremacy over the entire world.⁴⁵ YHWH's supremacy is particularly demonstrated by his mandate to Elijah in 1 Kings 19:15–17 (Note: Paul has used 1 Kgs 19:14, 18 in Rom 11:2–4, which includes the mandate in the middle). YHWH gives Elijah three new duties: to anoint a new king of Aram, to anoint a new king of Israel, and to anoint a new prophet to take Elijah's own place. Walsh provides some appropriate comments on this section:

> First, sending Elijah to involve himself in the politics of Aram is unexpected; generally speaking, Israelite prophets respected the autonomy of other realms. This is reminiscent of chapter 17, where Yahweh demonstrated his power within Baal's own territory around Sidon by causing drought, miraculously sustaining Elijah and the widow, returning the widow's son to life, and protecting his prophet from pursuit. Beneath the surface story of struggle between Baal and Yahweh for divine supremacy in Israel lies the seed of a more universalist claim: Yahweh is supreme in all the earth. Yahweh's meddling in the politics of Aram also points forward to the remaining chapters of 1 Kings.⁴⁶

Therefore, although the prophet Elijah accuses Israel of rebellion (their idolatry and killing of God's prophets), God's response to him shows that God has a larger and grander picture for the world. In other words, Israel's idolatry would bring them judgment, which in turn would lead to God's divine execution over the world.⁴⁷

In addition, the figure of Elijah stands in the most important position in the literary presentation of the Deuteronomistic history,⁴⁸ particularly,

---

45. Walsh, *1 Kings*, 277–278.
46. Ibid.
47. Note that this thematic concept is manifest in parables (Matt 22:1–10; Luke 14:15–24). That is, the concept that salvation will go to the Gentiles because of Israel's rebellion is shared among early Christians.
48. Aernie, *Paul among the Prophets*, 17.

in the Mosaic succession.⁴⁹ Vanlaningham provides some of the parallels to connect the discourse of Moses at Sinai with Elijah's interaction with the Lord at Horeb in 1 Kings 19.⁵⁰ The role of Israel in the discourses of both Moses and Elijah relates to their falling into idolatry – golden-calf worship or Baal-worship. As Wagner correctly observes, this is particularly obvious in 1 Kings:

> The denunciation of Israel as idolatrous is a curiously persistent motif in many of the texts appropriated by Paul in Romans 9–11 to explain Israel's current plight. The sin of idolatry is particularly prominent in the Elijah story. But for the remnant, Israel has forsaken the Lord and gone over to Baal.⁵¹

One important question should be raised here: what is Paul's perspective toward the Elijah's story in 1 Kings? By explicitly pointing to Elijah, Paul seems to preserve the situational context of Elijah's encounter in Romans 11. He acknowledges the rebellion of Israel in his repeated criticism of Israel's sin (cf. Rom 9:30–10:21), but he also notices that God has a salvific plan for the world that goes beyond human limitations. Therefore, it is in God that Israel can find hope. In sum, through employing the prophet Elijah's voice, Paul depicts Israel's sin of idolatrous worship and, allying with the divine oracle, Paul demonstrates God's grace toward Israel. Also, through Elijah's story, Paul invokes the prophetic role of Elijah (1 Kgs 19:15–17): to anoint a new king of Aram, to anoint a new king of Israel, and to anoint a new prophet to take Elijah's own place. This invoking suggests God's supremacy over the world, and also indicates that not only can an Israelite prophet be involved in Jewish affairs, he can also be concerned

---

49. Walsh, *1 Kings*, 267–289.
50. Michael G. Vanlaningham, "Paul's Use of Elijah's Mt. Horeb Experience in Rom 11:2–6," *TMSJ* 6 (1995): 227–228: While Moses passed 40 days on Mt. Horeb (Exod 34:28), Elijah took 40 days to get there (1 Kgs 19:8); Elijah is in the cave, probably an allusion to the location in which Moses found himself in Exod 33:22; God is said to "pass by" both Moses (Exod 33:22) and Elijah (1 Kgs 19:11), and both receive a vision of God (Exod 34:4; 1 Kgs 19:11–13). Also, Elijah's theophany shared with the theophany given to Moses and Israel the elements of wind, earthquake, and fire (cf. Exod 19:9; 20:18–19; Deut 4:9–10; 5:24–25).
51. Wagner, *Heralds of the Good News*, 238.

with the Gentiles. Therefore, Paul may consider himself as sharing the prophetic role in both Jewish and Gentile affairs.

After contrasting Israel's idolatry and God's grace by employing 1 Kings 19, Paul takes the following scriptural texts from Deuteronomy 29:3, Isaiah 29:10, and Psalm 68:23 (LXX). In Romans 11:8 Paul "extracted the phrase 'a spirit of stupor' from Isaiah 29:10 and inserted it into Deuteronomy 29:3,"[52] which conflates Deuteronomy 29:3 and Isaiah 29:10 into one scriptural voice. In particular, the general projecting introductory formula (καθὼς γέγραπται) suggests that the statement of the projected clauses (the conflated Scriptures) have been made into a generalized normative statement. That is, for Paul, Israel's hard-heartedness has been a constant fact from the Sinai covenant up until his present.[53]

Now let us examine the two texts in their own co-texts. We discussed in the last chapter the fact that Deuteronomy 29–30 represents Moses' final covenant address, which explores blessings and curses. Deuteronomy 29 focuses on curses and punishment:[54] verses 1–8 is a historical review of the period from God's guiding Israel out of Egypt to the arrival in the Promised Land, Canaan,[55] and verses 9–14 confirms the identity of the covenant partners.[56] The rest of Deuteronomy 29 (vv. 15–27) highlights the Deuteronomic curses (vv. 15–20 covers the curses that threaten those who turn away from YHWH and adhere to idol worship; verses 21–27 describes the curse from the perspective of future observers and notes that

---

52. David Lincicum, *Paul and the Early Jewish Encounter with Deuteronomy* (Tübingen: Mohr Siebeck, 2010), 147.

53. Scott J. Hafemann, *Paul, Moses, and the History of Israel: The Letter/Spirit Contrast and the Argument from Scripture in 2 Corinthians 3* (Tübingen: Mohr, 1995), 375.

54. Miller observes, "The Second covenant at Moab . . . anticipates or reflects the new covenant that the prophets announce out of the experience of exile and punishment by God for failure to live according to the divine purpose. That is probably why, in this formulation of the covenant, we hear of curse and punishment first (29:20–28) and then of blessing that will come after that (30:1–10), a blessing that is found in the restoration of Israel's fortunes after exile and the overthrow of their enemies who persecuted them." See Patrick D. Miller, *Deuteronomy* (Louisville: Westminster John Knox, 1990), 208.

55. Three stages of the history: "(1) the deliverance from Egypt, (2) the guidance through the wilderness, and (3) the defeat of Sihon and Og and the taking of the land." See Miller, *Deuteronomy*, 202.

56. See Richard D. Nelson, *Deuteronomy: A Commentary*. OTL. (Louisville: Westminster John Knox, 2002), 337; Miller, *Deuteronomy*, 208–210.

the devastation of the land results from abandoning the covenant of the Lord and turning to the worship of other gods).[57] Moses' address attributes Israel's curse or exile (vv. 21–27) to their dull hearts and deaf ears (v. 3). This can be seen from the contrast of verses 1–2 and verse 3, in which Moses gives a historical review of God's way of doing things. Moses repeatedly refers to Israel's direct witness of God's power against the Egyptians on their behalf, but Israel cannot understand in their heart, their eyes do not see, and their ears do not hear.[58]

Isaiah 29:10 belongs to the section 28:1–29:24, which interweaves the themes of judgment and salvation. It begins with the denouncement of the northern kingdom (28:1–13); verses 1–6 denounce the rulers of the northern kingdom and predict their doom, and then verses 7–13 make the accusation more specific.[59] The focus shifts to Jerusalem in 28:14 to 29:14. The rulers of Jerusalem are depicted as so senseless that they have made a covenant with "death" in hope of protecting themselves (28:14–22),[60] and "the priest and the prophets are as drunken and blind" (29:9–14).[61] In contrast, 29:17–24 affirms God's intention and ability to save Israel after the folly of their distrust of God. The interweaving of the denunciation of Israel with God's salvation occurs in 29:1–8 as well (vv. 1–4 vs. vv. 5–8). The contrast suggests that the people of Israel do not understand God's way in history, so they resort to the aid of foreign countries (e.g. Egyptians); however, even though they misconstrue God's words, God still offers to

---

57. McConville, *Deuteronomy*, 414.
58. We should note that the key word "heart" in 29:3, which makes a bridge with Deut 30 that the circumcised heart will return them to God (from curse to bless), is replaced with "spirit" ("no heart to understand" in Deut 29:3 with "a spirit of stupor" in Rom 11:8).
59. John Oswalt, *The Book of Isaiah: Chapters 1–39*. NICOT (Grand Rapids: Eerdmans, 1986), 505–509.
60. According to Sweeney, "The references to the covenant with 'death' or Sheol in vv. 15 and 18 relate to Hezekiah's attempts to form an alliance with other powers in order to revolt against the Assyrians." See Marvin A. Sweeney, *Isaiah 1–39: With an Introduction to Prophetic Literature* (Grand Rapids: Eerdmans, 1996), 367. Some commentators argue that the reference to death refers to the Egyptians (cf. Isa 30). See R. E. Clements, *Isaiah 1–39* (Grand Rapids: Eerdmans, 1980), 230.
61. Oswalt, *Isaiah*, 515.

strike the multitude of the nations, their attackers (vv. 5–8).[62] Therefore, God's grace to his people is stressed.

Therefore, both texts (Deut 29:3 and Isa 29:10) are concerned with the fact that Israel does not understand God's way of doing things; even though God has shown them the power of his salvation repeatedly, they still turn away from God to idol worship or to dependence on foreign alliances. Israel's dullness or senselessness occurs time and again in their history. In Romans 11:8, the voices of Moses and Isaiah have been closely merged to form one scriptural voice, which is also Paul's voice depicting Israel's dullness and hard-heartedness. In other words, for Paul, distrust of God by depending on foreign forces is no different than the sin of idolatrous worship. Israel's sin from the past until the present remains the same, that is, their disbelief of God.

When referring to Psalm 68:23 LXX, Paul employs the projecting introductory clause, Δαυὶδ λέγει (c9A, v. 9), which seems to preserve David's voice for the following projected statement, the quotation from Psalm 68:23. In this sense, the psalmist's situational context is of importance to understanding his voice. We can infer from verses 35–36 that the Psalm was produced or collected sometime after the Babylonian exile,[63] for the two verses "speak from the perspective that Jerusalem and its cities are not only in ruins but also that their inhabitants are in a foreign land."[64] Psalm 68 is a psalm of individual lament. Both in its beginning and ending, the psalmist asks for God's salvation: "Save me, O God" (v. 1) and asserts, "God will save Zion" (v. 35). The Psalm can be divided into four sub sections: verses 1–12 interweaves the petition with laments concerning the speaker's plight, verses 13–21 focuses on petition to God, verses 22–29 records the speaker's request for God to bring retribution on the wicked,

---

62. As Oswalt observes, "Those who should be gifted with discernment, who should be able to perceive the mysterious workings of God in history, are so stupid that they cannot understand God's ways even when they are presented to them in plain script. As a result, the ordinary people are led astray by spurious wisdom and the nation is sunk in degradation. The result is that God will once again, as in Egypt, have to do something shocking to show himself." Oswalt, *Isaiah*, 530.

63. Craig C. Broyles, *Psalms*. NIBCOT 11. (Peabody: Hendrickson, 1999), 285; cf. Goldingay, *Psalms*, 2:339.

64. Broyles, *Psalms*, 286.

even to curse them so they are blotted out the book of the living, and verses 30–36 concludes with praise.[65] The verse (Ps 68:23 LXX) that Paul employs in Romans 11:9–10 comes from the section that appeals for retribution on the wicked (vv. 22–29). In Psalm 68, we can see that the attackers of the speaker could refer to people within the Jewish community;[66] similarly, the people that Paul scorns are those from within Israel who have been hardened. The voice of David enters here in order to give a comment on the seriousness of Israel's sin, and that they deserve curses. However, this cursing voice is put in the mouth of David, not Paul, which hints that the cursing by David is restricted to his situational context and is not a normative statement valid forever.

Therefore, Paul may be confirming the voice of the psalmist (David) that these hardened Israelites deserve to be cursed and to be blotted out of the book of the living. However, it is worthy of note that Paul preserves the voice of the psalmist (David). In other words, Paul does not generalize the psalmist's voice into a normative statement or into his own. This would suggest that Paul may have reservations about allying with the psalmist's dark curse on Israel.

We have discussed the scriptural texts that are employed in Romans 11:1–10 in their own original co-texts. However, Paul articulates the scriptural voices in his own way. With the interactional voices of Elijah and the divine oracles (1 Kgs 19), Paul confirms Israel's sin of idolatry and God's grace toward the remnant in the past and applies the situation to his present time (Rom 11:5). Through the conflated voices of Deuteronomy 29:3 and Isaiah 29:10, Paul states Israel's hard-heartedness as a normative fact, that is, a constant fact from the Sinai covenant up until his present time. However, Paul distances his voice from cursing Israel's rebellion by explicitly using the voice of the psalmist instead of his own.

---

65. Goldingay, *Psalms*, 2:338–356; Broyles, *Psalms*, 285–288.
66. See Ps 68:9, "I became strange to my brothers, and a stranger to my mother's children." It is the psalmist's pious zeal that brought him alienation. See Schaefer and Cotter, *Psalms*, 166.

5.2.3 Thematic-organizational Meaning

Two main interweaving thematic formations go through Romans 11:1–10: [God's Faithfulness] and [Israel's Sin]. At first, God's non-abandonment of Israel (God's faithfulness) governs the main tone of this passage. Through the interactions of the voice of Elijah and the divine oracle, the two contrasting thematic formations [Israel's Sin: Idolatry] and [Gracious Election: Remnant] corresponds with each other in the divine voice; that is, even if Israel has sinned, there is still grace upon them.

Corresponding to the thematic formation [Israel's Sin: Idolatry], the formation [Israel's Sin: Heart-hardening] is brought into view, confirmed by the conflated scriptural voices. Again, Paul allies ancient Israel's sin of idolatry with their heart-hardening in terms of their disbelief of gospel. In sum, through the interweaving thematic formations [God's Faithfulness] and [Israel's Sin], Paul's voice conveys that God shows grace toward Israel even if they have sinned and are hardened. In this sense, Paul's view of God's faithfulness and Israel's salvation is no different from that of his Jewish contemporaries.

5.2.4 Multiple Voices: Paul's Jewish Contemporaries' Viewpoints on God's Faithfulness and Israel's Sinfulness

Part of the *Psalms of Solomon* (henceforth *Pss. Sol.*) contains similar themes to Romans 11:1–10:[67] God has not abandoned his people, although Israel is sinful. Therefore, we will focus on *Pss. Sol.* 7–9 to see the psalmist's viewpoints about God's faithfulness and Israel's sin.

Regarding the date of *Pss. Sol.*, the earliest possible date is around one century earlier than Paul's letter to the Romans and the latest should be before AD 70.[68] According to Wright:

> The earliest direct allusion in the psalms to a specific historical event is to Pompey's invasion (63 BC). The latest is to his

---

67. See *Pss. Sol.* 7–9.
68. "That Jerusalem has been desecrated but not destroyed suggests that the psalms reached their final form before 70 AD." See Robert B. Wright, "The Psalms of Solomon," in *The Old Testament Pseudepigrapha*, ed. James H. Charlesworth (New York: Doubleday, 1985), 641.

death, in 48 BC. The widest limits for dating are between 125 BC and the early first century AD. Narrow limits would be about 70 to 45 BC, with the caveat that the undatable psalms may have been earlier or later and the collection as a whole was certainly later.[69]

The eighteen *Psalms of Solomon* are a collection of hymns produced by a Jewish community.[70] But what kind of Jewish community? It could be either a Pharisaic or an Essene-like community.[71]

In the following, we will discuss *Pss. Sol.* 7–9 to see the psalmists' viewpoints on God's faithfulness and Israel's sin and fate. *Psalm of Solomon 7* was likely written just prior to Pompey's siege of Jerusalem in 63 BC,[72] so the psalm implies the psalmist's care for the temple and fear of its possible destruction by Gentiles.[73] Let us investigate *Pss. Sol.* 7 first:[74]

1.	μὴ ἀποσκηνώσῃς ἀφ' ἡμῶν ὁ θεός ἵνα μὴ ἐπιθῶνται ἡμῖν οἳ ἐμίσησαν ἡμᾶς δωρεάν	Do not move away from us, O God, lest those who hate us without cause attack us
2.	ὅτι ἀπώσω αὐτούς ὁ θεός μὴ πατησάτω ὁ πούς αὐτῶν κληρονομίαν ἁγιάσματός σου	For you have rejected them, O God; let their feet not trample the inheritance of your sanctuary.
3.	σὺ ἐν θελήματί σου παίδευσον ἡμᾶς καὶ μὴ δῷς ἔθνεσιν	Discipline us, you yourself, as you wish, but do not give (us) to the Gentiles

---

69. Ibid.
70. The writer or the collector speaks of and for a community under persecution, and with hopes for the future. Wright, "The Psalms of Solomon," 645.
71. For example, Ryle and James titled *Pss. Sol.* as *Psalms of the Pharisees*. See Wright, "The Psalms of Solomon," 642.
72. Kenneth Atkinson, *I Cried to the Lord: A Study of the Psalms of Solomon's Historical Background and Social Setting*, SJSJ, (Leiden: Brill, 2004), 111.
73. Ibid.
74. The Greek texts and their translations (LXE) come from Bibleworks 9. Italics mine. For a discussion of the Greek texts, see Robert Wright, *The Psalms of Solomon: A Critical Edition of the Greek Text* (London: T & T Clark, 2007).

4.	ἐὰν γὰρ ἀποστείλῃς θάνατον σὺ ἐντελῇ αὐτῷ περὶ ἡμῶν	For if you sent death you would give it instructions about us
5.	ὅτι σὺ ἐλεήμων καὶ οὐκ ὀργισθήσῃ τοῦ συντελέσαι ἡμᾶς	because you are kind, and will not be (so) angry to destroy us
6.	ἐν τῷ κατασκηνοῦν τὸ ὄνομά σου ἐν μέσῳ ἡμῶν ἐλεηθησόμεθα καὶ οὐκ ἰσχύσει πρὸς ἡμᾶς ἔθνος	While your name dwells among us, we will receive mercy and the Gentile will not prevail over us
7.	ὅτι σὺ ὑπερασπιστὴς ἡμῶν καὶ ἡμεῖς ἐπικαλεσόμεθά σε καὶ σὺ ἐπακούσῃ ἡμῶν	For you are our protector. We will call to you, and you will hear us
8.	ὅτι σὺ οἰκτιρήσεις τὸ γένος Ισραηλ εἰς τὸν αἰῶνα καὶ οὐκ ἀπώσῃ	For You will have compassion on the people Israel forever and You will not reject them
9.	καὶ ἡμεῖς ὑπὸ ζυγόν σου τὸν αἰῶνα καὶ μάστιγα παιδείας σου	And we are under your eternal yoke, and (under) the whip of your discipline
10.	κατευθυνεῖς ἡμᾶς ἐν καιρῷ ἀντιλήψεώς σου τοῦ ἐλεῆσαι τὸν οἶκον Ιακωβ εἰς ἡμέραν ἐν ᾗ ἐπηγγείλω αὐτοῖς	You will guide us aright in the time of your help to show mercy to the house of Jacob on the day when You promised (it) to them.

Pss. Sol. 7 is the psalmist's prayer of appeal for God's protection. The chain of phrases belongs to the type of discourse [God's Faithfulness: Non-abandonment]: μὴ ἀποσκηνώσῃς (not move away), σὺ ὑπερασπιστὴς ἡμῶν (you are our protector), οὐκ ἀπώσῃ (not reject [Israel]), κατευθυνεῖς ἡμᾶς (you guide us), and ἐλεῆσαι τὸν οἶκον Ιακωβ (have mercy on the house of Jacob). All these show the psalmist's viewpoint about God, which is that God will be faithful to Israel and protect them from harm from the Gentiles. In contrast, the Gentiles will be rejected by God: ἀπώσω αὐτούς ὁ θεός (God rejected them [the Gentiles]). Like Romans 11:1–10, this discourse of [God's Faithfulness: Non-abandonment] interweaves with the discourse of [Israel's Sin].

In *Pss. Sol.* 8, the psalmist acknowledges that the people are sinful (cf. vv. 7–13).[75] As he states:

> [8] God exposed their sins before the sun; the whole earth knew the righteous judgments of God.
> [9] In secret underground *places* were their outrageous transgressions of the law: son involved with mother and father with daughter.
> [10] Everyone committed adultery with his neighbor's wife; they made with them contracts with an oath about these things.
> [11] They plunder the sanctuary of God as if there were no heir who could redeem.
> [12] They trampled on the place of sacrifice of the Lord, *coming* from all kinds of uncleanness and with menstrual blood. They defiled the sacrifices as if *they were* vulgar meat.
> [13] They did not leave any sin which they would not commit, exceeding *in this* the Gentiles.[76]

In other words, these Israelites, the leaders of Israel, have sinned even more seriously than the Gentiles (v. 13). The psalmist expresses that judgment has been poured over Israel (vv. 14–23), that Israel was led away in exile to a foreign country, and that it was scattered in every Gentile nation when they abandoned the Lord (*Pss. Sol.* 9:1–2); however, this punishment does not last forever. When Israel repents, God will have mercy and compassion on them again. The psalmist's voice is that God's mercy is upon "the house of Israel forever and ever" (v. 11).[77]

---

75. Mikael Winninge, *Sinners and the Righteous: A Comparative Study of the Psalms of Solomon and Paul's Letters*. ConBNT. (Stockholm: Almqvist & Wiksell International, 1995), 60.

76. The translation is from LXE.

77. Here is the psalmist's prayer in *Pss. Sol.* 9:7–11, translated by Wright: "And whose sins will he forgive, except those who have sinned? You will bless the righteous, and not accuse them for their sin. Because your kindness is upon those that sin, when they repent. Now, then, you are God and we are the people whom you have loved: Look, and be compassionate, O God of Israel, because we are yours, and don't take your mercy from us, lest they set upon us. Because you have chosen the descendants of Abraham over all other nations; you put your name upon us, O Lord, and that will not cease forever. You made

Therefore, the psalmist's voice of God's non-abandonment of Israel is similar to Paul's voice. Although Israel has sinned and judgment falls upon them for a while, God will not everlastingly neglect them. He will save them in the future (cf. Rom 11:26). However, the psalmist's voice concerning the Gentiles remains distinguished from Paul's. This will be considered in the next section, when the Gentiles are brought into view.

5.3 Romans 11:11–32

In contrast to the first section (Rom 11:1–10), the dominant type of clause relationship in this section is hypotactic.[78] Also, relational clauses play as significant a role as material clauses in terms of the process type. This suggests that the relationship among participants is one main theme of this section. The participants of the relational clauses involve salvation, the Gentiles, Israel, etc. These facts demonstrate that the relationship between the Gentiles and Israel in regard to salvation is one of the main concerns in this section. Paul's argumentation proceeds with the identification and characterization of relationships at first (vv. 11–16). The material clauses center on verses 18–24, which present the metaphor of wild/natural branches and their root. The combination of material and relational clauses happens in verses 25–32, which speaks of God's salvific actions toward Israel and the Gentiles, and the relationships between Israel and the Gentiles. In sum, the relationship between the Gentiles and Israel in terms of salvation is unfolded by both relational and outer material experiences of the world.

5.3.1 Presentational Meaning

In the previous section (11:1–10), Paul reviews Israel's sin of idol-worship (11:1–4), and through the generalized voices of Moses and Isaiah and the

---

a covenant with our ancestors about us, and we will place our hope in you, when we turn ourselves toward you. May the Lord's mercy be upon the house of Israel forever and ever." See Wright, *Psalms of Solomon*, 131–132.

78. According to appendix 10, there are 20 hypotactic enhancements, 8 hypotactic extensions and 1 hypotactic elaboration (compare to 18 paratactic clause complexes).

voice of the psalmist David, he demonstrates that, because of Israel's heart-hardening, they deserve God's judgment (vv. 8–10). The following argumentative flow could be a further statement about what Paul, the apostle of the Gentiles, considers that judgment to be. One might conclude that the Gentiles now replace the role of Israel as God's people. However, Paul reverses this logic. He speaks to remind the Gentiles (cf. v. 13) that God's judgment of Israel is temporary, and that salvation is still awaiting Israel until all Israel will be saved. The following texts (vv. 11–32) proceed to remind or warn the Gentiles from three perspectives not to boast over Israel: the positive result of Israel's failure (vv. 11–15), the metaphor of olive root and branches (vv. 16–24), and Israel's final salvation (vv. 25–32).

Paul first directly addresses the Gentiles to indicate the positive result of Israel's failure. The conjunction οὖν in verse 11 indicates an inference from the previous argument. The verbal verb λέγω signals that a projected locution clause follows. The structure of the projected clause, verse 11a (cc10A-B), is similar to that of verse 1a: the rhetorical question λέγω οὖν μὴ ἔπταισαν ἵνα πέσωσιν; (did Israel's sin make them fall into final ruin?), followed by emphatic rejection μὴ γένοιτο. If we read these clauses as interweaving, we can infer that God has not rejected his people, so when they sinned (πταίω), they will not fall into ruin, a final failure.[79] With the contrastive particle ἀλλὰ (v. 11b, c11A), Paul's voice then further explains the positive result of Israel's trespass: that salvation had come to the Gentiles, but would then turn back again to Israel.[80] The preposition εἰς brings in a sub-clause (εἰς τὸ παραζηλῶσαι αὐτούς [v. 11b, c11B]) in a purpose relation with the primary clause (ἡ σωτηρία τοῖς ἔθνεσιν). It is interesting to note the use of the lexical term παραζηλόω in verse 11b

---

79. Most translations and commentaries regard πταίω as "stumble." See RSV, ASV, CEB, NAS, NET, NIV etc, and also Moo, *The Epistle to the Romans*, 686–687; Cranfield, *Romans*, 555; Dunn, *Romans 9–16*, 652–653, etc. However, it does not occur with the meaning "stumble" in the NT. The occurrences of Jas 2:10; 3:2 and 2 Pet 1:10 do not refer to "stumble," but to "sin" (cf. Louw and Nida, "πταίω," 774). Second, ἔπταισαν corresponds to the phrase τῷ αὐτῶν παραπτώματι in v. 11b. Moreover, when Paul speaks of "stumble" in previous passages (9:31-33), he uses προσκόπτω. Therefore, the meaning of πταίω is more likely "to sin, to err."

80. Moo has a similar idea, setting a three-stage process: "Israel's sin is the starting point of process that will lead back to blessing for Israel. The middle stage of this process involves the Gentiles." See Moo, *The Epistle to the Romans*, 687.

(c11B), which is the key term in Deuteronomy 32:21 and Romans 10:19.[81] The focus of Deuteronomy 32 is the final salvation of Israel.[82] Therefore, Israel's sin is not the end of the story, but it "is the first step in an unfolding process."[83] Why does Paul make the effort to show the positive result of Israel's trespass? Paul is probably reminding the Gentile Christians not to look down upon the Israelites (cf. v. 18). This can be seen clearly in his following articulations.

The structure of the argument in verse 12 corresponds to a *qal wahomer* (how much more) argument, arguing from the lesser to the greater.[84] In other words, if the protasis (the two propositions, c12A) is valid, "the apodosis that conveys its consequence is effectually more true."[85] The main items of the conditional clauses can be shown in the following chart:

The first proposition	τὸ παράπτωμα αὐτῶν	πλοῦτος κόσμου
The second proposition	τὸ ἥττημα αὐτῶν	πλοῦτος ἐθνῶν
The apodosis (consequence)	πόσῳ μᾶλλον τὸ πλήρωμα αὐτῶν	

---

81. Cf. Moo, *The Epistle to the Romans*, 688; Bell, *Provoked to Jealousy*, 112; Cranfield, *Romans*, 556.

82. The overall thematic patterns of Deut 32: God's care for Israel, Israel's apostasy, God's judgment on Israel through the Gentiles, and God's restoration of them.

83. Moo, *The Epistle to the Romans*, 683. Note that Moo puts a three-stage process at the heart of Rom 11: vv. 11–12: "trespass of Israel" – "salvation for the Gentiles" – "their fullness"; v. 15: "their rejection" – "reconciliation of the world" – "their acceptance"; vv.17–23: "natural branches" broken off – "wild shoots" grafted in – "natural branches" grafted back in; vv. 30–31: Disobedience of Israel – Mercy for Gentiles – Mercy to Israel. See Moo, *The Epistle to the Romans*, 684.

84. Ellis, *The Old Testament in Early Christianity*, 87; Terence L. Donaldson, "'Riches for the Gentiles' (Rom 11:12): Israel's Rejection and Paul's Gentile Mission," *JBL* 112 (1993): 89.

85. Waetjen, *Romans*, 266.

Paul speaks of Israel's παράπτωμα (trespass) again in the first proposition. It parallels with ἥττημα (defeat).[86] The use of the terms παράπτωμα and its cognate ἥττημα point to some sense of Israel's failure – a disobedience toward God.[87] Contrary to the Gentiles' expectation, the consequence of Israel's failure leads to rich blessings (πλοῦτος) for the world.

After presenting his apostolic role to the Gentiles in verses 13–14,[88] Paul resumes the *qal wahomer* argument in verse 15: if their ἀποβολή (rejection) means the reconciliation of the world,[89] what will their πρόσλημψις (acceptance) mean but life from the dead (εἰ μὴ ζωὴ ἐκ νεκρῶν)?[90] We can see that the semantic patterns of verses 11b–12 are similar to the patterns in verse 15. The chain of phrases – their (Israel's) trespass, their failure, their rejection – denotes a type of discourse pattern [Israel's Rebellion]. In contrast, the lexical chain riches (πλοῦτος), fullness (πλήρωμα), reconciliation (καταλλαγή), life from the dead (ζωὴ ἐκ νεκρῶν), and save (σῴζω)[91] would

---

86. It is rarely used, only occurring twice in other places, Isa 31:8 and 1 Cor 6:7, in both of which it may be translated as "defeat." Moo, *The Epistle to the Romans*, 688, n. 26; Cranfield, *Romans*, 557. Louw and Nida define it as follows: "a lack of attaining a desirable state or condition – 'to fail, to lack, failure.'" Louw and Nida, "ἥττημα," 152.
87. Cf. Bell, *Provoked to Jealousy*, 271.
88. We will discuss these two verses later, which seem to be inserted into a series of the rhetorical structure – *qal wahomer* argument. Moo considers that "these verses are something of an aside, a parenthesis that anticipates the hortatory direction that Paul takes his argument in vv. 17–24." See Moo, *The Epistle to the Romans*, 690–91.
89. The term ἀποβολή could be defined as "the event of ceasing to exist – 'loss, destruction;'" or "the removal of someone from a particular association – 'rejection, elimination.'" A good many commentators prefer the second interpretation, but differ in their opinion as to whether God takes the initiative. See Louw and Nida, "ἀποβολή," 160, 451. The only other occurrence of this term in the NT (Acts 27:22) probably means loss. Jewett takes the meaning of "their [Israel's] discarding [the gospel] (see Jewett, *Romans*, 680–681); Moo sees God's initiative in the process, that is, Israel's rejection by God (see Moo, *The Epistle to the Romans*, 692–93; cf. Louw and Nida, "ἀποβολή," 451). Jewett follows Fitzmyer's argument that in 11:1 Paul has repudiated the idea that God has rejected his people. However, Israel's rejection by God in this verse does not refer to the final abandonment by God, but to the temporary rejection in the process of God's whole redemptive plan.
90. Note that there is a different syntactical and logical structure with the *qal wahomer* argument in vv. 11–12: the "if... how much more" sequence in v. 12 gives way to an "if... what" sequence in v. 15, and different terminology. See Moo, *The Epistle to the Romans*, 692.
91. What does the phrase ζωὴ ἐκ νεκρῶν mean here? Many commentators noticed the kinship of Rom 11:15 and 5:10–11 in terms of the similar structure and terminologies (Moo, *The Epistle to the Romans*, 693–696; Jewett, *Romans*, 681. Note that Bell relates

appear in the ITF [God's Salvation]. Some Gentiles could conclude that Israel's rebellion excludes them from God's salvation. However, Paul sets [Israel's Rebellion] in a coherent relation with [God's Salvation] through the *qal wahomer* principle (the lesser to the greater). It is worthy of note that Paul does not approve [Israel's Rebellion] *per se*, but he perceives an overall picture of God's salvific plan so that he can put [Israel's Rebellion] into perspective.[92] In addition, it is God who can work to reverse the negative effect into a positive one.[93]

Verses 13–14 looks like an insertion, but it has a tight connection to both the preceding and following discourses. First, through the "jealousy" issue that has been introduced in verse 11b, Paul points out that his ministry (διακονία) as an apostle to the Gentiles has a significant impact on Israel.[94] Second, Paul's self-introduction as an apostle to the Gentiles lays the groundwork for the following injunction to the Gentiles in the metaphor of the olive branches (vv. 16–24).

The direct address "the Gentiles" has been emphasized by putting the pronoun ὑμῖν in the emphatic position in verse 13. Paul attempts to catch the attention of the Gentiles in order to direct them into the right way of thinking about their relationship with Israel. He asserts his role as an apostle to the Gentiles for the first time within Romans 9–11, but with the concessive expression ἐφ' ὅσον[95] and the following phrase μὲν οὖν,[96] Paul

---

Deut 32:39, "I kill and I make alive," to the expression "life from the dead" in Rom 11:15). If so, the expression "life from the dead" probably refers to the general resurrection at the end of time, "or to the blessed life that will follow that resurrection." See Jewett, *Romans*, 681; Moo, *The Epistle to the Romans*, 695.

92. God brings in a positive result from his temporary rejection of Israel, that is, the reconciliation of the world.

93. Waetjen sees a pattern of God's reversal indicated in the stories of Joseph as well as Jesus. For the former, "God did not abandon Jacob after his sons sold Joseph into Egyptian slavery, but used Joseph to bring deliverance, first to the Egyptians and subsequently to Jacob and his family." Analogous to Joseph, Jesus "was betrayed and handed over to the Romans for execution but resurrected from the dead and glorified by being seated on the right hand of God to become the Savior of the Gentiles as well as the present remnant of Israel." Waetjen, *Romans*, 265.

94. Moo, *The Epistle to the Romans*, 690–692.

95. See Louw and Nida, "ὅσος," 693: To some degree, as much as; In Rom 11:13, ὅσος is strengthened by ἐπί.

96. See Cranfield, *Romans*, 559; Dunn, *Romans 9–16*, 655–666; Moo, *The Epistle to the Romans*, 691; Jewett, *Romans*, 678, etc.

has expressed an idea which is contrary to what some of his addressees (the Gentile Christians), may be tempted to think: Paul, although a Jew, in turning his efforts to the Gentiles, has given up on his own people, for he disdained his people.[97] Contrary to what the Gentiles may expect, however, Paul points out that his ministry to the Gentiles will serve to save some Jewish people (σώσω τινὰς ἐξ αὐτῶν) by provoking their jealousy.[98] Note that it is Paul who makes his fellow Jews jealous in order to save some of his kinsmen (v. 14). Paul consistently identifies himself as an Israelite, and is concerned about his people (9:1–5; 10:1–2; 11:1–2, 13–14). Although he identifies his ministry as an apostle to the Gentiles, Israel still can benefit from his ministry: "in order to make my fellow Jews jealous, and thus save some of them" (v. 14). The lexical chain – Gentiles, apostle, ministry – can denote a type of discourse [Gentile Ministry]. Therefore, Paul displays his role as the apostle to the Gentiles, but he consistently insists on his concern for Israel, his kinsmen. In some sense, Paul's Gentile ministry is for the salvation of his own people. Thus far, Paul, by showing the significance of the role of Israel, attempts to warn the Gentiles not to boast over Israel, for they belong to the original root (ἡ ῥίζα).[99]

In Romans 11:16–24, Paul employs a metaphor of Ancient Grafting Oleiculture to warn the Gentiles of any projections of arrogant superiority. Starting from verse 16, the lexical chain shifts to the items of ancient Oleiculture of grafting: οἱ κλάδοι (branches), ἡ ῥίζα (root), ἀγριέλαιος/τῆς ἐλαίας (a wild olive shoot/tree), ἐξεκλάσθησαν (be broken off), ἐνεκεντρίσθης (be grafted in), etc. Similar descriptions of the process of grafting olive branches have been provided by Theophrastus of Eresus (371–287 BC).[100] In other words, this type of discourse can be labeled as ITF [Ancient

---

97. Moo, *The Epistle to the Romans*, 691.
98. Ibid.
99. There are controversial issues about what ἀπαρχὴ, φύραμα, ῥίζα and κλάδοι in v.16 refer to. Regarding ἀπαρχὴ, some identify it with "Christ." Although some church fathers took this position, it is not natural here to read it as "Christ." Others identify it with "the patriarchs," and still others with "Jewish Christians." We agree with most commentators and go with "the patriarchs." See Cranfield, *Romans*, 563–565; Moo, *The Epistle to the Romans*, 699–700; Bell, *Provoked to Jealousy*, 118–119.
100. See Philip F. Esler, "Ancient Oleiculture and Ethnic Differentiation: The Meaning of the Olive-Tree Image in Romans 11," *JSNT* 26 1 (2003): 113.

Grafting Oleiculture].[101] Another set of lexical allocations is as follows: ἀπιστία (unbelief), τοὺς πεσόντας (those who have fallen). In the co-text, the participants here refer to Israel. Therefore, we can consider them as belonging to the ITF [Israel's Rebellion]. Compared with the set of lexical allocations of Israel's rebellion, there is a chain of imperative phrases (the participants here refer to the Gentiles) – μὴ κατακαυχῶ (do not boast), μὴ ὑψηλὰ φρόνει (do not be proud) – which can belong to the ITF [Warning to the Gentiles]. We should note that Paul's comparing [Israel's Rebellion] and [Warning to the Gentiles] here is not to criticize his kinsmen, the Israelites, as he has done in Romans 9:30–10:4. On the contrary, Paul warns the Gentiles not to boast over Israel, otherwise they would be cut off from the tree just as those unbelieving-rebelling Israelites were (cf. v. 18), and he reminds the Gentiles that their being saved is due to God's kindness. In other places, like Ephesians 2:11–14, there is a similar thematic pattern to remind the Gentiles of their being aliens in the citizenship of Israel.[102]

Now let us investigate the text in detail. Verse 16 moves from discursive argument and scriptural quotations into metaphors: the metaphor of the first fruits and the lump of dough (ἀπαρχὴ and φύραμα),[103] and the meta-

---

101. The procedure of grafting branches is from cultivated olive trees into wild olive trees. However, Paul reverses this procedure. Some scholars (e.g. W. D. Davies, Dodd) state that Paul simply did not understand ancient Oleiculture; some defend Paul by arguing that occasionally a wild olive shoot can be grafted into a cultivated olive tree (W. M. Ramsay, A. G. Baxter and J. A. Ziesler, and P. F. Esler, etc.). See Esler, "Ancient Oleiculture," 103–124; J. A. Ziesler and A. G. Baxter, "Paul and Arboriculture: Romans 11:17–24," *JSNT* 24 (1985):25–32; cf. Moo, *The Epistle to the Romans*, 703.

102. Eph 2:12 reads, "At that time you were without Christ. You were aliens rather than citizens of Israel, and strangers to the covenants of God's promise. In this word you had no hope and no God." (CEB).

103. Note that the expression ἀπαρχὴ φύραμα only appears in Num 15:20 (LXX). There are several reasons that Paul refers to Num 15:20. First, Num 15:15–20 speaks of the religious law applied to the Israelite and the non-Israelite foreigner as well (גֵּר refers to the non-Israelite foreigner; see R. J. D. Knauth, "Alien, Foreign Resident," in *Dictionary of the Old Testament: Pentateuch*, ed. T. Desmond Alexander and David W. Baker [Downers Grove: InterVarsity, 2003], 27); second, in the following texts, it is an instruction when Israel fails to observe God's commandments (Num 15:22–29), thus the issue of Israel's failure is in the context; third, Num 15 considers under which conditions the Israelites and the foreigners residing among them shall be cut off (Num 15:30–31). The theme of "cutting off" corresponds to Paul's argument in Rom 11:17–24. In addition, Num 14 is a narrative about Israel's rebellion, when they disbelieved God's promise and complained against Moses, and God's forgiveness of them through Moses' intercession and their

phor of the root and branches.[104] The subsequent text (vv. 17–24) continues to explain the second metaphor, focusing on "branches." The metaphor of root and branches expresses the idea that some unbelieving Jews were cut off from the family whereas the Gentile believers have been adopted into the family; if the Gentiles do not remain in the faith, however, they can be broken off.

The conditional clauses (vv. 17–18a, cc16A-C) consist of a three-part protasis in verse 17, followed by an apodosis in verse 18a: "do not boast over the branches." This implies that some of the Gentile Christians may boast over Israel. Paul now turns to criticize the Gentiles. In the protasis (v. 17), Paul directly addresses Gentile Christians and points out the facts that, first, some of the branches (the unbelieving Jews) were cut off (ἐξεκλάσθησαν)[105] and, second, you, the wild olive shoot (Gentile Christians) were grafted in (ἐνεκεντρίσθης)[106] and have become participants in the richness of the root.[107] Regarding the metaphor of branches, there are two points to be noted: Paul reminds the Gentile Christians not to boast over the broken off branches, and to remain in faith since they were cut off because of

---

repentance (Num 14:39–40). Budd has argued that the story in Num 14:11b–23, which was edited after the fall of Jerusalem, and narrative of the golden calf are archetypal in the Deuteronomistic tradition, which explains Israel's dispossession. "It was important to point out that possession was contingent upon obedience, to explain what had happened, and also to set the tone for the future . . . The command to Israel not to enter from the south, but to turn back (v. 25), is a significant act of rejection. The Yahwist's final perspective, however, is far from somber. In the providence of God, the tragic failures of one generation can be retrieved in the experiences of the next. The purpose of God cannot ultimately be defeated. Nevertheless the reversal of the Judah tradition by the Yahwist adds a new and serious dimension to disaffection at this stage of the story." Philip J. Budd, *Numbers*. WBC 5. (Waco: Word Books, 1984), 162–164. Therefore, the seemingly "accidental" employment of ἀπαρχή and φύραμα indicates a profound implication.

104. Esler, "Ancient Oleiculture," 108.

105. The term ἐξεκλάσθησαν is a divine passive verb. It suggests that God is the one who had done the cutting off. See Moo, *The Epistle to the Romans*, 701, n. 23.

106. The verb ἐγκεντρίζω occurs only in this passage of New Testament (vv.17, 19, 23^{x2}, and 24^{x2}). It is a technical arboricultural term. Note that grafting is not known in some cultures. See Louw and Nida, "ἐγκεντρίζω," 517; Moo, *The Epistle to the Romans*, 701, n. 24.

107. Some scholars indicate that it is the reverse of the usual process to graft a wild or uncultivated tree into a cultivated one, and then point out that Paul simply did not know arboriculture because of his urban background. See Moo, *The Epistle to the Romans*, 702–703.

their unbelief (v. 20),[108] and, second, their being grafted into the cultivated olive tree happens solely because of God's kindness to them (v. 22). If they seek to justify a feeling of superiority over the Jews (v. 19: "Branches were broken off so that I might be grafted in"), and the Jews do not persist in their unbelief, God could cut them off and graft those Jews back into their own root.

Therefore, it remains possible for the cut away branches (the unbelieving Jews) to be grafted back into their own root. If the Jews do not persist in their unbelief, God has the power to re-graft them back into their root. In other words, the abandoning of the Jews is temporary; when they turn from unbelief to belief, they will be saved. In sum, the metaphor warns Gentile Christians not to boast over Jewish Christians, which paves the way for the following argument about the inclusion of all Israel in salvation.

After the metaphor of the grafted branches, Paul continues to address the Gentile Christians in order to remind them of the fact that God will have mercy over all Israel and all of them will be saved (vv. 25–32). Starting with a mental clause (Οὐ . . . θέλω ὑμᾶς ἀγνοεῖν, v. 25, c23A) and a nominal noun of address (ἀδελφοί), Paul expresses his intimacy with his audience, the Gentile Christians.[109] This type of personally intimate expression occurred in 10:1, in which Paul showed his concern about the salvation of Israel to his audience. Note that the key term in the second part of the mystery (σωθήσεται) corresponds to Paul's previous intercessory prayer toward God (Rom 10:1: εἰς σωτηρίαν).[110] Paul seems to predict that his interces-

---

108. Faith is a necessary condition for ultimate salvation, as Moo comments, "The person who ceases to believe forfeits any hope of salvation." See Moo, *The Epistle to the Romans*, 707.

109. Cranfield considers this expression as Paul's "emphasis [on] something which he regards as of special importance." Cf. Cranfield, *Romans*, 573. Both Moo and Cranfield agree that "brothers" here refer to the Gentile Christians (See Moo, *The Epistle to the Romans*, 714; Cranfield, *Romans*, 451). Contra Jewett, who argues that "brothers" refers to the Christian community consisting of Jews as well as Gentiles (see Jewett, *Romans*, 697). Tobin holds a similar view to Jewett. As he states, "the 'brothers' whom he is directly addressing are the Roman Christians, both Gentile and Jewish. The 'you' (plural) in 11:25, then, should not be confused with the 'you' (plural and singular) of the imaginary Gentile interlocutor(s) of 11:13–24" (Tobin, *Paul's Rhetoric*, 369).

110. In the following we divide the content of the mystery into two parts. For the correspondence with Rom 10:1, see also Karl Olav Sandnes, *Paul, One of the Prophets? A Contribution to the Apostle's Self-Understanding*. WUNT 43. (Tübingen: Mohr, 1991), 178.

sion will be answered, that is, all Israel will be saved in the eschatological future.[111]

The inferential conjunction γὰρ also connects with the preceding argument of 11:16–24,[112] whose main concern is to warn the Gentile Christians not to boast over Jewish Christians.[113] Particularly, in the last two verses (11:23–24), Paul implies a hope for Israel that the natural branches (those Israelites who have fallen) can be grafted back into cultivated olive trees.[114] In this way, Paul demonstrates to the Gentile Christians his concern for all his kinsmen, even if these Israelites are the fallen ones. The following ἵνα clause (ἵνα μὴ ἦτε [παρ'] ἑαυτοῖς φρόνιμοι, c23D, v. 25) is in a purpose relation with the primary clause οὐ . . . θέλω ὑμᾶς ἀγνοεῖν, ἀδελφοί, τὸ μυστήριον τοῦτο (c23A, v. 25), denoting that Paul's purpose to show the mystery to the Gentile Christians is to warn them not to think too highly of themselves. This warning is consistent with Paul's previous argument embedded in the metaphor of branches and roots. In a word, Paul uses an intimate personal tone to warn the Gentile Christians not to feel superior over the Jews. The way that Paul warns the Gentile Christians is similar to the way he critiques Israel in 9:30–10:21, proceeding from his concern for God's people. The manner of warning or critique stands not as if from an outsider, but from a heartfelt prophet.

With the ὅτι projection clauses (cc23BC, vv. 25–26a), Paul discloses a mystery (μυστήριον), that is, (1) πώρωσις ἀπὸ μέρους τῷ Ἰσραὴλ γέγονεν; (2) πᾶς Ἰσραὴλ σωθήσεται. The two aspects of the mystery seem to be placed in a tension of conflict: Israel's hardening and Israel's salvation. How do these two aspects relate to each other? This will need further lexicogrammatical investigation. The noun πώρωσις corresponds to the cognate verb πωρόω in verse 7.[115] As mentioned previously, hardness of the heart relates

---

111. Paul's first intercessory prayer in 9:2–3 is for Israel's connection with/recognition of Christ. Also, the thematic formations related to εἰς σωτηρίαν and σωθήσεται in 10:9–13 refer to belief in Jesus Christ. In other words, for Paul all Israel's salvation is possible through Messianic faith.

112. Cf. Moo, *The Epistle to the Romans*, 714.

113. Ibid., 715.

114. Ibid.

115. As aforementioned, hardness of the heart is related to idolatrous worship in v. 7, so it probably implies here that Israel has not obeyed God because of an idolatrous preference

to idolatrous worship.[116] The phrase ἀπὸ μέρους is likely used to place a numerical limit on Israel's hardening,[117] for the numerical meaning of the phrase is more consistent with the immediate co-text: first, the part of Israel (who were hardened) contrasts with the following "all Israel" (who will be saved); second, the concept that part of Israel was hardened is in agreement with the previous idea that "some of the branches were broken off" (v. 17).[118] Therefore, Paul places a numerical restriction on Israel's heart-hardening. Also, the following temporal clause ἄχρι οὗ τὸ πλήρωμα τῶν ἐθνῶν εἰσέλθῃ (c23Bb, v. 25) explicates the limit of Israel's hardening in terms of time span. In other words, at a certain point, Israel's hardening will be finished. The meaning of the phrase τὸ πλήρωμα τῶν ἐθνῶν very likely refers to the full number of the Gentiles.[119] Therefore, Paul indicates that part of Israel's hardening will be ended when the full number of Gentiles comes to be saved. It is worth mentioning that Sandnes has observed the prophetic connotation of the ἄχρι οὗ in verse 25, for it corresponds formally with Isaiah's question (How long, O Lord [Isa 6:11]), a cry of lamentation over

---

for other objects of faith. See also Meadors, *Idolatry and Hardening*, 152.

116. In light of v. 28, Israel's hardness is manifested in their refusal of the gospel. Therefore, for Paul, the act of refusing the gospel is analogous to idolatrous worship.

117. Grammatically, the phrase ἀπὸ μέρους could be adjectival, modifying Ἰσραὴλ, or adverbial, modifying either πώρωσις or the verb γέγονεν. But it is awkward to attach the phrase in an adverbial manner to the noun πώρωσις (What does "partial hardness" refer to? Does it contrast with a "full hardness"?). If attached to the verb γέγονεν, it could contain a temporal meaning. That is, it works together with the temporal clause (ἄχρι οὗ τὸ πλήρωμα τῶν ἐθνῶν εἰσέλθῃ) to denote the time limitation of Israel's hardening: Israel's hardening is temporary and will be finished at τὸ πλήρωμα τῶν ἐθνῶν εἰσέλθῃ. However, it would be redundant to see the adverbial use of ἀπὸ μέρους as temporal, since the temporal phrase ἄχρι οὗ already indicate a range of time. Therefore, the phrase ἀπὸ μέρους is used to denote numerical limitations. See Moo, *The Epistle to the Romans*, 717, n. 28; Jewett, *Romans*, 700, etc. Cf. Dunn, *Romans 9–16*, 679; Bell, *Provoked to Jealousy*, 128–129.

118. Cf. Rom 11:7: the elect obtained it (righteousness), but the rest were hardened.

119. The noun πλήρωμα has three types of meanings in the New Testament: first, a quantity which fills a space – "that which fills, contents"; second, a total quantity, with emphasis upon completeness – "full number, full measure, fullness"; third, the totality of a period of time, with the implication of proper completion – "end, completion." (see Louw and Nida, "πλήρωμα" 597–598, 638). The second understanding of the word πλήρωμα suits the co-text better. Most commentators and translators prefer a quantitative meaning of πλήρωμα (full number). See Moo, *The Epistle to the Romans*, 718–719; Jewett, *Romans*, 700; Bell, *Provoked to Jealousy*, 130–134, etc.

Israel's fate.[120] In other words, the mystery of the *ending* of Israel's hardening, when the *full number of the Gentiles* comes in, proceeds from Paul's prophetic perception.[121]

The second part of the mystery, καὶ οὕτως πᾶς Ἰσραὴλ σωθήσεται (v. 26, c23C), has become a contentious topic in current scholarship.[122] Among the four most popular understandings of the reference to πᾶς Ἰσραὴλ,[123] the most appropriate is to interpret it as all Israel as a whole, denoting a large and representative number from ethnic Israel but not necessarily every single member.[124] As regards the adverb οὕτως, it is appropriate to understand it as "with reference to that which follows – 'the following, as

---

120. Sandnes, *Paul, One of the Prophets*, 178.

121. Italics mine.

122. See Jason A. Staples, "What Do the Gentiles Have to Do with 'All Israel'? A Fresh Look at Romans 11:25–27," *JBL* 130 (2011):371–390. Dongsu Kim, "Reading Paul's καὶ οὕτως πᾶς Ισραήλ Σωθήσεται (Rom11:26a) in the Context of Romans," *CTJ* 45 (2010): 317–334; Cornelis P. Venema, "'In This Way All Israel Will Be Saved': A Study of Romans 11:26," *MAJT* 22 (2011):19–40; Christopher Zoccali, "'And So All Israel Will Be Saved': Competing Interpretations of Romans 11.26 in Pauline Scholarship," *JSNT* 30 (2008): 289–318; J. R. Daniel Kirk, "Why Does the Deliverer Come ἐκ Σιών (Romans 11:26)?" *JSNT* 33 (2010): 81–99; Christopher D. Stanley, "'The Redeemer Will Come ἐκ Σιών': Romans 11.26–27 Revisited," in *Paul and the Scriptures of Israel*, ed. Craig A. Evans and James A. Sanders (Sheffield: JSOT Press, 1993), 118–142; Bruce W. Longenecker, "Different Answers to Different Issues: Israel, the Gentiles and Salvation History in Romans 9–11," *JSNT* 36 (1989):95–123.

123. There are four types of reference to all Israel: (1) It refers to all the elect, including both Jews and Gentiles (this ecclesiological interpretation lacks solid support, since Paul's use of the term refers to ethnic Israel more than ten times in Rom 9–11, for instance, 9:[4], 6, 27, 31; 10:19, 21; 11:[1], 2, 7, 25 etc.); (2) the elect within the nation Israel (this view can be denied, since it requires that Paul shifts the meaning of "Israel" from v. 25b to 26a, and also it makes Paul's prediction purposeless); (3) the whole nation throughout history, including every single member (this view can be confirmed only when all Israel are saved irrespective of faith in Christ, which is the so-called 'two-covenant' interpretation. However, this is the least plausible. For a detailed argument, see Zoccali, "So All Will Be Saved," 297–298); (4) the nation Israel generally, not necessarily "every Israelite." See Zoccali, "So All Will Be Saved," 289–314; Bell, *Provoked to Jealousy*, 136–139; Moo, *The Epistle to the Romans*, 720–726, etc.

124. Moo gives a good argument that the phrase occurs 136 times in the LXX and few of these refer to every Israelite. In other words, the connotation of the phrase is the corporate meaning. See Moo, *The Epistle to the Romans*, 722, n. 55. Also, Bell gives a striking example in Mishnah Sanh.10.1, in which example all Israel refers to the corporate sense without including every single Israelite, since there is a long list of exceptions. See Bell, *Provoked to Jealousy*, 137–138.

follows.'" [125] That is, the adverb οὕτως denotes the statement πᾶς Ἰσραὴλ σωθήσεται as part of the mystery. In addition, salvation in Paul's mind must be a future or eschatological event. One key question that arises is, in what way can all Israel be saved? Some scholars argue that Israel's salvation is irrespective of faith in Jesus Christ (e.g. L. Gaston, S. Stowers, and J. Gager hold to the two-covenant salvation theory). However, this is the least possible in terms of Paul's overall argument flow in Romans 9–11:[126] Paul is willing to be accursed and cut off from Christ for the sake of his kinsmen, Israel, if they come to believe in Christ (Rom 9:1–5); Israel's lostness/stumbling lies in their not pursuing righteousness from faith (Rom 9:30–10:4); Paul urges preaching the gospel in the hope that Israel will believe in it (Rom 10:14–21); some Israelites were broken off because of their unbelief, but if they do not persist in their unbelief, they will be grafted back into their own olive tree again (Rom 11:17–24); and according to the gospel of Christ, Israel's unbelief makes them enemies of God (11:28–32). In light of this, the manner of the salvation of Israel must be through Messianic faith.[127]

It is worth noticing that the theme of all Israel's repentance during the eschaton is widespread in early Judaic literature.[128] Note that the structure of the content of the mystery can be characterized as a prophetic insight:

πώρωσις ἀπὸ μέρους τῷ Ἰσραὴλ γέγονεν

---

125. There are three other possible meanings for the word: referring to that which follows; a relatively high degree, presumably in keeping with the context – "so, so much"; and a temporal meaning (Louw and Nida, "οὕτως," 610, 685; Moo, *The Epistle to the Romans*, 719–720; Bell, *Provoked to Jealousy*, 134–136). In addition, Cranfield understands it as an emphatic word. See Cranfield, *Romans*, 576. For a detailed analysis for the preference of the meaning of "thus, in this way," see the arguments in Bell, *Provoked to Jealousy*, 134–136; Moo, *The Epistle to the Romans*, 719–720.

126. Cf. Terence L. Donaldson, "Jewish Christianity, Israel's Stumbling and the *Sonderweg* Reading of Paul," *JSNT* 29 (2006): 27–52.

127. Most scholars understand all Israel's salvation as a messianic salvation. See Longenecker, "Different Answers," 95–123; Moo, *The Epistle to the Romans*, 720–726; Cranfield, *Romans*, 574–577; Bell, *Provoked to Jealousy*, 128–139; Jewett, *Romans*, 702.

128. According to Johnson, "Both 4 Ezra and 2 Baruch speak of the 'full number' of the elect as a prelude to the eschaton, even as Paul discusses the πλήρωμα of Israel (11:12) and of the Gentiles (11:25) . . . Furthermore, the belief that the eschaton will follow 'all' Israel's repentance was apparently widespread in early Judaism, particularly apocalyptic texts." Johnson, *Function of Apocalyptic*, 125. Cf. T. Dan. 6:4; T. Sim. 6:2–7; T. Jud 23:5; As. Mos. 1:18; 2 Bar 78;6–7; Apoc. Abr. 23:5, etc.

ἄχρι οὗ τὸ πλήρωμα τῶν ἐθνῶν εἰσέλθῃ
καὶ οὕτως πᾶς Ἰσραὴλ σωθήσεται

The structure is threefold,[129] referring to three different time-dimensions: the hardening of Israel in the past (cf. Rom 10:16, 21), the ongoing Gentile mission, and the future salvation of Israel.[130] The prophetic formula, past-present-future, characterizes this as a prophetic oracle.[131]

With a projecting introductory clause καθὼς γέγραπται (c24A, v. 26), Paul generalizes the voice of the two conflated Isaianic texts (Isa 59:20; 27:9) into his own voice. Although the combined citation of Isaiah 59:20–21 with 27:9 in Romans 11:26b–27 follows the LXX texts closely, there is one significant revision: from ἕνεκεν Σιων (Isa 59:20, for the sake of Zion) to ἐκ Σιών.[132] This adjustment suggests to erase the situational context of Isaiah 59:20 (ἕνεκεν Σιων on account of Zion), which can denote the exclusive role of Zion in God's salvation.[133] The phrase ἐκ Σιών is more common, and conveys the connotation that something comes from Zion to somewhere else. This corresponds to Paul's voice that the gospel comes from the Jewish community and will be delivered to the Gentiles.

---

129. Cf. Getty, "Paul and the Salvation of Israel," 458; Moo, *The Epistle to the Romans*, 716.
130. Sandnes, *Paul, One of the Prophets*, 174–175.
131. Ibid.
132. Wagner argues that the shift and the conflation of the two Isaianic verses are Paul's doing (see Wagner, *Heralds of the Good News*, 281–286). On the contrary, Stanley considers that the revisions and conflation are from some Jewish oral tradition in which these two verses had already been conflated (See Stanley, "The Redeemer Will Come," 118–142 (126). Bell also argues that the conflation existed in pre-Pauline tradition. See Bell, *Provoked to Jealousy*, 142 and n. 195. However, it does not matter whether the combined Scripture of Isa 59:20–21 and 27:9 existed before Paul or not. The significance is that Paul at least endorses their conflation. In addition, when comparing Wagner's and Stanley's argumentation, Wagner's is more convincing (for Stanley's arguments, also see Stanley, *Paul and the Language of Scripture*, 166–171). Regarding the basic survey of the shift, see Kirk, "Romans 11:26," 81–99.
133. As Stanley has observed, "Both Isaiah 27 and Isaiah 59 portray Yahweh as a military hero who comes to rescue his people from a state of 'darkness' and 'captivity.' Both passages include references to the forgiveness of Israel's sin, the judgment and subjection of her enemies, and the return of her dispersed children from the surrounding nations." See Stanley, "The Redeemer Will Come," 120.

In another place, Paul alters the singular form of sin into the plural.[134] This revision must be necessitated by the co-text: the plural ἁμαρτίας parallels ἀσεβείας, both referring to Israel's sinfulness.[135] In sum, these few adjustments make the situational connotation into a normative one, that is, the voice of Isaiah is now a generalized one.[136]

Thus, this is the scheme of the mystery of the salvation of all Israel: the hardening of part of Israel, the inclusion of the Gentiles, and the salvation of all Israel. Therefore, Israel's rebellion provides a benefit for the Gentiles, who can now be included in the people of God, and the inclusion of the Gentiles in turn opens a way for all Israel to be saved. In terms of salvation, the Gentiles and Israel are interdependent. Now let us turn to verses 28–32. These verses can be grouped together as a sub-section of verses 25–32: first, there is an asyndeton between verses 25–27 and verse 28,[137] which suggests a possible break between verses 25–27 and verse 28;[138] second, verses 28–32 is internally closely connected with each other;[139] third, there is also a break before the subsequent doxology. However, the aim of this sub-section is to explain further the previous prophetic mystery statement regarding Israel's salvation, which suggests a semantic connection of verses 25–27 and verses 28–32.[140] This connection can be shown from the

---

134. According to Jewett, "The plural form was required to refer not to sin in general but rather the particular acts of violent opposition against the gospel and its messengers on the part of zealous Jews. See Jewett, *Romans*, 706.

135. Some argue that the plural form of ἁμαρτίας is not Pauline style. However, this plural form occurs together with the possessive pronoun. Actually, Paul uses the plural ἁμαρτίας seven times, six out of which are modified by a possessive of some sort. In other words, the possessive pronoun with the plural ἁμαρτίας must be Pauline style (see also Wagner, *Heralds of the Good News*, 283, n. 203). Note that the word ἀσεβείας is used by Paul in Rom 1:18 to condemn all those who worship man-made idols instead of God.

136. The detailed situational context of Isa 59:20 and 27:9 will be explored in the section of Scriptural Voices.

137. On the asyndeton, see *BDF* §463.

138. See also, Cranfield, *Romans*, 579; Moo, *The Epistle to the Romans*, 729; Bell, *Irrevocable Call*, 278; Bell, *Provoked to Jealousy*, 145, etc.

139. The argument flow will be discussed below. Note that the main participants focus on "you" (the Gentile Christians) and "they" (Israel as a whole), much more simply than the previous section. Also, a chiasm structure interweaves vv. 30–31 together. See Moo, *The Epistle to the Romans*, 732–733; Bell, *Provoked to Jealousy*, 147–148.

140. A good many commentators hold them together as a section of "the salvation of 'all Israel,'" not only as the climax of ch. 11, but also of chs. 9–11. See Moo, *The Epistle to the Romans*, 712–713; Cranfield, *Romans*, 572–573; Jewett, *Romans*, 695–696.

thematic flow of verses 28–32. In the following, the semantic meaning of verses 28–32 will be explored.

From the following chart, it can be seen that the two relational clauses in verse 28 are parallel with each other, and denote the relationship of Israel with God from different perspectives:

| c25A | κατὰ μὲν τὸ εὐαγγέλιον | ἐχθροὶ | δι' ὑμᾶς |
| c25B | κατὰ δὲ τὴν ἐκλογὴν | ἀγαπητοὶ | διὰ τοὺς πατέρας |

The preposition κατὰ denotes that with regard to the gospel, they (Israel) are enemies of God.[141] The word ἐχθροὶ denotes Israel's enmity with God.[142] With the prepositional phrase δι' ὑμᾶς, Paul points out that this enmity is for the sake of "you," the Gentile Christians (the audience). In other words, Paul implicitly warns the Gentiles to treasure the gospel and not to boast over Israel (cf. 11: 18).[143] Clause 25B (v. 28b) shares a similar semantic pattern with c25A (v. 28a). It indicates that in regard to election, they (Israel) are beloved because of the patriarchs. Note that the lexical allocations – ἐκλογὴν, ἀγαπητοὶ and τοὺς πατέρας – in the second clause (c25B, v. 28b) correspond to the semantic pattern in Romans 9:10–13 (Ἰσαὰκ τοῦ πατρὸς ἡμῶν, ἡ κατ' ἐκλογὴν πρόθεσις τοῦ θεοῦ, and

---

141. The cognate word of εὐαγγέλιον occurs in 10:15–16 (τῶν εὐαγγελιζομένων and τῷ εὐαγγελίῳ), which refers to the righteousness of faith or faith in Christ (10:14–17, cf. 9:30–33).

142. See Louw and Nida, "ἐχθρός," 493: "pertaining to being at enmity with someone – 'being an enemy, in opposition to.'" There are controversies about whether the definition of ἐχθρός is passive or active. Bell argues for the passive meaning, "those who hated by God," based on its parallel word ἀγαπητοὶ having the passive meaning. See Bell, *Provoked to Jealousy*, 146. Jewett considers it as active, "That zealous Israelites . . . make themselves into God's 'enemies' by warring against the gospel and its proclaimers require an active rather a passive definition of ἐχθρός." See Jewett, *Romans*, 707. However, the concern here is not passive or active enemies, but that Israel's enmity is *for the sake of the Gentiles*.

143. Moo makes this verse carry too much meaning. He says that κατὰ . . . τὸ εὐαγγέλιον ἐχθροί, "succinctly summarizes the point that Paul has made in 9:30–10:21: through their failure to respond to the revelation of God's righteousness in Christ, the heart of the gospel, Israel as a whole has failed to attain the eschatological salvation manifested in the gospel." See Moo, *The Epistle to the Romans*, 730.

τὸν Ἰακὼβ ἠγάπησα). In other words, the thematic meaning, that Israel is God's beloved because of the patriarchs, allies with that of the discourse in 9:6–13.[144] With the inferential conjunction γάρ, verse 29 further explains the reason why Israel is God's beloved. The gifts (τὰ χαρίσματα) here correspond to Romans 9:4–5, in which the privileges of Israel have been enumerated.[145] The call of God (ἡ κλῆσις τοῦ θεοῦ) has a connection with the seed of Isaac (cf. 9:7) and God's special election of Israel to be in a relationship with him (cf. 11:28).[146] In this sense, Paul confirms that God's word has not failed (cf. 9:6a), since God will keep his promise to the patriarchs. Note that the word ἀμεταμέλητα occurs rarely in the NT.[147] The employment of this word brings in new thematic meaning: that both Israel's privilege and its election are irrevocable (ἀμεταμέλητα) and without regret.[148] This confirms Paul's statements that "God has not rejected his people" (11:1) and "all Israel will be saved" (11:26). The lexical chains in the following indicate that they belong to the type of discourse pattern [Gracious Election: Patriarchs]: ἐκλογὴν, ἀγαπητοί, πατέρας, χαρίσματα, κλῆσις, and θεοῦ. The ITF [Gracious Election: Patriarchs] shares a similar thematic meaning with [Promise: Patriarchs] in 9:6–9.

With an inferential conjunction γάρ, Paul continues to explain how salvation will return to Israel; this is the focus of chapter 11. As Moo observes, "The argument recapitulates the process that Paul has described several times already, according to which God works out his purposes of salvation

---

144. Contra Jewett. For him, election here does not refer to the remnant as it does in 9:6–13 (cf. 9:11 ἡ κατ' ἐκλογὴν πρόθεσις τοῦ θεοῦ) and 11:7 (ἡ ἐκλογὴ vs. οἱ δὲ λοιποὶ), but to the general nation of Israel as "all Israel" in v. 26. See Jewett, *Romans*, 707. Jewett indicates that "it is the status and not the quality of Israel's election that is in view here."

145. Most commentators would agree with this understanding (see Moo, *The Epistle to the Romans*, 732; Cranfield, *Romans*, 581; Jewett, *Romans*, 708). Some would argue for an alternative, for instance, Bell regards the gifts as "the election of and promise to Abraham and his descendants." See Bell, *Provoked to Jealousy*, 146, note 217. Bell must take καὶ as an instance of hendiadys, in which the phrase τὰ χαρίσματα is used to introduce an aspect of the divine calling. However, the natural understanding of καὶ is as a copulative connection. See also Cranfield, *Romans*, 581; Moo, *The Epistle to the Romans*, 732.

146. The word κλῆσις cognates to ἐκλογή. See Moo, *The Epistle to the Romans*, 732, n. 90; Jewett, *Romans*, 708.

147. The other occurrence is in 2 Cor 7:10, which means "without regret." See also Moo, *The Epistle to the Romans*, 732, n. 94.

148. This word is derivative of μεταμέλομαι, "to regret," with a negative prefix, meaning "not regretful, not feeling sorry about." See Louw and Nida, "μεταμέλομαι," 318.

in history through an oscillation between Jews and Gentiles (cf. vv. 11–12, 15, 17–24, 25)."[149] The structure of verses 30–31 is formed by the two connective particles ὥσπερ (just as) and οὕτως (so also): "just as" the Gentiles have experienced (v. 30), "so" Israel will also experience (v. 31).[150] In other words, it expresses that as you (the Gentile Christian) once disobeyed God, now you have been shown mercy because of their (the unbelieving Jews) disobedience (in the sense of instrument, cause or manner).[151] So, in a similar way, they are disobedient now so that they will, in the near future (the second νῦν in v. 31),[152] be shown mercy, which has been shown to you. This parallel reading fits with Paul's argument that Israel has temporarily been hardened by God, but due to their trespass, salvation comes to the Gentiles (Rom 11:11). After the fulfillment of the Gentiles, salvation will take place among Israel in general because they will be provoked by jealousy because of the Gentiles' salvation (cf. vv. 11–12, 15, 25–26).[153] In other words, Paul demonstrates that you (the Gentile believers) are not better than Israel, for you were disobedient when God showed mercy to you (cf. 30a). In a similar way, although Israel is disobedient now, they will be grafted back to their own root due to God's mercy.

With an inferential conjunction γὰρ, clause 28A (v. 32a) makes it clear that God enclosed (συνέκλεισεν) all, including the Gentiles and Israel,[154] into disobedience. Therefore, it is not only that Israel is disobedient or rebellious, but that the Gentiles are also disobedient (cf. 11:16–24). To

---

149. Moo, *The Epistle to the Romans*, 732.
150. Ibid.
151. Many commentators differentiate the instrumental dative from the cause dative (see Cranfield, *Romans*, 583), but it is difficult to separate them (see Porter, *Idioms of the Greek New Testament*, 98–99).
152. Some good Greek MSS read the νῦν here in v.31 (a, B, D*, 1506), some omit it (P[46,] A, D², F, G, Ψ), and still others add ὕστερον instead (33, 365). See also Fitzmyer, *Romans*, 628. According to the MSS tradition, νῦν is possibly original. It's meaning is like ὕστερον (later). As Bell has appropriately argued, "νῦν refers to the near future when Israel will be saved, the assumption being that Paul expected the parousia in the near future." See Bell, *Provoked to Jealousy*, 150.
153. Cf. Cranfield, *Romans*, 582–586; Moo, *The Epistle to the Romans*, 732–735.
154. Note that τοὺς πάντας should not be understood as every single person. In the context, it refers to the corporate meaning. Moo indicates that it refers to the unbelieving Jews implied in vv. 30–31 and "you" to the Gentiles in the church at Rome whom Paul addressed. See Moo, *The Epistle to the Romans*, 736–737; Cranfield, *Romans*, 587–588.

a certain degree, Paul shows that his critique of Israel's disobedience can apply to the Gentiles as well. Both Israel and the Gentile believers, who are God's people, deserve a prophetic warning, which proceeds from Paul's deep concern for them. Then with a ἵνα purpose clause ἵνα τοὺς πάντας ἐλεήσῃ (so that he may have mercy upon all) in c28B (v. 32b), God's mercy is brought into view, which evokes the thematic meaning of God's nature in 9:14–18.

From the above analysis, we can see that verses 28–32 confirm the mystery that Israel has been hardened for their disobedience, but she will be saved in the future. Also, Paul's argument about Israel's final salvation serves to warn the Gentile believers away from their feeling of superiority. We have seen that in Romans 9:30–10:21 Paul sharply criticizes Israel's rebelliousness, but we can see that, in 11:11–31, Paul also criticizes the Gentile believers as well. Then finally in verse 32, he concludes that God consigns both Israel and the Gentiles to disobedience. In other words, the Gentiles are not better than Israel, for they were disobedient just the same as Israel.

In conclusion, Paul orients himself to speak to the Gentiles in verses 11–32. He warns them away from a feeling of superiority over Israel. First, Paul demonstrates the positive result of Israel's negative rebellion, that is, the inclusion of the Gentiles; next, through the metaphor of the olive branches, Paul reminds the Gentile Christians not to boast over Israel; finally, through the prophecy concerning the mystery of the salvation of all Israel, Paul argues that God will have mercy over all Israel just as he has mercy over the Gentile Christians. We should note that Paul's warning or reminding the Gentiles is from the perspective of inner circle relations, e.g. I am an apostle to the Gentiles (v. 13b); I do not want you not to know the mystery, brothers (v. 25). Paul's warning to the Gentile Christians is not like that of an outsider, but comes from a prophet with a personal concern for them; this is similar to his method of critique toward Israel (cf. Rom 9:30–10:21).

5.3.2 Scriptural Voices

In Romans 11:11–32, Paul transforms the prophetic voice of Isaiah 59:20 and 27:9 into his own. First let us explore the voice of the two Isaianic texts in their own co-texts.

The immediate co-text of Isaiah 59:20 is Isaiah 59,[155] which can be divided into three sub-sections: verses 1–8, verses 9–15a, and verses 15b–21.[156] In verses 1–8, there is a concentrated description of Israel's sin, e.g. iniquities, sins, defiled, lies, wickedness, no one . . . justly, no one . . . honestly, empty, violence, crooked, etc. All these can belong to the ITF [Israel's Sin], which is "the prophetic accusation of Israel's fundamental apostasy."[157] In verses 9–15a, the participants change from "you" and "they" into "we," and correspondingly the theme turns to Israel's confession of their sin. As Childs points out, "In verses 9–13 the complaint is sounded in the first person plural and thereby a completely different perspective is presented as the voice of faithful Israel transforms the complaint into a confession."[158] In the last subsection, God's salvation is brought into view. This salvation refers to God's repaying Israel's enemies and the rendering of his wrath against distant peoples (vv. 18–20).[159] The text that Paul uses comes from this last subsection, which portrays God's coming to Zion as redeemer of Israel.[160] If we can see these three subsections as three thematic formations, that is, [Israel's Sin], [Israel's Confession], and [God's Salvation: Israel], then they are quite a common thematic procession found in Jewish literature dealing with God's salvation. We should note that salvation here refers to the subjection of Israel's enemies, who are the Gentile nations.

Paul allies Isaiah 59:20 with 27:9 in Romans 11:26–27. It is significant to investigate Isaiah 27:9 in its own co-text. Isaiah 24–27 has been considered

---

155. See Childs, *Isaiah*, 481–486.
156. Cf. Peter D. Quinn-Miscall, *Isaiah* Readings. (Sheffield: JSOT Press, 1993), 134–135; Childs, *Isaiah*, 484; Paul, *Isaiah 40–66*, 497.
157. Childs, *Isaiah*, 487.
158. Childs, *Isaiah*, 488; See also Quinn-Miscall, *Isaiah*, 135.
159. Childs, *Isaiah*, 489.
160. Note that Paul's use of Isa 59:20 is close to the LXX, not the MT. The MT expresses that God's salvation comes to Zion to *those in Jacob who turn from transgression*, which contradicts Paul's argument for all Israel's salvation (Italics mine). See also Wagner, *Heralds of the Good News*, 286–294.

as the "Isaiah apocalypse" or "apocalyptic-eschatological prophecies."[161] Bound together by the repeated eschatological formula "in that day" (27:2, 12, and 13), chapter 27 interprets the eschatological deliverance of Israel. Verse 1 refers to the slaying of the dragon, and the destruction of this evil power signals a new age of divine rule that is to come.[162] Verses 2–5 are a transformation of the song of the vineyard (Isa 5:1–7), and verse 6 is the prophetic interpretation of the song, that in the future Israel shall blossom.[163] This reinterpreted song expresses God's caring about Israel, and his intimate relationship with Israel.[164] If verses 2–6 anticipates the eschatological hope of Israel through the metaphor of the vineyard, then verses 12–13, with the same eschatological formula "in that day" twice repeated, confirms explicitly what that hope is: the re-gathering of dispersed Israel from exile.[165] In other words, salvation for the Jewish Diaspora is to return to their homeland, to Zion. The middle part (vv. 7–11) is interwoven with judgment and salvation. Verses 7–8 starts with questions that raise the issue of YHWH's punishment of Israel, because of their idol worship, by dispersing them into the nations (cf. v. 9b). Then verse 9 states that "the punishment served to atone for the guilt of Jacob," on condition that Israel responds by abandoning their idol worship.[166] Verses 10–11 turns to the judgment of a people without discernment, the inhabitants in the fortified city, which most likely refers to the nations.[167] Therefore, the thematic flow

---

161. John F. A. Sawyer, *Isaiah*. DSBOT. (Edinburgh: Saint Andrew, 1984), 222; Widyapranawa, *Lord Is Savior*, 163.

162. Childs, *Isaiah*, 197; Widyapranawa, *Lord Is Savior*, 159.

163. Childs, *Isaiah*, 197; Quinn-Miscall, *Isaiah*, 71.

164. As Childs observes, "Accordingly, instead of the garden being left on its own, now Yahweh is its keeper. Instead of its dying from drought, now God himself waters it constantly. Instead of thorns and thistles being a sign of punishment and neglect, now they have become symbols of Israel's enemies against whom God fights. Instead of the garden being filled with cries of oppression and bloodshed, now it is the focus of God's peace. Instead of a verdict of final judgment, now God has no wrath left toward his people. Thus Jacob is not a wasteland, but a plant taking root with blossoms filling the whole world." See Childs, *Isaiah*, 197.

165. Childs, *Isaiah*, 198.

166. Ibid.

167. There is controversy about who "the people without understanding" are or what the fortified city refers to. Some say it refers to Jerusalem and others to Samaria. However, according to the thematic flow, it most likely refers to the nations who oppressed Israel. See also, Childs, *Isaiah*, 198; Widyapranawa, *Lord Is Savior*, 162–163.

in Isaiah 27 is as follows: the destruction of evil, God's concern for Israel, God's punishment of Israel for their sin of idol worship, God's salvation of Israel when they are repentant, God's judgment on the nations, and Israel's eschatological restoration. This flow preserves the basic elements of the discourse pattern in Isaiah 59: [Israel's Sin], [Israel's Confession] and [God's Salvation: Israel]. In other words, this pattern of thematic formation is not uncommon in the book of Isaiah. As Stanley has observed, Israel's salvation in both Isaiah 59 and 27 "includes references to the forgiveness of Israel's sin, the judgment and subjection of her enemies, and the return of her dispersed children from the surrounding nations."[168] In other words, Paul silences the voice of punishment of the nations in Isaiah 59 and 27, but preserves the thematic meaning of God's salvation of Israel and forgiveness of her sins. In this sense, Paul utilizes the generalized projecting clause (καθὼς γέγραπται, v. 26) to turn the voice of Isaiah into a normative one, which states that, although Israel has fallen into sin, God will finally save them. The specific situations of the two texts have been blurred. For Paul, the voice of Isaiah concerning the salvation of Israel is a general voice from Scripture as a whole, and it also becomes his own voice that Israel will be saved.

5.3.3 Thematic-organizational Meaning

In Romans 11:11–32, Paul addresses the Gentile Christians (cf. vv. 13, 25) not to think more highly of themselves than Israel in terms of God's salvific plan for the world. Just as he views his Gentile ministry as being interrelated to the salvation of his fellow Jews (vv. 13–14), he does not separate the process of the Gentiles' salvation from the role of Israel throughout verses 11–32. In other words, Paul views the Gentiles' and Israel's salvation as interdependent with each other. In verses 11–15, Paul represents Deuteronomy 32 in a way that makes it appear to be his own voice. Paul's discourse pattern of the relationships between the salvation of the Gentiles and Israel is: [Israel's Failure] makes [Inclusion of the Gentiles], which results in [Israel's Jealousy] so as to enter into [Full Inclusion of Israel]. A similar discourse pattern occurs again in verses 25–27: [Israel's Heart

---

168. Stanley, "The Redeemer Will Come," 120.

Hardening], [Inclusion of the Gentiles] and then [Salvation of All Israel].[169] In other words, Israel's failure, the inclusion of the Gentiles, and the salvation of all Israel depend on one another.

Second, the thematic meaning of the metaphor of the root and branches (vv. 16–24) expresses that the fate of the Gentile believers intertwines with that of Israel: [Israel's Failure], that part of the branches was broken off due to their unbelief; similarly, if the Gentile believers will not stand fast in faith, they will also be cut off, and the natural branches grafted back if they return to faith. In this sense, the fate of the Gentiles is similar to Israel, in that it relies on whether they believe in the gospel of Christ.

Third, the full inclusion of Israel comes after the inclusion of the Gentiles (vv. 25–26), and the way that Israel will receive mercy is not different from that of the Gentiles (vv. 30–31). Therefore, throughout the whole section, the theme of the salvation of the Gentiles is interwoven with the theme of the salvation of Israel. Their interrelationships are expressed through the three sub sections of verses 11–32.

5.3.4 Multiple Voices: Paul's Jewish Contemporaries' Viewpoints on the Role of the Gentiles in the Salvation of Israel

The history of Israel is her history with reference to other nations. In particular, the Israelites (not only in the Diaspora, but also in Jerusalem) interacted daily with the Gentile nations during the Second Temple Period. Therefore, these interactions would cause the Israelites to consider the role of the Gentiles in relation to God and their own salvation. However, different communities held different views about the role of the Gentiles in God's salvific plan. We have shown that Paul considers the Gentiles' role to be a significantly positive one in the economy of God's salvific plan; that is, the inclusion of the full number of the Gentiles will finally lead to the salvation of all Israel. In the following, we will present some non-Christian Jewish communities' views of the role of the Gentiles with reference to the salvation of Israel. We will investigate the *Psalms of Solomon* (henceforth

---

169. The discourse [Salvation of All Israel] is similar to that of [Full Inclusion of Israel].

Pss. Sol.) and *4 Ezra* to compare their viewpoints on the role of the Gentiles in regard to the salvation of Israel with that of Paul.

The *Psalms of Solomon* represent a significant piece of literature, probably produced a century before Paul, which presents a Jewish community's view of the relationship between the Gentiles and Israel. The sharp contrast between the righteous and the sinners stands as one of the most striking features of *Pss. Sol.*,[170] and, accordingly, the psalmist of *Pss. Sol.*, appeals to God to save the righteous and denounces the sinners.[171] These sinners, in the psalmist's eyes, shall be destroyed forever, as he states in *Pss. Sol.* 3:9–12: "The sinners stumble and curse their life . . . the destruction of sinners is forever and they will not be remembered when God looks after the righteous." But who are these sinners? Surely, the Gentiles are part of the company of the sinners.[172] They are those who trample Jerusalem in destruction (*Pss. Sol.* 17:22).[173] In *Pss. Sol.* 17:23–24, the psalmist clearly indicates that God, in righteousness, will destroy the sinners – the lawless Gentiles – with the word of his mouth (ὀλεθρεῦσαι ἔθνη παράνομα ἐν λόγῳ στόματος αὐτοῦ). However, in the view of the psalmist, the leaders of the Hasmonean dynasty, not only the Gentiles, are also sinners that God condemns.[174] This can be perceived in *Pss. Sol.* 17:6–9:[175]

---

170. Terence L. Donaldson, *Judaism and the Gentiles: Jewish Patterns of Universalism* (Waco, TX: Baylor University Press, 2007), 138.

171. Note that the righteous, in the view of the psalmist, are not those without sin. There is a category of "the sinfully righteous." See the discussion in Winninge, *Sinners and the Righteous*, 181–195.

172. We should note that "the line between sinners and the righteous does not coincide exactly with that between Jew and Gentile." See Donaldson, *Judaism and the Gentiles*, 138.

173. "In addition to denouncing the Gentiles as 'lawless' (*Pss. Sol.* 17:24), the writer views them as 'people of mixed origin' (*Pss. Sol.* 17:15) who are not part of the covenant community. He asks God to 'purge Jerusalem from nations that trample her down in destruction' (*Pss. Sol.* 17:22). According to the writer, Jerusalem's destruction by the Gentiles will soon be reversed. When the Davidic messiah rules Jerusalem he will destroy them by the 'word of his mouth' (*Pss. Sol.* 17:24)." See Atkinson, *I Cried to the Lord*, 134–135.

174. According to the psalmist, the sinners can be identified as the leaders of Hasmonean dynasty and the Gentile conqueror as Pompey. Donaldson, *Judaism and the Gentiles*, 137.

175. The translations are from Wright. Italics mine. "A man" here most probably refers to Pompey. See Wright, *Psalms of Solomon*, 179–181; Donaldson, *Judaism and the Gentiles*, 137; Winninge, *Sinners and the Righteous*, 97–98. This is also probable if we read *Pss. Sol.* 17 together with *Pss. Sol.* 8:16–20, in which the psalmist depicts the leaders of the country

> In their pride they flamboyantly set up their own royal house. Their arrogant substitution desolated David's throne. And they did not glorify your honorable name. But you, O God, will throw them down, and root up their descendants from the earth, for there will rise up against them *a man* alien to our race. You will repay them according to their sins O God; it will happen to them according to their deeds. God showed them no mercy. He hunted down their descendants and did not let even one of them escape.

Therefore, both the Gentiles and the leaders of Hasmonean dynasty are condemned by God. They are the sinners who are outside the psalmist's Jewish community. However, it is uncertain whether the term "Israel" includes the leaders of the Hasmonean dynasty, since the psalmist states that God will cause the ingathering of the tribes (of Israel), hasten his mercy to Israel, and shield them from the contamination of enemies (cf. 17:44–45). It is clear, however, that the psalmist's community, the Lord's people, will be blessed and ruled by the Lord Messiah forevermore (17:32, 46).[176]

To conclude, from the psalmist's perspective, the Gentile sinners, those who oppressed Israel, shall be destroyed forever. In the reign of the Lord Messiah, all Israel will be blessed with wisdom, happiness, and holiness forever. Therefore, the psalmist views the role of the Gentiles negatively in terms of their bringing destruction to Jerusalem, breaking the law, and bringing Israel their cultic worship of gods. However, as the people of God, Israel will be under the reign of the Lord Messiah, who will bring happiness and holiness to Israel forever. In this sense, the psalmist views the Gentiles as outside the Jewish community and condemns them to everlasting

---

who welcome the coming of the enemy, Pompey. See Winninge, *Sinners and the Righteous*, 98; Wright, *Psalms of Solomon*, 119.

176. It is interesting to note that the psalmist seems to indicate that in the Messianic reign, the Gentiles who fear God can share God's mercy; as he said, "The Lord himself is his king, the hope of the one who hopes in God. He will be merciful to all the Gentiles that fearfully stand before him" (17:34). However, the meaning of this verse in its co-text is ambiguous, since in the following verse, the psalmist states, "He [God] will strike the earth [all the Gentiles] with the word of his mouth forever; He will bless the Lord's people with wisdom and happiness." Since the main concern of the psalmist is not about mercy to the Gentiles, we will not get into a detailed discussions on this point.

destruction. The position of the psalmist is to promote the political sovereignty of the land of Israel. On the contrary, Paul views the Gentiles as included in the inner circle of God's people. His critique of the Gentiles and his instructions that they should not boast over Israel come from his heartfelt concern for them. In this sense, Paul's view of the role of the Gentiles differs from that of his Jewish contemporaries.

Not only *Pss. Sol.*, but also *4 Ezra* concerns God's faithfulness and the relationship of Israel and the Gentile nations. An investigation of *4 Ezra* shows that the main body of *4 Ezra* (chs. 3–14) was a late first-century Jewish writing. The original Jewish document was composed about AD 100,[177] which was within approximately fifty years of the composition of Romans. The author of *4 Ezra* reflects on the destruction of Jerusalem in AD 70, engaging with Jewish concepts of God's faithfulness and justice.[178] Both *4 Ezra* and Paul's letter to the Romans have been viewed as outside the common pattern of early Judaism.[179] Longenecker's book, *Eschatology and the Covenant: A Comparison of 4 Ezra and Romans 1 – 11*, demonstrates that there are some features common to *4 Ezra* and Romans. We will focus on the two authors' views of the role of the Gentiles in terms of their relationship with God and Israel.

In the opening of the first vision (3:4–36), Ezra questions God about "the fate of Israel and the destruction of Zion," which sets forth the central concerns of the whole book.[180] It is in this first vision that Ezra's question draws out God's attitude toward Israel and the nations (the Gentiles). Therefore, we will focus on the related parts of *4 Ezra* for our synoptic reading. Verses 4–36 can be divided into two main sections: a narration of the historical stories from the creation of Adam to the destruction of the Jewish

---

177. See C. A. Evans, *Ancient Texts for New Testament Studies: A Guide to the Background Lliterature* (Peabody: Hendrickson, 2005), 34. There are four chapters that were added near the middle or in the second half of the third century: two at the beginning and two at the end, by one or more unknown Christian writers (see Metzger, "Fourth Book of Ezra," 520).
178. Longenecker, *Eschatology and the Covenant*, 40.
179. We do not hold Sanders's view that there is a common pattern in early Judaism, but the two books, to a certain extent, do show some connections. See Longenecker, *Eschatology and the Covenant*, 21.
180. Stone, *Fourth Ezra*, 61.

temple (vv. 4–27) and Ezra's challenge to God concerning the victory of the Gentiles over Israel (vv. 28–36).[181]

In verses 12–27, Ezra tells Israel's history from the patriarchs down to David: God's promise to Abraham, Isaac, and Jacob of the multitudes of descendants, the delivery out of Egypt (the Exodus), the giving of the law, Israel's transgressions out of their evil heart, and the exile (Israel was delivered into the hands of their enemies).[182] In this part, Ezra demonstrates the relationship between God and Israel throughout history: God was faithful to Israel, but Israel failed to keep his commandments. Therefore, the punishment of Israel was their exile into the nations.

In the following section, Ezra compares the nations with Israel, asking "Is Babylon better than Zion?" (v. 32). Ezra first complains that God preserved the nations but destroyed his people, Israel, even though the nations were "unmindful of your commandments" (v. 33). In other words, Ezra assumes that the nations were aware of God's law,[183] but that they rejected it. Therefore, from the perspective of Ezra, the nations also transgressed the law and did not keep the commandments, but God seemed to spare those who acted wickedly rather than Israel.

From the above, it can be seen that Ezra sets the same requirement in order for both Israel and the nations to be involved in God's blessings: obedience to God's commandments. In a certain sense, Ezra is more like Paul in seeing the equality between Israel and the nations, and differs from the psalmist of *Pss. Sol.*, who considers the priority of Israel. Also, both Paul and Ezra acknowledge God's faithfulness to Israel – offering Israel the promise, the law, the Messiah – but Israel has sinned;[184] at this point, the Gentiles are brought into view. For Ezra, although Israel has sinned, the

---

181. Ibid., 60.
182. Ibid.
183. Elsewhere, through the voice of Uriel, it states that t humans as a whole have received the law. See 7:72–74, "Those who dwell on earth shall be tormented, because though they had understanding they committed iniquity, and though they received the commandments they did not keep them, and though they obtained the law they dealt unfaithfully with what they received. . . . For how long the time is that the Most High has been patient with those who inhabit the world, and not for their sake, but because of the times which he has foreordained!" The translations are from Metzger. See Metzger, "Fourth Book of Ezra," 539.
184. Ezra lists David as God's servant for the city of Israel, but Israel still transgressed.

Gentiles are no better than Israel at keeping the commandments; therefore, the Gentiles should be punished as well. If Ezra stresses the negative side of Israel's and the Gentiles' transgressions, Paul emphasizes the positive result of their failures based on the power of God. For Paul, Israel's failure results in the inclusion of the Gentiles as the people of God through their faith in the gospel of Christ, and the inclusion of the Gentiles ironically provokes Israel to return to the gospel. Therefore, both Israel and the Gentiles will be saved on the basis of the gospel of Christ.

In sum, the psalmist of *Pss. Sol.* views the Gentiles who oppress Israel as sinners; and God shall destroy them forever. Therefore, the role of the Gentiles in the view of the psalmist's community is very negative. Gentiles appear as outsiders, who are the source of their present sufferings. Although Ezra also sees the negative side of the Gentiles, he seems to place the Gentiles on equal status with Israel. However, the standard Ezra set for the Gentiles is the common Jewish requirement of obedience to God's commandments. Ezra places the Gentiles into the cultic system of Israel in order to achieve salvation. In other words, for Ezra, if the Gentiles wish to be saved by God, they need to be converted and become Israelites. In contrast, Paul places the Gentiles and Israel in a mutually dependent position. Israel's failure results in the inclusion of the Gentiles, and in turn, the Gentiles' inclusion leads the rest of Israel back to God. Also, unlike Ezra, the basis for salvation for Paul is faith in the gospel of Jesus Christ, so that the Gentiles do not need to become Jews in order to be saved. This viewpoint about the role of the Gentiles in salvation distinguishes Paul from his Jewish contemporaries.

5.4 Conclusion

Romans 11:1–32 is divided into two sections. In the first section, Paul contends that God has not rejected his people, ethnic Israel. He uses different scriptural voices to illustrate his view of God's acceptance of Israel. Paul's voice seeks to blend harmoniously with the scriptural voices: 1 Kings 19, Deuteronomy 29, Isaiah 29, and Psalm 68. He sees Israel's failure as the result of idolatrous worship and distrust of God, but he does not arrive at the conclusion that Israel will be destroyed and rejected by God forever. On the contrary, Paul prophesied the mystery of the salvation of all Israel in the eschatological future.

In the second section, Paul turns to the Gentile believers to warn them not to boast over Israel and to show them that Israel, as God's people, will be saved in the eschatological future, when all sins will be removed and salvation for both the Gentiles and Israel will be fulfilled in Christ. If in Romans 9:30–10:21 Paul criticizes his kinsmen for their rebellion, then in 11:11–32 he attempts to remind the Gentile believers of the necessity of standing fast in the faith of Christ. For Paul, both Israel and the Gentile believers are within the community of God's people, and they are interdependent on each other. The way Paul addresses Israel and the Gentiles resembles a prophetic speech pattern.[185] It is worthy of note that the thematic waves running through Romans 11 can be itemized as follows: God's faithfulness to Israel, Israel's idolatrous worship, the hardening of Israel, the inclusion of the Gentiles, Israel's jealousy, and salvation of all Israel. Paul considers the relationships between Israel and the Gentiles positively based on his reading of Scriptures. Moreover, if we bring in the Second Temple Literature of *Pss. Sol.* and *4 Ezra* and read intertextually about viewpoints regarding the relationship of Israel and the Gentiles, we can see that both Paul and some other Jewish communities would view Israel's position in God's salvific plan positively. However, Paul diverges from his Jewish contemporaries with his understanding that the Gentiles are of God's people on the basis of the gospel of Jesus Christ.

---

185. Some of the prophetic books include a tripartite structure: "The prophetic or divine voice is described as announcing (a) punishment against Israel, (b) punishment against nations other than Israel, and (c) salvation for Israel, or for both Israel and the nations." See Ehud Ben Zvi, "Prophetic Book: A Key Form of Prophetic Literature," in *The Changing Face of Form Criticism for the Twenty-First Century*, edited by Marvin A. Sweeney and Ehud Ben Zvi, (Grand Rapids: Eerdmans, 2003), 285. For a criticism of the "tripartite structure," see Sweeney et al., *The Twelve Prophets*, v. 2:494.

5.5 Additional Note: Verses 33–36

After Paul repeats his discourse patterns about God's salvific plan which involves both Israel and the Gentiles, this last hymnic section (vv. 33–36) is in praise of God, whose ways of salvation are beyond human grasp.[186] The hymnic character of this section is demonstrated in its repeatedly triadic pattern. The three basic units of the hymn are the opening exclamation (v. 33), the scriptural rhetorical questions (vv. 34–45), and the concluding doxology (v. 36).[187] Each unit also consists of a triadic structure: the three divine attributes of God's depth (v. 33a: πλούτου καὶ σοφίας καὶ γνώσεως θεοῦ), three rhetorical questions (vv. 34–35) that correspond to the description of God in verse 33 in reverse order, and three prepositional phrases (ἐξ αὐτοῦ καὶ δι' αὐτοῦ καὶ εἰς αὐτόν) applied to τὰ πάντα (v. 36a).[188] The two elements outside this triadic pattern are "the double exclamation making up the second part of verse 33 and the concluding doxology (v. 36b)."[189] They all praise God's doing (his judgment and his ways of salvation are inscrutable) and his being (God is glorified).

The βάθος of God is referred in 1 Corinthians 2:10, and there are numerous scriptural references to the depth of the sea. The "depth" of God here expresses Paul's awe and wonder at God's deeds. God's riches are demonstrated in his saving power for both the Jews and the Gentiles (cf. Rom 9:23; 10:12; 11:12), which "has proved capable of reversing the universal human bind in 'disobedience' and sin."[190] Wisdom in the context probably refers to God's mysterious plan to save all Israel in verses 25–26.[191] God's knowledge is closely linked with wisdom, referring to the fact that God's

---

186. Cf. Moo, *The Epistle to the Romans*, 742.
187. Byrne, *Romans*, 358.
188. According to Moo, "The concept of God as the source (ἐκ), sustainer (διά), and goal (εἰς) is all things particularly strong among the Greek Stoic philosophers." See Moo, *The Epistle to the Romans*, 743.
189. Byrne, *Romans*, 358.
190. Ibid., 359.
191. According to Jewett, "That this mystery has 'depth' that no human can penetrate without mystical disclosure is self-evident, not just because of the limitation of finite intelligence but also because of cultural biases that the preceding argument of Romans has sought to overcome." See Jewett, *Romans*, 717.

salvific wisdom is beyond human understanding (Rom 10:3, 19; 11:2b, 25 vs. 11:2a [οὐκ ἔγνω/ ἀγνοεῖν vs. προέγνω]). The thematic formation of verse 33 is paralleled in 2 *Apoc. Bar.* 14:8–9: "O Lord, my Lord, who can understand your judgment? Or who can explore the depth of your way? Or who can discern the majesty of your path? Or who can discern the beginning and the end of your wisdom?"[192] In other words, this type of doxological hymn is quite common among Paul's contemporaries.

The second strophe of the hymn consists of three τίς questions, borrowing from Isaiah 40:13 and Job 41:3.[193] They correspond to the description of God in verse 33 in reverse order. Some scholars argue that the quotation part was added at a later stage,[194] but the quotation most likely comes from Paul's hand.[195] The three prepositions ἐκ, διά, and εἰς that modify αὐτός (God) in verse 36 convey the concept that God is the source (ἐκ), the sustainer (διά), and the goal (εἰς) of all things.[196]

The final usage of Scripture in verses 33–35 is from Isaiah 40:13 and probably Job 41:3. The core theme is the depth of God's wisdom demonstrated in God's way of salvation for all. This last section is most likely a liturgical conclusion to God's unfathomable wisdom expressed in the salvific plan for both Israel and the Gentiles. As Johnson rightly observes:

> The hymn combines with the introductory oath of 9:1–5 to create an *inclusio* for the argument of chapters 9–11, beginning and ending with ascriptions of praise to the omnipotent

---

192. See Johnson, *Function of Apocalyptic*, 168–171.

193. The rendering of Isa 40:13 is close to the LXX text, but Paul's wording of Job 41:13 differs significantly from the LXX text. Probably Paul translated it himself from a non-LXX text source. See Moo, *The Epistle to the Romans*, 742, n. 19.

194. According to Jewett, "The hymn without the citations focuses entirely on God's attributes with no gesture of human response, no human involvement. The LXX citations baldly introduce human responses vis-à-vis God's greatness and raise the question about whether God would require a counselor or recompense." Jewett, *Romans*, 714, n.6.

195. Jewett, *Romans*, 714. Contra Johnson, *Function of Apocalyptic*, 168. Johnson together with Hanson suggests a pre-Pauline Jewish combination of the two verses (Isa 40:13 and Job 41:3).

196. Moo, *The Epistle to the Romans*, 743.

God (cf. ἐπὶ πάντων, 9:5; τὰ πάντα, 11:36). The doxology ascribes glory to the One blessed in 9:5.[197]

---

197. Johnson, *Function of Apocalyptic*, 173. Italics original. See also Moo, *The Epistle to the Romans*, 743.

CHAPTER SIX

Conclusion

This study has focused on Paul's discourse patterns regarding the relationship of God, Israel and the Gentiles in Romans 9–11 by means of thematic intertextual analysis. In our introduction, we showed that previous intertextual study of Romans 9–11 remains still in its infancy. No one up to now has established an appropriate intertextual methodological control to analyze Paul's discourse in Romans 9–11. Therefore, in order to remedy this situation, in chapter 2 we adapted Lemke's linguistic intertextual thematic theory as a methodological control to examine the entire discourse of Romans 9–11. Moreover, this discourse has been placed within its social culture, including the communities of the Second Temple Period, particularly those of Paul's time, both Christian and Jewish. This methodological approach and textual analysis has produced significant insights regarding Paul's viewpoint on God, Israel, and the Gentiles, as well as the intertexual relationships between these important voices which resonated during this period. The following summarizes the study and offers proleptic directions for further studies regarding Paul's viewpoints on God, Israel and the Gentiles.

Through the investigation of Romans 9:1–29 in chapter 3, we demonstrated that the focus of Romans 9 is on God himself and who God's people are. At first, Paul re-contextualizes the traditional Jewish discourse patterns, such as [Lament over Israel], [Martyr-like Intercession for Israel], and [Heritage of Israel], by allying them with the element of Christ*ness*. He reframes the traditional Jewish discourses through a Christian viewpoint, for example, allying Israel's sin of disbelief in Paul's time with their idol worship of the calf in Moses' time. This reframing is followed by the interweaving of the discourse formations of [God's Nature] and [God's People]. The thematic formation [God's Nature] – including his faithfulness, his mercy and his authority – represents the carrier formation, which interweaves with the formation of [God's People]. In other words, Paul in Romans 9:1–29 argues that "who God is" decides "who God's people are." Through the use of Scripture, Paul traces back the basic history of Israel as God's people: God's promise to the patriarchs in Genesis, Israel's rebellion (depicted in Exodus), and God's mercy to them (depicted in the prophetic books). Therefore, Paul converges the Mosaic tradition with a certain tradition of prophetic literature, confirming that "who can belong to God" has been revealed by God on the basis of the salvific history of Israel. By doing so, Paul embraces the Gentiles in the community of God's people. To justify this dealing with Israel and the Gentiles, Paul has implicitly characterized his identity as that of a Mosaic prophet in order to justify the fact that his words are from God and are therefore valuable (cf. Rom 9:3). In our investigation with Romans 9, the heteroglossic voices of Paul's Jewish contemporaries have been examined as well. The Jewish literature of *Jubilees*, *Philo*, *Wisdom of Ben Sira*, and *4 Ezra*, whose discourse patterns regarding the issues of God's promise to the patriarchs, and their depiction of the relation of Israel and the Gentiles, display contrasting viewpoints with Paul's discourse on Romans 9. Paul deviates from his Jewish contemporaries in that he includes the Gentiles as God's people and vessels of God's mercy.

Our chapter 4, Romans 9:30–10:21, concentrates on the rebellion of Israel and Paul's critique of them. His critique of Israel's rebellion proceeds from his formation of the relationship between faith and righteousness and his dissection of the bond between law and righteousness on the basis of Christ. Paul generalizes the voices of Moses and Isaiah so as to sharply criticize Israel's rebellion in refusing his gospel, as well as to proclaim the revelation of the inclusion of the Gentiles in the scope of salvation. From Paul's viewpoint, Israel's disbelief and disobedience to the gospel is the same sin as their idolatry in the past: this way of understanding of Israel's sin constituted a new pattern in constructing the discourse relations. Paul allies himself with the prophetic tradition of Moses and Isaiah in order to testify against Israel's rebellion, the idol-worship shown in their disbelief of the gospel and their exclusion of the Gentiles from the scope of salvation.

The Jewish literature – for instance *Baruch*, the works of Philo, and *Wisdom of Solomon* – share similar themes with Romans 9:30–10:21with special regard to the scope of salvation. The Jewish literature argues for God's favoring of Israel (*Baruch*, *Wisdom*), indicates that the Gentiles need to be converted or become proselytes in order to join the Jewish community (the works of Philo), and contends that it is the Gentiles who sinned by idolatry (*Wisdom*). Therefore, our intertextual comparative reading of Romans 9:30–10:21 with this related Jewish literature indicates that Paul's viewpoint on the relation of Israel and the Gentile, and the entire scope of salvation, is divergent from his Jewish contemporaries, which makes Paul's voice unique in his time.

Chapter 5 demonstrates that Romans 11 responds to Paul's previous critique of Israel, confirming that God has not rejected his people (vv. 1–6). If in Romans 9:30–10:21 Paul criticizes his kinsmen for their rebellion, then in 11:11–26, he alerts the Gentile believers of the necessity of standing fast in the faith of Christ. In other words, Paul prophetically critiques the Christian Gentiles as well to warn them against arrogance. Finally, Paul prophesies concerning the mystery of the salvation of Israel and the Gentiles in the eschatological future (vv. 26–32). It is worthy of note that the thematic waves running through Romans 11 can be itemized as follows: God's faithfulness to Israel, Israel's idolatrous worship, the hardening of Israel, the inclusion of the Gentiles, Israel's jealousy, and the salvation of all Israel, which resembles the prophetic discourse patterns demonstrated in Deuteronomy 32 and Isaiah 65. Moreover, when we bring in the Second Temple Literature of *Pss. Sol.* and *4 Ezra* and read them intertextually regarding their viewpoints on the relationship of Israel and the Gentiles, we see that both Paul and these other Jewish communities view Israel's position in God's salvific plan positively. However, Paul diverges from his Jewish contemporaries with his understanding that the Gentiles are of God's people on the basis of the gospel of Christ.

We can now conclude the findings of our investigation of Romans 9–11. First, we have adjusted Lemke's intertextual thematic analysis, as an indispensable tool, to analyze Paul's viewpoints of the relationships of God, Israel and the Gentiles in Romans 9–11 within the backdrop of Second Temple Literature. Second, Paul re-contextualizes the Jewish discourse patterns regarding the topics of intercession, Israel, God's promise, God's people, righteousness and law. It can be seen that Paul's discourse patterns share some continuity with his Jewish contemporaries, but the core of his value regarding how to include the Gentiles as God's people stands in a discontinuous relationship with contemporary Judaism(s). Third, this study has demonstrated that although Paul uses Jewish styles of scriptural hermeneutics, and though his discourse patterns resemble some Jewish literature in important aspects, Paul's viewpoint on the relationship of God, Israel and the Gentiles in Romans 9–11 is dissociated from his Jewish contemporaries in key ways. In other words, the core value of early Christian discourse has been embedded in Romans 9–11. Paul's viewpoint on the relationship of God, Israel and the Gentiles takes a divergent stance away from his Jewish contemporaries since Gentile inclusion is rooted in the gospel of Christ. Finally, Romans 9–11 not only provides Paul's self-presentation as a Mosaic prophet figure, but also its overall discourse patterns appear as a prophetic discourse: In each section (Rom 9:1–29; 9:30–10:4; 11:1–36) Paul designates his identity or his concerns for Israel (Rom 9:1–3, 10:1; 11:1–2) before he enters into the argumentation, which demonstrates the relation between Paul's self-understanding and his message in these three chapters; also, the overall discourse pattern in Romans 9–11 resembles a prophetic discourse pattern,[1] which expresses the idea that Paul's self-understanding as a prophetic figure serves to confirm that his word comes from divine authority.

---

1. Some significant prophetic books share a pattern of a tripartite organization, though each book has its own style and content: "(a) a section that primarily concerns announcements of judgment against Judah/Israel, (b) oracles against the "nations" (OAN) in medial position, and (c) a section that contains mainly announcements of salvation." Regarding the "oracles against the nations," "the nations are described as boasting because of their power or their wealth or both, as rejoicing in the fall of Judah, . . . In any case, the nations are described as being in better shape than Israel because they have not suffered the awesome punishment that Israel has suffered." See Ehud Ben Zvi, "Understanding the Message of the Tripartite Prophetic Books," *RQ* 35 (1993), 93–95.

APPENDIX 1

Halliday has provided three main conjunctive relations and their subtype-relations, as follows, (1) ELABORATION: Apposition and Clarification; (2) EXTENSION: Addition, Adversative and Variation; and (3) ENHANCEMENT: Temporal, Causal, Conditional, Means, Comparative, and Respective.[1] In his article, "The Cohesiveness of Discourse," Reed has supplied diagram lists for these relations and their corresponding expressions in Greek. Here we will display some significant relations and their Greek indicator:[2]

---

1. Halliday and Matthiessen, *An Introduction to Functional Grammar*, 541.
2. Cf. Reed, *A Discourse Analysis of Philippians*, 91–93.

ELABORATION	Apposition	expository	ὅτι, ἵνα, τοῦτο ἐστιν (in other words, that is, I mean, to put it another way)
		exemplifying	οὕτως, οὕτω, γέγραπται, ῥητῶς (for example, for instance, thus, to illustrate)
	Clarification	corrective	μᾶλλον, μενοῦν, μενοῦνγε, ἀλλά, ὅτι οὐχ (or rather, at least, to be more precise, on the contrary, however)
		particularizing	μάλιστα (in particular, more especially)
		summative	λοιπὸν, οὖν (in short, to sum up, in conclusion, briefly)
		verifactive	ὅλως, ὄντως (actually, as a matter of fact, in fact)
EXTENSION	Addition	positive	καί, δέ, τέ, πάλιν, εἶτα, ἐπί, καί . . . καί, τέ . . . καί, τέ . . . τέ, μέν . . . τέ (and, also, moreover, in addition)
		negative	οὐδὲ, μηδὲ (nor)
	Adversative		ἀλλά, δὲ, μενοῦν, μενοῦνγε, μέντοι, πλήν, παρὰ (but, yet, on the other hand, however)
	Variation	replacive	ἀντὶ, τοὐναντίον, μέν . . . τέ (on the contrary, instead)
		substractive	ἐκτὸς, εἰ μὴ (apart from that, except for that)
		alternative	ἤ, ἤ . . . ἤ, ἤτοι . . . ἤ (alternatively, or)
ENHANCEMENT	Temporal		δέ, ὡς, ὅτε, πότε, καθώς, εὐθέως, ταχὺς, σήμερον, ἕως, ἐν τῷ μεταξὺ, νῦν (then, afterwards, previously, immediately, meanwhile, until, at this moment)
	Comparative		ὅμοιος, ὡς, καθώς, ἤ, ἤπερ (likewise, similarly, in a different way)
	Causal	result	διό, πρός, εἰς, ἵνα, οὖν, ὡς, ὥστε (in consequence, as a result)
		purpose	ἵνα, ὅπως, ὥστε, μήποτε, μή πως (for that purpose, with this in view)
		reason	ὅτι, γάρ, διά, διότι, χάριν, ἕνεκεν, ἐκεῖ (on account of this, for that reason)
		basis	ἐπί, νή (on the basis of, in view of)
	Conditional	general	εἰ, εἴπερ, ἐάν, εἴτε . . . εἴτε, εἰ μὴ, ἐὰν μὴ (in that case, if, under the circumstances, otherwise, if not)
		concessive	καίπερ, καίτοι, κἄν (yet, still, though, however, nevertheless)
	Respective		ὧδε, ἐνθάδε, ἀλλαχοῦ (here, there, as to that, in that respect, in other respects, elsewhere)

All the above relations can be applied to the clausal or clause-complexing relations. Moreover, it is possible that some relations can also be applied to the bigger unit of text (beyond clause-complexes, e.g. TTFs, paragraphs or discourses). Several examples of clausal or clause-complexing relations will be construed in the following. After this, some often-used relational categories will be employed to discuss the relations at the rank beyond clauses, e.g. TTFs or discourses.

First are examples of Elaborative relations. A first subtype relation is Apposition, in which the same proposition is restated or re-presented in other words for emphasis, for example:

> ἄφετε τὰ παιδία ἔρχεσθαι πρός με καὶ μὴ κωλύετε αὐτά (Let the children come to me, and do not hinder them; Luke 18:16 RSV)

> Ἀλήθειαν λέγω ἐν Χριστῷ, οὐ ψεύδομαι (I am speaking the truth in Christ, I am not lying; Rom 9:1 RSV)

A second subtype is Clarification, in which the proposition is made precise or summarized. Here are several examples:

> Ἀνὴρ . . . εὐσεβὴς καὶ φοβούμενος τὸν θεὸν σὺν παντὶ τῷ οἴκῳ αὐτοῦ, ποιῶν ἐλεημοσύνας πολλὰς τῷ λαῷ καὶ δεόμενος τοῦ θεοῦ διὰ παντός (There was a devout man who feared God with all his household, gave alms liberally to the people, and prayed constantly to God; Acts 10:1–2 RSV)

> Ἄρα οὖν, ἀδελφοί, στήκετε καὶ κρατεῖτε τὰς παραδόσεις ἃς ἐδιδάχθητε εἴτε διὰ λόγου εἴτε δι' ἐπιστολῆς ἡμῶν (So then, brethren, stand firm and hold to the traditions which you were taught by us, either by word of mouth or by letter; 2 Thess 2:15 RSV)

> λοιπόν, ἀδελφοί, χαίρετε, καταρτίζεσθε, παρακαλεῖσθε, τὸ αὐτὸ φρονεῖτε, εἰρηνεύετε (Finally, brethren, farewell. Mend

your ways, heed my appeal, agree with one another, and live in peace; 2 Cor 13:11 RSV)

The first two cases are examples of clarification to make precise. "There was a devout man" in Acts 10:1 has been explained more precisely in Acts 10:2 as a man "who feared God with all his household, gave alms liberally to the people, and prayed constantly to God." Likewise, the clause "stand firm" has been expressed more precisely as "hold to the traditions . . ." in 2 Thessalonians 2:15. The third case is an example of summary. The term λοιπόν (in sum, finally) indicates the following clauses are in a summarized relationship with the previous text.

Second, we will provide illustrations for Extensive relations. Four subtypes are worthy of our attention. First, an Addition relation can be seen from Mark 15:20:

(1) ἐξέδυσαν αὐτὸν τὴν πορφύραν (they stripped him of the purple cloak)
(2) καὶ ἐνέδυσαν αὐτὸν τὰ ἱμάτια αὐτοῦ (and put his own clothes on him)

The two clauses are regarded as in sequence, for we can recognize that the actions occur in a succession relationship.

An Adversative relation is a second subtype of Extension in common usage. Matthew 5:17 is one good case for this relationship: οὐκ ἦλθον καταλῦσαι ἀλλὰ πληρῶσαι (I do not come to abolish [the law or the prophets], but to fulfill them. Matt 5:17). In opposition to the idea that Jesus came to abolish or destroy the law, he actually came to fulfill them. The two clauses are in an Adversative relation, signaling by the conjunction ἀλλά.

Another subtype is the Replacive relation, for example, μὴ ἀποδιδόντες κακὸν ἀντὶ κακοῦ ἢ λοιδορίαν ἀντὶ λοιδορίας, τοὐναντίον δὲ εὐλογοῦντες (Do not pay back evil with evil or reviling for reviling, instead, pay back with a blessing; 1 Pet 3:9). A second good illustration can be seen in Galatians 1:12: οὐδὲ γὰρ ἐγὼ παρὰ ἀνθρώπου παρέλαβον αὐτὸ . . . ἀλλὰ δι' ἀποκαλύψεως Ἰησοῦ Χριστοῦ (I did not receive it from any human being . . . but I received it through a revelation of Jesus Christ).

The fourth subtype is Alternative. An Alternation relation appears quite often in New Testament texts. Take 1 Corinthians 4:21 as an example:

(1) ἐν ῥάβδῳ ἔλθω πρὸς ὑμᾶς (shall I come to you with a rod?)
(2) ἢ ἐν ἀγάπῃ πνεύματί τε πραΰτητος; (or [shall I come to you] with love in a spirit of gentleness?)

In Alternation relations, only one of the two statements applies, not both.[3] The audience can only choose one choice between the two contrasting options.

The above Extensive relations, especially the Adversative, the Replacive, and the Alternative relations, are one of the most common linguistic sources for constructing Opposition relationship in Lemke's ITF system.

Now let us investigate Enhancement Relations: Comparative, Causal, and Conditional, etc., which are among the most common types of relationship to be found in the expository or argumentative discourses of the New Testament, particularly, in the Pauline epistles.

In regard to the Comparative relation, some linguistic markers have been spoken of above. Here are two cases: μηδὲ γογγύζετε, καθάπερ τινὲς αὐτῶν ἐγόγγυσαν (Do not grumble as some of them grumbled; 1 Cor 10:10) and ἀνεκτότερον ἔσται γῇ Σοδόμων καὶ Γομόρρων ἐν ἡμέρᾳ κρίσεως ἢ τῇ πόλει ἐκείνῃ (It shall be more tolerable on the day of judgment for the land of Sodom and Gomorrah than for that town; Matt 10:15 RSV).

The Causal relation is one of the most common types of relationship in argumentative discourses. It has been further sub-categorized into Result, Purpose, Reason, and Basis. There are many examples that can be found in the New Testament; we will provide only a few cases in the following.

1) Reason Relation
γάλα ὑμᾶς ἐπότισα, οὐ βρῶμα· οὔπω γὰρ ἐδύνασθε (I fed you with milk, not with solid food, for you were not ready for it; 1 Cor 3:2): The γὰρ

---

3. Other examples, Matt 6:24, Rom 6:16, etc. Cf. Louw and Nida, *Greek-English Lexicon*, 794–796; Peter Cotterell and Max Turner, *Linguistics & Biblical Interpretation* (Downers Grove: InterVarsity, 1989), 208.

indicates a Reason relation between the two clauses, The reason that "I fed you with milk" is expressed in the following clause, "you were not ready."

2) Result Relation
εἰ δὲ ἐν πνεύματι θεοῦ ἐγὼ ἐκβάλλω τὰ δαιμόνια, ἄρα ἔφθασεν ἐφ' ὑμᾶς ἡ βασιλεία τοῦ θεοῦ (If by the Spirit of God I cast out of demons, then the kingdom of God has come upon you; Matt 12:28 RSV).
τὰ γὰρ ἀόρατα αὐτοῦ ἀπὸ κτίσεως κόσμου τοῖς ποιήμασιν νοούμενα καθορᾶται, ἥ τε ἀΐδιος αὐτοῦ δύναμις καὶ θειότης, εἰς τὸ εἶναι αὐτοὺς ἀναπολογήτους (Ever since the creation of the world his invisible nature, namely, his eternal power and deity, has been clearly perceived in the things that have been made. So they are without excuse; Rom 1:20 RSV).

In Matthew 12:28, a linguistic marker begins a result clause, "the kingdom of God has come upon you," which is an inference from what has preceded, "by the Spirit of God I cast out of demons." Likewise, in Romans 1:20, all the evidence that can be seen results in no excuse for those who still refuse God. The marker εἰς also indicates a Result relation.

3) Purpose
αὐτοῦ γάρ ἐσμεν ποίημα, κτισθέντες ἐν Χριστῷ Ἰησοῦ ἐπὶ ἔργοις ἀγαθοῖς οἷς προητοίμασεν ὁ θεός, ἵνα ἐν αὐτοῖς περιπατήσωμεν (For we are his workmanship, created in Christ Jesus for good works, which God prepared beforehand, that we should walk in them; Eph 2:10 RSV). Both the primary clause and the relative clause (leading by οἷς) contain Purpose relations. In the primary clause, we are created in Christ Jesus for the purpose of good works, which is indicated by the linguistic marker ἐπὶ. In the relative clause, God prepared us beforehand for the purpose that we can walk in them [good works].

4) Basis
ἐπὶ στόματος δύο μαρτύρων ἢ τριῶν σταθῇ πᾶν ῥῆμα· (On the basis of what two or three witnesses say, every word shall be established; Matt 18:16). The linguistic marker ἐπὶ indicates the relation of basis here.

All the above four relations – Reason, Result, Purpose, and Basis – belong to the Causal relations group. They can be used to describe clausal relations and also relations beyond clauses and clause complexes as well, e.g. ITFs, paragraphs, and even some sorts of discourse.

Last but not least is the Conditional relation. I sub-type it into two: General and Concessive. The General Condition relation is always indicated by εἰ, εἴπερ, ἐάν, and εἰ μὴ, etc. In Matthew 4:3, εἰ υἱὸς εἶ τοῦ θεοῦ, εἰπὲ ἵνα οἱ λίθοι οὗτοι ἄρτοι γένωνται (If you are the son of God, command these stones to become bread), the "if" clause provides a condition for the following action.

The Concessive relation acknowledges a potential or apparent incompatibility between the concessive clause and primary clause in order to enhance the point that the text wants to make. An example from Colossians 1:21–22 will illustrate how to specify Concessive relations between two parts of a text. Colossians 1:21–22 can be divided into two text spans:

(1) Καὶ ὑμᾶς ποτε ὄντας ἀπηλλοτριωμένους καὶ ἐχθροὺς τῇ διανοίᾳ ἐν τοῖς ἔργοις τοῖς πονηροῖς (you, being formerly alienated and enemy in mind through the evil work)

(2) νυνὶ δὲ ἀποκατήλλαξεν ἐν τῷ σώματι τῆς σαρκὸς αὐτοῦ διὰ τοῦ θανάτου (now he has reconciled in his body of flesh by his death)

Units (1) and (2) are in a Concession relation. We can see a potential incompatibility between these two units ("alienated with God" is potentially incompatible with "reconciled with God"). However, the author, by pointing out the contrasted timing ποτε and νυνὶ, views them compatibly: he is not denying that you were alienated from and an enemy of God in the past time in unit (1), and has recognized the positive regard for the claim that he [God] has reconciled [you] now in unit (2). In this sense, the point in unit (2) has been enhanced.

In sum, all the above relations have been used in the clausal and clause-complexing relations in Halliday's work; however, most of these relations can be applied to the relations of TTFs and ITFs.

APPENDIX 2[1]

Chart for Romans 9:1–5

Chart 1

Verse no.	Greek Clauses	Clause no.
1	Ἀλήθειαν λέγω ἐν Χριστῷ,	c1A
	οὐ ψεύδομαι,	c2A
	συμμαρτυρούσης μοι τῆς συνειδήσεώς μου ἐν πνεύματι ἁγίῳ,	c2B
2	ὅτι λύπη μοί ἐστιν μεγάλη	c2Ca
	καὶ ἀδιάλειπτος ὀδύνη τῇ καρδίᾳ μου.	c2Cb
	ηὐχόμην γὰρ αὐτὸς ἐγὼ	c3A
3	ἀνάθεμα εἶναι ἀπὸ τοῦ Χριστοῦ ὑπὲρ τῶν ἀδελφῶν μου τῶν	c3B
	συγγενῶν μου κατὰ σάρκα,	c3C
4	οἵτινές εἰσιν Ἰσραηλῖται,	c3Da
	ὧν ἡ υἱοθεσία καὶ ἡ δόξα καὶ αἱ διαθῆκαι καὶ ἡ νομοθεσία καὶ ἡ	c3Db
5	λατρεία καὶ αἱ ἐπαγγελίαι,	c3Dc
	ὧν οἱ πατέρες	c3E
	καὶ ἐξ ὧν ὁ Χριστὸς τὸ κατὰ σάρκα,	
	ὁ ὢν ἐπὶ πάντων θεὸς εὐλογητὸς εἰς τοὺς αἰῶνας, ἀμήν.	

---

1. Notes for appendices 2–10 are found on page 288.

Chart 2

V and C no.	Token	Process type	T/A/V/M[1]
v. 1, c1A	λέγω	verbal	Present/impf/act/ind
v. 1, c2A	οὐ ψεύδομαι	verbal	Present/impf/mid/ind
v. 1, c2B	συμμαρτυρούσης	mental: percep	Present/impf/act/part.
v. 2, c2Ca	ἐστιν	Relational: attr.	Present/?/ act/ind
v. 2, c2Cb	ellipsis	Relational: attr.	
v. 3, c3A	ηὐχόμην	verbal	Imperf/impf/act/ind
v. 3, c3B	εἶναι	Relational	Present/?/act/inf
v. 4, c3C	εἰσιν	Relational	Present/?/act/ind
v. 4, c3Da	ellipsis	Relational	
v. 5, c3Db	ellipsis	Relational	
v. 5, c3Dc	ellipsis	Relational	
v. 5, c3E	ὤν	Relational	Present/?/act/part.

Chart for Romans 9:1–5

Clausal relations	participants
Paratactic elaboration: c1A ^ =c2A; Paratactic extension: c2Ca ^ +c2Cb; c3Da ^ +c3Db ^ +c3Dc Hypotactic enhancement: (c1A ^ =c2A) ^ xc2B	I:[2] I (Paul)^{x2}, R:[3] my (Paul) ^{x2} G:[4] Christ, conscience, holy spirit

Hypotactic extension:
c3Da ^ +c3Db ^ +c3Dc;
Projection: idea:
c2B ^ '(c2Ca ^ +c2Cb);
c3A ^ '3B (infinitive clause)
Embedded elaboration
c3B ^ =[[c3C]];
c3C ^ =[[c3Da]];
c3C ^ =[[c3Db]];
c3C ^ =[[c3Dc]];
c3Dc ^ =[[c3E]]
	R: me, my^{x3}, I, myself, (Paul); whom (Israelites) ^{x3}, he (ὁ ὢν): Christ
	I: I (Paul)
	G: heart, Christ ^{x2}, brothers, kinsmen, flesh ^{x2}, Israelites, sonship, glory, covenants, the giving of the law, the worship, the promise, the patriarchs, all, God

APPENDIX 3

Charts for Romans 9:6–13

Chart 1

Verse no.	Clauses	Clause no.
6	Οὐχ οἷον δὲ ὅτι ἐκπέπτωκεν ὁ λόγος τοῦ θεοῦ	c4A
	οὐ γὰρ πάντες οἱ ἐξ Ἰσραὴλ οὗτοι Ἰσραήλ	c5A
7	οὐδ' ὅτι εἰσὶν σπέρμα Ἀβραὰμ πάντες τέκνα	c5B
	ἀλλ᾽ ἐν Ἰσαὰκ κληθήσεταί σοι σπέρμα	c5C
8	τοῦτ᾽ ἔστιν οὐ τὰ τέκνα τῆς σαρκὸς ταῦτα τέκνα τοῦ θεοῦ	c6A
	ἀλλὰ τὰ τέκνα τῆς ἐπαγγελίας λογίζεται εἰς σπέρμα	c6B
9	ἐπαγγελίας γὰρ ὁ λόγος οὗτος	c7A
	κατὰ τὸν καιρὸν τοῦτον ἐλεύσομαι	c7Ba
	καὶ ἔσται τῇ Σάρρᾳ υἱός	c7Bb
10–13	Οὐ μόνον δέ	c8A
	ἀλλὰ καὶ Ῥεβέκκα	c8B①
	ἐξ ἑνὸς κοίτην ἔχουσα, Ἰσαὰκ τοῦ πατρὸς ἡμῶν	c8C
	μήπω γὰρ γεννηθέντων	c8Da
	μηδὲ πραξάντων τι ἀγαθὸν ἢ φαῦλον	c8Db
	ἵνα ἡ κατ᾽ ἐκλογὴν πρόθεσις τοῦ θεοῦ μένῃ οὐκ ἐξ ἔργων	c8E
	ἀλλ᾽ ἐκ τοῦ καλοῦντος	c8B②
	ἐρρέθη αὐτῇ	c8F
	ὅτι ὁ μείζων δουλεύσει τῷ ἐλάσσονι	c8G
	καθὼς γέγραπται	c8Ha
	τὸν Ἰακὼβ ἠγάπησα	c8Hb
	τὸν δὲ Ἠσαῦ ἐμίσησα	

Chart 2

Verse and Clause no.	Token	Process type	T/A/V/M	Clause complex relations	Participants
v. 6, c4A	ἐκπέπτωκεν	Material: action	Perfect/stative/act/ind.	paratactic enhancement: c4A ^ x c5	G: ὁ λόγος τοῦ θεοῦ, οὐ πάντες οἱ ἐξ Ἰσραήλ, Ἰσραήλ, σπέρμα Ἀβραάμ, πάντες (refer to Abraham's seed), τέκνα, σπέρμα, τὰ τέκνα τῆς σαρκός, τὰ τέκνα τοῦ θεοῦ, τὰ τέκνα τῆς ἐπαγγελίας, σπέρμα, ἐπαγγελίας ὁ λόγος, τῇ Σάρρᾳ υἱός, Ῥεβέκκα, Ἰσαὰκ τοῦ πατρὸς ἡμῶν, ἡ κατ' ἐκλογὴν πρόθεσις τοῦ θεοῦ, τὸν Ἰακώβ, τὸν Ἠσαῦ
v. 6, c5A	Ellipsis	Relational: id		Paratactic extension: c5A ^ +c5B ; c6A ^ +c6B; c7Ba ^ + c7Bb	
v. 6, c5B	εἰσὶν	Relational: id	Present/impf/act/ind.		
v. 7, c5C	κληθήσεταί	Relational: id	Future/ (?)/pass/ind.	paratactic elaboration: (c5A ^ +c5B) ^ = (c6A ^ +c6B)¹	
v. 8, c6A	ἔστιν ellipsis	Relational: id Relational: id	Present/impf/ act/ind.	c6B ^ =c7	
v.8, c6B	λογίζεται	Relational: id	Present/impf/pass/ind.		
v. 9, c7A	ellipsis	Relational: id		Projection: locution: c7 A^ "(c7Ba + c7Bb)	
v. 9, c7Ba	ἐλεύσομαι	Material: action	Future/ (?)/ mid/ind.		
v. 9, c7Bb	ἔσται	Relational: id	Future/ (?)/ mid/ind.		
v. 10, c8C	ἔχουσα	Relational: att	Present/impf/act/ part.	Paratactic extension: c8A ^ +c8B; c8Da ^ +c8Db; c8Ha ^ +c8Hb	
v. 11, c8Da	γεννηθέντων	Material: action	Aorist/perf/pass/part.	hypotactic enhancement: c8C ^ xc8D; c8D ^ xc8E projection: locution: c8B ^ c8E; c8G ^ ʻ(c8Ha ^ +c8Hb)	I: it (refer to ὁ λόγος), They (l κληθήσεταί), refer to the children of Isaac), They (l λογίζεται), refer to the children (of the promise), I (l ἐλεύσομαι] refer to God's messenger), I (l ἠγάπησα] refer to God) I (l ἐμίσησα] refer to God)
v. 11, c8Db	πραξάντων	Material: action	Aorist/perf/act/part.		
v. 11, c8E	μένῃ	Relational: att	Present/impf/act/sub.		
v. 12, c8B①②	ἐρρέθη	verbal	Aorist/perf/pass/ind.		
v. 12, c8F	δουλεύσει	Material: action	Future/(?) act/		
v. 13, c8G	γέγραπται	Material: action	Perfect/stative/pass/ind		
v. 13, c8Ha	ἠγάπησα	Mental: emotion	Aorist/perf/act/ind.		
v. 13, c8Hb	ἐμίσησα	Mental: emotion	Aorist/perf/act/ind.		R: οὗτοι, ταῦτα, οὗτος, αὐτῇ (Rebbeca), ὁ μείζων (Esau), τῷ ἐλάσσονι (Jacob)

APPENDIX 4
Charts for Romans 9:14–29

Chart 1

Verse no.	Clauses	Clause no.
14	Τί οὖν ἐροῦμεν;	c9A
	μὴ ἀδικία παρὰ τῷ θεῷ;	c9B
	μὴ γένοιτο.	c9C
15	τῷ Μωϋσεῖ γὰρ λέγει	c10A
	ἐλεήσω ὃν ἂν ἐλεῶ	c10Ba
	καὶ οἰκτιρήσω ὃν ἂν οἰκτίρω	c10Bb
16	ἄρα οὖν οὐ τοῦ θέλοντος οὐδὲ τοῦ τρέχοντος ἀλλὰ τοῦ ἐλεῶντος θεοῦ	c11A
17	λέγει γὰρ ἡ γραφὴ τῷ Φαραὼ	c12A
	ὅτι εἰς αὐτὸ τοῦτο ἐξήγειρά σε	c12B
	ὅπως ἐνδείξωμαι ἐν σοὶ τὴν δύναμίν μου	c12Ca
	καὶ ὅπως διαγγελῇ τὸ ὄνομά μου ἐν πάσῃ τῇ γῇ	c12Cb
18	ἄρα οὖν ὃν θέλει ἐλεεῖ	c13A
	ὃν δὲ θέλει σκληρύνει	c13B
19	Ἐρεῖς μοι οὖν	c14A
	τί [οὖν] ἔτι μέμφεται;	c14Ba
	τῷ γὰρ βουλήματι αὐτοῦ τίς ἀνθέστηκεν;	c14Bb
20	ὦ ἄνθρωπε, μενοῦνγε σὺ τίς εἶ	c15A
	ὁ ἀνταποκρινόμενος τῷ θεῷ;	c15B
	μὴ ἐρεῖ τὸ πλάσμα τῷ πλάσαντι·	c16A
	τί με ἐποίησας οὕτως;	c16B
21	ἢ οὐκ ἔχει ἐξουσίαν ὁ κεραμεὺς τοῦ πηλοῦ	c17A
	ἐκ τοῦ αὐτοῦ φυράματος ποιῆσαι	c17Ba
	ὃ μὲν εἰς τιμὴν σκεῦος ὃ δὲ εἰς ἀτιμίαν;	c17Bb

22-26	εἰ δὲ . . . ὁ θεὸς	c18①
	θέλων ἐνδείξασθαι τὴν ὀργὴν	c18A
	καὶ γνωρίσαι τὸ δυνατὸν αὐτοῦ	c18B
	ἤνεγκεν ἐν πολλῇ μακροθυμίᾳ σκεύη ὀργῆς κατηρτισμένα εἰς	c18②
	ἀπώλειαν	c18C
	καὶ ἵνα γνωρίσῃ τὸν πλοῦτον τῆς δόξης αὐτοῦ ἐπὶ σκεύη ἐλέους	c18D
	ἃ προητοίμασεν εἰς δόξαν;	c18E
	Οὓς καὶ ἐκάλεσεν ἡμᾶς οὐ μόνον ἐξ Ἰουδαίων ἀλλὰ καὶ ἐξ ἐθνῶν	c19A
	ὡς καὶ ἐν τῷ Ὡσηὲ λέγει	c19Ba
	καλέσω τὸν οὐ λαόν μου λαόν μου	c19Bb
	καὶ τὴν οὐκ ἠγαπημένην ἠγαπημένην	c19Ca
	καὶ ἔσται ἐν τῷ τόπῳ	c19Cb
	οὗ ἐρρέθη αὐτοῖς	c19Cc
	οὐ λαός μου ὑμεῖς	c19D
27	ἐκεῖ κληθήσονται υἱοὶ θεοῦ ζῶντος	c20A
	Ἠσαΐας δὲ κράζει ὑπὲρ τοῦ Ἰσραήλ	c20B
	ἐὰν ᾖ ὁ ἀριθμὸς τῶν υἱῶν Ἰσραὴλ ὡς ἡ ἄμμος τῆς θαλάσσης	c20C
28	τὸ ὑπόλειμμα σωθήσεται	c20D
29	λόγον γὰρ συντελῶν καὶ συντέμνων ποιήσει κύριος ἐπὶ τῆς γῆς	c21A
	καὶ καθὼς προείρηκεν Ἠσαΐας	c21B
	εἰ μὴ κύριος σαβαὼθ ἐγκατέλιπεν ἡμῖν σπέρμα	c21Ca
	ὡς Σόδομα ἂν ἐγενήθημεν	c21Cb
	καὶ ὡς Γόμορρα ἂν ὡμοιώθημεν	

Chart 2

Verse and Clause no.	Token	Process type	T/A/V/M
v. 14, c9A	ἐροῦμεν	verbal	Future/(?)/act/ind
v. 14, c9B	Ellipsis	Relational: attr.	
v. 14, c9C	γένοιτο		Aorist/perf/mid/opt
v. 15, c10A	λέγει	verbal	Present/impf/act/ind
v. 15, c10Ba	ἐλεήσω, ἐλεῶ	Mental: emotion Mental: emotion	Future/(?)/act/ind Present/impf/act/sub
v. 15, c10Bb	οἰκτιρήσω οἰκτίρω	Mental: emotion Mental: emotion	Future/(?)/act/ind Present/impf/act/sub
v. 16, c11A	θέλοντος τρέχοντος ἐλεῶντος	Mental: desid[1] Behavior: action Mental: emotion	Present/impf/act/part. Present/impf/act/part. Present/impf/act/part.
v. 17, c12A	λέγει	verbal	Present/impf/act/ind
v. 17, c12B	ἐξήγειρά	Material: action	Aorist/perf/act/ind
v. 17, c12Ca	ἐνδείξωμαι	Material: action	Aorist/perf/mid/sub
v. 17, c12Cb	διαγγελῇ	Material: action	Aorist/perf/pass/sub

Clause complex relations	Participants
Projection: locution: c10A ^ "(c10Ba ^ +c10Bb); c12A ^ "(c12B ^ x(c12Ca ^ +c12Cb)); c14A ^ "(c14Ba ^ +c14Bb); c16A ^ "c16B; c20A ^ "((c20B ^ xc20C) ^ xc20D); c21A ^ "(xc21B ^ (c21Ca ^ +c21Cb)) paratactic extension: c9A ^ +c9B ^ +c9C; c10Ba ^ +c10Bb; c13A ^ +c13B; c14 ^ +c15; c16A ^ +c17A; c18A ^ +c18B; c19Ba ^ +c19Bb; c19C ^ +c19D; c21Ca ^ +c21Cb	G: Μωϋσεῖ, τοῦ θέλοντος, τοῦ τρέχοντος, τοῦ ἐλεῶντος θεοῦ, ἡ γραφή, Φαραώ, τὴν δύναμίν μου, τὸ ὄνομά μου, ἄνθρωπε, θεῷ, τὸ πλάσμα, τῷ πλάσαντι, ὁ κεραμεύς, τοῦ αὐτοῦ φυράματος, τιμὴν σκεῦος, ἀτιμίαν (a vessel of dishonored), ὁ θεός, τὴν ὀργήν, τὸ δυνατὸν αὐτοῦ, λαόν μου^{X3}, ἠγαπημένην^{X2}, υἱοὶ θεοῦ ζῶντος, Ἡσαΐας, ὁ ἀριθμὸς τῶν υἱῶν Ἰσραήλ, ἡ ἄμμος τῆς θαλάσσης, τὸ ὑπόλειμμα, κύριος, λόγον, Ἡσαΐας, κύριος, σπέρμα, Σόδομα, Γόμορρα

Verse and Clause no.	Token	Process type	T/A/V/M
v. 17, c13A	θέλει	Mental: desid	Present/impf/act/ind
	ἐλεεῖ	Mental: emotion	Present/impf/act/ind
v. 18, c13B	θέλει	Mental: desid	Present/impf/act/ind
	σκληρύνει	Material: action	Present/impf/act/ind
v. 19, c14A	ἐρεῖς	verbal	Future/(?)/act/ind
v. 19, c14Ba	μέμφεται	Material: action	Present/impf/mid/ind
v. 19, c14Bb	ἀνθέστηκεν	Material: action	Perfect/stative/act/ind
v. 20, c15A	εἶ	Relational: id	Present/?/act/ind
v. 20, c15B	ἀνταποκρινόμενος	verbal	Present/impf/mid/part
v. 20, c16A	ἐρεῖ	verbal	Future/(?)/act/ind
v. 20, c16B	ἐποίησας	Material: action	Aorist/perf/act/ind
v. 21, c17A	ἔχει	Relational: attr	Present/impf/act/ind
v. 21, c17Ba	ποιῆσαι	Material: action	Aorist/perf/act/inf.
v. 22, c18A	θέλων	Mental: desid	Present/impf/act/part
	ἐνδείξασθαι	Material: action	Aorist/perf/mid/inf
v. 22, c18B	γνωρίσαι	Mental: cog²	Aorist/perf/act/inf
v. 22, c18	ἤνεγκεν	Material: action	Aorist/perf/act/inf
	κατηρτισμένα	Material: action	Perfect/stative/pass/part
v. 23, c18C	γνωρίσῃ	Mental: cog	Aorist/perf/act/sub
v. 23, c18D	προητοίμασεν	Material: action	Aorist/perf/act/ind
v. 24, c18E	ἐκάλεσε	Material: action	Aorist/perf/act/ind
v. 25, c19A	λέγει	verbal	Present/impf/act/ind
v. 25, c19Ba	καλέσω	Relational: id	Future/?/act/ind
v. 25, c19Bb	ἠγαπημένην (x2)	Mental: emotion	Perfect/stative/pass/part
v. 26, c19Ca	ἔσται	Relational: attr	Future/?/mid/sub
v. 26, c19Cb	ἐρρέθη	verbal	Aorist/perf/pass/ind
v. 26, c19D	κληθήσονται	Material: action	Future/?/pass/ind
v. 27, c20A	κράζει	verbal	Present/impf/act/ind
v. 27, c20B	ᾖ	Relational: id	Present/?/act/sub
v. 27, c20C	σωθήσεται	Material: action	Future/?/pass/ind
v. 28, c20D	συντελῶν	Material: action	Present/impf/act/ind
	συντέμνων	Material: action	Present/impf/act/ind
	ποιήσει	Material: action	Future/?/act/ind
v. 29, c21A	προείρηκεν	verbal	Perfect/stative/act/ind
v. 29, c21B	ἐγκατέλιπεν	Material: action	Aorist/perf/act/ind
v. 29, c21Ca	ἐγενήθημεν	Relational: id	Aorist/perf/pass/ind
v. 29, c21Cb	ὡμοιώθημεν	Relational: id	Aorist/perf/pass/ind

Clause complex relations	Participants
paratactic enhancement: c10 ^ xc11A; c12 ^ x(c13A ^ +c13B); hypotactic enhancement: c18① ② ^ xc18C; xc20A ^ c20B; c20B ^ xc20C; xc21B ^ (c21Ca ^ +c21Cb) hypotactic elaboration: c18C ^ =c18D;[3] c18C ^ =c18E;[4] embedded elaboration: c18① ^ =[[c18A ^ +c18B]][5] c19Ca ^ =[[19Cb]] Summary: projection: locution (x6); paratactic extension (x9); paratactic enhancement (x2); hypotactic enhancement (x4); hypotactic elaboration (x2); embedded elaboration (x2)	I: we, he (refers to God), I (refers to God)[x4], I ([ἐξήγειρά] refers to God), I ([ἐνδείξωμαι] refers to God), it ([διαγγελῇ] refers to God's name), he (refers to God)[x4], you ([Ἐρεῖς] refers to Paul's interlocutor), he ([μέμφεται] refers to Paul), he ([ἤνεγκεν] refers to God), he ([γνωρίσῃ] refers to God), he ([ἐκάλεσεν] refers to God), he ([λέγει] refers to God), I ([καλέσω] refers to God), we ([ἐγενήθημεν] refers to the Israel),), we ([ὡμοιώθημεν] refers to the Israel), R: σε (refers to Pharaoh), αὐτὸ, μοι (refers to Paul), τί, αὐτοῦ (God's), τίς, σὺ, τίς, ὁ ἀνταποκρινόμενος, τί, με, ἡμᾶς, αὐτοῖς, ὑμεῖς, ἡμῖν

Chart 3

¹⁴ Τί οὖν ἐροῦμεν; μὴ ἀδικία παρὰ τῷ θεῷ; μὴ γένοιτο.

¹⁵ τῷ Μωϋσεῖ γὰρ λέγει· ἐλεήσω ὃν ἂν ἐλεῶ καὶ οἰκτιρήσω ὃν ἂν οἰκτίρω.

¹⁶ ἄρα οὖν οὐ τοῦ θέλοντος οὐδὲ τοῦ τρέχοντος ἀλλὰ τοῦ ἐλεῶντος θεοῦ.

¹⁷ λέγει γὰρ ἡ γραφὴ τῷ Φαραὼ ὅτι εἰς αὐτὸ τοῦτο ἐξήγειρά σε ὅπως ἐνδείξωμαι ἐν σοὶ τὴν δύναμίν μου καὶ ὅπως διαγγελῇ τὸ ὄνομά μου ἐν πάσῃ τῇ γῇ.

¹⁸ ἄρα οὖν ὃν θέλει ἐλεεῖ, ὃν δὲ θέλει σκληρύνει.

¹⁹ Ἐρεῖς μοι οὖν· τί [οὖν] ἔτι μέμφεται; τῷ γὰρ βουλήματι αὐτοῦ τίς ἀνθέστηκεν;

²⁰ ὦ ἄνθρωπε, μενοῦνγε σὺ τίς εἶ ὁ ἀνταποκρινόμενος τῷ θεῷ; μὴ ἐρεῖ τὸ πλάσμα τῷ πλάσαντι· τί με ἐποίησας οὕτως;

²¹ ἢ οὐκ ἔχει ἐξουσίαν ὁ κεραμεὺς τοῦ πηλοῦ ἐκ τοῦ αὐτοῦ φυράματος ποιῆσαι ὃ μὲν εἰς τιμὴν σκεῦος ὃ δὲ εἰς ἀτιμίαν;

²² εἰ δὲ θέλων ὁ θεὸς ἐνδείξασθαι τὴν ὀργὴν καὶ γνωρίσαι τὸ δυνατὸν αὐτοῦ ἤνεγκεν ἐν πολλῇ μακροθυμίᾳ σκεύη ὀργῆς κατηρτισμένα εἰς ἀπώλειαν,

²³ καὶ ἵνα γνωρίσῃ τὸν πλοῦτον τῆς δόξης αὐτοῦ ἐπὶ σκεύη ἐλέους ἃ προητοίμασεν εἰς δόξαν;

²⁴ Οὓς καὶ ἐκάλεσεν ἡμᾶς οὐ μόνον ἐξ Ἰουδαίων ἀλλὰ καὶ ἐξ ἐθνῶν,

²⁵ ὡς καὶ ἐν τῷ Ὡσηὲ λέγει· καλέσω τὸν οὐ λαόν μου λαόν μου καὶ τὴν οὐκ ἠγαπημένην ἠγαπημένην·

²⁶ καὶ ἔσται ἐν τῷ τόπῳ οὗ ἐρρέθη αὐτοῖς· οὐ λαός μου ὑμεῖς, ἐκεῖ κληθήσονται υἱοὶ θεοῦ ζῶντος.

²⁷ Ἠσαΐας δὲ κράζει ὑπὲρ τοῦ Ἰσραήλ· ἐὰν ᾖ ὁ ἀριθμὸς τῶν υἱῶν Ἰσραὴλ ὡς ἡ ἄμμος τῆς θαλάσσης, τὸ ὑπόλειμμα σωθήσεται·

²⁸ λόγον γὰρ συντελῶν καὶ συντέμνων ποιήσει κύριος ἐπὶ τῆς γῆς.

²⁹ καὶ καθὼς προείρηκεν Ἠσαΐας· εἰ μὴ κύριος σαβαὼθ ἐγκατέλιπεν ἡμῖν σπέρμα, ὡς Σόδομα ἂν ἐγενήθημεν καὶ ὡς Γόμορρα ἂν ὡμοιώθημεν.

Chart 4

Hos 2:1 καὶ ἦν ὁ ἀριθμὸς τῶν υἱῶν Ἰσραηλ ὡς ἡ ἄμμος τῆς θαλάσσης Isa 10: 22 καὶ ἐὰν γένηται ὁ λαὸς Ἰσραηλ ὡς ἡ ἄμμος τῆς θαλάσσης τὸ κατάλειμμα αὐτῶν σωθήσεται λόγον γὰρ συντελῶν καὶ συντέμνων ἐν δικαιοσύνῃ	Rom 9: 27 ἐὰν ᾖ ὁ ἀριθμὸς τῶν υἱῶν Ἰσραηλ ὡς ἡ ἄμμος τῆς θαλάσσης, τὸ ὑπόλειμμα σωθήσεται·
Isa 10: 22–23 καὶ ἐὰν γένηται ὁ λαὸς Ἰσραηλ ὡς ἡ ἄμμος τῆς θαλάσσης τὸ κατάλειμμα αὐτῶν σωθήσεται λόγον γὰρ συντελῶν καὶ συντέμνων ἐν δικαιοσύνῃ ὅτι λόγον συντετμημένον ποιήσει ὁ θεὸς ἐν τῇ οἰκουμένῃ ὅλῃ Isa 28:22 καὶ ὑμεῖς μὴ εὐφρανθείητε μηδὲ ἰσχυσάτωσαν ὑμῶν οἱ δεσμοί διότι συντετελεσμένα καὶ συντετμημένα πράγματα ἤκουσα παρὰ κυρίου σαβαωθ ἃ ποιήσει ἐπὶ πᾶσαν τὴν γῆν	Rom 9: 28 λόγον γὰρ συντελῶν καὶ συντέμνων ποιήσει κύριος ἐπὶ τῆς γῆς.

(Note: <u>double underline</u>: agreement between Hos 1:10, Isa 10:22 and Rom 9:27a; **<u>thick underline</u>**: agreement between Isa 10:22 and Rom 9:27b; <u>single underline</u>: agreement between Isa 10:22 and Rom 9:28a; wave underline: agreement between Isa 10:23 and Rom 9:28b)

APPENDIX 5
Charts for Romans 9:30–10:4

Chart 1

Verse no.	Clauses	Clause no.
30	Τί οὖν ἐροῦμεν;	c1A
	ὅτι ἔθνη . . . κατέλαβεν δικαιοσύνην . . .	c1B
	τὰ μὴ διώκοντα δικαιοσύνην δικαιοσύνην δὲ τὴν ἐκ πίστεως	c1Ca//c1Cb
	Ἰσραὴλ δὲ . . . εἰς νόμον οὐκ ἔφθασεν	c2A
31	διώκων νόμον δικαιοσύνης	c2B
	διὰ τί;	c3A
32	ὅτι οὐκ ἐκ πίστεως	c3Ba
	ἀλλ᾿ ὡς ἐξ ἔργων·	c3Bb
	προσέκοψαν τῷ λίθῳ τοῦ προσκόμματος	c4A
	καθὼς γέγραπται·	c4B
33	ἰδοὺ τίθημι ἐν Σιὼν λίθον προσκόμματος καὶ πέτραν σκανδάλου,	c4C
	καὶ ὁ πιστεύων ἐπ᾿ αὐτῷ οὐ καταισχυνθήσεται	c4D
1	ἀδελφοί,	c5A
	ἡ μὲν εὐδοκία τῆς ἐμῆς καρδίας	c5Ba
	καὶ ἡ δέησις πρὸς τὸν θεὸν ὑπὲρ αὐτῶν	c5Bb
	εἰς σωτηρίαν	c5Bc
	μαρτυρῶ γὰρ αὐτοῖς	c6A
2	ὅτι ζῆλον θεοῦ ἔχουσιν	c6Ba
	ἀλλ᾿ οὐ κατ᾿ ἐπίγνωσιν	c6Bb
	ἀγνοοῦντες γὰρ τὴν τοῦ θεοῦ δικαιοσύνην	c7Aa
3	καὶ τὴν ἰδίαν [δικαιοσύνην] ζητοῦντες στῆσαι,	c7Ab
	τῇ δικαιοσύνῃ τοῦ θεοῦ οὐχ ὑπετάγησαν	c7B
	τέλος γὰρ νόμου Χριστὸς	c8A
4	εἰς δικαιοσύνην παντὶ τῷ πιστεύοντι	c8B

Chart 2

V and C no.[1]	Token	Process type	T/A/V/M	Clause Complex relations	Participants
v. 30, c1A	ἐροῦμεν	verbal	Future/(?)/act/ind	Paratactic extension: (X8) c1A ∧ +c2A; c1A ∧ + (c1B ∧ +c2A); c3Ba ∧ +c3Bb; c3A ∧ + (c3Ba ∧ +c3Bb); c4C ∧ +c4D; c6Ba ∧ +c6Bb; c7Aa ∧ +c7Ab; c6B ∧ +c7;	I: we
v. 30, c1B	κατέλαβεν	Material: action	Aorist/perf/act/ind		G: ἔθνη, δικαιοσύνηx2 I: she (ἔθνη)
v. 30, c1Ca	διώκοντα	Material: action	Present/impf/act/part.		G: δικαιοσύνην
v. 31, c2A	ἔφθασεν	Material: action	Aorist/perf/act/ind		G: Ἰσραήλ, νόμον I: she (Ἰσραήλ)
v. 31, c2B	διώκων	Material: action	Present/impf/act/part.		G: νόμον δικαιοσύνης
v. 32, c4A	προσέκοψαν	Material: action	Aorist/perf/act/ind		I: they (Ἰσραήλ)
v. 33, c4B	γέγραπται	Material: action	Perfect/Stative/act/ind	Embedded elaboration: (X3) c1B ∧ =c1Ca (on ἔθνη); c1B ∧ =c1Cb (on δικαιοσύνην); c2A ∧ =c2B (on Ἰσραήλ);	I: it (the Scripture)
v. 33, c4C	τίθημι	Material: action	Present/impf/act/ind		I: I (YHWH)
v. 33, c4D	πιστεύων	Mental: percep[2]	Present/impf/act/part.		G: ὁ πιστεύων ἐπ᾽ αὐτῷ
v. 33, c4D	καταισχυνθήσεται	Mental: emotion	Future/(?)/pass/ind	Hypotactic enhancement: (X3) c4A ∧ xc4B; xc7A ∧ c7B; c8A ∧ xc8B	R: ἐμῆς (Paul)
v. 1, c5B	Ellipsis	Relational: id			I: I (Paul)
v. 2, c6A	μαρτυρῶ	verbal	Present/impf/act/ind		I: I (Paul)
v. 2, c6Ba	ἔχουσιν	Relational: attr	Present/impf/act/ind		I: they (Ἰσραήλ)
v. 3, c7Aa	ἀγνοοῦντες	Mental: cog	Present/impf/act/part.	Projection: locution: (X2) c4B ∧ "(c4C ∧ c4D); c6A ∧ "(c6B ∧ +c7)	G: θεοῦ δικαιοσύνην
v. 3, c7Ab	ζητοῦντες στῆσαι	Material: action	Present/impf/act/part.		I: they (Ἰσραήλ)x2 G: τὴν ἰδίαν δικαιοσύνην
v. 3, c7B	ὑπετάγησαν	Material: action	Aorist/pf/act/ind		I: they (Ἰσραήλ) G: δικαιοσύνῃ τοῦ θεοῦ
v. 4, c8A	Ellipsis	Relational: id			G: Χριστός, νόμου
v. 4, c8B	πιστεύοντι	Mental: percep	Present/impf/act/part.		

APPENDIX 6
Charts for Romans 10:4–13

Chart 1

Verse no.	Clauses	Clause no.
4	τέλος γὰρ νόμου Χριστὸς	c8A
	εἰς δικαιοσύνην παντὶ τῷ πιστεύοντι	c8B
5	Μωϋσῆς γὰρ γράφει τὴν δικαιοσύνην τὴν ἐκ [τοῦ] νόμου	c9A
	ὅτι ὁ ποιήσας αὐτὰ ἄνθρωπος ζήσεται ἐν αὐτοῖς	c9B
6	ἡ δὲ ἐκ πίστεως δικαιοσύνη οὕτως λέγει·	c10A
	μὴ εἴπῃς ἐν τῇ καρδίᾳ σου·	c10B
	τίς ἀναβήσεται εἰς τὸν οὐρανόν;	c10Ca
	τοῦτ' ἔστιν Χριστὸν καταγαγεῖν	c10Cb
	ἤ· τίς καταβήσεται εἰς τὴν ἄβυσσον;	c10Da
7	τοῦτ' ἔστιν Χριστὸν ἐκ νεκρῶν ἀναγαγεῖν	c10Db
	ἀλλὰ τί λέγει;	c11A
8	ἐγγύς σου τὸ ῥῆμά ἐστιν ἐν τῷ στόματί σου καὶ ἐν τῇ καρδίᾳ σου,	c11B
	τοῦτ' ἔστιν τὸ ῥῆμα τῆς πίστεως	c11Ca
	ὃ κηρύσσομεν	c11Cb
	ὅτι ἐὰν ὁμολογήσῃς ἐν τῷ στόματί σου	c12Aa
	κύριον Ἰησοῦν	c12Ab
9	καὶ πιστεύσῃς ἐν τῇ καρδίᾳ σου	c12Ba
	ὅτι ὁ θεὸς αὐτὸν ἤγειρεν ἐκ νεκρῶν,	c12Bb
10	σωθήσῃ	c12C
	καρδίᾳ γὰρ πιστεύεται εἰς δικαιοσύνην,	c13A
11	στόματι δὲ ὁμολογεῖται εἰς σωτηρίαν	c13B
	λέγει γὰρ ἡ γραφή·	c14A
	πᾶς ... οὐ καταισχυνθήσεται	c14Ba
	ὁ πιστεύων ἐπ' αὐτῷ	c14Bb
12	οὐ γάρ ἐστιν διαστολὴ Ἰουδαίου τε καὶ Ἕλληνος,	c15A
	ὁ γὰρ αὐτὸς κύριος πάντων,	c15Ba
	πλουτῶν εἰς πάντας	c15Bb
13	τοὺς ἐπικαλουμένους αὐτόν·	c15Bc
	πᾶς γὰρ ... σωθήσεται	c16A
	ὃς ἂν ἐπικαλέσηται τὸ ὄνομα κυρίου	c16B

Chart 2

V and c no.	Token	Process type	T/A/V/M
v. 5, c9A	γράφει	Material: action	Present/impf/act/ind
v. 5, c9B	ζήσεται ποιήσας	Material: action Material: action	Future/?/mid/ind Aorist/pf/act/part.
v. 6, c10A	λέγει	Verbal	Present/impf/act/ind
v. 6, c10B	εἴπῃς	verbal	Aorist/pf/act/subj
v. 6, c10Ca	ἀναβήσεται	Material: action	Future/?/mid/ind
v. 6, c10Cb	ἔστιν; καταγαγεῖν	Relational: id Material: action	Present/?/act/ind Aorist/pf/act/inf
v. 7, c10Da	καταβήσεται	Material: action	Future/?/mid/ind
v. 7, c10Db	ἔστιν; ἀναγαγεῖν	Relational: id Material: action	Present/?/act/ind Aorist/pf/act/inf
v. 8, c11A	λέγει	Verbal	Present/impf/act/ind
v. 8, c11B	ἐστιν	Relational: id	Present/?/act/ind
v. 8, c11Ca	ἔστιν	Relational: id	Present/?/act/ind
v. 8, c11Cb	κηρύσσομεν	verbal	Present/impf/act/ind
v. 9, c12Aa	ὁμολογήσῃς	verbal	Aorist/pf/act/subj
v. 9, c12Ab	Ellipsis	Relational: id	
v. 9, c12Ba	πιστεύσῃς	Mental: percep	Aorist/pf/act/subj
v. 9, c12Bb	ἤγειρεν	Material: action	Aorist/pf/act/ind
v. 9, c12C	σωθήσῃ	Material: action	Future/?/pass/ind
v. 10, c13A	πιστεύεται	Mental: percep	Present/impf/mid/ind
v. 10, c13B	ὁμολογεῖται	Verbal	Present/impf/mid/ind
v. 11, c14A	λέγει	Verbal	Present/imf/act/ind
v. 11, c14Ba	καταισχυνθήσεται	Mental: emotion	Future/?/pass/ind
v. 11, c14Bb	πιστεύων	Mental: percep	Present/impf/act/part
v. 12, c15A	ἐστιν	Existential	Present/?/act/ind
v. 12, c15Ba	Ellipsis	Relational: id	
v. 12, c15Bc	ἐπικαλουμένους	verbal	Present/impf/mid/part
v. 13, c16A	σωθήσεται	Material: action	Future/?/pass/ind
v. 13, c16B	ἐπικαλέσηται	verbal	Aorist/pf/mid/subj

Charts for Romans 10:4–13

Clausal relationships	Participants
Hypotactic projection: (x5) c9A ^ "c9B; c10B ^ "(c10Ca ^ +c10Cb); c10A ^ "(c10B ^ "(c10BCa^ +c10Cb)); c12Aa ^ "c12Ab; c12Ba ^ 'c12Bb Paratactic projection: (x1) c14A ^ "c14B; Hypotactic enhancement: (x4) c10Ca ^ xc10Cb; c10D a^ x10Db; x(c12A ^ + c12B) ^ 12C; c15Ba ^ xc15Bb Paratactic extension: (x4) c11A ^ + c11B; c12A ^ + c12B; c13A ^ + c13B; c15A ^ + c15B Paratactic elaboration: (x1) c11B ^ =c11Ca hypotactic elaboration: (x1) c11Ca ^ =c11Cb	G: Μωϋσῆς; δικαιοσύνην νόμου
	G: ὁ ἄνθρωπος
	G: πίστεως δικαιοσύνη
	I: you ; R: σου
	R: τίς (who)
	G: Χριστὸν
	R: τίς (who)
	G: Χριστὸν
	I: it (Scripture); R: τί
	G: σου τὸ ῥῆμά
	G: τὸ ῥῆμα τῆς πίστεως I: we (Paul and audience) R: ὃ (ῥῆμά τῆς πίστεως)
	I: you (audience)
	G: κύριον; Ἰησοῦν
	I: you (audience)
	G: ὁ θεὸς; R: αὐτὸν (Jesus)
	I: you (audience)
	I: he (general)
	I: he (general)
	G: ἡ γραφή
	G: πᾶς ὁ πιστεύων
	R: αὐτῷ (Jesus)
embedded elaboration: (x3) c14Ba ^ =c14Bb (on πᾶς); c15Bb ^ =c15Bc (on πάντας); c16A ^ =c16B (on πᾶς)	G: Ἰουδαίου; Ἕλληνος
	G: ὁ αὐτὸς κύριος (Jesus); τοὺς ἐπικαλουμένους αὐτόν R: πάντων^{X2}
	R: αὐτόν (Jesus)
	R: πᾶς
	R: ὃς (πᾶς) G: τὸ ὄνομα κυρίου

APPENDIX 7

Baruch Text

Chapters	Greek	RSV
1:15–21 Sin against God	¹⁵ καὶ ἐρεῖτε τῷ κυρίῳ θεῷ ἡμῶν ἡ δικαιοσύνη ἡμῖν δὲ αἰσχύνη τῶν προσώπων ὡς ἡ ἡμέρα αὕτη ἀνθρώπῳ Ιουδα καὶ τοῖς κατοικοῦσιν Ιερουσαλημ . . . ¹⁷ ὧν ἡμάρτομεν ἔναντι κυρίου ¹⁸ καὶ ἠπειθήσαμεν αὐτῷ καὶ οὐκ ἠκούσαμεν τῆς φωνῆς κυρίου θεοῦ ἡμῶν πορεύεσθαι τοῖς προστάγμασιν κυρίου οἷς ἔδωκεν κατὰ πρόσωπον ἡμῶν ¹⁹ ἀπὸ τῆς ἡμέρας ἧς ἐξήγαγεν κύριος τοὺς πατέρας ἡμῶν ἐκ γῆς Αἰγύπτου καὶ ἕως τῆς ἡμέρας ταύτης ἤμεθα ἀπειθοῦντες πρὸς κύριον θεὸν ἡμῶν καὶ ἐσχεδιάζομεν πρὸς τὸ μὴ ἀκούειν τῆς φωνῆς αὐτοῦ ²⁰ καὶ ἐκολλήθη εἰς ἡμᾶς τὰ κακὰ καὶ ἡ ἀρά ἣν συνέταξεν κύριος τῷ Μωυσῇ παιδὶ αὐτοῦ ἐν ἡμέρᾳ ᾗ ἐξήγαγεν τοὺς πατέρας ἡμῶν ἐκ γῆς Αἰγύπτου δοῦναι ἡμῖν γῆν ῥέουσαν γάλα καὶ μέλι ὡς ἡ ἡμέρα αὕτη ²¹ καὶ οὐκ ἠκούσαμεν τῆς φωνῆς κυρίου τοῦ θεοῦ ἡμῶν κατὰ πάντας τοὺς λόγους τῶν προφητῶν ὧν ἀπέστειλεν πρὸς ἡμᾶς	¹⁵And you shall say: "Righteousness belongs to the Lord our God, but confusion of face, as at this day, to us, to the men of Judah, to the inhabitants of Jerusalem, . . . ¹⁷ because we have sinned before the Lord, ¹⁸and have disobeyed him, and have not heeded the voice of the Lord our God, to walk in the statutes of the Lord which he set before us. ¹⁹ From the day when the Lord brought our fathers out of the land of Egypt until today, we have been disobedient to the Lord our God, and we have been negligent, in not heeding his voice. ²⁰ So to this day there have clung to us the calamities and the curse which the Lord declared through Moses his servant at the time when he brought our fathers out of the land of Egypt to give to us a land flowing with milk and honey. ²¹ We did not heed the voice of the Lord our God in all the words of the prophets whom he sent to us, but we each followed the intent of his own wicked heart by serving other gods and doing what is evil in the sight of the Lord our God.

Chapters	Greek	RSV
2:21, 24, 26 Sin against God – Exile	οὕτως εἶπεν κύριος κλίνατε τὸν ὦμον ὑμῶν καὶ ἐργάσασθε τῷ βασιλεῖ Βαβυλῶνος καὶ καθίσατε ἐπὶ τὴν γῆν ἣν ἔδωκα τοῖς πατράσιν ὑμῶν . . . καὶ οὐκ ἠκούσαμεν τῆς φωνῆς σου ἐργάσασθαι τῷ βασιλεῖ Βαβυλῶνος καὶ ἔστησας τοὺς λόγους σου οὓς ἐλάλησας ἐν χερσὶν τῶν παίδων σου τῶν προφητῶν τοῦ ἐξενεχθῆναι τὰ ὀστᾶ βασιλέων ἡμῶν καὶ τὰ ὀστᾶ τῶν πατέρων ἡμῶν ἐκ τοῦ τόπου αὐτῶν . . . καὶ ἔθηκας τὸν οἶκον οὗ ἐπεκλήθη τὸ ὄνομά σου ἐπ' αὐτῷ ὡς ἡ ἡμέρα αὕτη διὰ πονηρίαν οἴκου Ισραηλ καὶ οἴκου Ιουδα	"Thus says the Lord: Bend your shoulders and serve the king of Babylon, and you will remain in the land which I gave to your fathers." . . . "But we did not obey thy voice, to serve the king of Babylon; and thou hast confirmed thy words, which thou didst speak by thy servants the prophets, that the bones of our kings and the bones of our fathers would be brought out of their graves." . . . And the house which is called by thy name thou hast made as it is today, because of the wickedness of the house of Israel and the house of Judah.

Chapters	Greek	RSV
2:27–35 Repentance – Return	²⁷ καὶ ἐποίησας εἰς ἡμᾶς κύριε ὁ θεὸς ἡμῶν κατὰ πᾶσαν ἐπιείκειάν σου καὶ κατὰ πάντα οἰκτιρμόν σου τὸν μέγαν ²⁸ καθὰ ἐλάλησας ἐν χειρὶ παιδός σου Μωυσῇ ἐν ἡμέρᾳ ἐντειλαμένου σου αὐτῷ γράψαι τὸν νόμον σου ἐναντίον υἱῶν Ισραηλ λέγων ²⁹ ἐὰν μὴ ἀκούσητε τῆς φωνῆς μου ἦ μὴν ἡ βόμβησις ἡ μεγάλη ἡ πολλὴ αὕτη ἀποστρέψει εἰς μικρὰν ἐν τοῖς ἔθνεσιν οὗ διασπερῶ αὐτοὺς ἐκεῖ ³⁰ ὅτι ἔγνων ὅτι οὐ μὴ ἀκούσωσίν μου ὅτι λαὸς σκληροτράχηλός ἐστιν καὶ ἐπιστρέψουσιν ἐπὶ καρδίαν αὐτῶν ἐν γῇ ἀποικισμοῦ αὐτῶν ³¹ καὶ γνώσονται ὅτι ἐγὼ κύριος ὁ θεὸς αὐτῶν καὶ δώσω αὐτοῖς καρδίαν καὶ ὦτα ἀκούοντα ³² καὶ αἰνέσουσίν με ἐν γῇ ἀποικισμοῦ αὐτῶν καὶ μνησθήσονται τοῦ ὀνόματός μου ³³ καὶ ἀποστρέψουσιν ἀπὸ τοῦ νώτου αὐτῶν τοῦ σκληροῦ καὶ ἀπὸ πονηρῶν πραγμάτων αὐτῶν ὅτι μνησθήσονται τῆς ὁδοῦ πατέρων αὐτῶν τῶν ἁμαρτόντων ἔναντι κυρίου ³⁴ καὶ ἀποστρέψω αὐτοὺς εἰς τὴν γῆν ἣν ὤμοσα τοῖς πατράσιν αὐτῶν τῷ Αβρααμ καὶ τῷ Ισαακ καὶ τῷ Ιακωβ καὶ κυριεύσουσιν αὐτῆς καὶ πληθυνῶ αὐτοὺς καὶ οὐ μὴ σμικρυνθῶσιν ³⁵ καὶ στήσω αὐτοῖς διαθήκην αἰώνιον τοῦ εἶναί με αὐτοῖς εἰς θεὸν καὶ αὐτοὶ ἔσονταί μοι εἰς λαόν καὶ οὐ κινήσω ἔτι τὸν λαόν μου Ισραηλ ἀπὸ τῆς γῆς ἧς ἔδωκα αὐτοῖς.	²⁷ "Yet thou hast dealt with us, O Lord our God, in all thy kindness and in all thy great compassion, ²⁸ as thou didst speak by thy servant Moses on the day when thou didst command him to write thy law in the presence of the people of Israel, saying, ²⁹ If you will not obey my voice, this very great multitude will surely turn into a small number among the nations, where I will scatter them. ³⁰ For I know that they will not obey me, for they are a stiff-necked people. But in the land of their exile they will come to themselves, ³¹ and they will know that I am the Lord their God. I will give them a heart that obeys and ears that hear; ³² and they will praise me in the land of their exile, and will remember my name, ³³ and will turn from their stubbornness and their wicked deeds; for they will remember the ways of their fathers, who sinned before the Lord. ³⁴ I will bring them again into the land which I swore to give to their fathers, to Abraham and to Isaac and to Jacob, and they will rule over it; and I will increase them, and they will not be diminished. ³⁵ I will make an everlasting covenant with them to be their God and they shall be my people; and I will never again remove my people Israel from the land which I have given them."

Chapters	Greek	RSV
3:9–14, 29–30 The fulfillment of law in wisdom	⁹ ἄκουε Ισραηλ ἐντολὰς ζωῆς ἐνωτίσασθε γνῶναι φρόνησιν ¹⁰ τί ἐστιν Ισραηλ τί ὅτι ἐν γῇ τῶν ἐχθρῶν εἶ ἐπαλαιώθης ἐν γῇ ἀλλοτρίᾳ ¹¹ συνεμιάνθης τοῖς νεκροῖς προσελογίσθης μετὰ τῶν εἰς ᾅδου ¹² ἐγκατέλιπες τὴν πηγὴν τῆς σοφίας ¹³ τῇ ὁδῷ τοῦ θεοῦ εἰ ἐπορεύθης κατῴκεις ἂν ἐν εἰρήνῃ τὸν αἰῶνα ¹⁴ μάθε ποῦ ἐστιν φρόνησις ποῦ ἐστιν ἰσχύς ποῦ ἐστιν σύνεσις τοῦ γνῶναι ἅμα ποῦ ἐστιν μακροβίωσις καὶ ζωή ποῦ ἐστιν φῶς ὀφθαλμῶν καὶ εἰρήνη . . . ²⁹ τίς ἀνέβη εἰς τὸν οὐρανὸν καὶ ἔλαβεν αὐτὴν καὶ κατεβίβασεν αὐτὴν ἐκ τῶν νεφελῶν ³⁰ τίς διέβη πέραν τῆς θαλάσσης καὶ εὗρεν αὐτὴν καὶ οἴσει αὐτὴν χρυσίου ἐκλεκτοῦ	⁹ <u>Hear the commandments of life, O Israel; give ear, and learn wisdom!</u> ¹⁰ <u>Why is it, O Israel, why is it that you are in the land of your enemies, that you are growing old in a foreign country, that you are defiled with the dead,</u> ¹¹ <u>that you are counted among those in Hades?</u> ¹² <u>You have forsaken the fountain of wisdom.</u> ¹³ <u>If you had walked in the way of God, you would be dwelling in peace for ever.</u> ¹⁴ Learn where there is wisdom, where there is strength, where there is understanding, that you may at the same time discern where there is length of days, and life, where there is light for the eyes, and peace. . . . ²⁹ <u>Who has gone up into heaven, and taken her, and brought her down from the clouds?</u> ³⁰ <u>Who has gone over the sea, and found her, and will buy her for pure gold?</u>
Chapters	Greek	RSV
3.36–4:4 Wisdom is for Israel alone	³⁷ ἐξεῦρεν πᾶσαν ὁδὸν ἐπιστήμης καὶ ἔδωκεν αὐτὴν Ιακωβ τῷ παιδὶ αὐτοῦ καὶ Ισραηλ τῷ ἠγαπημένῳ ὑπ' αὐτοῦ ³⁸ μετὰ τοῦτο ἐπὶ τῆς γῆς ὤφθη καὶ ἐν τοῖς ἀνθρώποις συνανεστράφη 4:1 αὕτη ἡ βίβλος τῶν προσταγμάτων τοῦ θεοῦ καὶ ὁ νόμος ὁ ὑπάρχων εἰς τὸν αἰῶνα πάντες οἱ κρατοῦντες αὐτῆς εἰς ζωήν οἱ δὲ καταλείποντες αὐτὴν ἀποθανοῦνται ² ἐπιστρέφου Ιακωβ καὶ ἐπιλαβοῦ αὐτῆς διόδευσον πρὸς τὴν λάμψιν κατέναντι τοῦ φωτὸς αὐτῆς ³ μὴ δῷς ἑτέρῳ τὴν δόξαν σου καὶ τὰ συμφέροντά σοι ἔθνει ἀλλοτρίῳ ⁴ μακάριοί ἐσμεν Ισραηλ ὅτι τὰ ἀρεστὰ τῷ θεῷ ἡμῖν γνωστά ἐστιν	³⁶ He found the whole way to knowledge, and gave her to Jacob his servant and to Israel whom he loved. ³⁷ Afterward she appeared upon earth and lived among men. ¹She is the book of the commandments of God, and the law that endures forever. All who hold her fast will live, and those who forsake her will die. ² Turn, O Jacob, and take her; walk toward the shining of her light. ³ Do not give your glory to another, or your advantages to an alien people. ⁴ Happy are we, O Israel, for we know what is pleasing to God.

APPENDIX 8
Charts for Romans 10:14–21

Chart 1

Verse no.	Clauses	Clause no.
4	πῶς οὖν ἐπικαλέσωνται εἰς ὃν οὐκ ἐπίστευσαν;	c17A
	πῶς δὲ πιστεύσωσιν οὗ οὐκ ἤκουσαν;	c17B
	πῶς δὲ ἀκούσωσιν χωρὶς κηρύσσοντος;	c17C
	πῶς δὲ κηρύξωσιν ἐὰν μὴ ἀποσταλῶσιν;	c17D
15	καθὼς γέγραπται·	c17Ea
	ὡς ὡραῖοι οἱ πόδες τῶν εὐαγγελιζομένων [τὰ] ἀγαθά.	c17Eb
	Ἀλλ' οὐ πάντες ὑπήκουσαν τῷ εὐαγγελίῳ.	c18A
16	Ἠσαΐας γὰρ λέγει·	c18Ba
	κύριε, τίς ἐπίστευσεν τῇ ἀκοῇ ἡμῶν;	c18Bb
	ἄρα ἡ πίστις ἐξ ἀκοῆς,	c19A
17	ἡ δὲ ἀκοὴ διὰ ῥήματος Χριστοῦ	c19B
	ἀλλὰ λέγω,	c20A
18	μὴ οὐκ ἤκουσαν;	c20B
	μενοῦνγε·	c20Ca
	εἰς πᾶσαν τὴν γῆν ἐξῆλθεν ὁ φθόγγος αὐτῶν	c20Cb
	καὶ εἰς τὰ πέρατα τῆς οἰκουμένης τὰ ῥήματα αὐτῶν	c20Cc
	ἀλλὰ λέγω,	c21A
	μὴ Ἰσραὴλ οὐκ ἔγνω;	c21B
19	πρῶτος Μωϋσῆς λέγει·	c21Ca
	ἐγὼ παραζηλώσω ὑμᾶς ἐπ' οὐκ ἔθνει,	c21Cb
	ἐπ' ἔθνει ἀσυνέτῳ παροργιῶ ὑμᾶς.	c21Cc
	Ἠσαΐας δὲ ἀποτολμᾷ καὶ λέγει·	c22A
	εὑρέθην [ἐν] τοῖς ἐμὲ μὴ ζητοῦσιν,	c22Ba
20	ἐμφανὴς ἐγενόμην τοῖς ἐμὲ μὴ ἐπερωτῶσιν.	c22Bb
	πρὸς δὲ τὸν Ἰσραὴλ λέγει·	c23A
	ὅλην τὴν ἡμέραν ἐξεπέτασα τὰς χεῖράς μου	c23Ba
	πρὸς λαὸν ἀπειθοῦντα καὶ ἀντιλέγοντα.	c23Bb
21		

Chart 2

V and C no.	Token	Process type	T/A/V/M
v.14, c17A	ἐπικαλέσωνται ἐπίστευσαν	Verbal Mental: percep	Aorist/pf/mid/subj Aorist/pf/act/ind
v. 14, c17B	πιστεύσωσιν ἤκουσαν	Mental: percep Material: action	Aorist/pf/mid/subj Aorist/pf/act/ind
v. 14, c17C	ἀκούσωσιν κηρύσσοντος	Material: action verbal	Aorist/pf/mid/subj Present/impf/act/part
v. 15, c17Da	κηρύξωσιν ἀποσταλῶσιν	Verbal Material: action	Aorist/pf/mid/subj Aorist/pf/pass/subj
v. 15, c17Db	γέγραπται	Material: action	Perfect/stative/pass/ind
v. 15, c17Dc	Ellipsis εὐαγγελιζομένων	Relational: attr verbal	Present/impf/mid/ind
v. 16, c18A	ὑπήκουσαν	Material: action	Aorist/pf/act/ind
v. 16, c18Ba	λέγει	verbal	Present/impf/act/ind
v. 16, c18Bb	ἐπίστευσεν	Mental: percep	Aorist/pf/act/ind
v. 17, c19A	Ellipsis	Relational: attr	
v. 17, c19B	Ellipsis	Relational: attr	
v. 18, c20A	λέγω	verbal	Present/impf/act/ind
v. 18, c20B	ἤκουσαν	Material: action	Aorist/pf/act/ind
v. 18, c20Cb	ἐξῆλθεν	Material: action	Aorist/pf/act/ind
v. 19, c21A	λέγω	verbal	Present/impf/act/ind
v. 19, c21B	ἔγνω	Mental: cog	Aorist/pf/act/ind
v. 19, c21Ca	λέγει	verbal	Present/impf/act/ind
v. 19, c21Cb	παραζηλώσω	Material: action	Future/?/act/ind
v. 19, c21Cc	παροργιῶ	(?)	Future/?/act/ind
v. 20, c22A	ἀποτολμᾷ λέγει	Relational: attr verbal	Present/impf/act/ind Present/impf/act/ind
v. 20, c22Ba	εὑρέθην ζητοῦσιν	Material: action Material: action	Aorist/pf/pass/ind Present/impf/act/part.
v. 20, c22Bb	ἐγενόμην ἐπερωτῶσιν	Relational: attr material: action	Aorist/pf/mid/ind Present/impf/act/ind
v. 21, c23A	λέγει	verbal	Present/impf/act/ind
v. 21, c23Ba	ἐξεπέτασα	Material: action	Aorist/pf/act/ind
v. 21, c23Bb	ἀπειθοῦντα ἀντιλέγοντα	Material: action verbal	Present/impf/act/part. Present/impf/act/part.

Clausal relations	Participants
Paratactic extensions: (x8) c17A ^ +c17B ^ +c17C ^ +c17D; c19A ^ +c19B; c20B ^ +c20Ca; c20Cb ^ +c20Cc; c20 ^ +c21; c21B ^ +C21Ca; c21Cb ^ +c21Cc; c22Ba ^ +c22Bb;	I: they^{x2}
	I: they ^{x2}
	I: they I: he (someone)
	I: they^{x2}
	I: it (Scripture)
paratactic projection: (x7) c17Ea ^ "c17Eb; c18Ba ^ "c18Bb; c20A ^ "(c20B ^ +c20Ca); c21Ca ^ "(c21Cb ^ +c21Cc); c21A ^ "(c21B ^ +c21Ca); c22A ^ "(c22Ba ^ +c22Bb); c23A ^ "c23B	G: οἱ πόδες G: οὐ πάντες (not all); G: τῷ εὐαγγελίῳ
	G: Ἠσαΐας
	R: τίς (who)
	G: ἡ πίστις G: ἡ ἀκοή
hypotactic enhancement: (x2) c17D ^ x(c17Ea ^ "c17Eb); c18A ^ x(c18Ba ^ "c18Bb)	I: I (Paul)
	I: they
	G: ὁ φθόγγος; τὰ ῥήματα R: αὐτῶν (their)x2
	I: I (Paul)
	G: Ἰσραὴλ
	G: Μωϋσῆς
	I: I (Moses) R: ὑμᾶς (Israel)
	I: I (Moses) R: ὑμᾶς (Israel)
	G: Ἠσαΐας
	I: I (Isaiah) R: ἐμὲ (Isaiah)
	I: I (Isaiah) R: ἐμὲ (Isaiah)
	I: he (Isaiah); G: τὸν Ἰσραὴλ
	I: I (Isaiah); G: τὰς χεῖράς μου
	G: λαὸν (Israel)

APPENDIX 9
Charts for Romans 11:1–10

Chart 1

Verse no.	Clause	Clause no.
1	Λέγω οὖν	c1Aa
	μὴ ἀπώσατο ὁ θεὸς τὸν λαὸν αὐτοῦ;	c1Ab
	μὴ γένοιτο·	c1B
	καὶ γὰρ ἐγὼ Ἰσραηλίτης εἰμί ἐκ σπέρματος Ἀβραάμ, φυλῆς Βενιαμίν	c2
		c3A
2	οὐκ ἀπώσατο ὁ θεὸς τὸν λαὸν αὐτοῦ	c3B
	ὃν προέγνω	c4A
	ἢ οὐκ οἴδατε	c4Ba
	ἐν Ἠλίᾳ τί λέγει ἡ γραφή	c4Bb
3	ὡς ἐντυγχάνει τῷ θεῷ κατὰ τοῦ Ἰσραήλ;	c4Ca
	κύριε, τοὺς προφήτας σου ἀπέκτειναν,	c4Cb
	τὰ θυσιαστήριά σου κατέσκαψαν	c4Cc
4	κἀγὼ ὑπελείφθην μόνος καὶ ζητοῦσιν τὴν ψυχήν μου.	c4D
	ἀλλὰ τί λέγει αὐτῷ ὁ χρηματισμός;	c4Ea
	κατέλιπον ἐμαυτῷ ἑπτακισχιλίους ἄνδρας,	c4Eb
5	οἵτινες οὐκ ἔκαμψαν γόνυ τῇ Βάαλ.	c5
6	οὕτως οὖν καὶ ἐν τῷ νῦν καιρῷ λεῖμμα κατ' ἐκλογὴν χάριτος γέγονεν·	c6A
		c6B
7	εἰ δὲ χάριτι, οὐκέτι ἐξ ἔργων,	c7A
	ἐπεὶ ἡ χάρις οὐκέτι γίνεται χάρις.	c7Ba
	Τί οὖν;	c7Bb
	ὃ ἐπιζητεῖ Ἰσραήλ, τοῦτο οὐκ ἐπέτυχεν,	c7Bc
8	ἡ δὲ ἐκλογὴ ἐπέτυχεν·	c8A
	οἱ δὲ λοιποὶ ἐπωρώθησαν	c8Ba
	καθὼς γέγραπται·	c8Bb
9	ἔδωκεν αὐτοῖς ὁ θεὸς πνεῦμα κατανύξεως	c9A
	ὀφθαλμοὺς τοῦ μὴ βλέπειν καὶ ὦτα τοῦ μὴ ἀκούειν, ἕως τῆς σήμερον ἡμέρας	c9B
10	καὶ Δαυὶδ λέγει	c9Ca
	γενηθήτω ἡ τράπεζα αὐτῶν εἰς παγίδα καὶ εἰς θήραν καὶ εἰς σκάνδαλον καὶ εἰς ἀνταπόδομα αὐτοῖς,	c9Cb
	σκοτισθήτωσαν οἱ ὀφθαλμοὶ αὐτῶν	c9D
	τοῦ μὴ βλέπειν	
	καὶ τὸν νῶτον αὐτῶν διὰ παντὸς σύγκαμψον.	

Chart 2

V and C no.	Token	Process type	T/A/V/M
v. 1, c1Aa	λέγω	Verbal	Present/impf/act/ind
v. 1, c1Ab	ἀπώσατο	Material: action	Aorist/pf/act/mid
v. 1, c1B	γένοιτο	Existential	Aorist/perf/mid/opt
v. 1, c2	εἰμί	Relational: id	Present/?/act/ind
v. 2, c3A	ἀπώσατο	Material: action	Aorist/pf/act/mid
v. 2, c3B	προέγνω	Mental: cog	Aorist/pf/act/mid
v. 2, c4A	οἴδατε	Mental: cog	Perfect/stative/act/ind
v. 2, c4Ba	λέγει	verbal	Present/impf/act/ind
v. 2, c4Bb	ἐντυγχάνει	verbal	Present/impf/act/ind
v. 3, c4Ca	ἀπέκτειναν	Material: action	Aorist/pf/act/ind
v. 3, c4Cb	κατέσκαψαν	Material: action	Aorist/pf/act/ind
v. 3, c4Cc	ὑπελείφθην ζητοῦσιν	Relational: att Material: action	Aorist/pf/pass/ind Present/impf/act/ind
v. 4, c4D	λέγει	Verbal	Present/impf/act/ind
v. 4, c4Ea	κατέλιπον	Material: action	Aorist/pf/act/ind
v. 4, c4Eb	ἔκαμψαν	Material: action	Aorist/pf/act/ind
v. 5, c5	γέγονεν	Relational: id	Perfect/stative/act/ind
v. 6, c6B	γίνεται	Existential	Present/impf/act/ind
v. 7, c7Ba	ἐπιζητεῖ ἐπέτυχεν	Material: action Material: action	Present/impf/act/ind Aorist/pf/act/ind
v. 7, c7Bb	ἐπέτυχεν	Material: action	Aorist/pf/act/ind
v. 7, c7Bc	ἐπωρώθησαν	Material: action	Aorist/pf/pass/ind
v. 8, c8A	γέγραπται	Material: action	Perfect/stative/pass/ind
v. 8, c8Ba	ἔδωκεν	Material: action	Aorist/pf/act/ind
v. 8, c8Bb	βλέπειν ἀκούειν	Material: action Material: action	Present/impf/act/inf Present/impf/act/inf
v. 9, c9A	λέγει	verbal	Present/impf/act/ind
v. 9, c9B	γενηθήτω	Relational: id	Aorist/pf/pass/imp
v. 10, c9Ca	σκοτισθήτωσαν	Material: action	Aorist/pf/pass/imp
v. 10, c9Cb	βλέπειν	Material: action	Present/impf/act/inf
v. 10, c9D	σύγκαμψον	Material: action	Aorist/pf/pass/imp

(Note: there are 30 clauses in total: 17 material clauses, 5 verbal clauses, 4 relational clauses, 2 mental

Clause Complex relations	Participants
Paratactic projections: locution (x6) c1Aa ^ "c1Ab; c4B ^ "c4C; c4D ^ "c4E; c7A ^ "c7B; c8A ^ "c8B; c9A ^ "(c c9B ^ +c9C ^ +c9D)	I: I (Paul)
	G: God, his (God's) people
	G: I (Paul), an Israelite, a descendant of Abraham, a member of Benjamin
	G: God, his people
Paratactic extension: (x7) c1A ^ +c1B; c1 ^ +c3; c4Ca ^ +c4Cb ^ +c4Cc; c4B ^ +c4D; c7Ba ^ +c7Bb ^ +c7Bc; c9B ^ +c9C ^ +c9D; c8 ^ +c9	I: he (God)
	I: You (pl.); G: the Scripture, Elijah I: it (the Scripture)
	I: he (Elijah)
	I: they (Israel)^{x3}; I: I (Elijah);
Paratactic enhancement: (x4) c1 ^ xc2; c4Ba ^ xc4Bb; c4 ^ xc5; c6A ^ +c6B;	G: the divine oracle
	I: I (God); R: myself (God); G: 7000 men
Paratactic elaboration: (x1) c5 ^ =c6;	I: they (7000 men)
	G: Baal
Hypotactic projection: idea (x1) c4A ^ 'c4B	G: remnant, Grace^{x4}, work
	G: Israel, the chosen ones, the rest
Hypotactic enhancement: (x2) c8Ba ^ xc8Bb; c9Ca ^ xc9Cb	
Hypotactic elaboration: (x1) c3A ^ =c3b	I: it (the Scripture)
Embedded elaboration: (x1) c4Ea ^[[c4Eb]]	G: God; R: them (the hardening);
	G: David
	R: their ^{x3}; them

existential clauses.)

APPENDIX 10
Charts for Romans 11:11–32

Chart 1

Verse no.	Clause	Clause no.
11	Λέγω οὖν	c10Aa
	μὴ ἔπταισαν ἵνα πέσωσιν;	c10Ab
	μὴ γένοιτο	c10B
	ἀλλὰ τῷ αὐτῶν παραπτώματι ἡ σωτηρία τοῖς ἔθνεσιν	c11A
	εἰς τὸ παραζηλῶσαι αὐτούς	c11B
12	εἰ δὲ τὸ παράπτωμα αὐτῶν πλοῦτος κόσμου	c12Aa
	καὶ τὸ ἥττημα αὐτῶν πλοῦτος ἐθνῶν	c12Ab
	πόσῳ μᾶλλον τὸ πλήρωμα αὐτῶν	c12B
13	ὑμῖν δὲ λέγω τοῖς ἔθνεσιν·	c13A
	ἐφ' ὅσον μὲν οὖν εἰμι ἐγὼ ἐθνῶν ἀπόστολος,	c13B
	τὴν διακονίαν μου δοξάζω	c13C
14	εἴ πως παραζηλώσω μου τὴν σάρκα	c13Da
	καὶ σώσω τινὰς ἐξ αὐτῶν	c13Db
15	εἰ γὰρ ἡ ἀποβολὴ αὐτῶν καταλλαγὴ κόσμου	c14A
	τίς ἡ πρόσλημψις εἰ μὴ ζωὴ ἐκ νεκρῶν;	c14B
16	εἰ δὲ ἡ ἀπαρχὴ ἁγία,	c15Aa
	καὶ τὸ φύραμα	c15Ab
17	καὶ εἰ ἡ ῥίζα ἁγία,	c15Ba
	καὶ οἱ κλάδοι.	c15Bb
	Εἰ δέ τινες τῶν κλάδων ἐξεκλάσθησαν	c16A
	σὺ δὲ ἀγριέλαιος ὢν ἐνεκεντρίσθης ἐν αὐτοῖς	c16Ba
	καὶ συγκοινωνὸς τῆς ῥίζης τῆς πιότητος τῆς ἐλαίας ἐγένου	c16Bb
18	μὴ κατακαυχῶ τῶν κλάδων·	c16C
	εἰ δὲ κατακαυχᾶσαι	c16D
	οὐ σὺ τὴν ῥίζαν βαστάζεις	c16Ea
	ἀλλὰ ἡ ῥίζα σέ	c16Eb
19	ἐρεῖς οὖν·	c17A
	ἐξεκλάσθησαν κλάδοι	c17Ba
	ἵνα ἐγὼ ἐγκεντρισθῶ	c17Bb

20	καλῶς·	c18
	τῇ ἀπιστίᾳ ἐξεκλάσθησαν	c18A
	σὺ δὲ τῇ πίστει ἕστηκας	c18B
	μὴ ὑψηλὰ φρόνει	c18Ca
	ἀλλὰ φοβοῦ	c18Cb
21	εἰ γὰρ ὁ θεὸς τῶν κατὰ φύσιν κλάδων οὐκ ἐφείσατο	c19A
	[μή πως] οὐδὲ σοῦ φείσεται	c19B
22	ἴδε οὖν χρηστότητα καὶ ἀποτομίαν θεοῦ·	c20A
	ἐπὶ μὲν τοὺς πεσόντας ἀποτομία,	c20Ba
	ἐπὶ δὲ σὲ χρηστότης θεοῦ	c20Bb
	ἐὰν ἐπιμένῃς τῇ χρηστότητι	c20Ca
	ἐπεὶ καὶ σὺ ἐκκοπήσῃ.	c20Cb
23	κἀκεῖνοι δέ . . . ἐγκεντρισθήσονται	c21A
	ἐὰν μὴ ἐπιμένωσιν τῇ ἀπιστίᾳ	c21B
	δυνατὸς γάρ ἐστιν ὁ θεὸς πάλιν ἐγκεντρίσαι αὐτούς.	c21C
24	εἰ γὰρ σὺ ἐκ τῆς κατὰ φύσιν ἐξεκόπης ἀγριελαίου	c22Aa
	καὶ παρὰ φύσιν ἐνεκεντρίσθης εἰς καλλιέλαιον,	c22Ab
	πόσῳ μᾶλλον οὗτοι οἱ κατὰ φύσιν ἐγκεντρισθήσονται τῇ ἰδίᾳ	c22B
25	ἐλαίᾳ	c23A
	Οὐ γὰρ θέλω ὑμᾶς ἀγνοεῖν, ἀδελφοί, τὸ μυστήριον τοῦτο,	c23D
	ἵνα μὴ ἦτε [παρ'] ἑαυτοῖς φρόνιμοι,	c23Ba
	ὅτι πώρωσις ἀπὸ μέρους τῷ Ἰσραὴλ γέγονεν	c23Bb
26	ἄχρι οὗ τὸ πλήρωμα τῶν ἐθνῶν εἰσέλθῃ	c23C
	καὶ οὕτως πᾶς Ἰσραὴλ σωθήσεται	c24A
	καθὼς γέγραπται·	c24Ba
	ἥξει ἐκ Σιὼν ὁ ῥυόμενος,	c24Bb
27	ἀποστρέψει ἀσεβείας ἀπὸ Ἰακώβ.	c24Bc
	καὶ αὕτη αὐτοῖς ἡ παρ' ἐμοῦ διαθήκη	c24Bd
	ὅταν ἀφέλωμαι τὰς ἁμαρτίας αὐτῶν.	
28	κατὰ μὲν τὸ εὐαγγέλιον ἐχθροὶ δι' ὑμᾶς,	c25A
	κατὰ δὲ τὴν ἐκλογὴν ἀγαπητοὶ διὰ τοὺς πατέρας·	c25B
29	ἀμεταμέλητα γὰρ τὰ χαρίσματα καὶ ἡ κλῆσις τοῦ θεοῦ.	c25C
30	ὥσπερ γὰρ ὑμεῖς ποτε ἠπειθήσατε τῷ θεῷ,	c26A
	νῦν δὲ ἠλεήθητε τῇ τούτων ἀπειθείᾳ,	c26B
31	οὕτως καὶ οὗτοι νῦν ἠπείθησαν τῷ ὑμετέρῳ ἐλέει,	c27A
	ἵνα καὶ αὐτοὶ [νῦν] ἐλεηθῶσιν.	c27B
32	συνέκλεισεν γὰρ ὁ θεὸς τοὺς πάντας εἰς ἀπείθειαν,	c28A
	ἵνα τοὺς πάντας ἐλεήσῃ.	c28B

Chart 2

V and C no.	Token	Process type	T/A/V/M	
v. 11, c10Aa	λέγω	verbal	Present/impf/act/ind	
v. 11, c10Ab	ἔπταισαν	Material: action	Aorist/pf/act/ind	
	πέσωσιν	Material: action	Aorist/pf/act/sub	
v. 11, c10B	γένοιτο	Existential	Aorist/pf/mid/opt	
v. 11, c11A	Ellipsis	Relational: att		
v. 11, c11B	παραζηλῶσαι	Material: action	Aorist/pf/act/inf	

Clause Complex relations	Participants
Paratactic projection: locution (x4) c10Aa ^ "c10Ab; c13A ^ "(c13B ^ +c13C); c17A ^ "(c17Ba ^ xc17Bb); c24A ^ 'c24B	I: I (Paul)
	I: they (Israel)
	G: salvation, the Gentiles
	R: them (Israel)

V and C no.	Token	Process type	T/A/V/M
v. 12, c12Aa	Ellipsis	Relational: id	
v. 12, c12Ab	Ellipsis	Relational: id	
v. 12, c12B	Ellipsis	Relational: id	
v. 13, c13A	λέγω	verbal	Present/impf/act/ind
v. 13, c13B	εἰμι	Relational: id	Present/?/act/ind
v. 13, c13C	δοξάζω	Material: action	Present/impf/act/ind
v. 14, c13Da	παραζηλώσω	Material: action	Future/?/act/ind
v. 14, c13Db	σώσω	Material: action	Future/?/act/ind
v. 15, c14A	Ellipsis	Relational: id	
v. 15, c14B	Ellipsis	Relational: id	
v. 16, c15Aa	Ellipsis	Relational: id	
v. 16, c15Ab	Ellipsis	Relational: id	
v. 16, c15Ba	Ellipsis	Relational: id	
v. 16, c15Bb	Ellipsis	Relational: id	
v. 17, c16A	ἐξεκλάσθησαν	Material: action	Aorist/pf/pass/ind
v. 17, c16Ba	ὧν ἐνεκεντρίσθης	Relational: id Material: action	Present/?/act/ind Aorist/pf/pass/ind
v. 17, c16Bb	ἐγένου	Relational: id	Aorist/pf/mid/ind
v. 18, c16C	κατακαυχῶ	Verbal	Present/impf/mid/imp
v. 18, c16D	κατακαυχᾶσαι	verbal	Present/impf/mid/ind
v. 18, c16Ea	βαστάζεις	Material: action	Present/impf/act/ind
v. 18, c16Eb	Ellipsis	Material: action	
v. 19, c17A	ἐρεῖς	verbal	Future/?/act/ind
v. 19, c17Ba	ἐξεκλάσθησαν	Material: action	Aorist/pf/pass/ind

Clause Complex relations	Participants
Paratactic extension: (x10) c10A ^ +c10B; c10 ^ +c11; c11 ^ +c12; c13B ^ +c13C; c15A ^ +c15B; c18A ^ +c18B; c24Ba ^ +c24Bb ^ +c24Bc; c25A ^ +c25B; c26A ^ +c26B; c26 ^ +c27	R: their^{x3}, G: world, God. I: I (Paul)^{x2}; G: the Gentiles^{x2}; apostle (Paul) R: I (Paul), you (the Gentiles), I: I (Paul)^{x2}; R: my(Paul's) ^{x2}, some of them (Israel), their, G: rejection, world, acceptance
Paratactic Enhancement: (x4) (c18A ^ +c18B) ^ xc18C; c23B ^ xc23C; c25B ^ xc25C; (c26 ^ +c27) ^ xc28	G: dough, lump, root, branches G: some of branches, R: you (a Gentile), them (the Israel) G: wild olive, the root of the olive tree
Hypotactic extension: (x8) c12Aa ^ +c12Ab; c13Da ^ +c13Db; c16Ba ^ +c16Bb; c16A ^ +c16B; c16Ea ^ +c16Eb; c18Ca ^ c18Cb; c20Ba ^ c20Bb; c22Aa ^ c22Ab	G: branches, the root^{x2}, R: you (the Gentiles)^{x2}
	I: you (a Gentile), they (the Israel) G: branches, R: I (a Gentile)

V and C no.	Token	Process type	T/A/V/M
v. 19, c17Bb	ἐγκεντρισθῶ	Material: action	Aorist/pf/pass/sub
v. 20, c18A	ἐξεκλάσθησαν	Material: action	Aorist/pf/pass/ind
v. 20, c18B	ἕστηκας	Existential	Perfect/stative/act/ind
v. 20, c18Ca	φρόνει	Mental: percep	Present/impf/act/imp
v. 20, c18Cb	φοβοῦ	Mental: emotion	Present/impf/act/imp
v. 21, c19A	ἐφείσατο	Material: action	Aorist/pf/mid/ind
v. 21, c19B	φείσεται	Material: action	Future/?/mid/ind
v. 22, c20A	ἴδε	Material: action	Aorist/pf/act/imp
v. 22, c20Ba	Ellipsis	Relational: att	
v. 22, c20Bb	Ellipsis	Relational: att	
v. 22, c20Ca	ἐπιμένῃς	Relational: id	Present/impf/act/sub
v. 22, c20Cb	ἐκκοπήσῃ	Material: action	Future/?/pass/ind
v. 23, c21A	ἐγκεντρισθήσονται	Material: action	Future/?/pass/ind
v. 23, c21B	ἐπιμένωσιν	Relational: id	Present/impf/act/sub
v. 23, c21C	ἐστιν	Relational: id	Present/?/act/ind
	ἐγκεντρίσαι	Material: action	Aorist/pf/act/inf
v. 24, c22Aa	ἐξεκόπης	Material: action	Aorist/pf/pass/ind
v. 24, c22Ab	ἐνεκεντρίσθης	Material: action	Aorist/pf/pass/ind
v. 24, c22B	ἐγκεντρισθήσονται	Material: action	Future/?/pass/ind
v. 25, c23A	θέλω	Mental: desid	Present/impf/act/ind
	ἀγνοεῖν	Mental: cog	Present/impf/act/inf
v. 25, c23C	ἦτε	Relational: att	Present/?/act/sub
v. 25, c23Ba	γέγονεν	Relational: att	Perfect/stative/act/ind
v. 25, c23Bb	εἰσέλθῃ	Material: evt[1]	Aorist/pf/act/sub
v. 26, c23C	σωθήσεται	Material: act	Future/?/pass/ind
v. 26, c24A	γέγραπται	Material: act	Perfect/stative/pass/ind
v. 26, c24Ba	ἥξει	Material: act	Future/?/act/ind
v. 26, c24Bb	ἀποστρέψει	Material: act	Future/?/act/ind
v. 27, c24Bc	Ellipsis	Relational: id	
v. 27, c24Bd	ἀφέλωμαι	Material: act	Aorist/pf/mid/sub
v. 28, c25A	Ellipsis	Relational: id	
v. 28, c25B	Ellipsis	Relational: id	
v. 29, c25C	Ellipsis	Relational: att	
v. 30, c26A	ἠπειθήσατε	Material: act	Aorist/pf/act/ind
v. 30, c26B	ἠλεήθητε	Mental: emo	Aorist/pf/pass/ind
v. 31, c27A	ἠπείθησαν	Material: act	Aorist/pf/act/ind
v. 31, c27B	ἐλεηθῶσιν	Material: act	Aorist/pf/pass/sub
v. 32, c28A	συνέκλεισεν	Material: act	Aorist/pf/act/ind
v. 32, c28B	ἐλεήσῃ	Mental: emo	Aorist/pf/act/sub

Clause Complex relations	Participants
Hypotactic enhancement: (x20) c11A ^ xc11B; xc12A ^ c12B; c13C ^ xc13D; xc14A ^ c14B;	I: they (the Israel), you (a Gentile)^{x2} R: you (a Gentile)
xc15Aa ^ c15Ab; xc15Ba ^ c15Bb; x(c16A ^ +c16B) ^ c16C;	G: God, natural branches, R: you (a Gentile) I: he (God)
xc16D ^ (c16Ea ^ +c16Eb); c17Ba ^ xc17Bb; xc19A ^c19B; c20Ca ^ xc20Cb; c20Bb ^ c20Ca; c21A ^ xc21B;	I: you (a Gentile), G: God^{x2}, the falling (the Israel) R: you (a Gentile) ^{x2}
(c21A ^ xc21B) ^ x21C; xc22A ^ c22B; c23A ^ xc23D; c23Ba ^ xc23Bb; c24Bc ^ xc24Bd; c27A ^ xc27B; c28A ^ xc28B	R: they (the Israel) ^{x2}, you (a Gentile), these (the natural branches) I: they (the Israel) ^{x2}, G: God, wild olive tree, cultivated olive tree, the natural branches, olive tree
Hypotactic Elaboration: (x1) c20A ^=c20B;	I: I (Paul), you (the Gentiles)
Embedded Projection: idea (x1) c23A ^ '(c23B ^ xc23C);	R: you (the Gentiles); yourself (the Gentiles); G: brothers (the Gentiles), mystery, Israel, full number of the Gentiles
	G: all Israel, the deliver, Jacob, covenant, sin I: it (the Scripture), he (the deliver), I (God), R: my (God), them (Israel), their (Israel), this (covenant)
	G: Gospel, enemies (Israel), election, the beloved (Israel), the patriarchs, gift, call, God^{x3}, R: you (the Gentiles), they (Israel) ^{x2}, your (thee Gentiles), all men (Israel and the Gentiles) ^{x2} I: you (the Gentiles)

Appendix Endnotes

Appendix 2
1. They stand for Tense/Aspect/Voice/Modality.
2. "I" stands for "Implied participant reference," which includes the morphological features of person and number with a finite verb form. See http://opentext.org/model/guidelines/wordgroup/0-2.html#d13.
3. "R" stands for "Reduced participant reference," which involves the use of a pronoun or other referring expression to point to a participant. See http://opentext.org/model/guidelines/wordgroup/0-2.html#d13.
4. "G" stands for "Grammaticalized participant reference," which involve a full, substantive reference to a participant. See http://opentext.org/model/guidelines/wordgroup/0-2.html#d13.

Appendix 3
1. I see the phrase τοῦτ' ἔστιν as an idiomatic expression, like "in a word, that is . . ." Therefore, I keep c6A and c6B in the same position as c5A and c5B. See other NT examples: Matt 27:46; Mk 7:2; Act 1:19; Rom 7:18; Rom 10:6–8; Phlm 2:12; Heb 2:14, 7:5, 9:11, 10:20, 11:16, 13:15; 1 Pet 3:20.

Appendix 4
1. It stands for "desiderative."
2. It stands for "cognitive."
3. c18D elaborates the nominal phrase σκεύη ἐλέους.
4. c18E further describes the nominal phrase σκεύη ἐλέους.
5. c18A and c18B describe God's desideration.

Appendix 5
1. Verse and clause numbers.
2. It stands for "perception."

Appendix 10
1. The abbreviation "evt" stands for "event."

Bibliography

Aageson, James W. "Paul's Use of Scripture: A Comparative Study of Biblical Interpretation in Early Palestinian Judaism and the New Testament with Special Reference to Romans 9–11." Unpublished D Phil Thesis, University of Oxford, 1983.

Abasciano, Brian J. "Paul's Use of the Old Testament in Romans 9:1–9: An Intertextual and Theological Exegesis." Unpublished D Phil Thesis, University of Aberdeen, 2004.

———. *Paul's Use of the Old Testament in Romans 9:1–9: An Intertextual and Theological Exegesis*. LNTS 301. New York: T&T Clark, 2005.

———. *Paul's Use of the Old Testament in Romans 9:10–18: An Intertextual and Theological Exegesis*. LNTS 317. New York: T & T Clark, 2011.

Aernie, Jeffrey W. *Is Paul Also among the Prophets?: An Examination of the Relationship between Paul and the Old Testament Prophetic Tradition in 2 Corinthians*. LNTS 467. New York: T & T Clark, 2012.

Aichele, George. "Canon as Intertext: Restraint or Liberation?" In *Reading the Bible Intertextually*, edited by Richard B. Hays, Stefan Alkier and Leroy Andrew Huizenga, 139-156. Waco: Baylor University Press, 2009.

Allen, Graham. *Intertextuality*. NCI. New York: Routledge, 2000.

Atkinson, Kenneth. *I Cried to the Lord: A Study of the Psalms of Solomon's Historical Background and Social Setting*. SJSJ. Leiden: Brill, 2004.

Badenas, Robert. *Christ the End of the Law: Romans 10.4 in Pauline Perspective*. JSNTSup 7. Sheffield: JSOT Press, 1985.

Baker, Murray. "Paul and the Salvation of Israel: Paul's Ministry, the Motif of Jealousy, and Israel's Yes." *CBQ* 67 (2005): 469–84.

Barclay, John M. G. "Unnerving Grace: Approaching Romans 9–11 from the Wisdom of Solomon." In *Between Gospel and Election: Explorations in the Interpretation of Romans 9–11*, edited by Florian Wilk, J. Ross Wagner and Frank Schleritt, 91–109. Tübingen: Mohr Siebeck, 2010.

———. "Paul's Story: Theology as Testimony." In *Narrative Dynamics in Paul: A Critical Assessment*, edited by Bruce W. Longenecker, 133–156. Louisville: Westminster John Knox, 2002.

Barthes, Roland. "Theory of the Text." In *Untying the Text: A Post-Structuralist Reader*, edited by Robert Young, 30–47. London: Routledge & Kegan Paul, 1981.

Basser, Herbert W. *Midrashic Interpretations of the Song of Moses*. American University Studies 2. New York: Peter Lang, 1984.

Bauckham, Richard. *Jesus and the God of Israel: God Crucified and Other Studies on the New Testament's Christology of Divine Identity*. Grand Rapids: Eerdmans, 2008.

Beal, Timothy K. "Ideology and Intertextuality: Surplus of Meaning and Controlling the Means of Production." In *Reading between Texts*, edited by Danna Nolan Fewell, 27–39. Louisville: Westminster John Knox 1992.

Beale, G. K. *John's Use of the Old Testament in Revelation*. JSNTSup 166. Sheffield: Sheffield Academic, 1998.

Beetham, Christopher A. *Echoes of Scripture in the Letter of Paul to the Colossians*. BibInt 96. Leiden: Brill, 2008.

Bekken, Per Jarle. *The Word Is Near You: A Study of Deuteronomy 30:12–14 in Paul's Letter to the Romans in a Jewish Context*. BZNW 144. New York: Walter de Gruyter, 2007.

Bell, Richard H. *The Irrevocable Call of God: An Inquiry into Paul's Theology of Israel*. WUNT 184. Tübingen: Mohr Siebeck, 2005.

———. *Provoked to Jealousy: The Origin and Purpose of the Jealousy Motif in Romans 9–11*. WUNT 63. Tübingen: Mohr Siebeck, 1994.

Belli, Filippo. *Argumentation and Use of Scripture in Romans 9–11*. Anbib 183. Rome: Gregorian & Biblical Press, 2010.

Ben Zvi, Ehud. *Hosea*. FOTL 21A. Grand Rapids: Eerdmans, 2005.

———. "The Prophetic Book: A Key Form of Prophetic Literature." In *The Changing Face of Form Criticism for the Twenty-First Century*, edited by Marvin A. Sweeney and Ehud Ben Zvi, 276–297. Grand Rapids: Eerdmans, 2003.

———. "Understanding the Message of the Tripartite Prophetic Books." *RQ* 35 (1993): 93–100.

Black, Stephanie L. *Sentence Conjunction in the Gospel of Matthew: καί, δέ, τότε, γάρ, οὖν and Asyndeton in Narrative Discourse*. JSNTSup 216. London: Sheffield Academic, 2002.

Boda, Mark. "Quotation and Allusion." In *Dictionary of Biblical Criticism and Interpretation*, edited by Stanley E. Porter, 296–297. London: Routledge, 2007.

Breech, E. "These Fragments I Have Shored against My Ruins: The Form and Function of 4 Ezra." *JBL* 92 (1973): 267–274.

Brodie, Thomas L., Dennis Ronald MacDonald, and Stanley E. Porter. "Conclusion: Problems of Method." In *The Intertextuality of the Epistles: Explorations of Theory and Practice*, edited by Thomas L. Brodie, Dennis Ronald MacDonald and Stanley E. Porter, 284–296. Sheffield: Sheffield Phoenix, 2006.

Broyles, Craig C. *Psalms*. NIBCOT 11. Peabody: Hendrickson, 1999.

Brueggemann, Walter. *1 & 2 Kings*. SHBC. Macon: Smyth & Helwys, 2000.

———. *Isaiah 40–66*. 2 vols. WestBC. Louisville: Westminster John Knox, 1998.

Budd, Philip J. *Numbers*. WBC 5. Waco: Word Books, 1984.

Byrne, Brendan. *Romans*. SP 6. Collegeville: Liturgical Press, 1996.

Campbell, Douglas Atchison. *The Deliverance of God: An Apocalyptic Rereading of Justification in Paul*. Grand Rapids: Eerdmans, 2009.

Campbell, William S. *Paul and the Creation of Christian Identity*. LNTS 322. New York: T & T Clark, 2008.

Capes, David B., Rodney Reeves, and E. Randolph Richards. *Rediscovering Paul: An Introduction to His World, Letters, and Theology*. Downers Grove: IVP Academic, 2007.

Carraway, George. *Christ Is God over All: Romans 9:5 in the Context of Romans 9–11*. LNTS 489. London: T & T Clark, 2013.

Chae, Daniel Jong-Sang. *Paul as Apostle to the Gentiles: His Apostolic Self-Awareness and Its Influence on the Soteriological Argument in Romans*. PBTM. Carlisle: Paternoster, 1997.

Charlesworth, James H. "From Messianology to Christology: Problems and Prospects." In *The Messiah: Developments in Earliest Judaism and Christianity*, edited by James H. Charlesworth, 3–35. Minneapolis: Fortress, 1992.

———, ed. *The Messiah: Developments in Earliest Judaism and Christianity*. Minneapolis: Fortress, 1992.

Childs, Brevard S. *Isaiah*. Louisville: Westminster John Knox, 2001.

Chilton, Bruce D. "Romans 9–11 as Scriptural Interpretation and Dialogue with Judaism." *ExAud* 4 (1988): 27–37.

Clarke, Ernest G. *The Wisdom of Solomon: Commentary*. CBCA. Cambridge: University Press, 1973.

Clement, Ronald E. "'A Remant Chosen by Grace' (Romans 11:5): The Old Testament Background and Origin of the Remnant Concept." In *Pauline Studies: Essays Presented to Professor F.F. Bruce on His 70th Birthday*, edited by Donald Alfred Hagner and Murray J. Harris, 106–21. Exeter: Paternoster, 1980.

Clements, R. E. *Isaiah 1–39*. NCBC. Grand Rapids: Eerdmans, 1980.

Cohn-Sherbok, Dan. *The Jewish Messiah*. Edinburgh: T&T Clark, 1997.

Collins, J. J. "Joseph and Aseneth: Jewish or Christian?" *JSP* 14 (2005): 97–112.

Cotterell, Peter, and Max Turner. *Linguistics & Biblical Interpretation*. Downers Grove: InterVarsity, 1989.

Craigie, Peter C., Page H. Kelley, and Joel F. Drinkard. *Jeremiah 1–25*. WBC 26. Dallas: Word Books, 1991.

Cranfield, C. E. B. *A Critical and Exegetical Commentary on the Epistle to the Romans*. ICC 31A. Edinburgh: T. & T. Clark, 1979.

Crenshaw, James L. *Joel: A New Translation with Introduction and Commentary*. AB 24C. London: Doubleday, 1995.

Danker, Frederick W., et al. *A Greek-English Lexicon of the New Testament and Other Early Christian Literature*. 3rd ed. Chicago: University of Chicago Press, 2000

Das, A. Andrew. *Paul, the Law, and the Covenant*. Peabody: Hendrickson Publishers, 2001.

———. *Solving the Romans Debate*. Minneapolis: Fortress Press, 2007.

Dearman, J. Andrew. *The Book of Hosea*. NICOT 29. Grand Rapids: Eerdmans, 2010.

DeSilva, David Arthur. *Introducing the Apocrypha: Message, Context, and Significance*. Grand Rapids: Baker Academic, 2002.

Di Lella, Alexander A., and Patrick W. Skehan. *The Wisdom of Ben Sira: A New Translation with Notes*. AB 39. Garden City: Doubleday, 1987.

Dinter, Paul E. "The Remnant of Israel and the Stone of Stumbling According to Paul (Romans 9–11)." Unpublished D Phil Thesis, Union Theological Seminary in New York, 1979.

Dodd, C. H. *The Epistle of Paul to the Romans*. MNTC. London: Hodder & Stoughton, 1932.

Donfried, Karl P., ed. *The Romans Debate*. Grand Rapids: Baker Academic, 1991.

Donaldson, Terence L. "'Riches for the Gentiles' (Rom 11:12): Israel's Rejection and Paul's Gentile Mission." *JBL* 112 (1993): 81–98.

———. "Jewish Christianity, Israel's Stumbling and the *Sonderweg* Reading of Paul." *JSNT* 29 (2006): 27–54.

———. *Jews and Anti-Judaism in the New Testament: Decision Points and Divergent Interpretations*. Waco: Baylor University Press, 2010.

———. *Judaism and the Gentiles: Jewish Patterns of Universalism (to 135 CE)*. Waco, TX: Baylor University Press, 2007.

———. *Paul and the Gentiles: Remapping the Apostle's Convictional World*. Minneapolis, MN: Fortress, 1997.

Dozeman, Thomas B. *Commentary on Exodus*. ECC. Grand Rapids: Eerdmans, 2009.

Dunn, James D. G. "Did Paul Have a Covenant Theology? Reflections on Romans 9. 4 and 11.27." In *The Concept of the Covenant in the Second Temple Period*, edited by Stanley E. Porter and Jacqueline C. R. De Roo, 287–307. Leiden: Brill, 2003.

———. *The Partings of the Ways: Between Christianity and Judaism and Their Significance for the Character of Christianity*. 2nd ed. London: SCM, 2006.

———. *Paul and the Mosaic Law*. Grand Rapids: Eerdmans, 2001.

———. "Righteousness from the Law and Righteousness from Faith: Paul's Interpretation of Scripture in Romans 10:1–10." In *Tradition and Interpretation in the New Testament*, edited by Earle E. Ellis and Gerald F. Hawthorne, 216–228. Grand Rapids: Eerdmans, 1987.

———. *Romans 9–16*. WBC 38. Dallas: Word Books, 1988.

Durham, John I. *Exodus*. WBC 3. Waco: Word Books, 1987.

Eddinger, Terry. *Malachi: A Handbook on the Hebrew Text*. BHHB. Waco: Baylor University Press, 2012.

Elliott, Neil. *The Arrogance of Nations: Reading Romans in the Shadow of Empire*. PCC. Minneapolis: Fortress, 2008.

Ellis, E. Earle. *The Old Testament in Early Christianity: Canon and Interpretation in the Light of Modern Research*. Grand Rapids: Baker, 1991.

Esler, Philip F. "Ancient Oleiculture and Ethnic Differentiation: The Meaning of the Olive-Tree Image in Romans 11." *JSNT* 26 1 (2003): 103–124.

Evans, C. A. *Ancient Texts for New Testament Studies: A Guide to the Background Lliterature*. Peabody: Hendrickson, 2005.

———. "Paul and the Hermeneutics of 'True Prophecy': A Study of Romans 9–11." *Bib* 65 (1984): 560–570.

———. "Paul and the Prophets: Prophetic Criticism in the Epistle to the Romans." In *Romans and the People of God: Essays in Honor of Gordon D. Fee on the Occasion of His 65th Birthday*, edited by Sven Soderlund, Gordon D. Fee and N. T. Wright, 115–128. Grand Rapids: Eerdmans, 1999.

Fisk, Bruce N. "Paul among the Storytellers: Reading Romans 11 in the Context of Rewritten Bible." In *Paul and Scripture: Extending the Conversation*, edited by Christopher D. Stanley, 55–94. Atlanta: Society of Biblical Literature, 2012.

Fitzmyer, Joseph A. *Romans: A New Translation with Introduction and Commentary*. AB 33. New York: Doubleday, 1993.

Friedman, Susan Stanford. "Weavings: Intertextuality and the (Re)Birth of the Author." In *Influence and Intertextuality in Literary History*, edited by Jay Clayton and Eric Rothstein, 146–180. Madison: University of Wisconsin Press, 1991.

Fruchtenbaum, Arnold G. *The Book of Genesis*. ABC. San Antonio: Ariel Ministries, 2009.

Gadenz, Pablo T. *Called from the Jews and from the Gentiles: Pauline Ecclesiology in Romans 9–11*. WUNT 267. Tübingen: Mohr Siebeck, 2009.

Gaston, Lloyd. *Paul and the Torah*. Vancouver: University of British Columbia Press, 1987.

Gaventa, B. R. "The Rhetoric of Death in the Wisdom of Solomon and the Letters of Paul." In *The Listening Heart: Essays in Wisdom and the Psalms in Honor of Roland E. Murphy*, edited by Kenneth G. Hoglund and Roland E. Murphy, 127–145. Sheffield: JSOT Press, 1987.

Getty, Mary Ann. "Paul and the Salvation of Israel: A Perspective on Romans 9–11." *CBQ* 50 (1988): 456–469.

Gilbert, Maurice. "Methodological and Hermeneutical Trends in Modern Exegesis on the Book of Ben Sira." In *The Wisdom of Ben Sira: Studies on Tradition, Redaction, and Theology*, edited by Angelo Passaro and Giuseppe Bellia, 1–20. Berlin: Walter de Gruyter, 2008.

Glazier-McDonald, Beth. *Malachi, the Divine Messenger*. SBLDS. Atlanta: Scholars Press, 1987.

Goldingay, John. *Psalms*. 3 vols. BCOTWP. Grand Rapids: Baker Academic, 2006.

Goodman, Martin. *The Apocrypha*. OBC. Oxford: Oxford University Press, 2012.

Goodwin, Mark. *Paul, Apostle of the Living God: Kerygma and Conversion in 2 Corinthians*. Harrisburg: Trinity Press International, 2001.

Grafe, E. "Das Verhältnis der paulinischen Schriften zur Sapientia Salomonis." In *Theologische Abhandlungen*, edited by Adolf von Harnack, 251–286. Freiburg, 1892.

Hafemann, Scott J. *Paul, Moses, and the History of Israel: The Letter/Spirit Contrast and the Argument from Scripture in 2 Corinthians 3*. WUNT 81. Tübingen: Mohr, 1995.

Hall, Winfield Scott, II. "Paul as a Christian Prophet in His Interpretation of the Old Testament in Romans 9–11." Unpublished PhD Dissertation. Lutheran School of Theology at Chicago, 1982.

Halliday, M. A. K., and Ruqaiya Hasan. *Language, Context, and Text: Aspects of Language in a Social-Semiotic Perspective*. 2nd ed. Language Education. Oxford: Oxford University, 1989.

Halliday, M. A. K., and Christian M. I. M. Matthiessen. *An Introduction to Functional Grammar*. 3rd ed. London: Arnold, 2004.

Harrington, D. J. "Pseudo-Philo: A New Translation and Introduction." In *The Old Testament Pseudepigrapha*, edited by James H. Charlesworth, 297–377. Peabody: Hendrickson, 2011.

Harris, Murray J. *Jesus as God: The New Testament Use of Theos in Reference to Jesus*. Grand Rapids: Baker, 1992.

Hartley, John E. *Leviticus*. WBC 4. Dallas: Word Books, 1992.

Hasel, Gerhard F. *The Remnant: The History and Theology of the Remnant Idea from Genesis to Isaiah*. 2nd ed. AUMSR. Berrien Springs: Andrews University Press, 1974.

Hatina, Thomas R. "Intertextuality and Historical Criticism in New Testament Studies : Is There a Relationship?" *BibInt* 7 (1999): 28–43.

Hays, Richard B. *Echoes of Scripture in the Letters of Paul*. New Haven: Yale University Press, 1989.

Heil, J. P. "From Remnant to Seed of Hope for Israel: Romans 9:27–29." *CBQ* 64 (2002): 703–720.

Hengel, Martin. *The Pre-Christian Paul*, translated by J. Bowden. London: SCM, 1991.

Hill, Andrew E. *Malachi: A New Translation with Introduction and Commentary*. AB 25D. New York: Doubleday, 1998.

Hofius, Otfried. "'All Israel Will Be Saved': Divine Salvation and Israel's Deliverance in Romans 9–11." *PSB* 11 (1990): 19–39.

Horbury, William. *Jewish Messianism and the Cult of Christ*. London: SCM, 1998.

Janowski, Bernd, and Peter Stuhlmacher, eds. *The Suffering Servant: Isaiah 53 in Jewish and Christian Sources*, translated by Daniel P. Bailey. Grand Rapids: Eerdmans, 2004.

Jewett, Robert. *Romans: A Commentary*. Hermeneia. Minneapolis: Fortress, 2007.

Johnson, Dan G. "The Structure and Meaning of Romans 11." *CBQ* 46 (1984): 91–103.

Johnson, E. Elizabeth. *The Function of Apocalyptic and Wisdom Traditions in Romans 9–11*. Atlanta: Scholars, 1989.

Käsemann, Ernst. *Commentary on Romans*. Grand Rapids: Eerdmans, 1980.

Kim, Dongsu. "Reading Paul's καὶ οὕτως πᾶς Ισραηλ Σωθήσεται (Rom11:26a) in the Context of Romans." *CTJ* 45 (2010): 317–334.

Kim, Johann D. *God, Israel, and the Gentiles: Rhetoric and Situation in Romans 9–11*. Atlanta: SBL, 2000.

Kim, Seyoon. *The Origin of Paul's Gospel*. 2nd ed. WUNT 4. Tübingen: Mohr, 1984.

Kirk, J. R. Daniel. "Why Does the Deliverer Come ἐκ Σιὼν (Romans 11:26)?" *JSNT* 33 (2010) 81–99.

Knauth, R. J. D. "Alien, Foreign Resident." In *Dictionary of the Old Testament: Pentateuch*, edited by T. Desmond Alexander and David W. Baker, 26–33. Downers Grove: InterVarsity, 2003.

Kristeva, Julia. *Revolution in Poetic Language*, translated by Margaret Walker. New York: Columbia University press, 1984.

Lemke, J. L. "Discourses in Conflict: Heteroglossia and Text Semantics." In *Systemic Functional Approaches to Discourse: Selected Papers from the 12th International Systemic Workshop*, edited by James D. Benson and William S. Greaves, 29–50. Norwood: Ablex 1988.

———. "Ideology, Intertextuality, and the Notion of Register." In *Systemic Perspectives on Discourses*, edited by J. D. Benson and W.S. Greaves, 275–294. Norwood: Ablex, 1985.

———. "Interpersonal Meaning in Discourse: Value Orientations." In *Advances in Systemic Linguistics: Recent Theory and Practice*, edited by Martin Davies and Louise Ravelli, 82–104. London: Pinter, 1992.

———. "Intertextuality and Text Semantics." In *Discourse in Society Systemic Functional Perspectives*, edited by Peter Howard Fries, Michael Gregory and M. A. K. Halliday, 85–114. Norwood: Ablex, 1995.

———. "Intertextuality and the Project of Text Linguistics." *TEXT* 20 (2000): 221–225.

———. "Resources for Attitudinal Meaning: Evaluative Orientation in Text Semantics." *Functions of Language* 5 (1998): 33–56.

———. "Semantic and Social Values." *Word* 40 (1989): 37–50.

---. "Text Structure and Text Semantics." In *Pragmatics, Discourse and Text*, edited by Erich H. Steiner, 158–170. London: Pinter, 1988.

---. *Textual Politics: Discourse and Social Dynamics*. CPLE. London: Taylor & Francis, 1995.

---. "Thematic Analysis: Systems, Structures, and Strategies." *SI* 3 (1983): 159–187.

Lincicum, David. *Paul and the Early Jewish Encounter with Deuteronomy*. WUNT 284. Tübingen: Mohr Siebeck, 2010.

Lindqvist, Pekka. *Sin at Sinai: Early Judaism Encounters Exodus 32*. SRB. Winona Lake: Eisenbrauns, 2008.

Linebaugh, Jonathan A. *God, Grace, and Righteousness in Wisdom of Solomon and Paul's Letter to the Romans: Texts in Conversation*. NovTSup 152. Leiden: Brill, 2013.

Litwak, Kenneth D. "Echoes of Scripture? A Critical Survey of Recent Works on Paul's Use of the Old Testament." *CurBS* 6 (1998): 260–288.

Lodge, John G. *Romans 9–11: A Reader-Response Analysis*. USFISFCJ. Atlanta: Scholars, 1996.

Longenecker, Bruce W. "Different Answers to Different Issues: Israel, the Gentiles and Salvation History in Romans 9–11." *JSNT* 36 (1989): 95–123.

---. *Eschatology and the Covenant: A Comparison of 4 Ezra and Romans 1–11*. JSNTSup 57. Sheffield: JSOT Press, 1991.

Louw, J. P., and Eugene A. Nida. *Greek-English Lexicon of the New Testament: Based on Semantic Domains*. 2nd ed. 2 vols. New York: UBS, 1989.

Manning, Gary T. *Echoes of a Prophet: The Use of Ezekiel in the Gospel of John and in Literature of the Second Temple Period*. JSNTSup 270. London: T & T Clark International, 2004.

Martin, J. R. *English Text: System and Structure*. Philadelphia: John Benjamins, 1992.

McConville, J. G. *Deuteronomy*. AOTC 5. Downers Grove: InterVarsity, 2002.

McDonald, Lee Martin, and Stanley E. Porter. *Early Christianity and Its Sacred Literature*. Peabody: Hendrickson, 2000.

Meadors, Edward P. *Idolatry and the Hardening of the Heart: A Study in Biblical Theology*. London: T&T Clark, 2006.

Metzger, B. M. "The Fourth Book of Ezra: A New Translation and Introduction." In *The Old Testament Pseudepigrapha*, edited by James H. Charlesworth, 517–559. Peabody: Hendrickson, 2011.

Meyers, Carol L. *Exodus*. NCamBC. Cambridge: Cambridge University Press, 2005.

Miller, Patrick D. *Deuteronomy*. IBC. Louisville: Westminster John Knox, 1990.

———. "'Moses My Servant': The Deuteronomic Portrait of Moses." *Int* 41 (1987): 245–255.

Moberly, R. W. L. *Prophecy and Discernment*. CSCD. Cambridge: Cambridge University Press, 2006.

Mohrmann, Douglas Carl. "Semantic Collisions at the Intertextual Crossroads: A Diachronic and Synchronic Study of Romans 9:30–10:13." Unpublished PhD Thesis, Durham University, 2001.

Moo, Douglas J. *The Epistle to the Romans*. NICOT. Grand Rapids: Eerdmans, 1996.

Moyise, Steve, ed.. *The Old Testament in the Book of Revelation*. JSNTSup 115. Sheffield: Sheffield Academic, 1995.

———. *Paul and Scripture*. Grand Rapids: Baker Academic, 2010.

Munck, Johannes. *Christ & Israel: An Interpretation of Romans 9–11*. Philadelphia: Fortress, 1967.

Müller, C. *Gottes Gerechtigkeit und Gottes Volk: Eine Untersuchung zu Romer 9–11*. Göttingen: Vandenhoeck & Ruprecht, 1964.

Nelson, Richard D. *Deuteronomy: A Commentary*. OTL. Louisville: Westminster John Knox, 2002.

Neusner, Jacob, William S. Green and Ernest Frerichs, eds. *Judaisms and Their Messiahs: At the Turn of the Christian Era*. Cambridge: Cambridge University Press, 1987.

Nickelsburg, George W. E. *Jewish Literature between the Bible and the Mishnah: A Historical and Literary Introduction*. 2nd ed, with CD-ROM. Minneapolis: Fortress, 2005.

Nygren, Anders. *Commentary on Romans*, translated by Carl C. Rasmussen. London: SCM, 1952.

Omanson, Roger L. *A Textual Guide to the Greek New Testament*. Stuttgart: Deutsche Bibelgesellschaft, 2006.

Osborne, Grant R. *Matthew*. ZECNT. Grand Rapids: Zondervan, 2010.

Oswalt, John. *The Book of Isaiah: Chapters 1–39*. NICOT. Grand Rapids: Eerdmans, 1986.

Pao, David W. *Acts and the Isaianic New Exodus*. WUNT 130. Tübingen: Mohr Siebeck, 2000.

Paul, Shalom M. *Isaiah 40–66: Translation and Commentary*. ECC. Grand Rapids: Eerdmans, 2012.

Philo. *The Works of Philo: Complete and Unabridged*. Translated by Charles Duke Yonge. Peabody: Hendrickson, 1993.

Piper, John. *The Justification of God: An Exegetical and Theological Study of Romans 9:1–23*. Grand Rapids: Baker, 1983.
Porter, Stanley E. "The Concept of Covenant in Paul." In *The Concept of the Covenant in the Second Temple Period*, edited by Stanley E. Porter and Jacqueline C. R. De Roo, 269–285. Leiden: Brill, 2003.
———. *Idioms of the Greek New Testament*. 2nd ed. BLG 2. Sheffield: Sheffield Academic, 1994.
———. "Paul and His Bible: His Education and Access to the Scriptures of Israel." In *As It Is Written: Studying Paul's Use of Scripture*, edited by Stanley E. Porter and Christopher D. Stanley, 97–124. Atlanta: SBL, 2008.
———. "The Use of the Old Testament in the New Testament: A Brief Comment on Method and Terminology." In *Early Christian Interpretation of the Scriptures of Israel*, edited by Craig A. Evans and James A. Sanders, 79–96. Sheffield: Sheffield Academic, 1997.
———. *Verbal Aspect in the Greek of the New Testament: With Reference to Tense and Mood*. SBG 1. New York: P. Lang, 1989.
———, ed. *The Messiah in the Old and New Testaments*. Grand Rapids: Eerdmans, 2007.
Porter, Stanley E., Jeffrey T. Reed, and Matthew Brook O'Donnell. *Fundamentals of New Testament Greek*. Grand Rapids: Eerdmans, 2010.
Propp, William Henry. *Exodus 19–40: A New Translation with Introduction and Commentary*. AB 2A. New York: Doubleday, 2006.
Quesnel, Michel. "La figure de Moïse en Romains 9–11." *NTS* 49 (2003):321–335.
Quinn-Miscall, Peter D. *Isaiah*. Readings. Sheffield: JSOT Press, 1993.
Räisänen, Heikki. *Paul and the Law*. 2nd ed. WUNT 29. Tübingen: Mohr, 1987.
Reasoner, Mark. "Romans 9–11 Moves from Margin to Center, from Rejection to Salvation: Four Grids for Recent English-Language Exegesis." In *Between Gospel and Election: Explorations in the Interpretation of Romans 9–11*, edited by Florian Wilk, J. Ross Wagner and Frank Schleritt, 73–89. Tübingen: Mohr Siebeck, 2010.
Reed, Jeffrey T. *A Discourse Analysis of Philippians : Method and Rhetoric in the Debate over Literary Integrity*. JSNTSup 136. Sheffield: Sheffield Academic, 1997.
Ruiten, Jacques T. A. G. M. van. *Abraham in the Book of Jubilees: The Rewriting of Genesis 11:26–25:10 in the Book of Jubilees 11:14–23:8*. SJSJ. Leiden: Brill, 2012.

Salvesen, Alison. "Baruch." In *The Apocrypha*, edited by Martin Goodman, John Barton and John Muddiman, 112–17. Oxford: Oxford University press, 2012.

Sanday, W., and Arthur C. Headlam. *A Critical and Exegetical Commentary on the Epistle to the Romans*. ICC 32. New York: C. Scribner's Sons, 1923.

Sanders, E. P. *Paul, the Law, and the Jewish People*. Philadelphia: Fortress, 1983.

———. *Paul and Palestinian Judaism: A Comparison of Patterns of Religion*. Philadelphia: Fortress, 1977.

Sanders, James A. *From Sacred Story to Sacred Text: Canon as Paradigm*. Philadelphia: Fortress, 1987.

Sandnes, Karl Olav. *Paul, One of the Prophets? A Contribution to the Apostle's Self-Understanding*. WUNT 43. Tübingen: Mohr, 1991.

Sawyer, John F. A. *Isaiah*. DSBOT. Edinburgh: Saint Andrew, 1984.

———. *Prophecy and the Biblical Prophets*. Rev. ed. OB. Oxford: Oxford University Press, 1993.

Schaefer, Konrad, and David W. Cotter. *Psalms*. BO. Collegeville: Liturgical, 2001.

Scholer, David M. "Forward." In *The Works of Philo: Complete and Unabridged*, ix–xvii. Peabody: Hendrickson, 1993.

Schreiner, Thomas R. "Paul's View of the Law in Romans 10:4–5." *WTJ* 55 (1993): 113-135.

———. *Romans*. BECNT. Grand Rapids: Baker, 1998.

Sherwood, Aaron. *Paul and the Restoration of Humanity in Light of Ancient Jewish Traditions*. AJEC. Leiden: Brill 2013.

Shum, Shiu-Lun. *Paul's Use of Isaiah in Romans: A Comparative Study of Paul's Letter to the Romans and the Sibylline and Qumran Sectarian Texts*. WUNT 156. Tübingen: Mohr Siebeck, 2002.

Smith, Ralph L. *Micah-Malachi*. WBC 32. Waco: Word Books, 1984.

Spencer, F. Scott. "Metaphor, Mystery and the Salvation of Israel in Romans 9–11: Paul's Appeal to Humility and Doxology." *RE* 103 (2006): 113–138.

Sprinkle, Preston M. *Law and Life: The Interpretation of Leviticus 18:5 in Early Judaism and in Paul*. WUNT 241. Tübingen: Mohr Siebeck, 2008.

Stanley, Christopher D. *Arguing with Scripture: The Rhetoric of Quotations in the Letters of Paul*. New York: T&T Clark International, 2004.

———. "Paul's Use of Scripture: Why the Audience Matters." In *As It Is Written: Studying Paul's Use of Scripture*, edited by Stanley E. Porter and Christopher D. Stanley, 125–155. Atlanta: SBL, 2008.

———. *Paul and the Language of Scripture: Citation Technique in the Pauline Epistles and Contemporary Literature*. SNTSMS 69. Cambridge: Cambridge University Press, 1992.

———. "'The Redeemer Will Come ἐκ Σιών': Romans 11.26–27 Revisited." In *Paul and the Scriptures of Israel*, edited by Craig A. Evans and James A. Sanders, 118–142. Sheffield: JSOT Press, 1993.

Staples, Jason A. "What Do the Gentiles Have to Do with 'All Israel'? A Fresh Look at Romans 11:25–27." *JBL* 130 (2011): 371–390.

Starling, David Ian. *Not My People: Gentiles as Exiles in Pauline Hermeneutics*. BZNW 184. Berlin: de Gruyter, 2011.

Stegemann, Ekkehard W. "Coexistence and Transformation: Reading the Polictics of Identity in Romans in an Imperial Context." In *Reading Paul in Context: Explorations in Identity Formation: Essays in Honour of William S. Campbell*, edited by Kathy Ehrensperger and J. Brian Tucker. London: T & T Clark International, 2010.

Stegner, William R. "Romans 9:6–29 – A Midrash." *JSNT* 22 (1984): 37–52.

Steinmann, A. E. "Hardness of Heart." In *Dictionary of the Old Testament: Pentateuch*, edited by T. Desmond Alexander and David W. Baker, 381–383. Downers Grove: InterVarsity, 2003.

Stone, Michael E. *Fourth Ezra: A Commentary on the Book of Fourth Ezra*. Hermeneia. Minneapolis: Fortress, 1990.

Stuart, Douglas K. *Exodus*. NAC 2. Nashville: Broadman & Holman, 2006.

———. *Hosea-Jonah*. WBC 31. Dallas: Word, 1998.

Suggs, M. Jack. "The Word Is Near You: Romans 10:6–10 within the Purpose of the Letter." In *Christian History and Interpretation: Studies Presented to John Knox*, edited by John Knox, William Reuben Farmer and C. F. D. Moule, 289–312. Cambridge: University Press, 1967.

Sweeney, Marvin A. *Isaiah 1–39: With an Introduction to Prophetic Literature*. FOTL 16. Grand Rapids: Eerdmans, 1996.

Sweeney, Marvin A., David W. Cotter, Jerome T. Walsh, and Chris Franke. *The Twelve Prophets*. BO. Collegeville: Liturgical, 2000.

Thibault, Paul J. *Social Semiotics as Praxis: Text, Social Meaning Making, and Nabokov's Ada*. THL. Minneapolis: University of Minnesota Press, 1991.

Thielman, Frank. "Unexpected Mercy: Echoes of a Biblical Motif in Romans 9–11." *SJT* 47 (1994): 169–181.

Tobin, Thomas H. *Paul's Rhetoric in Its Contexts: The Argument of Romans*. Peabody: Hendrickson, 2004.

VanderKam, James C. *The Book of Jubilees: A Critical Text*. 2 vols. CSCO. Leuven: Peeters, 1989.

Vanlaningham, Michael G. "Paul's Use of Elijah's Mt. Horeb Experience in Rom 11:2–6." *TMSJ* 6 (1995): 223–232.

Venema, Cornelis P. "'In This Way All Israel Will Be Saved': A Study of Romans 11:26." *MAJT* 22 (2011): 19–40.

Vermès, Géza. *The Complete Dead Sea Scrolls in English*. New York: Allen Lane, 1997.

Waetjen, Herman C. *The Letter to the Romans: Salvation as Justice and the Deconstruction of Law*. Sheffield: Sheffield Phoenix, 2011.

Wagner, J. Ross. "The Heralds of Isaiah and the Mission of Paul: An Investigation of Paul's Use of Isaiah 51–55 in Romans." In *Jesus and the Suffering Servant*, edited by W. H. Bellinger and William Reuben Farmer, 193–222. Harrisburg: Trinity Press International, 1998.

———. *Heralds of the Good News: Isaiah and Paul "in Concert" in the Letter to the Romans*. NovTSup 101. Leiden: Brill, 2002.

Wakefield, Andrew H. "Romans 9–11: The Sovereignty of God and the Status of Israel." *RevExp* 100 (2003): 65–80.

Walsh, Jerome T. *1 Kings*. BO. Collegeville: Liturgical, 1996.

Waters, Guy Prentiss. *The End of Deuteronomy in the Epistles of Paul*. WUNT 221. Tübingen: Mohr Siebeck, 2006.

Watson, Francis. *Paul and the Hermeneutics of Faith*. Edinburgh: T & T Clark, 2004.

Watts, John D. W. *Isaiah 1–33*. WBC 24. Waco: Word, 1985.

———. *Isaiah 34–66*. WBC 25. Waco: Word, 1987.

Watts, Rikki E. *Isaiah's New Exodus and Mark*. WUNT 88. Tübingen: Mohr Siebeck, 1997.

Westermann, Claus. *Basic Forms of Prophetic Speech*. Louisville, KY: Westminster John Knox, 1991.

Westfall, Cynthia Long. *A Discourse Analysis of the Letter to the Hebrews : The Relationship between Form and Meaning*. LNTS 297. London: T & T Clark, 2005.

Widyapranawa, S. H. *The Lord Is Savior: Faith in National Crisis: A Commentary on the Book of Isaiah 1–39*. ITC. Grand Rapids: Eerdmans, 1990.

Wilk, Florian. *Die Bedeutung des Jesajabuches für Paulus*. FRLANT 179. Göttingen: Vandenhoeck & Ruprecht, 1998.

Wilson, Walter T. *On Virtues: Introduction, Translation, and Commentary*. PAC. Leiden: Brill, 2011.

Winninge, Mikael. *Sinners and the Righteous: A Comparative Study of the Psalms of Solomon and Paul's Letters.* ConBNT. Stockholm: Almqvist & Wiksell International, 1995.

Winston, David. *The Wisdom of Solomon: A New Translation.* AB 43. Garden City: Doubleday, 1979.

Wintermute, O.S. "Jubilees: A New Translation and Introduction." In *the Old Testament Pseudepigrapha,* edited by James H. Charlesworth, 35–142. Peabody: Hendrickson, 2011.

Wise, Michael Owen, Martin G. Abegg, and Edward M. Cook. *The Dead Sea Scrolls: A New Translation.* 2nd ed. London: Harper Collins, 2005.

Witherington, B. "Christ." In *Dictionary of Paul and His Letters,* edited by Gerald F. Hawthorne, Ralph P. Martin and Daniel G. Reid, 95–100. Downers Grove: InterVarsity Press, 1993.

Wolde, Ellen Van. "Trendy Intertextuality?" In *Intertextuality in Biblical Writings: Essays in Honour of Bas Van Ierse,* edited by Sipke Draisma, 43–49. Kampen: Kok, 1989.

Wright, N. T. *The Climax of the Covenant: Christ and the Law in Pauline Theology.* Minneapolis: Fortress Press, 1992.

———. *Paul: In Fresh Perspective.* Minneapolis: Fortress Press, 2005.

Wright, Robert B. "The Psalms of Solomon." In *The Old Testament Pseudepigrapha,* edited by James H. Charlesworth, 639–70. New York: Doubleday, 1985.

———. *The Psalms of Solomon: A Critical Edition of the Greek Text.* London: T & T Clark, 2007.

Zerbe, Gordon. "Jews and Gentiles as People of the Covenant: The Background and Message of Romans 11." *Direction* 12 (1983): 20–28.

Zetterholm, Magnus. *The Messiah: In Early Judaism and Christianity.* Minneapolis: Fortress, 2007.

Ziesler, J. A. *The Meaning of Righteousness in Paul: A Linguistic and Theological Enquiry.* SNTSMS 20. Cambridge: University Press, 1972.

Ziesler, J. A. and A. G. Baxter. "Paul and Arboriculture: Romans 11:17–24." *JSNT* 24 (1985): 25–32.

Zoccali, Christopher. "'And So All Israel Will Be Saved': Competing Interpretations of Romans 11.26 in Pauline Scholarship." *JSNT* 30 (2008): 289–318.

Langham Literature and its imprints are a ministry of Langham Partnership.

Langham Partnership is a global fellowship working in pursuit of the vision God entrusted to its founder John Stott –

> *to facilitate the growth of the church in maturity and Christ-likeness through raising the standards of biblical preaching and teaching.*

Our vision is to see churches in the majority world equipped for mission and growing to maturity in Christ through the ministry of pastors and leaders who believe, teach and live by the Word of God.

Our mission is to strengthen the ministry of the Word of God through:
- nurturing national movements for biblical preaching
- fostering the creation and distribution of evangelical literature
- enhancing evangelical theological education

especially in countries where churches are under-resourced.

Our ministry

Langham Preaching partners with national leaders to nurture indigenous biblical preaching movements for pastors and lay preachers all around the world. With the support of a team of trainers from many countries, a multi-level programme of seminars provides practical training, and is followed by a programme for training local facilitators. Local preachers' groups and national and regional networks ensure continuity and ongoing development, seeking to build vigorous movements committed to Bible exposition.

Langham Literature provides majority world pastors, scholars and seminary libraries with evangelical books and electronic resources through grants, discounts and distribution. The programme also fosters the creation of indigenous evangelical books for pastors in many languages, through training workshops for writers and editors, sponsored writing, translation, strengthening local evangelical publishing houses, and investment in major regional literature projects, such as one volume Bible commentaries like *The Africa Bible Commentary*.

Langham Scholars provides financial support for evangelical doctoral students from the majority world so that, when they return home, they may train pastors and other Christian leaders with sound, biblical and theological teaching. This programme equips those who equip others. Langham Scholars also works in partnership with majority world seminaries in strengthening evangelical theological education. A growing number of Langham Scholars study in high quality doctoral programmes in the majority world itself. As well as teaching the next generation of pastors, graduated Langham Scholars exercise significant influence through their writing and leadership.

To learn more about Langham Partnership and the work we do visit **langham.org**

www.ingramcontent.com/pod-product-compliance
Lightning Source LLC
Chambersburg PA
CBHW070234240426
43673CB00044B/1786